THE
HISTORY OF
ADVERTISING

40
MAJOR BOOKS
IN FACSIMILE

Edited by
HENRY ASSAEL
C. SAMUEL CRAIG
New York University

A
GARLAND
SERIES

FORTY YEARS AN
ADVERTISING
AGENT
1865–1905

GEORGE PRESBURY ROWELL
''

GARLAND PUBLISHING, INC.
NEW YORK & LONDON
1985

HF5813
U6
R578
1985

For a complete list of the titles in this series
see the final pages of this volume.

This facsimile has been made from a copy in
the Yale University Library.

Library of Congress Cataloging in Publication Data

Rowell, George Presbury.
    Forty years an advertising agent.
    (The History of advertising)
    Reprint. Originally published: New York : Printers'
Ink Pub. Co., 1906.
    1. Advertising—United States.   2. Advertising,
Newspaper—United States.   I. Title.   II. Series.
HF5813.U6R578   1985   659.13'2   84-46061
ISBN 0-8240-6755-X (alk. paper)

Design by Donna Montalbano

The volumes in this series are printed on
acid-free, 250-year-life paper.

Printed in the United States of America

FORTY YEARS AN
ADVERTISING AGENT

FORTY YEARS AN

ADVERTISING AGENT

1865-1905

BY

GEORGE PRESBURY ROWELL

FOUNDER OF THE ADVERTISING AGENCY OF GEO. P. ROWELL & CO.,
MARCH 5TH, 1865 — RETIRED AUGUST 31ST, 1905.
FOUNDER OF ROWELL'S AMERICAN NEWSPAPER DIRECTORY IN 1869, THE FIRST
SERIOUS EFFORT EVER MADE TO ASCERTAIN AND MAKE KNOWN
THE CIRCULATIONS OF NEWSPAPERS THAT COMPETE
FOR ADVERTISING PATRONAGE.
FOUNDER OF PRINTERS' INK IN 1888: A JOURNAL FOR ADVERTISERS,
THE FIRST PERIODICAL EVER ESTABLISHED FOR THE
SERIOUS DISCUSSION OF ADVERTISING
AS A BUSINESS FORCE.

PRINTERS' INK PUBLISHING CO.
NEW YORK
1906

FOREWORD

The fifty-two chapters or papers that make up the contents of this volume were not begun with a thought of preserving them in any more permanent or accessible form than would be accomplished by their appearance in the columns of *Printers' Ink*. When the first installment was given out the writer had not decided to attach his name. His feelings were expressed in a paragraph which preceded the initiatory installment and which read as follows:

A man, whose name will occur to many as one who for nearly half a century has been closely in touch with newspapers and advertising, has consented to tell the story of his experience in a series of papers to be published in *Printers' Ink*. The first installment is here given; others will follow from week to week until it appears that readers fail to find in them very much of instruction or interest, or the writer tires of his self-imposed task, or the editor should conclude that a pressure of matter of more importance will forbid the further devotion of so much space to old stories and ancient history.

As the work progressed there were evidences that the papers were being read with interest, not only by men of the writer's generation, but, in business houses where advertising formed a part of the conduct of affairs, it was made to appear that they had the attention of clerks and office boys, from among whom the advertising men of the future are likely to be recruited. On this account the writer's interest in his work grew more pronounced, and eventually he thought it might be possible to continue the papers through the fifty-two numbers of *Printers' Ink* that would make up the volume for the year 1905.

That ambition having been achieved, and the series completed, a review of the many comments and suggestions, made and sent in by correspondents, appeared to indicate an interest in the story greater than would be expected for material usually considered so dry and uninteresting. Ex-

tracts from some of the comments that led to the final
decision to make a book out of the papers are here reproduced:

Advertising literature would have lost much if Mr. Rowell had
not written these papers.

They bring so freshly to mind men who in a past generation
left their mark and imprint on our history's page.

They set forth the inception, the development, and the growth
of the art (or science) of advertising in a practical way that none
of to-day's theories can possibly do.

They bring back old *times* when the future looked bright and
radiant.

They are the most interesting papers that have ever appeared
in any publication devoted to advertising.

The papers are practical and inspiring; they are nothing short
of an education to the beginner who would succeed.

The work has permanent value as a contribution to the history
of American journalism, and particularly as a clear exposition of
one of its comparatively little understood but most important phases.

My wife doesn't know much about advertising, but she shares
the great interest I feel in these naively written reminiscences.

They are written in a style peculiar to the author and can hardly
fail to attract attention.

They are too good to pass without emphasis and hearty approbation. Every newspaper man in the Union feels an interest in that
familiar name which carries so much influence among advertisers.

There seems to be a charm about them that I have not been
able precisely to analyze.

They are written in language most captivating and tell a story
full of interest to every newspaper man.

I thought as I read those very instructive and interesting articles
I was just sitting beside Mr. Rowell and could hear him explaining.

The style could not be better for the subject. It will be a real
book; there are few of them, most are a rehash or warmed over.

What particularly impresses me in reading them all is the absence
of any remark or comment that could be construed as an ill-natured
criticism or wound the feelings of any one whose name is mentioned.

There is scarcely a man who made his own first start in a modest
way who will not be taken back to his own early experiences by
those of Mr. Rowell.

They're the best ever.

After all, what more agreeable reading can there be than the con-
fessions of an old sinner?

I must express sincere admiration for the simplicity of the style
as well as the easy run of the narrative.

Being of the younger school of advertising I particularly appreciate Mr. Rowell's reminiscences, as there is food for thought in
every year of his long experience.

I appreciate the extreme care he is taking in the preparation of
these articles and their refreshing, reminiscent, humorous style. It
has been my pleasure to meet and know well many of the persons
he is describing. and I must say he "hits the nail squarely on the
head" in these descriptions.

They are very interesting to me, because, as a new advertiser, I want to know something about advertising in days gone by, and about the men who made advertising what it is to-day.

They are a review of old times, old friends, and show to the present young men what patience, privations and hard work it took to get a foothold on that ladder of fame that we all strive to climb. If those letters could be read by every young man in the land it would be a God-send to many a parent; for they would cause many a young man to realize what honesty of purpose were required to stand well with his fellow-man and secure, honestly, sufficient to make his declining years a pleasure.

They offer a very valuable contribution to the history of newspapers and advertising in America.

They are full of instruction and profitable suggestions to every man who prints and thinks; and they are written in English that Washington Irving would have delighted in could he but have dipped into them.

Are the most interesting articles that have appeared in the advertising world.

I want to add my voice to the chorus which acclaims the unequalled interest of Mr. Rowell's recollections.

To the young man who is following the advertising game they are worth more than can be measured in mere dollars and cents.

These letters have given me thoughts and ideas for reflection that I could not have secured in any manner except by purchase through years of "bumping" experience. Of course, experience is the only real teacher, but the man who goes for a slide down the toboggan, having been informed in advance of a steep incline at a given point that is bound to take his breath, can in a measure prepare for the "bump" and only needs to give half a gasp, while the fellow who goes uninformed gives a gasp and a half.

They are an excellent piece of history writing, but particularly interesting to those who have ever had any hand in the business.

What funny stories! I nearly had hysterics over the man who saw *bugs*.

To a young man it presents ideals in the business world that are seldom revealed in so clear a manner. Let it be said that this story will reach down as a triumph of its kind.

I do not suppose the younger portion of the fraternity take as much interest in it as we old-timers do.

I like to read them. It leaves a nice taste in your mouth, to say nothing of the information to be gained.

The manner of setting forth the stages through which advertising has passed during the last forty years helps one to understand more fully why certain conditions now exist.

I think the advertising world can be congratulated that Mr. Rowell was one of the first—and therefore the pacemaker—of the advertising agency.

I heartily appreciate the remarkable felicity in narration, and in the happy blending of sententious humor and sound sense with which these unique "recollections" are fairly saturated.

While what he tells is readable, the way he tells it is delightful.

As to the correctness of Mr. Rowell's recollections, I am pleased to say that they have the admiration of every man familiar with the period that he has been describing.

I have found them most delightful, at times even fascinating.

He certainly knows how to tell a story in the most entertaining way.

The reminiscences have great interest for me, not only because they are so entertainingly written, and bring to mind so many interesting facts relating to men and events long forgotten, but also because they throw strong sidelights upon the business of the advertising agent as it was formerly conducted.

His characterization of men whom I know has been so perfect that an artist ought to be able to make a picture of them from his word-painting.

After reading his letters I would like very much to meet him. I have formed a high opinion of his force of character and worth as a successful business man with high ideals.

I think that no piece of literature that has appeared for a number of years has proven as interesting to advertising men.

They are the most charmingly written and intensely interesting chapters of business history ever published.

It seems as though each one was better than the last.

Probably the best history of the growth of the advertising business that has ever appeared in print.

I am neither a publisher nor an advertising agent, but I have derived a very great deal of valuable information from Mr. Rowell's papers. He has the rare gift of imparting knowledge in an entertaining manner. I can imagine I hear his kindly voice as I read. I am quite sure he is a man who is honored and respected by his associates. He is so intensely human.

It is an incentive, a help to any one at all discouraged, to read such cheering words.

The story is mightily interesting, and especially so to newspaper men.

Though not an advertising man, they hold my interest as very few reminiscent recitals do. My guess is that it is because he has something to tell and knows how to tell it in words "without trimmings."

I don't know how it is about these papers, but if you begin one you can't lay it down until you have read it all.

I enjoyed the article relating to fishing and hunting very much. It has the true flavor of the woods about it, and I am passing it around among my fishing and hunting friends.

The world lost a facile writer of good English when Mr. Rowell lost himself in the advertising business.

These reminiscences are the first readable articles of a personal nature which have appeared in the advertising field. They light up the dry routine of "Essays on the Theory of Advertising," "Studies of Systems," and criticisms from boy archers who know *so* much.

Interesting in themselves, they are expressed in such frank stories of success and mistake, of victory and defeat, that no reader in or out of the craft of advertising can fail to be attracted by the personality of the man who remembers so well and spares himself so little.

I can scarcely conceive it possible that better advice can be given to a young canvasser. And, moreover, the whole is written in a style so delightful and simple that it would be pleasing to the outsider to read. The whole series has been pervaded by a charming and educating mode of writing, and carry hope, encouragement and precious wisdom to young newspaper men and others all over the English-speaking world.

The possible republication in book form of Mr. Rowell's reminiscences is a consummation devoutly to be wished.

Bring it to book—to not do so would be a crime.

In my opinion, they will bring him a more lasting fame than either the American Newspaper Directory or the Great Advertising Agency of which he has been the successful head.

With so many commendations before him, worded in language indicating both earnestness and good faith, and conscious not only of a wish to see his recollections in a form more conveniently accessible and more likely to be preserved than when scattered through the pages of fifty-two issues of a weekly paper, and also of an only half-admitted desire to see his name appear as author on the title page of a real book, the writer finally decided that he might venture to put the papers into the form in which they are now presented. If the matter, as a whole, is as well received as has been its serial appearance, from week to week, he hardly knows whether he will be more pleased or amazed. One effect of the many kind words with which his work has been favored has been to recall a memory of two young people, whom he knew in boyhood, who, displaying the beauty and perfection of their first baby, in the sunshine of a Sunday morning—in a perambulator newly purchased for the purpose—showed a great deal of appreciation of every compliment bestowed upon the result of their efforts, admitting without hesitation that, having had no previous experience, they had not expected they would be able to do so well, and they were on that account all the more gratified with the result.

Forty Years an Advertising Agent

FIRST PAPER

The first newspaper I remember was the *Caledonian*. It was published at St. Johnsbury, the place where the Fairbanks scales are made. The name came from that of the county, Caledonia, one of the northern tier in the little New England border State of Vermont. My father was a Whig in politics. The *Caledonian* was naturally of that stripe and complexion. Our nearest neighbor, a man named May, was a Democrat, and he, too, took a paper that sustained his political views. His paper became known to me about as soon as the other. It was called the *North Star* and was printed at Danville, a town of more importance then than now. One of these papers carried at its head a verse which I still recall. It read:

> Here shall the press
> The people's rights maintain,
> Unawed by influence
> And unbribed by gain.

My memory does not distinctly recall which paper it was that proclaimed these high, brave and virtuous principles, probably it was the *North Star,* for it ceased to exist half a century ago, while the *Caledonian* continues even until this day.

There was not much occasion for newspapers in that primitive forest region in the northern part of the Green Mountain State at the time my memory first began to take note of affairs. Our nearest neighbor was very near indeed, for both his family and ours found shelter under the hospitable roof of a single log cabin. No advertisement, story, or editorial, made any lasting impression on a nascent brain that recalls with distinctness the spicy taste of the bark of the yellow birch twigs that grew in the woods near by and the beauty of the miniature trout in the little pool in the brook, where the water was dipped up for family consumption, which allowed itself to be impounded within the shiny tin pail and revealed the vermilion spots on its sides to the admiring eyes of the boy of four or five. That must have been about the time of these first memories, for the mind's eye still brings before it the cover pages of the Thomas Almanacs of that period, bearing, as the most conspicuous line, the figures 1842 and 1843. Now and then in literature one comes across a reference to the latch string which, when it hung out, was an evidence of open hospitality, an invitation to enter, and which, when withdrawn, closed the door even more effectively than a lock; and it is always a joy to remember that our house, too, had a latch string and that it *always* hung out.

Although the mind recalls no newspaper advertisement at this time there is a memory of the presence in the house of a bottle containing a liquid of a golden pomegranate color, enclosed in a paper wrapper somewhat approaching the same shade, the taste of the liquid suggesting something akin to the flavor of the meats in the black cherry stones with which a country boy was likely to be acquainted on account of their close connection with a delicacy known as cherry rum. This wonderful patent medicine is still to be found at drug stores, still has the same color, same wrapper and is still known as Ayer's Cherry Pectoral. The only other result of advertising that made an impression on the memory that time has not effaced was a certain poster picture of a sort of calico horse of Arabian pattern and vast grace and beauty, all calculated to emphasize benefits that might be derived from a compound known as Merchants' Gargling Oil. This preparation, too, I am led to believe is still to be found in the drug stores of the country. Not Rosa Bonheur's "Horse Fair," to my maturer and more critical eyes in later years, ever equaled the grace and beauty nor the coloring of that splendid Arabian steed. Having a bearing upon the comparative merits of the two pictures here referred to, there comes to mind a story that used to be told by that eminent advertising agent, scholarly gentleman and prince of raconteurs, the late James H. Bates. "A boy from the western section of the State," he said "had come for a visit to New York City and a whilom schoolmate, who had for some time held a clerkship in the metropolis, took him in hand to show him the sights. Nothing, however, excited his wonder nor aroused any enthusiasm until at last when he had been taken to the great store of A. T. Stewart & Co., at Broadway and Tenth street (now Wanamaker's), after inspecting the display of merchandise, the army of clerks, the crowd of shoppers, the two finally stood in the great central rotunda, where looking upward the eye counted story after story, balcony above balcony, all surmounted by the great skylight overhead, a gleam of satisfaction appeared in the country boy's eyes and he admitted to his friend 'This is something like Rochester.'"

In the matter of newspapers and advertisements that made an impression on the memory, there seems to have been an interim until, in the early fifties of the last century, the parental home had moved across the Connecticut into the Granite State. Lancaster, New Hampshire, was the capital and principal town of Coos County, situated in the northern part of New Hampshire. New Hampshire was a Democratic State, Coos County was the most Democratic portion of the State and Lancaster more intensely Democratic than any other town in the County. There did not live anywhere a more earnest Democrat than James M. Rix and he edited and printed a small weekly paper known, and still known at this day (1905), as the Coos County *Democrat*. It used to be said by those who had an opportunity to take note of such matters that in every remote homestead in Upper Coos (pronounced Co-os), in the best room, there would be found a "light stand" covered with a white cloth, and on the cloth the family Bible and on the Bible a folded copy of Rix's Coos *Democrat*. From his office went out into the wider world many men who became prominent. Col. Edward F. Cross, of the New Hampshire Fighting Fifth, was a printer boy in Rix's office and there, too, served for a time the inimitable Charles F. Browne, who afterwards became known everywhere as Artemus Ward. Browne was finally discharged by Rix on account of a fight with another apprentice, during which they overturned the imposing stone and succeeded in pying a page of that week's paper. Browne's other exploits, as reported by those who still remember him, were limited to striping a sign post in front of the temperance tavern, transforming it into a barber's pole, and in substituting a green pumpkin for a great watermelon that Editor Rix had grown with care from a seed furnished by a friendly Congressman, watched with pride, boasted of with complacency, and finally had promised should regale his guests on an auspicious occasion to occur on a specified date. It is related that so well did the substitute pumpkin match the purloined melon, so judiciously was the stem adjusted, that the exchange was not noticed nor suspected until the grand occasion came, the company had assembled, and Mr. Rix proceeded to cut the melon.

Of the advertisements in the *Democrat* only a few are recalled. One had a picture of a soldier and a horse, and announced the merits of Redding's Russia Salve. Another told of Wistar's Balsam of Wild Cherry and a third offered for sale a certain house in the village, the owner being about to go West; the remarkable thing about this announcement being that the house was not at the time for sale, the alleged owner who advertised it having actually sold it and actually gone West some years before, but the advertisement still stood and did occasional service in filling out a column.

Most citizens who wished for a paper of wider range read the New Hampshire *Patriot*, published at Concord, the State Capital, a paper of an even more rabid stripe of Democracy than Thomas Jefferson would have desired, while those of Whig proclivities subscribed to the *Independent Statesman*, also published at Concord. My father read the Boston *Journal* and there was a considerable package of New York *Tribunes* regularly received at the postoffice. All of these were weekly issues. The daily was not then much of a factor in farming regions or village communities.

SECOND PAPER

The Arab hopes at some period of his life to make a pilgrimage to Mecca. Good Americans, it has been said, go to Paris when they die. More certain than either is it that the boy of Northern New England, when the time arrives for entering upon a business or professional career, will go to Boston. It was to Boston then that the writer made his way in the Spring of 1856, to return to the parental home after losing a situation with attendant salary on account of the financial panic of 1857. During the Winter that followed it is remembered that the Want advertisements in the Boston Daily *Journal* were read with care, while he who perused them was earning, or leastwise receiving, twenty dollars a month for teaching a district school in a neighboring town, the salary being supplemented by free food and lodging on the plan of "boarding around," staying with each family from a day to a week according to the number of pupils coming from that house.

I have always thought I derived much benefit and instruction from a book presented to me by a relative that Winter called *Freedley's Essay on Business*. It was mainly a compilation, but told much of interest about men and methods. In it I read that it was not an unusual thing for the living expenses of a successful wholesale merchant doing business in a great city to reach the sum of $5,000 in a year. Much that the book contained seemed wise and reasonable, but this particular paragraph was turned down as preposterously impossible. How a single family could run through so great a sum in so short a time was beyond my comprehension. Why, not half a dozen persons in the town where I was teaching had acquired so considerable a property as to be worth a total of $5,000, and the few who had were considered wealthy men. Possibly the figures were a misprint. It is perhaps needless to admit that the accuracy of

Freedley was afterwards acquiesced in and that, too, long before the late Pierre Lorillard had proclaimed that no gentleman ought to be expected to live on a lesser expenditure than $1,000 a day.

Among the advertisements in the daily Boston *Journal,* that were read with so much care, those that spoke of opportunities offered to young men to earn money by becoming agents for the sale of books seemed most attractive. The Spring of 1858 found me in Boston again, and it came about that living in apartments in the house where I boarded was a certain Mrs. Bailey, a lady of advanced years, a sister of Col. Charles Gordon Greene, the editor of the Boston *Post* and at that time naval officer of the port of Boston. She was also the mother of Edwin C. Bailey, then, if my memory serves me, Postmaster of Boston and owner of the Boston *Herald.* The good lady's girlhood had been passed in the Granite State and she took a kindly interest in the country boy just come out in the world to make his fortune. One morning she called me into her room and read to me from the *Post* an announcement of the death of a certain Mr. Slack who had been employed in that office as collector from a time to which the memory of man did not run to the contrary, and who, she told me, received the enormously lucrative salary of $2,000 a year. "Now," said she, "you go right down there and give Charles this note and I think he will give you the place." Charles was not as enthusiastic as his sister; furthermore, he was the editor and the vacancy was in the business office controlled by a partner. The partner was shocked beyond expression at the idea of filling Mr. Slack's place before he should have entered into his grave and, I thought, even more pained that the editor should assume to nominate a candidate for a counting room vacancy. The most surprising thing of all, however, was the fact that I did get the place, not at $2,000 a year, but at the more just and moderate compensation of $8 a week, and very good pay it was, and a very good place it proved.

And here for seven years I remained. I boarded in the last street below the Roxbury line and although the work of the day was walking, walking, walking, it was found that the 60 cents a week that might be saved on car fares formed an appreciable addition to that part of the salary left over after settling for board and washing. The walking done in those seven years gave me a pair of calves that would have been a source of pride had knickerbockers been in fashion, and they had hardly got down to normal when, twenty years later, knickerbockers did come into common use with the bicycle and game of golf.

At this time (1858), the best or most popular daily paper in Boston was the *Journal*. Charles O. Rogers was owner and supreme in its control. He was a wonder. Never to be found at his office, as it seemed to me, nearly always to be seen at some saloon near by, red of face, not always steady of gait, not a specially meritorious citizen as seen by an outsider, he was possessed of more business sense than found place in any other newspaper office in Boston, and his paper was run on a higher plane, I think, than any other, from the business, the literary, the ethical, in fact from every standpoint from which it could be viewed, and, while Rogers lived, it did not cease to be the best paper, the most popular, the least objectionable, the most profitable, and to have the largest circle of readers, that is the greatest circulation. Col. Rogers died in 1869. While he lived he held the position in advance of all competitors; but no sooner had he disappeared than the *Herald* advanced to first place.

At the time of my first recollection of it the most conspicuous feature of the Boston *Herald* was an entire first page filled full with the sort of advertisements that appeal to weak men or to such as have acquired diseases through giving away to weaknesses more human than moral. The *Herald* was a survival of numerous unsuccessful journalistic enterprises, and had the popular advantage of being sold at a lower price than any other Boston daily. Under the Bailey management it appeared to take on a lease of vigorous life, was toned down, and improved in every way, and afforded a moderately satisfactory income to its owner.

Besides the *Journal* and the *Herald* there was the *Bee*,

edited by Col. Schouler, a great friend of Col. Greene's in private and a vigorous enemy and savage critic in his editorial capacity. The *Bee* was Republican in politics, the *Post* Democratic. A story was often told of an indignant friend of Greene's who repaired to the office of the *Bee* on one occasion determined to chastise Schouler, but desisted because on entering he there found the two editorial enemies discussing some new story on the most friendly and intimate terms.

The *Post* was a good commercial paper and Democratic, as has been said. The *Advertiser* was also a good commercial paper and Republican. It was the more conservative and sometimes the advocates of the *Post* used to assert of the two that the Boston merchants read the *Post* and filed the *Advertiser*.

There was another commercial paper, the *Courier*. It had once held a high position in the people's regard, but was not prosperous at this time. It still exists, I think (1905), but is now issued weekly. From time to time during the last twenty years or more the New York *Sun* has, in its Sunday column of "Poems Worth Reading," published numerous specimens of witty, satirical verse credited to the Boston *Courier*, that have been of a quality to cause regret that no one has found it worth while to make and publish a collection of the productions of that man, whoever he may be. There is a humor about them that is inimitable.

Besides these there was the Boston *Transcript*, then as now a woman's paper, "the tea table paper of Boston." Col. Greene always caressingly referred to it as "Little Crino-line." Then as now it was about the cleanest, nicest thing in the way of a daily newspaper that anyone knew anything about.

And finally there was the *Traveler*, an evening paper that made a living, and was an extra good paper on Saturdays. Samuel Bowles, who achieved a marked success as publisher of the Springfield *Republican*, had come to Boston for a time and tried his hand on the *Traveler*, but succeeded no better than did Mr. Charles A. Dana when he left New York to see what he could do with a Chicago paper.

There were no Sunday papers then, but Col. W. W. Clapp (who long afterwards was in control of the Boston *Journal*) issued from an office in Franklin street the *Saturday Evening Gazette,* a clean family paper that had a fair circulation and earned a good living for its proprietor. It is alive to this day, as is the *Courier.* There is nothing in this world so hard to kill as a newspaper; and when one is dead that it will stay dead is an assertion that no prudent man will venture to make. It was on Col. Clapp's desk, in that Franklin street office, that for the first time in my life I saw exhibited the placard "This is My Busy Day."

The names of not many papers known at this time can now be recalled. *Gleason's Pictorial* had made a fortune for its owner and had become *Ballou's Pictorial* under the control of M. M. Ballou, who seemed to get as much fun out of it as any editor and publisher could ever hope for. Mr. Ballou afterwards became the founder of the Boston *Globe,* and it ruined him financially. There was a story paper known as the *Olive Branch* that had so many readers that the wonder is why it ceased to exist; also the *True Flag;* all made up of completed stories. *Harper's Magazine* was a pronounced success; the *Knickerbocker* had succumbed to lack of patronage; *Putnam's* appeared; but was making nobody rich. The *Atlantic Monthly* had just been launched upon the sea of popular favor. Bound copies of the first seven volumes have had a place on my library shelves for nearly fifty years, and there are few other books, among many hundreds, that would be more unwillingly parted with. In these appeared the *Autocrat of the Breakfast Table, Elsie Venner, The Minister's Wooing* by Mrs. Stowe; and I doubt if in any equal number of pages of the magnificent monthly periodicals of to-day (1905) can be found so much of literature that will survive the test of half a century.

From Augusta, Maine, a supposedly religious paper called the *Gospel Banner* is remembered, but as it was of a denomination called Universalists and argued that all mankind would eventually be saved, it was, I thought, looked upon with disfavor by self-respecting Christians who "hoped for better things."

A comic paper called *Nic Nax,* published in New York, extracted its price from my small surplus pretty regularly, and as much may be said of another of similar character called the *Picayune.* In the last named I recall a cartoon representing the Harper Brothers, who had achieved a marked success for their *Weekly* and launched their *Bazar* with such favor that it was said to have netted a profit of a hundred thousand dollars the first year of its life. The four earnest men were listening to a reporter who asserted that he had been at the office of the *Picayune,* and while there that the owner of that publication had been seen to laugh. "Laugh! did he," said the elder Harper—"we'll start a *Picayune!*"

Mr. Gilbert, in his operetta of H. M. S. Pinafore, causes the Admiral to say

> I believe that on the seas
> The expression "If you please"
> A particularly gentlemanly tone implants.

Some such idea as this prevailed concerning the influence of the New York *Home Journal,* then conducted by Gen. Geo. P. Morris and Nathaniel P. Willis. I read the paper weekly with profit, I trust, and never ceased to have a sort of reverential regard for Mr. Morris Phillips, who was no relative to Gen. Morris, but succeeded to the control of the paper, and continued it until its merger, in recent years, with the very excellent society journal known as *Town and Country.* Morris Phillips, if not a great man, was a kindly one. Of many good acts of his I have had knowledge and sorry I am that I shall see his face on earth no more.

A paper called *Brother Jonathan,* issued either monthly or occasionally, was more attractive than any other. Its size was enormous, exceeding the dimensions of any I have ever seen, and as to its pictures they were uncountable. The publisher, a man named Day, was also the founder of the New York *Sun,* which, by the way, was the first American daily ever sold for one cent a copy. He is reported to have made a fortune and numerous descendants of his are well known and highly regarded in New York society to-day.

The *Gleason's Pictorial* has been said to have been the first illustrated weekly in America; for years I retained copies containing a thrilling story called "The Robber of the Rhine Valley," concerning which I now only remember that the heroine was described as having "eyes as blue as London milk." Mr. Gleason, in the day of his success, secured from England the services of a man named Carter, who had originally been a bookbinder and later achieved some facility as an engraver on wood. This man afterwards came to New York and set up for himself, discarding the name of Carter and taking the prettier sounding one of Frank Leslie; under which he long exercised a tremendous influence upon the publication of picture papers, illustrated magazines and story books. He died, perhaps, twenty-five years ago and, after his death, his second wife assumed the name of Frank Leslie by Legislative permission and for a considerable time continued the business with perhaps more marked success than her husband had achieved. *Leslie's Weekly,* under different ownership, is to-day a remaining. monument to the energy and ability of the English Mr. Carter.

It is an interesting fact that *Harper's Magazine* was originally established solely as an advertising medium for promoting the sale of the books published by that enterprising firm. For many years all outside advertising patronage was refused and the writer remembers listening, with staring eyes, while Fletcher Harper the younger related that he had that week refused an offer of $18,000 for the use of the last page for a year for an advertisement of the Howe Sewing Machine. It was Commodore Alden B. Stockwell, son-in-law of Elias Howe, and at one time a conspicuous person in Wall Street, who made this offer.

Robert Bonner's New York *Ledger* was as conspicuous on the newsstands as Mr. Curtis's *Saturday Evening Post* is to-day. Bonner had been a compositor on the Hartford *Times.* Coming to New York he acquired the *Merchants' Ledger,* a commercial paper of no prominence or importance, changed its character and in part its name, filled it full of stories, engaged good writers, paid them well and, notwithstanding the admitted fact that novel reading was a wicked waste of time, probably there are few men or women to-day of the age of seventy or thereabouts who do not recall the thrilling interest with which, with or without parental approval, they absorbed the chapters of Sylvanus Cobb's "Gun Maker of Moscow" and "The Hidden Hand" by Mrs. E. D. E. N. Southworth. Fanny Fern wrote exclusively for the *Ledger*. When Edward Everett had accepted the presidency of the Ladies' Mount Vernon Society, having in hand the object of acquiring and preserving for posterity the home of Washington, he found himself unable to decline the, as it then seemed, princely offer of ten thousand dollars for a series of fifty-two articles to appear one column a week for the period of a year, the money to go to increase the funds of the Society. Admiration for Mr. Bonner's enterprise, when I read of it, caused me to become a regular reader of the *Ledger,* and such for numerous years I continued to be. Doubtless that $10,000 investment was a paying advertisement.

Mr. Bonner's most successful method of advertising was the publication of a page or so of a story in the columns of the leading papers having at the foot of the last paragraph the words *Continued in the New York Ledger.* The idea was new and took wonderfully. When he used display his method consisted of column after column and page after page sometimes of agate caps, wherein were repeated the same words over and over, something like this, which I well remember:

```
THE NEW YORK LEDGER
THE NEW YORK LEDGER
THE NEW YORK LEDGER
         WILL BE FOR SALE
         WILL BE FOR SALE
         WILL BE FOR SALE
TO-MORROW  MORNING
TO-MORROW  MORNING
TO-MORROW  MORNING
         THROUGHOUT THE
         THROUGHOUT THE
         THROUGHOUT THE
UNITED STATES
UNITED STATES
UNITED STATES
         AND NEW JERSEY
         AND NEW JERSEY
         AND NEW JERSEY
```

The suggestion that New Jersey is outside of the United States is not often touched upon nowadays, but for many years the references to it were as common as the recurrence of the mother-in-law joke. The origin of the idea came from a condition under which the Camden and Amboy Railroad held its charter, which provided that out of the railroad receipts one dollar should be paid into the State treasury for every through passenger. With that praiseworthy prudence that has raised railroad managers into such prominence among business men and financiers, the directors ordered that a dollar should be added to the regular fare on every through ticket. As transportation began at Jersey City, across the North River from New York, and ended at Camden, across the Schuylkill from Philadelphia in Pennsylvania, it became equivalent to a tax on any citizen of any State who had occasion to travel across the territory of New Jersey.

It has been related that Bonner was often heard to say, when speaking of his success as an advertiser, that over and over he would gather together all the money he could lay his hands on and "throw it all out to the newspapers" and that it seemed as though before he could get back to his office it would all be there again and a whole lot more with it. By and by he had gained riches, and bought trotting horses, which he enjoyed more than confinement to an office, and the paper fell off somewhat from its highest tide of success. More than once he made spasmodic efforts to renew the methods that had been so effective, but the novelty had departed and the money did not so readily return. Finally, when he had become old, he presented the paper to his sons, and they, too, tried to resuscitate its shrinking fortunes, but without success. Then it was changed to a monthly, but that did not go, and now (1905) it is not issued at all. It is a surprising fact that during the days of its great success, the days when it made a millionaire of its owner, it never inserted a single advertisement. It is the only instance I can recall wherein a paper has been specially prosperous without the aid of what is, on all sides, supposed to be the life and soul of a newspaper—the advertising patronage which its fame and circulation brings.

There arose and flourished, for a little time, emanating from New York, a certain paper named *Venus' Miscellany,* such a journal as would be appreciated by the cadets of the red-light district. The knowledge of the contents of a single number would cause the heart of Mr. Anthony Comstock

to beat,
And blossom in purple and red.

It soon ceased to appear, and the impression prevailed that on account of it more than one newsdealer was led to spend a longer or shorter period in a penitentiary.

There was also a weekly whose office of publication was not readily located, but which was as eagerly sought for as is our own *Town Topics* at the present time. It was called *Life in Boston* and was nothing like as nice as *Town Topics,* but seemed to be fully as interesting.

I also recall one other rather saffron journal published in New York by one George W. Matsell, who had once been chief of the city police. It was the New York *Police Gazette,* and it is still alive to-day (1905). I often think of a certain Sunday when I had carried a copy home, and my grandmother, a country bred New England woman then in her seventies, took it up and devoted considerable time to its perusal. To her a murder was a rare and dreadful occurrence, to be talked about for months. Here she found murders by the dozen and other outrages without number. Evidently her first thought was that an epidemic of crime had opened up about her. She wiped her glasses and read and read and wiped her glasses again until finally, in wonder and horror, she laid the paper down and looking at me, not unkindly but with staring eyes, exclaimed, with measured delay and emphasis on every word, "George! What—sort—of—a—paper—is—this?"

The only advertisements during this time that made any impression that has remained in my mind, as I now recall, were those of Geo. W. Simmons, proprietor of a clothing store in North Street, Boston, known as Oak Hall. The situation of this great mart was even more unfavorable than Chatham Square would be to-day in the City of New York, but Mr. Simmons had a great trade, made a fortune, and he and his family maintained an excellent social position in exclusive Boston. The announcements of the business seemed to be everywhere, on fences and rocks as well as in newspapers; and it used to be related that on one occasion a White Mountain tourist, at vast pains and some expense, had ascended Profile Mountain and caused himself to be let down with ropes until his feet finally rested upon the bridge of the nose of "the Old Man of the Mountain." He looked above, at the peaks at the right and left, at Profile Lake at his feet, and congratulated himself that where he stood the foot of man had never been before. Finally facing about, preparatory to permitting himself to be drawn up to the ledge from which he had descended, to his amazement and disgust, he read in bold letters painted on the smooth face of a rock close at hand, the words—VISIT OAK HALL, BOSTON.

THIRD PAPER

In the office of the Boston *Post* I was not long in coming to the conclusion that the value of advertising space was largely influenced by circumstances and conditions, some of which were difficult to understand. The basis of charge was the "square." Originally, doubtless, that word meant a space down the column equal to the width thereof, but when smaller type came to be used in the setting of advertisements the number of lines that had filled the space was still construed to be a proper equivalent for the square, and by and by a still smaller number of lines was adopted; until the square at last became an arbitrary measure, differing in each office, and having a range of anywhere between four and thirty-two lines. In the office of the *Post* a square was eight lines, and the cost of insertion one dollar for the first and fifty cents for each subsequent appearance. If advertisements were frequent or continued, a discount was allowed varying from 10 to 50 per cent, according as the gross total ranged between $10 and $100 within a period of three months. A gross bill of $100 might be reduced one-half and settled for $50, but a gross bill of $90 carried with it a right to no more than 33 1-3 per cent discount and, therefore, could not be liquidated for less than $60. Sometimes an advertiser would ask how much he must advertise to secure 100 per cent discount, but such inquiries were treated as frivolous. Once there was a lawsuit with a publisher who offered $50 in settlement of a gross bill of $97.50, while the office insisted upon receiving $65, and this contention the Court upheld. I was a witness in the case and, on taking my seat after leaving the stand, the defendant asked me, in a low tone, whether I had ever read the story of Ananias, and appeared too disgusted for anything when I told him I never had, and asked him who published it, and if it was good. I found it not customary to take off any discount from an advertising bill unless a discount was asked for. Sometimes after the money had been paid and the bill receipted, the belated inquiry about a discount would be made. The question was embarrassing at the moment, but in such a case there was never any discount.

There were certain classes, such as Wants, To Lets, Co-partnership and Legal advertisements, upon which no discount was ever allowed, and the same rule applied to announcements under the heading of Special Notices or a certain other caption, specified as Business Notices, that contained paragraphs set in reading matter type and charged for at twenty cents a line. The same rule of no discount also applied to any charge for real reading matter, for which fifty cents a line was demanded if it was to be paid for at all.

In addition to the scale of discounts outlined there was an established yearly rate under which a merchant might use the space of a square for $40 per annum or, if to the inquiry whether "inside" insertions were wanted, the answer should be affirmative, the price would in that case be $80 or about the equivalent of fifty per cent reduction from the gross rate charged at fifty cents a square for all insertions after the first.

I never could perceive that there was any special difference in the position actually given, whether the advertiser paid $40 or $80. There was a usage that assumed that the paper might omit yearly advertisements, in the case of an occasional press of matter, and, as an offset to this concession, the yearly advertiser might on occasion occupy space in excess of one square without paying additional. From this the transition was easy to now and then using overspace which, at times, in the case of some customers, would run up to more than half-a-dozen squares. I recall one case of a real estate man who, on such a contract, at $40 a year, used to run in a picture of his office building, occupying five inches of space down the column. And yet the paper was pretty stiff and held customers rather firmly to the letter of a contract. I was able to make excellent use of the possibilities under a flexible rate on an occasion when I negotiated a contract with Mr. Lewis Rice, proprietor of the American House, by which he gave me board and room for a year at $416, and the office, having the case of the real estate man brought up as a precedent, allowed me to balance the charge by a cash payment of $40.

The interest of all this is mainly in the establishment of the fact that advertising space had at that time no recognized measure or standard of value. Practically, within certain limits, it amounted to getting as much as possible and taking what one could get; and my memory does not remind me that those who paid a low price for a large space were, as a rule, any better satisfied than those were who paid a higher price for a smaller space. Then as now the idea that "advertising always pays" was promulgated and the assertion was made then as frequently as now, and is now made as frequently as then, that advertising does not amount to anything and is a waste of money.

I think the hotel incident illustrates that people will often make trades that are payable in swaps and exchanges when they would not for a moment think of paying for the thing obtained the actual money cost to them of the thing to be given in exchange.

The inconsistencies revealed by the methods of charging outlined are not more apparent than real, but they were no greater than is common to-day in a great majority of newspaper offices. Almost every man connected with the business office of a newspaper acquires a habit of speaking of this customer and that as "willing to pay a fair price" or "never willing to pay a fair price," seemingly oblivious of the fact that no such question would arise were the rates uniformly the same to everyone. It is only a first-rate paper that can afford to have a uniform rate of charge, but not every first-class paper by any means does have such a rate.

The New York *Herald*, at the present time (1905), will insert a three line Situation Wanted advertisement for a servant maid for fifteen cents, but will demand thirty cents from her mistress for the same number of words expressing that a servant is wanted. If the mistress should advertise under the heading of Personals, for information about an old servant, the charge for those lines would be ninety cents. If the master, a widower, should wish the address of an old servant and state matrimony as his object the clerk at the *Herald's* advertising counter will mulct him of $3 for three lines, or precisely twenty times as much as he would demand from the missing maid if she should advertise for a situation. Evidently it is not the space he occupies that an advertiser pays for, but an indefinite something the exact value of which neither the man who buys nor the man who sells quite understands.

Advertising is publicity, a means of causing it to be known what service you or I can render, what wants we can satisfy; and the reasons why that service should be sought at our hands. Sometimes a little publicity brings many customers and in that case advertising pays and pays well. An advertisement of a piano, inserted in the bulletin of a church fair, may cost a dollar or two, and its probable power to do good, as compared with other methods of publicity, may not be worth so many cents, but it may chance that the advertisement is seen by a girl whose father has promised to buy her a piano, while she is in the company of another girl whose opinion she values, and they both happen to notice the piano advertisement, and the other girl to remark that her own piano is of that make, and that she thinks it the best of all. Next day, it may be, the girl and the father visit the piano store, mention seeing the advertisement in the church fair bulletin and the dealer pockets a profit of $100 from an outlay of an inconsiderable fraction of that amount. He immediately concludes that advertising is profitable, and that church fair bulletins as advertising media cannot be surpassed. So, too, now and then some one invests a dollar or several dollars in the purchase of a lottery ticket and draws the grand prize or a portion of it, and then he and those who knew of his venture are inclined, for a while at least, to think a lottery a paying investment, although knowing full well that all the prizes do not amount to so much as one-half of the money paid for tickets.

It is the lottery feature about advertising that leads inexperienced persons to think the value of one paper about as great as that of any other, and to be willing to pay, say $5 each, for the service of twenty small papers, when they would hesitate long before consenting to pay $50 for a similar announcement in a single great paper that they know full well not only prints and circulates more copies than all the twenty, but know just as well that the average purchasing power of each reader of the great paper is more than twice that of the average purchasing power of each of the readers of the many smaller ones, and that the influence of the great paper is much larger on each of its readers, and their confidence in anything they see announced in its columns is many times greater. The science of advertising is still a puzzle, and those who give advice about it with greatest confidence are always to be found in the ranks of those whose experience is but moderate.

FOURTH PAPER

It has been already stated that my business in the office of the Boston *Post* was to look after the collection of bills and accounts due to the office. Naturally, however, it came about, there being no advertisement solicitor employed, that Mr. James H. Beals, my chief, would suggest that as I knew Mr. So-and-So by sight I should step into his place of business and ask him if the advertisement seen this morning in the *Journal*, the *Advertiser* or the *Courier* should not also appear in the *Post*. Every one who has been young, and while young has attempted to solicit orders for advertising, can appreciate the dread with which I approached this or that great man to beg his patronage and the feeling of something almost like joy that welled in my bosom when I discovered that the man with the requisite authority was out to luncheon, or, better still, out of town. There were exceptions, however. The experiences were not all disagreeable. Now and then the advertiser seemed to want to see me, and gave an order as though it was a favor to him; and out of acquaintances begun or improved in this way I found friends who were pleasant then and useful and profitable in after years. If a young man represents a newspaper of merit, and will tell his story clearly, distinctly, and without circumlocution, he will have few experiences that he need regard as disagreeable and many times will admit, when the day is over, that its hours have not only produced profit but pleasure and satisfaction as well.

Having become familiar with Boston, its crooked streets and alleyways, I had a longing for a sight of the great metropolis, the City of New York, and one time, in midsummer, in the year 1860, my ambition was gratified. I was given a list of persons to be called on and consulted on the subject of advertising in the *Post*. There was also a package of bills for varying amounts for services rendered, as it seemed to me, at a date that indicated neglect on the part of the office bookkeeper that they had not been sent in before. I had a pass on the railroad to Stonington, Connecticut, and on the steamer from that port to New York and, better than all, a due bill taken in payment for advertising done in the *Post* for the Fifth Avenue Hotel. It was a grand hotel in those days, the finest in America. It had one grave fault, it was too far up town, so far, in fact, that a business man could hardly afford the time needed to go and come. The Astor House, corner of Barclay street, the Metropolitan, near Prince street, and the St. Nicholas between were the popular houses.

Paran Stevens kept the Fifth Avenue, also the Revere House in Boston, the Continental in Philadelphia, the Battle House in Mobile, and I know not how many others, and the Fifth Avenue made more money than all the others, and more than any hotel had ever made before—and not many have ever made so much since. It was a gold mine. Amos R. Eno owned it. When Mr. Eno died his estate counted up numerous millions, but in the financial panic of 1857 he was "land poor" and became embarrassed. He had projected a great block of stores, the walls were built, he was in a quandary; when one day Mr. Stevens came to him, induced him to change his stores into a hotel and advanced the money to enable him to carry out the new suggestion. Who looks at a plan of the Fifth Avenue Hotel, either of the ground floor or any other, will not fail to note that it is intersected by thick walls running from front to rear; and everyone knows that the principal office or exchange is planned precisely as it would be for an ordinary store, being of uniform width throughout the entire length.

It was at the Fifth Avenue that the Western man was said to have had the experience I heard Senator Wolcott, of Colorado, relate to the New England Society on one occasion. The man had disappeared, his family, who had accompanied him to the city, became uneasy about him. At last he came to his room, and to the anxious inquiry of his wife, "Where in the world have you been all day?" he responded

calmly, "I've just been in the cuspidor walking pro and con."
Senator Platt, Senator Gorman, of Maryland, Senator
Aldrich, of Rhode Island, Governor Odell and many other
Senators and Governors may be often found at this house
to-day. It is perhaps the best specimen in the world (1905)
of a hotel conducted on the American plan. I am living
there myself this winter, but this is no paid notice. In this
house in 1860 the writer first saw and rode in a passenger
elevator or "lift," and in the place where it is situated there
is to-day a notice that in the year 1859 was installed in the
space, "the first passenger elevator ever used in any hotel,
or any other building, in this country or the world."

Paran Stevens was a Vermont man. It has been related
that while young he thought well of himself when he owned
and attended a well-known stallion, but, becoming a hotel
man, he soon made himself the best hotel man America had
ever seen. Late in life he married a beautiful girl who had
been a mill hand in a cotton factory at Lowell, Mass. She
long outlived her husband, became a leader in the ultra-
fashionable set in New York society, and the names of her
daughter and of her daughter's daughter are often seen in
society notes—the Hon. Mrs. Paget, etc., etc.

New York was different from Boston. One could stop
on Broadway without creating surprise, and might stand in
a doorway to look over memoranda without exciting attention or curiosity. The men whom I was to see about advertising orders were mainly out of town or out of business,
and those against whom I had bills to collect appeared to be
mainly out of business, or dead, or both. I located one man
in Morrisania, a place situated many miles away and approached by horse cars through Third avenue, fare five
cents each way. After three trips, two made by appointment, this good man paid over to me $2 on account. I never
saw him more, nor was the account ever balanced. Another
man, a hairdresser, after some demur, paid me $10, the
amount of the bill against him, and ordered his advertisement stopped. He seemed to be pretty earnest about it. I
got no other money. My feet were sore, my shoes were

somewhat depleted in the matter of thickness of sole, I had collected $12 and paid out thirty cents for car fare to and from Morrisania. I had my hotel bill entered on the back of the due bill I had in my pocket. It was $12.50, being $2.50 a day for five days (they charge more in 1905), and by means of my passes on boat and railroad was back in Boston after an absence of six days and six nights. I did not feel enthusiastic as I made my report to my employers and the office bookkeeper, but no fault was found, no unpleasant comments made; in fact, the tendency seemed rather in the direction of smiling acquiescence rather than any disposition to criticise. Some months afterward I learned that the wonder on the part of the manager, who usually attended personally to New York business, was, not that I only collected $12, but that I succeeded in getting so much as one dollar or, for that matter, so much as a cent.

"Mr. Batcheller said he wanted his advertisement stopped," I reminded Mr. Beals when credit for the payment had been posted on the ledger. He made no comment and I repeated the statement, whereupon he looked at me with an amused expression and said, "I guess Batcheller has ordered that advertisement stopped as often as four times a year for the last four years."

FIFTH PAPER

Du Maurier, in his story of "Trilby," that everybody once read and no one now knows anything about, resurrected the lines of a once popular ballad:

> Don't you remember
> Sweet Alice, Ben Bolt,
> Sweet Alice, whose hair
> Was so brown?

There was a later suggestion that Alice now lay in the churchyard. The thought may run on to a still later time when her boy sweetheart no longer expresses a remembrance because he has joined her and is not here to speak. The mind can look forward to another not very distant period when there will be few, or none, who can recall any memory of either Alice or Ben, because both of them had passed from human vision before those had come into being to whose memory the appeal would have to be addressed.

These thoughts come to mind in connection with recollections of persons with whose faces I became familiar in the years of that early connection with a newspaper office. I recall a bare room, not a very tidy one, with a single desk, two chairs, a man, not old but with thin hair—foretelling baldness—sitting, his face in his hands, his elbows resting upon the desk. It was Gen. Benjamin F. Butler, in his not much used Boston office, a year or two before the Civil War.

In a busier, better organized lawyer's office I recall a bright, round, kindly face, good wholesome color, dark hair, a brisk manner, and remember that the man became very conspicuous soon after as the great War Governor, John A. Andrew.

In still another office, not appearing so brisk as the last named but much more so than the first, I recall the kindly, thoughtful, wrinkled—oh! so wrinkled—face of Rufus Choate; and that the name on the check given in payment for a year's subscription resembled a spider track more than a signature.

The home of Wendell Phillips was in Essex, not far from Washington street, and the orator himself sometimes opened the door in answer to the ring. The quiet of the library, the dignity, the kindly dignity of the man, an air of refinement about the surroundings: a memory of all these comes before me when the name of the great Anti-Slavery champion is mentioned.

Over the Quincy market, that was an eighth of a mile in length, the old firm of Oliver Ames & Son, makers of shovels and that sort of thing, had a mammoth wareroom (this was before Oakes Ames and the days of the Credit Mobilier), and a partner of the house was Peter Harvey, a heavily built, florid man with, as it seemed to me, a choleric temper and a disposition to allow me to call numerous times to collect his subscription to the paper. He was generally known and spoken of as "the friend of Daniel Webster." In after years I often wondered how so chilly a personage as he appeared to be could have written so charming a book as his biography of Webster certainly is.

An elderly man with a brisk, nervous manner was in the counting room, from time to time, in the interest of life insurance, and I recall the pride and satisfaction with which he replied to inquiries about the progress of a son who had gone to New York, and became active in the line of business with which the father's interest seemed to be joined. That son was Henry B. Hyde, so long the head, almost the creator, of the great Equitable Life Assurance Society.

An older man, of reserved, dignified manner, came in now and then to look at files of the paper, to resurrect some paragraph that had interest for him, and I learned that his name was Motley, and that he had a son named John Lothrop Motley, then United States Minister at The Hague.

Still another old man, less active, less prosperous, less self-assertive than either of the others, was a Mr. Derby; and he, too, is remembered on account of his son, one of the earliest American humorists, known to those who remember him at all as John Phoenix.

The face of one other man comes before me, a tall, large, wholesome-looking personage, perhaps not quite up to the times in appearance and manner, always wearing a curious deprecating smile—not a frequent but an occasional visitor at the office. The business that brought him being gener-- ally an announcement of a railroad excursion of not any great importance to some point not far away. There seemed to be a disposition, on the part of the manager, to have fun with this man, always in a half bantering, but not wholly disrespectful way, and I remember that anything he really seemed to want to have done or said by the paper was usually acquiesced in ; and it was also understood that if his bills were not promptly paid no fuss would be made about it. I believe, however, that his bills were always paid, eventually. When he went from the office, on the first occasion that I recall seeing him, the manager, looking at the retreating figure rather quizzically, told me "That man has a charter from the Congress of the United States to build a railroad to the Pacific Ocean." San Francisco was not twenty years old then ; Omaha was the name of an Indian tribe, not of a city ; Los Angeles was a village inhabited by a few score people of Spanish origin, and Denver had no place on the map. By and by I heard of George Francis Train, Oakes Ames, the Credit Mobilier, and knew that a Pacific railroad had been built and that the charter, which had been Mr. Josiah Perham's cherished possession, and about which he was so often ridiculed, really did come into effective use in carrying forward the great enterprise. I never see the kindly but rather bucolic countenance of the venerable Mr. Russell Sage without being reminded of Perham ; the same face, the same smile, only Mr. Sage is much older—but then Mr. Perham is dead.

In one lawyer's office on Court street, the office of Stillman B. Allen, a considerable collection business was done, and there at one time appeared a square-shouldered, curly-haired, red-cheeked young man, who was always so polite, attentive, civil and prompt, that to have occasion to be brought into contact with him was a pleasure. Before I left Boston his name appeared on the sign, which became Allen & Long, and later I was glad to hear of him as Congressman, Governor and Secretary of the Navy. He was John D. Long, now as then of Hingham, Mass.

Fletcher Webster, a son of Daniel Webster, had an office in the Surveyor's Department of the Custom House. He may have held the office of Surveyor. He was slow pay and impressed one as a dull man, although rather fine looking, with black hair and eyes. He became Colonel of a regiment in the Civil War, but I do not remember that he distinguished himself either by the exhibition of great ability or the lack of it.

Then there was the Pension Commissioner, Isaac O'Barns, a man who had been, I think, a personal friend of and an appointee under President Franklin Pierce, and whom no subsequent President seemed to feel like displacing. He was a tall, broad-shouldered, white-haired old man, a typical old school gentleman. He boarded at the Bromfield House. His office was at the Custom House, where he went late and from whence he returned early. He had lost his voice and spoke only in a hoarse whisper, and the unexpected quality of his few sentences led to as many funny stories being attributed to him as, in later days, was the case with that famous Baltimorean who reformed and became a New Yorker, I mean the late William M. Travers. It was told of Isaac O'Barns that he promised to subscribe for the erection of a Baptist church somewhere on the one condition that they should "Baptize 'em in hot water;" that when he had asked at the Tremont House bar for 'rot gut" and been handed out the brandy decanter—the barkeeper knowing he always drank brandy—he remarked, after completing the transaction, "You keep a pretty good house here, don't you?" To which the man responding that such was the intention, asked "What do you find this morning to specially commend, Mr. O'Barns?" received for answer, "You give a man just what he calls for." Again, one day stopping on the edge of a crowd in State street, at the scene of the Boston massacre, just below the old State House, where an itinerant preacher was holding forth, he asked "What's this? What's this?" and was told that it was a meeting of Second Adventists. "What are they? What are they?" whispered the old gentleman, and being told that they looked for the second coming of Christ he seemed to wait several minutes with interest, but finally inquired in his loudest whisper, "Expect him to-day?" Finally on his death bed, or when he thought he was dying, and the doctor had pronounced his feet warm and said no one ever died with warm feet, the old gentleman inquired in his whisper whether the doctor had forgotten the case of John Rogers.

Of all the men of that day there are a few still remaining, and one of these I sometimes meet in recent years, I refer to J. Parker Whitney, who in 1858 was a dealer in paints in Union street near Hanover. I recall an occasion when a hotel man, proposing to do the honors of his place, asked whether we would drink claret or champagne, and Whitney said, in response, that we would as soon have both as either, and we had both. Whitney always seemed to get all there was to be had. He graduated from paints and oils, did something in mines, gold and copper, has a California ranch to-day with sixty miles of stone wall upon it, came near being the first United States Senator from Colorado, has long been rated a millionaire by the mercantile agencies, and has been made more or less conspicuous the past year or two on account of the frolics of a fun-loving son and a Hebe-like daughter, who, beautiful as she may be, can hardly compete in loveliness with the memory of her mother when, twenty years ago, she, too, was just out of school. Mr. Whitney is known to all who go fishing at the Rangeley Lakes, for his Camp there, at Mosquito Brook on Lake Molychuckamuck, has stood for more than forty years, and there has not been perhaps a single winter of them all that he has not been there, with good company, long enough to get a deer or two, a touch of zero weather, and to renew the memory of visits made before and friends who will not come

again because they have now gone beyond earth's boundary
lines. At one time Mr. Gilbert E. Jones, long of the New
York *Times,* was associated with Mr. Whitney in the man
agement of the Mosquito Brook Camp, as is evidenced in the
combination of their two monograms, still to be noted artis-
tically carved by Gillie's own hand, and affixed to the door
that fronts the Lake, as the writer well remembers.

An editorial writer on the *Post,* at this time, was B. P.
Shilliber, whose *nom de plume* was Mrs. Partington. His
humorous sayings had a wide vogue, but probably did not
produce much of an addition to his income, which was a
stated salary of $15 a week. The business of selling jokes
in the open market was not then established. Mrs. Partington was a Boston Mrs. Malaprop, and a great many of her
sayings were comments upon the conduct and experiences of
Ike, a grandson or nephew, who was a sort of pre-historic
Buster Brown. Ike had to be vaccinated, and the old lady,
mentioning the matter, said he was "noculated by an ocu-
list." A woman who said that she could not bear children
was comforted with the remark, "Perhaps if you could you
would like them better."

I have before referred to a Mrs. Bailey, to whom I was
indebted for a valuable service. It became a part of my
duty, as years went on, to collect a sum of money for this
good lady and to take it to her on a specified day each month,
Col. Greene, her brother, paying half and Edwin C. Bailey,
her son and owner of the Boston *Herald,* the other half.
The cashier at the *Herald* office, R. M. Pulsifer, by name,
had instructions to honor my demands. The draft was not
a heavy one, I think about seventeen dollars from each contributor. The lady then lived at Chestnut Hill, some miles
out of Boston, and in the goodness of her dear old heart she
would have me stay to drink a cup of tea with her on these
occasions, and more than likely there would be hot biscuits
and a slice of ham or cold tongue, a bit of jam or preserves,
and I would be called upon to tell as much of the world's
affairs as passed under my immediate eye, and in return was
often taken into her confidence, we being both from the

Granite State, and she as near her eighties as I to my twenties.

On one occasion there was mention made that Mr. Salmon P. Chase had retired from Lincoln's Cabinet and his successor as Secretary of the Treasury would be William Pitt Fessenden of Maine, and I came away with the impression that the new Secretary was a cousin or nephew of my good friend, Col. Greene of the *Post*. Next morning I stood in the counting room, behind the newspaper counter, when Col. Greene came in, as was his custom, to take a copy of the morning issue in his hand, and, as I handed him the paper and said good morning, I ventured to ask him about his relationship to the new Secretary. He looked at me through his gold-bowed spectacles with, I thought, a shade of annoyance, and turned away without answering, but, pausing at the door, he turned to me and said "Before you go out to-day come up to my room." I did this a little later. He sat at his desk, a pretty plain affair, in his editorial sanctum—decidedly primitive quarters he had—but he a handsome, stately, kindly, well-dressed, clean-shaven, healthy man of between fifty and sixty years of age. He did not ask me to be seated, but spoke in earnest tones. "You know my sister is much older than I. She was a young woman when I was a baby. When she was a young woman she had an experience of the sort that people, who have had such, do not talk about. The father of her son had been the principal of the Academy at Boscawen and from there went to another academy at Fryeburg, Maine, and there the boy was brought up. The father's name was Fessenden and Pitt was the son. He is about my own age and a mighty good fellow he is, too. Now," continued the Colonel, "you can see that if you had known a little more this morning you wouldn't have been asking questions, and now that you know so much I think I can trust you to keep your mouth shut." I would not have told the story here had it not come to me, many years later, from a very old man who, relating a personal interview had with Daniel Webster at the time he had failed to receive the

Presidential nomination that went to Gen. Scott, and the great expounder somewhat repiningly found fault with the bad faith, as he thought it, of a young politician in Maine, who had failed to support his claims ; and then the great man proceeded to tell of a certain horseback ride he had taken thirty years before, from Boscawen in New Hampshire, to interview the principal of the academy at Fryeburg, Maine, in the interest of a certain baby boy who, had he remembered and acknowledged the obligation now, might have been a help, but had not so proved himself.

SIXTH PAPER

There was one experience in connection with my service with the *Post* that has always impressed me as almost wonderful, and I mention it here believing it may encourage some young man to attempt to overcome a bad habit before it is too late. The outcome in my case is not as encouraging as I could wish, but there certainly was progress made; perhaps a stronger will would have achieved a permanent success. The case was this: from boyhood -I had been afflicted with a bad memory for names. I even forgot the names of boys who had been schoolmates. On one occasion, during my experiences in Boston in a thread and needle store in 1856, a young man from my own New Hampshire town had a job driving a market wagon, and occasionally called at the store where I was employed, and once came in to spend a Sunday with me and brought a watermelon for our personal delectation. Late in the afternoon of that Sunday I had to ask this friend to tell me his name. This weakness seemed so serious a fault that I thought very likely it might lead to my losing the good place I had fallen into, and I resolved to overcome the deficiency if I possibly could. So effective was that resolve that during the entire seven years of my employment there arose no case where I had difficulty about remembering a name; and there is no name that became known to me during that seven years that I cannot now recall without effort, after a lapse of more than forty years, and yet (and this is the discouraging part of the story) no sooner had I left the employment, wherein that resolve had been made, and commenced a business of my own, than the old infirmity reasserted itself, and has continued to this day; to such an extent that I confidently expect some day to have to consult my card case to ascertain my own name.

Pursuing my duties as collector, I conceived it to be important to keep appointments with care. If a man said "Call next Thursday and I will pay you," I was certain to be in evidence when Thursday came, and I noted, after long experience, that while young and hopeful I believed every man intended to do with me exactly as he promised. The fact that I did so believe had influence in inducing him to sustain the good opinion he could see he had impressed me with. Afterwards, when, from frequent disappointments, my faith had become somewhat dimmed, the efficacy of that promise became lessened to a degree that was quite perceptible. I made most painstaking efforts on certain quarter days, first of January, April, October, etc., to collect as many as one hundred different bills in one day, but on no occasion was I ever able to accomplish so much, although I now and then came very near to it. My work afforded a good opportunity to learn human nature. The man who was short of money when I called was likely always to be short of money. The man who failed to keep his promise to pay on a certain day generally failed to keep his promise. The man who paid the bill on presentation did the same next time and every time. This other man would have the bill left, that he might examine it, and then would pay the next time I called; and when I called again would have forgotten to look into the case, but, on account of his promise, would on the second occasion assume the accuracy of the account and pay it. With the next bill it would be the same story over again. In time I came to have the opinion that I could tell in advance what every bookkeeper, cashier or principal would say to me when I presented a bill, and in nearly every case I would be right.

Many persons came to know me by my occupation instead of by my name, and for years after that occupation had come to an end I would meet a familiar face here or there and be greeted with a "How are you, *Post?*" If people might be depended on to say the same thing on the recurrence of the same sort of an occasion, so, too, it was noted that the prosperous establishment, as a rule, remained prosperous and grew more so, while those of a different character became more and more down at the heel as years progressed. One man on Commercial street, named Bradshaw, was a dealer in flour, and on the stove in his office there would generally be little gobs or balls of dough, and I rarely ever saw him, either in his office or near by on the street, that he did not have a patch of flour, about the size of a wafer, on the end of his nose. Whenever I come across the name of Bradshaw the picture of that flour merchant arises before me, and always with the spot of flour on the end of his nose.

At the office of the Boston *Herald* my monthly visits made me acquainted with the cashier, a young man in the early twenties, bright of eye, civil and engaging of manner, of slight build, not above medium height, and having the general appearance of a good clerk who had plenty to do and was not growing wealthy from the compensation paid him. His name was R. M. Pulsifer, and a little later it became well known in newspaper circles. It has been stated that under the ownership and control of Edwin C. Bailey the *Herald* had entered upon a period of prosperity. Bailey was a man of superior intelligence; large, florid—not handsome —brusque, not over-generous, not over-popular, in general considered a supremely selfish man. He had trained several young men to manage the various departments of the paper, and they had learned to perform their tasks creditably. The paper seemed to have prospects of better days ahead. Mr. Bailey wished to go to Europe and enjoy a vacation. It had occurred to him that it would be a good thing to bind his young managers more closely to the paper by making it possible for each to acquire an interest in the property. The negotiations resulted in the sale of the paper for $300,000— a sum that seemed a preposterous price—to five young men, employees, no one of whom had ever possessed a thousand dollars in his life, each to be responsible for the others. And so it came about that the *Herald* changed hands. The new firm of R. M. Pulsifer & Co. was the owner, and Bailey went abroad with the comfortable feeling that the interest on the great indebtedness would be about as much as the paper could be made to produce. He could count on the boys doing their level best to carry the great burden, and, by and by, when his two years' mortgage matured, he would return, take back the property, and let the boys off. This was in 1869.

Well, Bailey went away, the new firm continued the business on the plans which Bailey had inaugurated; the affairs of the *Herald* had reached a stage where things had begun to come its way; the Civil War was ended. Everybody was prosperous. All newspapers made money, and the *Herald* more than any other in Boston; the obligations to Bailey were met out of the earnings and Bailey never had a ghost of a chance of owning it again. He retired to New Hampshire, where he exhibited some political ambition, but finally died while in the prime of life, a discontented and disappointed man. Pulsifer, on the other hand—gentle, lovable, rather competent than otherwise, stood at the head of the most important daily in Boston—was possessed of an income beyond the wildest dreams of a few years before. His influence was great, his credit good for anything he might wish, his name was sought here and there as director, manager, patron of this and that, and in time he found himself involved beyond his depth. Chagrined at what appeared to have been bad management or bad judgment; that his brilliant prospects had led to defeat and failure, he one day, in a despondent moment, took his life and was thought to have died a bankrupt. It turned out, however, when cooler heads assumed charge of his affairs, that they straightened themselves out amazingly, and in the end, every creditor received a hundred cents on the dollar, and a competence was in reserve for Pulsifer's family. Had it not been for his love of approbation, and desire to be of use to every one who sought his aid or influence; in other words, if he could have attended to the paper and let outside things alone, he might be alive to-day, a millionaire, the leading newspaper man of New England, and still have to his credit several of the allotted three score years and ten. As it is (as it was to be), however, poor Pulsifer has long rested peacefully in his grave; but none who remember him ever say a word to his discredit, or think of him as other than generous and lovable to a degree that is all too rare.

At the corner of Court street and Court Square, in a basement, there was in those days a roomy restaurant, rather dark, where one could get a better beefsteak than could be had elsewhere, and where everything on the bill of fare was good. It was a man's restaurant. The only entrance was through a saloon, passing the bar to reach the stairway leading down. On a corner in Cornhill Court, not far away, reached by two narrow lanes from Washington street and another from Court Square, was another place, perhaps equally excellent in its way, although I am not certain that its line extended beyond wines, liquors, cigars and the things that go with them. This place was known to everybody as George Young's, the other as Parker's or Harvey D. Parker's. Later Mr. Parker built the Parker House in School street, the first attempt in Boston to conduct a hotel on what is known as the European plan. It became a better hotel than Boston had ever had before; and at a much later period two stewards at Parker's, Hall and Whipple by name, secured the construction of a hotel in Cornhill Court, on the site of George Young's, and called the house Young's Hotel. It was an immediate success. At first the house entertained only men, but in time it spread over the whole space, and now the original site of both Young's and Parker's is covered by a great hostelry known as "Young's," and ladies, as well as men, are welcome guests.

Nothing succeeds like success. Messrs. Whipple and Hall revived the old Adams House on Washington street and of this Mr. Hall afterwards took personal charge, relinquishing his interest in Young's, and at a later day Mr. Whipple acquired the Parker House in School street, where both he and Hall had been trained, and this he retains, and has also acquired the Touraine, corner of Tremont and Boylston streets, which the writer, after a pretty wide experience, has at times felt like pronouncing, taking it all in all, the most complete and perfect hotel to be found to-day (1905) on the surface of the globe.

SEVENTH PAPER

There was one curious experience of rather trivial importance that made a lasting impression on my mind. I will endeavor to relate the circumstances as they transpired. A very respectable firm in Milk street was at that time promoting the sale of a dressing or blacking for ladies' shoes, and did a little advertising. Brown & Brother was the name of the concern. One day the senior Mr. Brown suggested to me that he would be glad to send a dozen bottles of the blacking to the editorial room of the *Post* and to have a short commendatory notice appear in the paper, setting forth the good qualities of the mixture as they should be revealed from a practical application. Being advertisers to some extent and likely to become better customers by and by, if the public should appreciate their goods, there was nothing unusual in the request, and I promised to speak with the editor about the matter. With this understanding the package was sent to me and under my supervision taken to the editorial room, where I told my story. It was not the editor-in-chief that I saw, but his son, and the younger man did not appear to be specially enthusiastic about the business. "They advertise in the *Post,* do they?" he asked. "They are a respectable firm, you say," continued he, and then, as a finality, "Well, I don't know anything about the stuff and they know all about it. Tell Mr. Brown to write such a notice as he thinks he ought to have and I'll print it." I thereupon waited upon Mr. Brown; but instead of being pleased he appeared greatly pained at the proposal. He had not intended to bribe the editor by a present of a dozen bottles of blacking. He had hoped the blacking would be taken home, that the women folks would use it, and, after a suitable test of its virtues, there would appear in the paper a short announcement that would be, in very truth, an editorial opinion of the merits of the compound; while what I was proposing was equivalent to printing in the *Post* not the editor's opinion, but Mr. Brown's opinion, and that was already before the public in the numerous advertisements that had been put forth.

I had never given the matter so much thought before, but I became interested. "What you want, Mr. Brown, is that the *Post* shall say a few words commendatory of your article. Now the *Post* is willing to do this, but it so happens that the managing editor is not so situated as to wish to invite public attention to the views of any females who may happen to be dwelling in his house. He, personally, has no acquaintance with your goods, and does not need to have any. He knows you, however, by reputation, and knowing that you have an intimate knowledge of all that can be said for your goods, he is willing to allow you to be the editor so far as the particular paragraph we have in mind is concerned. When the paragraph appears in the paper it will be an expression of the opinion of the paper, will it not, and what more do you want?"

But it would not do at all, and I think Mr. Brown's high ideas of the purity and value of an editorial opinion suffered a great jolt. For my own part I have never ceased, whenever I read in a paper, an expression of opinion or a record of a transaction, to almost unconsciously try to read between the lines, to see perhaps, or to try to imagine, what sort of a man or woman or boy it was that really wrote the article, and what were the conditions that allowed it to get into print, why its tone was this way, that, or the other. Still my conclusion is that an advertiser, who is offered an opportunity to puff his own goods in his own words, and have the matter appear without cost, in a paper of his selection, had better lose no time in availing himself of the opportunity. If the paper, in other days, should see fit to give expression to a contrary opinion what a joy it will be to confront it with an opposite view taken from its own columns. In my personal feelings, however, I am, after all these years, inclined to agree, and be in sympathy, with Mr. Brown, and for this reason: Mr. Brown, being so near to his goods, so saturated with his subject, so to speak, can only say what he has said many times before. There will be no freshness or spontaneity about his paragraph, and, being an honest, conscientious man, he will say nothing that is not absolutely and accurately true. The editor of the paper, on the other hand, knows little about the goods to be puffed and cares less. He wishes to say what will please the man who solicits the puff, and may be led to commit himself by ascribing or permitting one of his young men to ascribe certain virtues that the proprietor would not claim, although he would see no impropriety in using the notice on the strength of its being an editorial opinion. It has been said that there is no flattery so subtle as that which is undeserved, and, consequently that nothing pleases a man so much as to be praised for qualities that he is conscious he does not possess. After all, the supposed overstrained praise may turn out to be based upon solid grounds. Not every owner of a proprietary article knows in the beginning all the things his preparation will eventually be found to be good for.

When the famous Lord Timothy Dexter of Newburyport, Mass., sent his celebrated cargo of warming pans to the West Indies it is not probable that he would have asserted that the covers were good for skimmers and the basins for dippers. More probably it was the editor of the *Sugar Makers' Magazine* of that day who discovered these unexpected uses and proclaimed them at a time when skimmers and dippers were needed and none were to be had. The warming pans made very tolerable skimmers and dippers, and not to have commented on their value as such would have been a failure to render a good service to the sugarmakers who were subscribers for the magazine.

I have asserted that the business men with whom my occupation brought me into contact remained about the same from year to year, but there were occasional exceptions. Sometimes a new element crept in and disturbed the ordinary routine. In South Market street a certain Samuel Page did business, and it generally took about twenty calls to gather in the $8 due for his year's subscription. One day, however, there seemed to have been a change. A bright-eyed young man stood at the desk, talked a little, asked a question or two, paid the bill, and made some inquiries about advertising and its cost. Soon I began to hear about this young man. On the Fourth of July he released a bald eagle on Boston Common and got his name in the papers. Then he painted black the great iron fence, a mile long, that surrounded Boston Common, using a substance that was new then, produced from coal tar—a sort of by-product. Shortly after Boston became too small for George Shepard Page and he went to New York. Later he was rich and possibly (a little later) poor again; but he was heard of, and among the many good things he did was to draw public attention to the enormous brook trout to be found, and the good sport to be had in capturing them, in the waters of the Rangeley group of Lakes in the State of Maine, the head waters of the Androscoggin; and he it was that established there the Oquossoc Angling Association, that has existed from his time to this day, fully forty years; and many are the memories of pleasant hours and delightful fish stories that, in connection with that resort, will flood the minds of numerous good citizens, whenever an opportunity for such thoughts is invited or obtrudes itself.

Having the privilege of a free admission to the theatres and other places of amusement, in consideration of my newspaper connection, and not possessing a very wide social connection, nor having anything over-luxurious in the way of attractions at my lodgings, it came about that I acquired a pretty intimate acquaintance with the merits of the various plays, actors, singers, musicians and other entertainers in general. John Gilbert, afterwards so popular in New York, was a prime favorite at the Boston Theatre. There, too, the charms and merits of Mrs. Barrow and Mrs. John Wood were recognized and acknowledged. Edwin Booth, when scarcely more than a boy, was thought well of, but his brilliant future did not seem to be by any means assured; and the same may be said of Adelina Patti, a miss in her teens, wearing her hair hanging down her back in two long braids, as was once a common enough school-girl fashion. Brignoli was admired by the ladies on account of his good looks and magnificent tenor voice, and condemned for his stiff and awkward manners. Who was ever so fat and, at the same time, so amiable as Susini? Later two beautiful girls came on the operatic stage, Miss Hinkley and Clara Louise Kellogg. How vastly funny William Warren could be, at the Museum, and then, too, what a masterly actor he was when a great part was assumed by him. Never was there a nobler, a more lovable Sir Peter Teazle. Did any other person ever succeed in making everybody laugh as Dan Setchell did? Was ever anybody so fairy-like as Agnes Robertson? Maggie Mitchell and Lotta came later, and they, too, were very much admired and enjoyed. Burton in "Toodles" as he eyed the sharp point of his cravat that stuck up threateningly before his eyes, or reached out a second hand to grasp the candle, held in the other, as though there were two candles and, on investigation, pronouncing it "A sort of a double barreled cand'l." There was good George Holland, the preaching of whose funeral sermon afterwards gave its famous name to "The Little Church Around the Corner" in metropolitan New York. The elder Booth had passed away before my time. Forrest was so much a star that I rather think my free admission was held up while he appeared. Thalberg was master of the piano. Ole Bull made the violin speak and laugh and cry. Who that ever listened to him can forget the lectures of Artemus Ward? There was the one on "The Babes in the Wood," in which no reference was made to the babes nor robins nor woods nor leaves but when, at a point having to do with Shakespeare or Roman history, the lecturer ventured the statement that Brutus was killed by Cæsar and, after a pause, with a semi-idiotic smile added the words "and et tu," some persons who had not laughed before would burst into uncontrollable mirth, and everybody seemed to join in at last, whereupon the lecturer seemed to be both amazed and injured. There came a time when a handsome, black-haired, black-eyed young man gave, at the Howard Athenæum, a better exhibition of Richard III than was ever rendered elsewhere or by any other actor, either before or since, and one regrets to know that the youth who seemed to fit the part so well came afterwards into such unenviable notoriety. He was John Wilkes Booth, brother of Edwin, afterwards assassin of the beloved President Abraham Lincoln.

As the names are mentioned, scenes and portraits rise to the mind's view with more distinctness than those of John Drew or the "College Widow," seen last week or last night, and what a pleasure these pictures afford:

> For now when on my couch I lie
> In vacant or in pensive mood
> They burst upon that inward eye
> Which is the bliss of solitude.

EIGHTH PAPER

As years passed on there was an increase allowed on the $8-a-week salary. It reached $10 and $12 and finally $14, which, at the age of twenty-four, seemed to be an income that would warrant taking a wife and assuming the expenses of a possible family. The paper allowed frequent advertising contracts payable in goods, or part goods and part cash, and on such contracts the schedule of discount was held in abeyance. I remember making a deal with a furniture man over the office counter one day that was finally consummated on the basis of so many dollars and so many cents, payable at expiration of the service, one-half in cash and the balance in furniture to be bought at the store "per agreement." That phrase, "per agreement," covered manifold details in many cases and explained many discrepancies. When the man had gone the manager stepped forward, looked at the record in the book, and, in a way he had of saying a sentence over twice, expressed himself to me: "That's right, Mr. Rowell, that's right. When it's part cash and part trade get just about as much cash as you would if there were not to be any goods." With merchandise obtained on advertising account the office was rather liberal with its clerks. Many an overcoat, trunk, hat or umbrella came to me in that way; and I have to this day a handsome black walnut library table and chair that came out of a furniture deal about the time I was contemplating housekeeping possibilities. As the first pieces of furniture I owned I have ever valued these highly, and when, some time after, I established an advertising agency that table and that chair were all the furniture that went into the office, and they were all that was needed. By and by, with added expenses, it became hard to come out even on $14 a week, and advances to $16 and $18 hardly kept up with added wants, either imaginary, ideal or actual. There ought, it seemed, to somewhere be an opening for growth wherein genius might spread and expand.

It came about finally, in the autumn of the year 1864, that I was again in New York, this time intrusted with more promising matters than had occupied me during the visit already described. The hotel due bill this time was on the La Farge House, on Broadway, near Bond street, the same that afterward became, as it is to-day (1905), the Broadway Central. The work of the day having been satisfactorily performed, I decided to allow myself the relaxation of a visit to one of the New York theatres. I secured a seat in the balcony at Wallack's, then situated at the corner of Broadway and Thirteenth street. What the play was that evening I have never been able to recall, but that visit to the theatre changed the current of my life. I saw there something that was new to me. The playbill not only contained the programme of the performance, but down the side, and on the back, and on additional pages, were advertisements of New York shops, restaurants, hotels, drug stores, and what not. I thought I saw possibilities for me in that playbill. It could be introduced into Boston. The managers of the Boston theatres knew me, for I visited them regularly to collect weekly bills for advertising; furthermore, the manager of one of the most important, the Boston Museum, was R. Montgomery Field, long a reporter on the *Post,* and he knew me well, and would welcome an opportunity to do me a favor. There was the Boston Theatre, of which Mr. Jarrett was manager; the Howard Athenæum, over which the celebrated John Stetson exercised an influence, and the Minstrel Show of Morris Bros., Pell and Trowbridge. Lon and Billy Morris had always a friendly manner, and were a good sort, anyway. The playbill was so many inches long and three columns wide. If the programme could be condensed into two columns of the first page there would be a column left for advertisements, and it would be preferred space, and worth an extra price on that account. It would be advisable to have a little reading matter and an editor. The need of this was established by the presence of some

reading matter in the playbill in my hand. It did not occupy any great percentage of space, a single column, the central one, on the third page, would be enough. It need not
be very high-grade literature; that in the New York playbill did not seem remarkable on that score. I was confident
that, with the scissors, and perhaps an occasional puff for an
advertiser, the column could be filled by Dr. Hobbs, an
acquaintance of mine, a reporter on the *Post* ever since
Monte Field had given up the position to go with Mr. Kim-
ball at the Museum. Hobbs would not demand more than
$6 a week for the service, possibly no more than $3. His
regular stipend, as I knew, was $15, and this service would
be so much extra. There would be then a column of advertising space on the first page, three columns on the second,
two on the third, and two again on the fourth, and allow a
column there for free announcements of the theatres themselves, a total of eight columns to be disposed of, having a
total length of I do not know how many inches, which,
divided into "squares," of eight lines, and charged for at I
do not remember how much, would amount to a total number of dollars per week that must afford a considerable profit
over the cost of producing the playbills. The details I do
not now recall, but the conclusion finally arrived at was this:
It is now November; the holidays will soon be here. I do
not know that this thing will go anyway, consequently it will
not be safe for me to throw up a position that is paying me
$18 a week and perhaps find myself stranded a little later.
My work as a bill collector gave me a good deal of leisure.
My employers did not seem to care particularly where I was,
or what I was doing, so long as my work did not appear to
be neglected. I would see Monte Field, and with his countenance and approval would beard the great Mr. Jarrett, and
when both had been secured I felt confident that Lon Morris
would be easy, and that any old thing would answer for the
Howard Athenæum. If all went well I would, with the manager's consent, try the scheme for the three weeks of the
holiday season between December 10 and January 1, and, if
my calculations were correct, there would be for me a net

profit of $600, and I could judge from the outcome whether
or not it would be advisable to continue the scheme as a regular business. I recall that it was something past five o'clock
in the morning before the calculations could be gotten out of
my head to an extent that would permit of going to sleep.
They were gone over again and again on the boat and the
train on the return to Boston.

Next day I called on Harry McGlenen, who seemed to
have a cinch on the theatrical printing in the Boston of that
day. He was a noble fellow when at his best, and when he
was not was still superior to ordinary men. He listened to
my scheme, said the managers would have none of it, that
it was not new, had been tried before and would not go.
Furthermore, although he would not stand in the way of
my proposed three weeks' experiment, his knowledge of my
financial condition was not such as to warrant his recommending the office where he made headquarters to undertake the printing for me. Then I went to see my friend
Field. He had been ill for a day or two; nothing serious, but
would not be in town that day. Time was short. I went
out that afternoon to the place where he lived, rather far
toward the Dorchester line, in the then town of Roxbury.
He was rather surprised to have a visit from me, listened to
my story, said the thing was not new, would not go, and if it
were new and good the Museum would not have anything
to do with it, certainly would not allow another theatre to
be advertised in a playbill used in its own auditorium. In
fact, while McGlenen, who was practically a stranger, had
discouraged me, the one man whom I had counted on with
certainty turned me down flat, and so hard that I never ventured to reopen the subject with him.

Next I went to Mr. Jarrett. Jarrett is remembered by
myriads of old theatregoers. It was he who practically introduced the leg drama into America in the form of the ex-
travaganza called "The Black Crook," performed at Niblo's
Garden so long, so successfully, and so many years ago.
Well, Mr. Jarrett was not in his office the first nor the second time I called, so I told the story to his manager. I

wanted to supply the playbills, all the playbills they wanted, for three weeks between December 10 and 31. They would be supplied free. The programme would be changed daily or twice a day, as desired, and the theatre would also be advertised in the other places that should enter into the arrangement. Finally I saw Mr. Jarrett, a tall man, dark, with a smooth face. He wore a Prince Albert coat and a silk hat; everything was black. He looked at me with a rather tired expression in his eyes that seemed to change a little as I told my story over again; then he looked out of the window for a moment, and turning to me, said: "Look here, young man, we don't want that thing, but you seem to want it, and to be very much in earnest about it. I don't want to stand in the way of what might happen to be of some account to you. I understand we can close down on it at the end of three weeks if we don't like it, so if your heart is set on it, and it rests with me, you may go ahead." This was the giant of the combination. Lon Morris heard the story, and said "All right; count me in;" and the Stetson combination was quite willing to use any sort of a playbill that would save the theatre the expense of printing one. There was something going on at the Boston Music Hall at that season, and they, too, would use my programmes. The Museum could not be had. All the other places of amusement had acquiesced in my desire. Nothing now remained but to contract with the printer, an editor, and last, but not least, to get the advertisement orders that were to net me the $600 profit upon which my heart was set. The printer was easily found. He was one J. E. Farwell, having an office and plant on Congress street, directly opposite the *Post* counting room. Dr. Hobbs was willing to act as literary editor, but turned down the $3 a week proposal, demanding $6, and to that I agreed. I was hardly justified in setting up a business office in the counting room of the *Post,* where I was drawing a weekly salary for services rendered, so it was decided to make a post office box stand in lieu of an office. I put my name in the playbills as publisher, and, although I have no memory of any permission to attempt in this way to do a business of my own while receiving pay for attending to the business of others, I do not remember that I was at all called to account to explain my action.

The playbills being determined upon, and their production arranged for, the space must be filled. There were so many "squares," some had preferred positions and must be sold at a higher price. The cost of the work would be a specified sum, already ascertained. The $600 contemplated profit seemed to be an obligation that must be dealt with if the enterprise was to be a success. I must sell the space, and at the prices fixed, and do it quickly, too, for there was scarcely more than a week to do it in. I knew the advertisers of Boston, I knew the men who had the giving out of copy; but best of all, I believed I had the choicest advertising scheme that had ever been presented. I called at every place, saw the right man, there was no time to spare; the time to prepare the copy was now; give it to me or mail it to-day to my name and post office box. Some were not convinced. For these I was positively sorry, not so much for failing to get the order as at finding a man so dull of comprehension occupying a position where he would be expected to know a good thing when he saw it, and not knowing that he ought to seize this particular good thing before it passed beyond his reach. The space was limited; when it was sold there would be no more; now was the time to act, and act these people did. My first issue was full. My playbills were full for the first two weeks, but one thing I had overlooked. Christmas was the height of the season. Most of my contracts I secured for the full three weeks ending December 31, but a few dropped out with the issue of December 24, Christmas Eve. It was true that I had secured the cost of the enterprise and a profit, but the profit already secured did not reach the $600 upon which I had set my heart. I think it required more effort to sell the little space that remained vacant for the third week than it did to dispose of all the other; and finally some was sold to be paid for in goods; and early in the new year I was able to look with pride upon a pair of pantaloons from "Collins the Tailor," an alleged sole-leather trunk from Sage's Mart, a case of California wine from a Mr. Perkins, agent for the vineyard, but formerly a book publisher of the old firm of Phillips, Sampson & Co., founders of the *Atlantic Monthly,* then insolvent. But better than all, when bills were collected and paid, there did remain the contemplated $600 for profit, with about $24 additional, besides the wine, the trunk and the trousers.

Successful as the enterprise had proved the conclusion was forced upon me that I should not be able to make it a permanent success. It was not the new thing I had thought it. The difficulty found in filling the small space left over in the third week indicated what might be expected in the dull months of midwinter. I had lost the effective enthusiasm that had at first enabled me to capture an order from nine out of every ten men I talked with; furthermore, I was working on a salary for people who were entitled to my best services, and the new year is a time when a bill collector has occasion to get busy.

Well, my playbill experiment came to an end; but it caused me to think over and over that if I could make $600 in three weeks, working for myself, I ought to be too smart to work for other people for $900 a year; and so I told my employers that when the 4th of March should come that would complete a seven years' term in their service, I would give up the pleasant position I had held with them. To this no particular objection seemed to be urged, and in February I bought a little weekly publication called the *Dial,* that consisted of the tables of the various railroads running into and out of Boston, and was delivered to subscribers, revised and corrected, once a week, the carrier placing the sheet in a japanned tin frame prepared for its reception, and previously sold to the subscriber for half a dollar, and collecting also the subscription price of 10 cents a week. This enterprise was known to be easily managed by one or two low-priced men who looked after the carriers, made the needed corrections for the printer, and kept a record of unpaid subscriptions. There was known to be an annual profit of several hundred dollars on the publication, certainly not less than two or three hundred, and this would answer as a nucleus around which other business might be gathered. I think the price paid for the *Dial* was $300. The former owner, a compositor in the printing office that had issued my playbills, had fallen on the ice while skating, and was just then in need of ready money.

The possibility of obtaining advertisements in the city to be inserted in papers published in smaller cities and in county towns and country villages was one to which I had often devoted some thought. It had been learned that the average price demanded for a column of space in a country paper was no more than $100 a year, and that a commission or reduction of 25 per cent. was commonly allowed to the advertising agents in the city who secured the advertising orders; furthermore, that it was no unusual thing for such papers to sell a column for a good deal less than $100. I knew by observation that the average length of a column in a country paper was as much as twenty inches, and an examination of a few rate cards revealed that on short-time advertisements such papers, at that time just after the Civil War, generally demanded a dollar a "square" for the first insertion and fifty cents for each subsequent insertion, not exceeding three or four or half a dozen, and that the "square" in these papers was never more than an inch down the column.

From what has been said one may see that if twenty inches could be bought for $75 net for the period of a full year, one inch would, at that rate, cost no more than $3.75, and as there are fifty-two weeks in a year, the cost per inch per week would be less than eight cents; in fact, less than thirty cents for four weeks. Following out the calculation, it appeared that if the papers would sell the space and allow it to be subdivided, and would agree to change the matter twelve times in a year; and if a hundred papers could be secured in New England at the average price of $100 gross each, the whole service would cost no more than $7,500 net; while if the space could be peddled out at something less than half the monthly rate usually demanded, say $1 for four insertions of an advertisement occupying one inch of space; and as fifty-two weeks would allow for thirteen different sets of four weeks' advertisements, it was evident that (100 × 20 = 2,000 × 13 = $26,000) even if I could sell no more than half the space it would produce $13,000, or a profit of $5,500, with possibilities vastly beyond that sum.

I had arrived at the conclusion that I could accomplish something with such a scheme, and after a careful weighing of all the pros and cons my conclusion was that I could carry out such an enterprise and make a net profit of as much as $10,000 in a year. Still, I was aware that there were unforeseen difficulties that might have to be met, and I was by no means at ease at the prospect of being without the definite and certain $18 that I had heretofore been able to count on as regularly as Saturday came around.

And now a surprise awaited me. My employers would be glad to have me retain my present position and would advance the $18 to $30 per week. This was an eye opener, but I had bought the *Dial*. I would stay for the salary offered if I might publish the *Dial* as a side issue, and put my office address on it. This could not be permitted. Then I offered to dispose of the *Dial* and keep the old place if a salary of $40 a week might be paid to me, but this seemed to be beyond my employer's views of my probable value, and so on Saturday, March 3, 1865, I left the place I had filled precisely seven years, and started out on the hundred papers a month for $100 scheme, and with a good deal of misgiving, too.

Of one thing I was very glad. I left my old employers with the thought that they had been good to me, and that my stay with them had been always pleasant and agreeable. I had permission to refer to them, and it was understood that they would say to an inquirer that from their knowledge of me they would have confidence that I could be relied on to perform whatever I could be induced to promise to perform. In fact, I afterward had reason to believe that one of the partners, on more than one occasion, in answer to an inquiry about my financial ability, had been heard to say: "If he wants any money and comes to me he will get what he wants." I regard it as one of the most fortunate things that can happen to a young man that he should be able, in after life, to know that the good relation that existed between him and his employer, through a term of service, was not interrupted when that term of service ceased, nor ever afterward.

NINTH PAPER

On Monday, March 5, 1865, I took possession of a small office at No. 23 Congress street, in Boston, situated up two flights of stairs, in the rear of a building owned and occupied by a very respectable firm of liquor dealers; who sold goods in packages and over the bar as well. The rent of the office was $150 a year, payable monthly. It was a room about fifteen feet square with two windows looking out on a court, and contained no closet nor any additional space or conveniences.

Mr. Horace Dodd, a friend of some years' standing, but having no experience with advertising or newspapers, had expressed a willingness to join forces with me, if an opening wide enough for two to stand in could be developed. Horace had no money, but his uncle, also known as Horace Dodd, an old and respected Boston merchant, was willing to back his nephew to the extent of $1,000 in ready cash. I was also able to produce an equal amount, because I had the confidence of my father and one or two other relatives. It hurts me to admit, however, that had I not enjoyed that confidence, I could not have started out in trade at that time; for during the preceding years, and before the experiment with the playbills, I had, in an endeavor to improve my finances, by buying some stocks on a margin, succeeded in acquiring a net indebtedness of about $2,000 over and above any money I could lay my hands on. Possibly this disagreeable circumstance had something to do with forcing the conviction upon me that I must get out and hustle, and earn more money than I had done up to that time. Necessity has often been said to be the mother of invention.

The library table and the black walnut arm-chair, previously referred to, were taken to the new office. It was also embellished with a jute carpet, that developed the quality of getting fuller of dirt and holes than any other carpet it has ever been my fortune to become familiar with, and doing it quicker. Aside from the carpet, the only outlay for furniture was $1.25 paid for a waste paper basket; and Horace and I agreed that, as one entered the office, this basket gave something of a business air to the room. We were not quite decided that our shadowy plans would work out, so while I occupied that one chair and wrote letters to all the country papers in New England, whose names we could ascertain, Horace endeavored to enlarge the circulation of the *Dial* by canvassing for new subscribers, carrying around with him, for purpose of explanation and exhibition, one of the japanned skeleton frames, a purchase of which was a preliminary necessity, before the subscription at ten cents a week could be considered as established. Now and then he would meet an acquaintance on a street corner, and one of them hurt his feelings one day by inquiring "What the hell are you doing with that tin thing?"

Pretty soon a few papers began to reach us by mail. I remember how gratified I felt when the first copies of the Springfield *Republican* and of the Worcester *Spy* came to hand. To care for these, we invested as much as a dollar, possibly more, in the purchase of as many newspaper filing sticks as could be hung upon brass hooks across a vacant space in the wall where there was a closed door that separated our office from that of a real estate man, who came sometimes and sat in the room that adjoined ours.

The answers that came from the newspapers to the letter I had written indicated that they were favorably impressed with my proposal. They seemed to think very highly indeed of one rather novel feature I had injected into it. It was to the effect that although I expected to pay promptly, yet as I was a stranger I would be willing to send a check for the first month's advertising by return mail if, in addition to the 25 per cent belonging to all agents—by divine right—an additional three per cent would be allowed for money paid in advance. I know now that a five per cent allowance would have been granted just as freely, but I had not then learned all that an advertising agent ought to know and, to my inexperienced mind, it seemed to me that a rate of 36 per cent per annum, in consideration of expediting a payment some thirty days, was as much as it would be reasonable to ask. That extra three per cent continued to be allowed and taken in some cases for many years; and now, after forty years, it has become almost customary to allow a reduction of five per cent to agents for the same purpose by a majority of the greatest and best newspapers and magazines; and not infrequently the extra discount is all, or about all, the profit the agent makes on a considerable percentage of the business he sends out.

It was soon evident that I could secure the hundred New England papers I desired, without any trouble, and that the price would not exceed the net sum estimated in advance; consequently I made an advertising trade, with a house, sign and fresco painter of my acquaintance, by which he authorized me to have his name, business and street address inserted in our proposed list of one hundred papers, the same to occupy the space of half an inch, a space that would accommodate five lines of printed matter, and agreed to pay for the service the sum of $62.50 by painting, first a sign of blue and gold to decorate the wall at the top of the second flight of stairs, setting forth that thereabouts was the office of the *Dial,* and also to paint the two names

GEORGE P. ROWELL
HORACE DODD 2ND

in black letters on the glass pane in the office door, and in gold letters on a piece of black surfaced tin to be placed in position at the street entrance. Whatever balance remained to our credit could be wiped out by additional signs and painting, as business developed. We would not enter into a partnership until we were satisfied there would be something beside responsibility to divide.

When we had a list of one hundred papers decided on, there arose the question of securing advertising contracts to fill the space we had agreed to buy in them. Something to exhibit to customers and to base a contract on that would be more easily read and not so difficult to prepare as a written list seemed to be an absolute necessity. On the floor above us two young men (the firm was Babb & Stevens) had just established a one-room printing office, and had a small Gordon press. After numerous conferences on the subject of style of type, form of setting, quality of paper, etc., it was decided that a specified number of folders that would fit into a number six envelope could be had for the sum of $6. We were hardly in position to assume imprudent expenses, and I think there was more hesitation about the $6 outlay than there ever was afterward over any outlay whatever that seemed to be needed for the promotion of business.

The circulars were effective. It was a poor day when I did not secure at least one order, and as the average space used was not much less than an inch it was less than a month before the first installment of copy was ready to go out. There was full twenty inches of it, but some of the columns were twenty-two, twenty-four or even twenty-six inches long. It was the need of something to fill in these odd pieces of waste space that first led the Advertising Agency of Geo. P. Rowell & Co. to themselves become advertisers. If we could then have owned the recipe and trademark of Ripans Tabules it is probable that they would by this time have become much more famous than they ever have, or than is likely to ever come about in their case.

It was not very evident to me how my friend Needham, the painter, expected to get his money back out of announcements in country papers, and I asked him the question one day. In reply he said he thought he "might get a church;" having in mind fresco painting and appropriate decoration. I do not think his expectations were realized. He was a little man, not very well dressed, his clothes were generally too big for him, but he really was a first-class artizan, and with more business ability might have become almost famous. One cold sleety day Horace and I were walking down the north side of Court street and saw Needham, evidently caught out without an overcoat or an umbrella, feeling very chilly, apparently, and standing all hunched up in a stairway entrance on the opposite side of the street. I said to Horace "There's Needham over there." Horace looked, took in the general appearance of the man and said, with a sort of a laugh that was common with him when some funny thought was in his mind: "Looks as though he'd got a church!" The idea that the remark conveyed to me was that Dodd thought Needham had swallowed a country meeting house and that was what made him look so angular and so uncomfortable.

TENTH PAPER

Neither my partner nor I had ever had a day's experience in the conduct of an advertising agency. I doubt if Mr. Dodd had ever been inside of any such institution. The first advertising agent I ever heard of was Volney B. Palmer, and there was, in the earliest days of my knowledge of Boston, a sign bearing his name, on the south end of a structure called Scollays Building, that stood in the middle of the road, so to speak, at the place where Tremont street so mixed itself up with Court street that one side became Tremont Row, while the other remained Court street, and at a point, too, where Cornhill came to an end, losing itself in the combination. Palmer died perhaps half a century ago and the building he occupied was effaced from the surface of the earth, perhaps as much as a quarter of a century since. It had long stood there, conspicuous as a single tooth in a jaw with practically nothing opposite. Where Mr. Palmer did business, as did also his successor, for several years, there is now nothing but a widened roadway, in the centre of which stands a structure that serves as an entrance to some part of Boston's modern subway system.

At the time our enterprise was set on foot, in March, 1865, Mr. S. R. Niles was doing business in the old offices and the old building that had been the headquarters of his predecessor, the deceased Mr. Palmer. Mr. Niles had a clerk, Hallfelder by name, with whose face and figure I was well acquainted. He had the peculiarity ascribed in "Great Expectations" to Mr. Jaggers' clerk, of having a knowledge of something very much to the discredit of everybody. I think, however, no one ever knew anything that was really to the discredit of Hallfelder. I believe he is to-day in attendance at the office of some Boston advertising agency, and am inclined to think that the wisest man living would fail to concoct any question having to do with the business of an advertising agent that Hallfelder could not answer, exactly as it should be answered, if he could only be induced to answer it at all. I have not seen him in twenty years, but I know that he exists; and if I see him no more on earth, I am confident I shall find him on the right side on that day when all shall be separated into two great companies.

An eighth of a mile away from Scollays Building at No. 10 State street was the office of S. M. Pettengill & Co., considered a New York concern, but represented by U. L. Pettingill, a gentleman whose name was almost identical with that of his principal. One spelled it with an *e* in the center, while the other substituted an *i*. They were in no way related, but conducted a business together upon terms and conditions that showed that S. M. Pettengill had entire confidence in U. L. Pettingill and vice versa. S. M. Pettengill had been a clerk for Mr. Palmer, but had acquired the confidence of the great advertiser of the Boston of that day, **Mr. George W. Simmons of Oak Hall,** and of some other customers, and one day he left Mr. Palmer and set up an office of his own.

Mr. Palmer had prided himself that he was sole agent for all newspapers. He was of English origin; rather pompous; rather irascible. He had been known to tell that conspicuous newspaper man, Samuel Bowles of the famous Springfield *Republican,* that he, Palmer, could tell him (Bowles) the principles upon which business should be conducted, but could not attempt to furnish him (Bowles) with the intellect necessary for comprehending the same. Mr. Palmer not only demanded a commission of 25 per cent on all the advertisements he forwarded, but demanded the same allowance upon any advertisement that might be forwarded direct by one who had once been his customer. He also kept a neat little account and finally billed the paper for postage and stationery, and in conclusion acknowledged no responsibility to the paper for any service done for any advertiser from whom he (Palmer) had not been able to collect. Mr. Palmer had an office in New York also, and another in Philadelphia, and his stout figure, florid countenance, gray hair, bald head, blue coat with brass buttons, gold bowed spectacles, gold headed cane and bandanna handkerchief were known and, to some extent, respected by advertisers and publishers for a considerable term of years. After Palmer's death he was succeeded in Boston, as I have said, by Mr. S. R. Niles. In the other two cities the Palmer offices fell to a firm who did business under the name of Joy, Coe & Co. in both New York and Philadelphia. Their offices in New York were in the old Tribune building, where in later years the business passed over to Mr. W. W. Sharpe, who still does business in New York within a stone's throw of the offices of the writer and yet, so far as I can remember, we two have never met. I have often been told that Sharpe is a good man, doing a good and profitable business, and I understand that the same is true to-day, and cannot but regard it as a singular circumstance, although quite typical of life in New York, that we have never become acquainted.

In Philadelphia Mr. Coe eventually joined forces with two younger men of enterprise and character and for years did business under the firm name of Coe, Wetherell & Smith. Smith was the brains of the concern. He was young, perhaps not more than twenty-four. His lungs were weak. The firm had made money, but there came a time when Smith was ill and confined to his rooms. Out of door air was recommended for him—the more the better. He would buy a pair of horses, and drive daily in Fairmount Park; but when they had been selected he was not able to drive. Inspecting them from the window, he said, in a whisper, to his friend and partner, Mr. Wetherell, "I guess they'll do," wrote a check for the price, but never saw them nor his business office again. He was a charming fellow, handsome, well informed, well bred and every inch a gentleman. Mr. Wetherell continued along with the venerable Mr. Coe until in 1876, the Centennial year, he, too, contracted pulmonary disease. Mr. Coe was called hence a little in advance of the death of Mr. Wetherell and the Agency, what there was of it, passed into the hands of N. W. Ayer & Son, who had at that time acquired some prominence.

In attempting to deal so thoroughly with the estimable Mr. Palmer and those that came after him I have gotten far away from the Pettengill office in State street. Mr. Pettengill, as I have said, had left Palmer suddenly, and commenced sending business to the papers on his own account. The papers were quite willing to have him do this, for if one agent in a town could send some business it was natural to infer that two could send twice as much, and possibly at twice as good prices. That, however, did not matter much, for advertising space not only did not cost anything, but was an expense if not filled with an advertisement—preferably an electrotype—because in the case of vacant space there would be the necessity of setting up reading matter to fill the void and that would cost money. Mr. Palmer, however, issued a proclamation warning the press against "one Pettengill," and the publishers saved the document and when they went to Boston showed it to Pettengill to make him feel good, and then went around to tell Mr. Palmer that the new man was actually sending them more business than he was.

Thus in the early day there began to be competition between agents. Mr. Pettengill soon found that the larger part of his business came from New York, and he opened an office there, and New York soon became his principal office, the Boston branch being left in the charge of an employee, Mr. U. L. Pettingill, as has been said. In the course of time U. L. was given a share in the earnings of the Boston office, and later he paid a fixed sum per annum to S. M. and what was earned beyond that became his own. The arrangement held good for a great many years and was only terminated by the retirement of Mr. S. M. Pettengill from business about the year 1890. He died shortly after selling the good will of the New York office to his former partner, Mr. James H. Bates, then of the Bates & Morse Agency, and Mr. U. L. Pettingill, also dying about that time, was succeeded by his son, U. K. Pettingill, who thus fell into an old established business and inherited, it is said, a very pretty fortune in well invested securities, beside. It is now quite generally known that he expanded the business far beyond the lines that his conservative father would have thought the boundaries of prudence and, in the latter part of the year 1903, was compelled to suspend payment, owing the newspapers something more than a million dollars, a loss which was submitted to on all sides with characteristic good nature or indifference.

Besides those already named there was still one other agency in Boston in 1865. It was conducted by two young men under the style of Evans & Lincoln. Evans had been a soldier, had been wounded in the Civil War, and coming home had taken up for occupation the work of soliciting advertising patronage for a few religious papers, notably the *Watchman* and *Reflector* and the *Youths' Companion*. In this work the firm of Evans & Lincoln made a decided hit. Prices were high, the country was full of paper money, everybody was prosperous, the religious people were undoubtedly the best people, and the religious papers the best papers, but no one had ever before exploited their merits. These young men were industrious and did very well indeed. Evans was a Baptist, his heart was in his work. He was thoroughly in earnest, and Lincoln used to say that when Evans found himself liable to fail to secure the order he was seeking, he often successfully reinforced his other arguments by exhibiting his sore leg that remained an uncomfortable memento of his patriotic service to his country. Lincoln was a very handsome fellow, and prosperity was too much for him. He finally seceded from Evans, and becoming an independent agent, made the acquaintance of one Turner, who was then attempting to put on the market a proprietary remedy having the euphonious designation of Turner's Tic Doloreaux and Neuralgia Pill. It did not sell, but the advertisements continued ; people thought Lincoln would "get stuck" or would "stick" the papers, but neither happened ; bills were promptly paid by both Lincoln and Turner, and still the goods did not sell. At last it turned out that Turner had on some occasion or some pretence been allowed to overdraw his account at the bank, and being unable to make good the clerk by whose negligences the overdraft had been made possible, had not the courage to admit his fault, and Turner, seeing how the land lay, insisted on piling up his overdrafts until thcy amountcd to $400,000 or thereabouts; nearly all of which had gone into advertising the pill with the long name; a circumstance that goes to show that merit as well as money is needed to make an article sell. Well, Turner went to the penitentiary and Lincoln did even worse, for his habits became bad. He grew to be a chronic borrower, his handsome face and fine figure grew into something quite different, and finally he disappeared, and I never have met any one who could tell me what became of him. Evans continued the business and did very well, but as years went on he hardly kept up to the times, and eventually he failed.

The newspapers of America will, as a rule, acknowledge as an advertising agent anybody who has enterprise or capital enough to print his name on a letterhead, they will let an agent stave off payments till the day of doom; but, so far as I have observed, they will never forgive and further recognize as an agent a man who has once failed and left them absolutely in the lurch. Mr. Evans has died during the present year (1905), and I have been told that it was his good fortune to have a relative, a woman who was both rich and kind, in fact no less a person than she of whom Eli Perkins presumed to say that Bishop Potter married her for her widow's *mite* and she the Bishop for his Bishop's *mitre*. This good lady, I am glad to be told, saw to it that our old competitor did not want for any substantial need while his life was spared. It was in Mr. Evans' office, in Boston, that Mr. A. L. Thomas, now the head of the great Lord & Thomas advertising agency, and the principal owner of Cascarets, the wonderful medicine that works while the patient sleeps, obtained his first lessons in the science of advertising.

There was also at this time an advertising agency in Cincinnati conducted then, and long afterwards, by Mr. S. H. Parvin, who had secured and deserved the confidence of publishers. Long years afterward his son, in partnership with somebody else, came to grief and failure. In Chicago an agent had credit for doing a profitable business. The man's name had a German sound, but for a long time it not only entirely escaped my memory, but had fallen into such oblivion that for a dozen years or more I had met with no one who even remembered that such a man ever existed. Recently, however, Mr. N. M. Sheffield, who was himself one of the earliest advertising agents—being domiciled in St. Louis—has told me that the name of the forgotten Chicago agent was Charles H. Scriven. A little later the firm of Cook, Coburn & Mack was established in Chicago, and for many years did a considerable business. Carlos A. Cook had been a traveling man in the employ of J. C. Ayer & Co., of Lowell, Mass., who were then perhaps the largest advertisers of patent medicines in America. A brother of Cook's was, I think, a partner in the Ayer concern. The Mr. Mack of this firm was a brother of Mr. I. F. Mack, so long known, and at the present time as well, as publisher of the Sandusky, Ohio, *Register*. At a later date Mr. Mack came to New York and, with Leander H. Crall, also of Ohio, established the calling of Special Agent that has since been in such successful operation. Mack and Crall were the first Special Agents that attempted to represent Western dailies, maintaining permanent offices in the City of New York.

Finally there was (in the year 1865), in San Francisco, an established advertising agency conducted by one L. P. Fisher, who had the confidence of the few newspapers then issued on the Pacific Coast. Outside the City of New York I think the agencies then generally recognized have all been mentioned.

ELEVENTH PAPER

We got along very well in that little back office, up two flights of stairs. We commenced business in March, and March is in Spring time; Summer would soon come. The building was not heated, but the expense of coal and a stove might possibly be saved or delayed until Autumn. Somebody had advertised the enormous heating powers of a sheet iron cylinder, to be suspended over a gas jet—patent applied for—retail price 88 cents, and one of these moderated the March temperature of that small office to some degree. One particularly bad morning I started up the "heater," and, locking the door, sallied out to visit the post office for hoped for letters and papers. Evidently I had dropped the not fully extinguished match into the half filled basket containing waste paper; then worth five cents a pound. When I returned from the postoffice there had been a conflagration. The waste basket was gone, the contents had disappeared, and in the jute carpet, nearly new, near the end of the valued black walnut table, was a black bordered hole about as large as the bottom of a half bushel measure. The injury to the carpet was serious, but could be repaired by shoving under an extra half yard or so and fastening down the black edges of the circle with carpet tacks made and provided for such purposes. Plainly the office ought not to be left alone. Mr. Dodd knew a boy named Andrew, who was employed by a photographer who had some other business also, and only opened his studio afternoons. We secured Andrew's services for half of every day. He came in the morning, swept the office, brought the mail, and at twelve noon departed for his other place. I do not remember whether it was $2 a week or $3 that was paid to Andrew. I would be inclined to think it was $3, but really that seems dear for a boy who gave only half his time. Still this was War time and everything commanded a high price. The time came, later, when we needed the entire services of a whole boy, and Andrew, I think, returned with his parents to Scotland; but we never afterwards had a boy that got quite so close to us as Andrew did.

Things went pretty well in the office that first month. Fully twenty inches of advertising space, in the newspaper combinations, had been sold; and fully $2,000 charged up for the service to advertisers, all presumed to be good; and the knowledge that the net amount that would have to be paid to the newspapers was less than $600 did much to recon-

1856   1865

PORTRAITS OF THE AUTHOR.

cile the partners to the expenditure for the six dollar circular that has been already referred to.

Pretty soon it seemed a desirable thing to engage a solicitor, and in some way we were brought into relations with a compositor, once hailing from Nova Scotia, E. P. Fox by name. Fox was six feet two inches tall, and broad in proportion; especially if the measurement were to be taken across the centre, half way between the crown of his head and the soles of his feet. His hair was precisely the color of that of the red fox I had been familiar with in the New England pasture lands and wood borders. Fox was not well

79

dressed. His countenance was florid, but there was something about his manner that was irresistible. When he had appeared in an office no one could get him out until he had told his story, and if he had once gotten under way few cared to stop him before he was done; for he not only told his business story very well, but told also many others that had nothing whatever to do with business. I do not mean that he uttered untruths, although I do hope that all the stories he told were not absolute facts. Of all the funny stories I had ever heard, I think, in the course of a year, Fox had told me nine-tenths of them over again and told them better than I had heard them told before, and told twice as many others that were new to me, some of them so good that nowadays, forty years later, I occasionally venture one of them on an audience, and it generally passes as new. It is a good thing about an old story that if it is old enough it is likely to be accepted as the newest thing out. Mark Twain may not have been jesting when he asserts that in the writings of a classical Greek, who lived before the Christian era, he found the incident of the Jumping Frog that he honestly thought had originated with him. One morning Fox had something to relate that did not amuse. It was in April (1865), the War seemed to be nearly at an end. It was the horrible news of the assassination of President Lincoln (not found in the morning papers) that had just come over the wires. That was a sad day in the little back office, up two flights of stairs.

Pretty soon there were more papers to take care of than could be filed on sticks and hung on the door space that divided us from the alleged real estate man. We did not see the man often and I have an idea that he, on his part, failed to see the landlord as regularly as was provided and set down in the terms of his lease. One day I had an interview with this man. He was thinking seriously of giving up his office. I agreed to take it. He would sell the desk at which he sat. The price he demanded was three dollars and a half, and I agreed to take that, too. It has been worth it. If any one will take the trouble to look for me at No. 10

Spruce street, to-day, if the hour happens to be between 12 m. and 1 p. m. he is likely to find me in the northwest corner of the back office up two flights of stairs, sitting at that same little desk, and possibly engaged in re-reading these memories, for it would seem that while so much space is accorded to trifles; I shall never cease to think of other items that ought to have had mention, and to seek out the place where they should be injected if a new edition is ever called for.

It has been said that a peasant boy may become a learned man; president of a college may be, or governor of a province; but if he live to be old and have the misfortune to be feeble, there is a likelihood that his speech will revert to the patois of his childhood and his mind dwell upon the scenes that interested him then. The experiences in that little office, at the age of twenty-six, are vastly more interesting to-day, as I recall them, than any much more important matters that transpired at a later period, when a little success did not appear to be of one hundredth part as much consequence as the same would have seemed thirty or more years before.

Pretty soon we needed a bookkeeper. After one or two experiments that did not turn out well, we chanced upon a young man, George H. Pierce by name. He had recently come from Columbus, Ohio, where he had been employed for a time on the Ohio *State Journal.* He had much to tell of the conditions that obtained in a newspaper office in the City of Columbus. There was an advertisement solicitor connected with the *Journal,* Ward Beach by name, but in no way to be associated with that most eminent clergyman of that day, the celebrated Henry Ward Beecher, although one name seemed to contain the other. Then there was a shrewd man, business manager of the *Journal,* named F. W. Hurtt. I afterwards became personally acquainted with both of these men. Mr. Hurtt came to New York, made an arrangement with Dr. Humphreys of Homeopathic Specifics fame and took charge of affairs there to such purpose that the good old Doctor was glad to part with him even at the expense of allowing him to take away the most valuable trademark the concern had possessed, no less a trademark than "Pond's Extract," a preparation of Witch Hazel that is a household remedy from one end of America to the other. What a commentary it is on the value of a trademark. The Humphreys people had made Pond's Extract for years. It was admittedly a preparation of Witch Hazel: They could no longer sell it as Pond's Extract, that privilege had passed to Mr. Hurtt, but dozens of other people were selling extracts of Witch Hazel and the Humphreys people had still just as good a right to make and sell an extract as anybody else. They could call it Humphreys' Extract, but not Pond's. Everybody had heretofore bought Pond's Extract of the Humphreys concern, now they could buy Humphreys' Extract there, but not Pond's. To get Pond's they must go elsewhere. And yet the Humphreys' Extract was identical in composition with Pond's, was made by the same people that had always made Pond's, and was sold in larger bottles and at a lower price; and for all that the people would have none of it. They had learned to use Pond's and would have no other. I had knowledge in the early day of a similar case. Two men were part owners of a preparation for the hair called Hall's Hair Renewer. They were not agreed on business methods and one disposed of his interest in the concern to the other and that other became a millionaire doing business at Nashua, N. H. The first man knew just as well how to make the preparation, and did make it, and put it on the market, and he advertised it, too, only it was Plummer's Hair Renewer and not Hall's. Everybody wanted Hall's, nobody would have Plummer's, and the money spent in advertising it was wasted. After a time the owner of Hall's Hair Renewer, having become wealthy, had social aspirations that the patent medicine business did not aid, and the Renewer was sold for a great price to J. C. Ayer & Co., of Lowell, who had already exploited with some success practically the same thing under the name of Ayer's Hair Vigor, but could not make it compete with Hall's that had been earlier in the field.

To get back to Ward Beach. He, too, came eventually

to New York and was for a long time a canvasser for the *American Agriculturist*, which, under the management of Orange Judd, was one of the conspicuous journalistic successes of its time. People used to insist upon injecting an additional syllable into the name, and call it the *Agriculturalist*. It may be just as good a paper to-day as it was then —perhaps better—but people surely hear a great deal less of it now. It was, I think, the first paper to attempt to make good to a subscriber any loss incurred by trusting to the good faith of any advertisement that appeared in its pages. Well,

GEORGE H. PIERCE.

all there is to say of Beach is that he knew more good stories than a commercial traveler; such things seemed to seek him out; no one else could make the point so well; and so many new ones came to him that he had no time to retail old ones. I have been led to suppose that Beach, who seemed a good fellow, was led into some transaction or other that would not wash. He disappeared from New York many years ago, and I never knew what became of him.

Pierce, the bookkeeper engaged, remained with me for many years. He came with me from Boston to New York,

Pierce used to relate that about the time I dissolved partnership with Horace Dodd, he heard me say on one occasion that I would never have another partner. He said that it greatly discouraged him. He gave that as a reason for some shortcomings of his that I had noted about the time that I actually had taken another partner in the business. Finally I had to part with Pierce and he went to Maine, where for a long time he was in the employ of that Mr. E. C. Allen who was the father of that great publishing business of low-priced periodicals that has grown up in Augusta and been the *bête noir* of the Third Assistant Postmaster-General for the last quarter of a century. Later Pierce returned to Boston and entered the employ of a man who had been a clerk in the little Congress street office at the time of Pierce's own engagement there.

George Pierce was the most accomplished penman I ever knew. His books were beautiful to look at. For years we used, as a business card, a facsimile of one he drew with a pen on a piece of bristol board; and the handsome check of which my firm drew in the vicinity of two hundred thousand on the National Broadway Bank, before its merger with the Mercantile National, was also lithographed from a sketch made by Pierce that could not be improved upon. His skill with the billiard cue probably led to the termination of his engagement with me. I had at one time possessed some facility in handling a rifle at short range, but finding myself out of practice gave my gun to Pierce, who had at that time never had any experience as a marksman. He took the rifle with him when he went to Maine, and in later years became decorated with numerous medals and insignia, designating his prowess and victories over the riflemen of a State where good marksmen abound.

As we grew more busy I remembered a handsome boy I had known as a clerk in a New Hampshire postoffice, the son of a Methodist minister. I wrote to him, and he came to me, and proved just as competent as I had thought he would, and that means that he proved very competent indeed. When I changed my headquarters from Boston to New

84

York Mr. Dodd desired this youth to stay with him. His parents were also unwilling to have him exposed to the temptations of so wicked a city as New York, so he remained in Boston, becoming in time a partner with Mr. Dodd, finally his successor, and at present is conducting a successful advertising agency of his own. He was long the Secretary of the American Advertising Agents' Association and is widely known and liked by advertising men and publishers. He is not as handsome as he was when a boy. I was trying here to ring in the story of the boy who tickled the heels of a mule, and having been kicked in the face and knocked over the fence, had expressed to his father the fear that he would never be as good looking as he had been and the father had admitted that probability, but added "You'll know more." I am speaking of J. Wesley Barber, Advertising Agent, still of Boston. I would not assert that he knows much more to-day than he did forty years ago, for he was one of the most intelligent as well as one of the most attractive boys I ever knew. If he does not know any more now than he did then, every one who is as well acquainted with him as I am will admit that he knows a very great deal.

A REMARKABLE COINCIDENCE.

CHELSEA, MASS., March 4, 1905.

Editor of PRINTERS' INK:

I think you will be interested in this remarkable coincidence. To-day I was reading Mr. George P. Rowell's installment of "Forty Years an Advertising Agent," in the current number of your publication. I had just begun the second paragraph and was reading the words "Mr. Horace Dodd, a friend of some years' standing," etc., when I was interrupted by Mr. Daniel H. Sullivan, a real estate agent of Chelsea, in whose office I was and who wanted to show me a specimen of fine handwriting by a gentleman whom he knew to be about 70 years old. I glanced at the paper and saw that the signature was "Horace Dodd!" And the heading on the sheet was that of Horace Dodd, Advertising Agent, at 7 Water street, Boston.

And, furthermore, this happened to-day—March 4, 1905—within a few hours of exactly 40 years from the day of which Mr. Rowell wrote in the article which I chanced to be reading when Mr. Sullivan happened to show me Mr. Dodd's letter.

Yours truly,

CHAS. N. MORGAN.

TWELFTH PAPER

The business had not been established very long before it was noted that New York offered a more fruitful field than Boston for the securing of advertising orders. I was obliged to make frequent visits, and sometimes it began to seem that we ought to have an office and a resident representative in the great metropolis. Our youngest competitor, Mr. Evans, had opened an office in the old Herald building at 119 Nassau street, and Mr. Dodd, on a business trip, had it in mind to investigate the Evans branch, and take note of the progress it appeared to be making. He found this easy to do, without exposing a disposition to spy out the land; for the Evans office was confined to a single room, a view of which could be had from a hallway, through the transparent glass in the office door. Mr. Evans' representative was plainly to be seen, sitting at a white-wood table, with his hat on, and attempting, with a knife having opened blades at each end, to play, so far as one could do it alone, and on a table instead of the ground, the game that had been so popular when we all were boys and known as mumble the peg. Being told that Evans' New York branch was a success, and having concluded from observation that its operations were not complex, we looked about for a New York representative of our own, and here, as well as in numerous other ways, our salaried solicitor, Mr. E. P. Fox, came forward with information and advice. He had a large acquaintance among printers; and the best printer he ever knew had had some experience in canvassing for something, I do not now recall what. He was then in New York in the employ of a firm named Thitchener & Glastater, a rather successful house notwithstanding the unpronounceable character of the names of the partners. In Fox's opinion, if John A. Moore, his old friend, could be secured to represent the concern in New York all difficulties would disappear; and he proceeded to write to John, and tell him all about the opening for his abilities. Shortly after, I went to New York, called at the office where Moore was employed, and while waiting for him to come to the counting room had my attention directed to a conversation going on between Mr. Thitchener and a rather sallow, cadaverous man, who, it appeared, had a patented method of making a broom, by which every housewife could renew her own, and practice much economy, inasmuch as one handle would outwear many brooms, in fact, only one handle would be required in a lifetime; while the broom itself could be renewed yearly, quarterly, monthly or even hourly, if desired. Mentally I did not agree with the man's idea as to what would come about as soon as he should have distributed the handsome printed matter of which Mr. Thitchener was then exhibiting a perfected proof. In after years I had other views, differing from those held by this small sallow man—Charles A. Clegg was his name—and in the arguments that ensued between us, divers lawyers, judges and referees took part, until, eventually, I and those interested with me were not much less than $200,000 out of pocket; while our wily opponent, so far as I could learn, had just about enough left over, after settling all expenses incurred, to pay him day wages for the time he had devoted to the conduct of the case. I have rarely read of bankruptcy proceedings with more resignation than when I perused the line or two that recently came under my eye, announcing that such had just been inaugurated in the case of this acquaintance of that morning in the printing office counting room in the year 1866. Fortunately, perhaps, I could not foresee all the future on that early occasion, and soon John Moore came in, and I then met a man who became, I think, the most faithful, the most devoted and attached friend it has ever been permitted me to know.

Moore had looked into the scheme, whereby an inch advertisement might be inserted for a month in a hundred New England newspapers for $100, and thought it would go. He knew we already had it in successful operation. He had even gone out and talked about it to a few possible customers, and had the promise of one order and the prospect of another. He would take hold of the work; the wages he would demand was $40 a week. I hardly saw how it was possible for a journeyman printer to be worth so much money, but Moore was by no means an ordinary printer. He was unusual, as was shown by the fact that he was on friendly and even intimate terms with his employers, and they were at first quite unwilling to lose his services, although finally inclined to acquiesce because his health was not first rate, and it was believed that the out-of-door exercise incidental to canvassing for advertising orders would be of benefit to him. Furthermore he might possibly corral, now and then, a good order for job printing that he could turn over to them.

And so it was arranged that Moore should come with us. We shortly secured a small office at No. 58 Cedar street, with a small boy to answer questions, or say he did not know; and our New York branch was thereupon placed upon a level but little, if any, inferior to that occupied by our competitor, Mr. Evans. I wish to say at this place that John Moore earned the salary we paid him, and always earned all he received. He was the most successful advertisement solicitor I ever employed, although he labored under the serious disqualification that he could never manage the smallest computation in the matter of figures. He always made his customer do the figuring; and if at the office any discrepancy was discovered he was full of impatience, not with himself but with the bungling calculator, and it seemed to afford him an actual satisfaction to go back, point out the error, reprove the perpetrator for his carelessness, and bring a revised calculation that would pass examination. Curiously, too, he did this without ever giving offense or forfeiting the confidence of his clients whom he held with wonderful tenacity, in spite of efforts of business rivals to detach them from their allegiance to him. If I had, personally, made a calculation for him it was beyond the pale of discussion. It was right! could not be wrong! and there was no call for any revision, or for any more words on the subject. Discovering this tendency, I was extremely careful not to give any occasion for upsetting his confidence, and, so far as I can recall, it remained undisturbed to the end. He continued in my employ until he died, in the Centennial year, some ten years later. After he came with me he became a Free Mason, and grew to be very popular among the brotherhood; taking all the degrees up to the 32d degree, and holding numerous offices in Lodge, Commandery, Counsel, Consistory and what not; and it was

JOHN A. MOORE.

in conformity with his desire that I, who had long been a Master Mason, a Royal Arch Mason and a Knight Templar, was led to ask for and receive other degrees from the 11th degree to the 32d degree, becoming a Prince of Jerusalem and entitled to write myself a Knight of the East and West, Knight of the Eagle and Pelican and I know not how many other grand and noble things. When poor Moore passed away, the Masonic brethren paid him so much honor, and expressed so much love for him, and regard for his memory, that I thought at the time I would be quite content could the half be said for me at my demise; and have realized ever since that it would not be, no not a quarter. We took him to his home in the Granite State, where an old mother, a dear sister and an only brother mourned his taking off, and we buried him in the sandy soil of his native Manchester, and left him to that sleep that is to know no waking until the final day. I shall never have a more faithful, a more loyal friend, nor know many whose association can be so helpful.

A young man from my own New Hampshire village had lately completed his course of study at the Norwich University of Vermont—which by the way was Admiral Dewey's Alma Mater—and was in attendance at the Harvard Law School at Cambridge. He was five years younger than I. An older brother of his had married an older sister of mine. His father was richer than mine. He had been brought up in the village, I on the farm. We had long known each other and each found in the other some quality that he valued more perhaps because he realized its lack in himself. We were friends. The younger man was an indefatigable worker. While in his native village he had learned the printer's trade, without being attached to the office of the newspaper where he did it, or receiving any compensation for the services he rendered. He would just go in, get hold of a piece of available copy, put it in type, read the proof, make the corrections and all that, sometimes working as many hours as a journeyman and doing as much work. This was his method in his boyhood of disposing of spare hours and holidays. Now, at the law school, there were days that left him at leisure, and he took up the practice of coming to my office, where he would observe what was going on, and invariably lend a hand, whether the work happened to be addressing envelopes, sending out orders, examining papers or what not. He was a remarkably rapid worker, and exhibited unusual intelligence in comprehending the intricacies of the business, and he came so often and did much work that, although no compensation was given or expected, the office learned to depend upon him in a pinch, and he to know the business from A to Z nearly as well as either Mr. Dodd or I did. I recall that when his time at the law school was ended, and an engagement in a Boston law office would give full scope for his appetite for work, and in consequence he was not likely to confer his services upon us any more, Horace and I invested probably as much as six dollars, may be eight, in the purchase of a set of Plutarch's Lives, which we presented to our volunteer assistant, with a writing on a

CHARLES N. KENT.

blank page expressing our appreciation of his valuable services. I mention this man here because it came about when a year or two later I had removed to New York, and was without a partner, I felt the need of some one who knew the business and knew me, and whom I could trust; and remembering that this young lawyer had shown symptoms of entertaining such a feeling for a certain lady living in New York, as the young people in "Helen's Babies" designated as "respect," I wrote to him, telling him how much broader an opening New York offered to a young lawyer, how great an advantage a little experience in a business office was certain to be, offered to pay him a weekly salary of $30 for a year and hold him at liberty to start out for himself at the expiration of that time. He came and at the end of a year his "respect" for the young woman having grown, and she having acquired a somewhat similar sentiment in his favor, I sold him a quarter interest in the business, which consisted mainly in good will, for the very respectable sum of $12,500, which was only to be paid, however, out of the earnings. His father made no objection to the movement, but explained to the neighborhood that no cash capital had been invested. He was to draw $50 a week on the new deal, and any surplus earnings should go to liquidate his indebtedness. He married the lady whom he had respected so much, made the weekly stipend meet their moderate needs, and after twenty-one months, in which no accounting was had, a balancing of the books showed that his indebtedness had been wiped out and he was entitled to a considerable check from me to make our account even. This gentleman became known, for more than thirty years, to every one who had dealings with the Advertising Agency of Geo. P. Rowell & Co., and among all the items of good fortune that I have had occasion to be thankful for scarcely any, nay not one, in a purely business way, stands rated so high as my acquaintance and long association with this friend of my youth and my manhood, my long time partner, Charles Nelson Kent.

There remains one more employee of the Boston office that should be mentioned. In connection with the *Dial*, we found it advisable to issue an Express List, showing what company reached each New England town, where its office in Boston was situated, and some other matters. This sheet, surrounded with a border of paying advertisements, was presented to subscribers to the *Dial;* but was also in some demand in other offices, where the *Dial* was not taken. It was found that the demand would probably warrant an attempt to push the sale by a personal canvass, the seller taking copies along and delivering to the customer when found, on receiving the price, 10 cents. In answer to an advertisement for such a canvasser a young man named B. Frank Newton made application, was engaged, and did so well that, when the work was done, we were unwilling to part with him, and he came with me next year to the City of New York, and remained in my service, or closely connected with the office, for, I think, not less than thirty years.

THIRTEENTH PAPER

Some traveling had to be done in those days. An advertising agent, to be able to talk understandingly about the conditions in several States, should know something about them by personal observation. To-day and for nearly a score of years I have been able to truthfully assert some knowledge of every State and Territory, gained on the spot, with the single exception of South Dakota; but that was not the case in 1866. The experiences of one long journey, underaken for the accumulation of knowledge of the newspaper and advertising field, are still vividly in mind. One sunshiny afternoon I stood on the bank of the Mississippi—Father of Waters—at Alton, Illinois. I must have thought Alton a point of some consequence, partly perhaps on account of the prominence it received through its name being made a part of that of an important railroad—the Chicago and Alton. I had read of the Mississippi, dreamed of it. I recalled·a picture wherein the Spaniard DeSoto was represented taking his first view of it. La Salle had paddled and floated down its course. It had been a bone of contention between my country and Spain. And now I stood upon its shore. It was a moment to remember. A large log had been left on the shelving bank by a falling of the water. It was not of a sort familiar to me, and I wondered if it could be a Cottonwood. Almost every tree ever spoken of in the reports of the explorers of the West seemed to be a Cottonwood. I cut a small chip from the end with my penknife and can recall the sourish taste at this moment. I think a chip from a poplar log, after it had been soaking for a season in a New England mill pond, would have a similar flavor. I can identify by the taste most woods with which I have ever become acquainted, and I know now that the conclusion I arrived at, that the log was a Cottonwood, was correct. There were hours to wait at Alton before another train would pass that would take me to St. Louis. The newspapers of the town

94

could be sized up without much of a tax upon my time, but I became interested to see streets cut down through a bluff of considerable height, and had difficulty in deciding whether the material of the bluff was earth or stone. I could not scratch it with a thumb nail nor indent it with the toe of my boot, but there seemed little difficulty about carving a letter upon a smooth portion of its surface, without perceptible injury to the penknife blade. I am still uninformed about the geological construction of the vicinity of Alton.

At St. Louis water in the ewer in the hotel bedroom had a deposit of mud fully an inch and a half in thickness, and the drinking water seemed to suggest that it, too, would accomplish something very similar if not quickly put out of danger. It tasted well enough, however.

The leading papers of St. Louis were the *Republican* and the *Democrat*. The *Republican* was the best, that is the most successful paper, and was Democratic in politics. The *Democrat* was a close second in merit, and people were not few who thought it the better of the two. It was Republican in politics. At the office of the *Republican* Col. George Knapp seemed to be the supreme authority. He was a short, stout, florid man of reserved manner. His brother, Colonel John, was tall, lean, also florid, but amiable and friendly to a degree that was very gratifying to me. The name of the *Republican* has been curtailed in recent years. It is now the *Republic* and its destinies are at present presided over by Col. Charles W. Knapp, who is a son of the genial, kindly Colonel John, whom I so well remember. The *Democrat* flourished for a time, but was finally practically put out of business by the strategy, if I may call it that, of Col. Houser, who established the *Globe* and made things so lively in St. Louis that after a time the *Democrat* struck its colors and the two became one, the *Globe-Democrat,* and became also, and still remains, the best all-around specimen of a newspaper issued west of Chicago.

Minneapolis had only about 10,000 inhabitants then and the idea that it would ever compete with its Sister City in population or importance was so preposterous that no one ever thought of such a thing, or, if he did, would certainly have had sense enough not to mention the idea in the presence of a resident of St. Paul.

I was in Springfield, Ill., of an evening, and at the office of the *Journal* was alone with the manager. "Mr. Lincoln," said he, "sat in the chair where you sit now, when the dispatch came announcing his nomination for the Presidency. He had stayed away from the Convention because he said he thought he was a little too much of a candidate to make it good taste for him to go; and then he added 'I'm afraid I am hardly enough of a one to warrant me in staying away.'" The newspaper man, before saying good night, took me around and showed me the modest two-story house that had been Mr. Lincoln's home. I could see it well enough in the moonlight and remember it perfectly, with its green blinds, roof slanting to the street and the door yard fence painted white.

There was occasion to be at the station early next morning, I think 4.30 was the hour my train was advertised to start, and I was there. The station was well filled with a heterogeneous set of human beings who appeared to be bent on going somewhere; most of them talked about "going West" and were of the class of pioneers, nearly every one of them being apparently chuck full of days' works, courage and good nature. There was one exception, a man who had for sale, and had with him, in a basket, for immediate delivery, a remedy for fever and ague, price one dollar a bottle. It was a sure cure, never known to fail except in one instance and the exception proved the rule. The exception, however, was the man himself, who was, at that particular time, the best example of what they used in Illinois to call the "shakes" that I have ever seen. Still he was not only saturated with his remedy, but had reinforced it with another that was said to be also good for snake bites. He showed no evidence of bites, but as for ague, he made the story seem probable that such people were of use in the Autumn, because if one climbed a hickory tree his involuntary movements would shake off the nuts. The train was slow about starting that morning, or late about arriving, and the memory of that early hour or two in the station at Springfield is not a cheerful one. I sometimes think it a part of Mr. Lincoln's good fortune that he never went back to Springfield, for to pass through that station as it was then could have afforded him no pleasure.

Milwaukee was a clean, well-built town. I walked down a steep incline from the Newhall House to the office of the *Evening Wisconsin,* then situated at the river's edge, and there I met Mr. Andrew Jackson Aikens, a man who was then and is now (1905) business manager and part owner of the paper, as well as being the originator of the "patent inside" system that has made it possible to have a paper at every frontier outpost or county seat where there is a probability of sufficient legal advertising to be done to amount to $100 per annum. In later years I recall walking again down that incline toward the river accompanied by my old time competitor and long time friend, Mr. S. M. Pettengill. He stopped suddenly, grasped me by the arm and with the other hand pointed across the water. "Do you see that? I like that!" he asked and exclaimed. His eyes seemed to be fixed on a huge black and white sign that decorated the side of a great warehouse, and contained a single word. "What is it?" I asked, "What is it you like?" "Do you see that sign?" "Yes! What of it?" "Do you see what it says?" "Yes, it says COMMISSION." "Not only commission," said Mr. Pettengill, "but it is a very *large* commission!" The commissions allowed to agents at that time were larger than now, but the tendency to restrict them had made so much progress as to enable Mr. Pettengill to fully make up his mind as to what he particularly liked.

Less attractive, less orderly than Milwaukee, Chicago was not so nice in any way, only it was busier and had gotten past the period of being jealous of Milwaukee, which had long promised to be the place of greater importance. The sidewalks seemed to be mainly of wood; at every street crossing the foot passenger walked down or up a short flight of plank stairs, and if it were after dark and pedestrians not too plenty the rats would scurry in every direction as one passed up and down the rickety steps. The people seemed to live in story and a half wooden houses, and in the back yard of these a barrel set down in the spongy soil seemed to make a good enough well, and, if covered with a board, to keep out deceased rats and cats, no reasonable person would have occasion to find fault with the quality of the water; for he might go far, provided he confined his journeyings to the limits of the city, without finding any better.

Two papers in Chicago were of prime importance, the *Tribune* and the *Times*. The *Tribune* was just coining money, and had a handsome new building not less than three stories high. The manager, and a part owner of the paper, was a Mr. Cowles, a handsome, agreeable man with a crisp manner, who did not seem to have any undue enthusiasm about welcoming or recognizing a new advertising agent. "Who does the agent represent?" asked Mr. Cowles. I thought it a conundrum, and not being able to guess it declined to speak for others, but for myself would venture to say that I, as an agent, represented myself. That seemed to be a new idea to Mr. Cowles, but, on reflection, he admitted that such might also be the case with some of the others. He spoke, with some indications of a liking for him, of "Jim Bates." It was the first time I had ever heard of him, and Mr. Cowles told me he was the more active partner of the Pettengill concern. What Mr. Cowles had in mind when he propounded his conundrum was that the agent purported to represent the newspaper, that the newspaper paid him, but that in practice the agent represented the advertiser and worked for his interests all the time. The proposition was new to me. I had not carried my consideration of the question so far; but in after years I noted that although the agent's commission apparently does come in the shape of an allowance from the paper when the bill is paid, yet the actual money comes not from the paper but from the advertiser. I have also noticed that in all brokerage it is the buyer that the broker must seek, that without the buyer he can do nothing for the seller, and the loyalty is admitted to be due to the man who pays the broker money rather than to the man to whom the broker pays the money. It is the man with the money that is sought after by the agent and the newspaper and, for that matter, by almost everybody that is walking up and down the earth. Mr. W. H. Cowles, publisher of that excellent daily, the *Spokesman Review* of Spokane, in the State of Washington, is a son of the gentleman here mentioned as the business manager of the Chicago *Tribune.*

At the office of the Detroit *Tribune,* the evening when I called, there sat at a desk a kindly-faced, bearded man, evidently in the early forties. He told me much about Michigan and Detroit and the newspaper prospects, and I came away thinking him a nice man but one not at all likely to set the world on fire ; and for that matter he never has. But this was Mr. J. E. Scripps, who afterwards established the Detroit *News* and also the numerous papers that compose the Scripps-McRae League of to-day ; and perhaps has done as much, or more, toward forwarding the interests of one cent journalism than even the great and yellow Mr. Hearst of San Francisco, New York, Boston, Chicago and Los Angeles.

At Toledo I called at the office of the daily *Blade,* where I saw the proprietor, who told me that he was then issuing 1,800 copies. I had supposed the edition was larger and said so, whereupon he admitted quite willingly that it had not been nearly so large until very recently ; but told me he had lately secured, as editor, David R. Locke, who had become rather famous as the writer of the Nasby Letters. Since Mr. Locke came the circulation had increased.

The next forenoon, I remember it was a sunny morning, I stood on the street with Ralph H. Waggoner, Jr., whose father was editor of the Toledo *Commercial,* a paper that seemed then and often afterwards to be almost a success, but never quite arrived at it, and has finally died. Mr. Waggoner directed my attention to a man on the other side of the street who, he said, was Mr. Locke. I recall just how he looked. Probably 33 or 34 years of age, stout and heavy of build, not of more than medium height, wearing a pair of black pantaloons that were not creased but somewhat kneed, a pepper and salt sack coat, very short, and a silk hat that appeared to give evidence of considerable use in sleeping cars rather than of ironing or brushing. He was a good-looking man, on the whole, and seemed to be enjoying very much a conversation he was carrying on with his companion as they walked along toward the office of the *Blade*. I afterwards came to see and know a great deal of Mr. Locke. He certainly became a conspicuous figure in American journalism. It used at one time to be said that he made a good living by selling the *Blade* at one season of the year, when someone turned up who thought he could run it better than Locke did, and buying it back a few months later, when the purchaser found that he could not.

At Cleveland the best paper was the *Herald,* although Mr. Cowles of the *Leader* did not seem to think so. The *Herald* was controlled by A. W. Fairbanks, a practical printer. George A. Benedict was editor-in-chief, and his son, George S. Benedict, had charge of the advertising department. The last-named was a specially attractive and capable young man, who had business ideas concerning the management of a newspaper that were decidedly in advance of his time. On the occasion of a visit to New York he was so unfortunate as to be on a sleeping car on the Hudson River Railroad, on a train that collided with an oil train somewhere in the neighborhood of Poughkeepsie, and he and many other passengers perished in the conflagration. After young Benedict's death the *Herald* ceased to hold its pre-eminence, which was eventually assumed by the *Leader,* presided over by a Mr. Cowles, and was afterwards merged in the *Leader.* The Mr. Cowles of Cleveland was a brother of that Mr. Cowles who has been mentioned as business manager and part owner of the Chicago *Tribune.* He had a peculiar defect of speech, conveying to a hearer the impression that he had no palate. There was no real deficiency in his organs of speech, however, but the trouble arose from the ear, which was deficient in a peculiar way, inasmuch as, though he could hear most sounds perfectly well, any sound of S, or as he expressed it, any hissing sound, was absolutely lost to him, and he told me once that he had never in his life heard a bird sing, and was man grown before he realized that there really was any such thing as the song of birds, of which so much was said in literature, but had supposed it was all a sort of poetic license.

Coming east from Cleveland I found myself in a seat with a red-faced, stout, handsome, elderly man whom I recognized as Henry Wilson, Senator from Massachusetts—colleague of Charles Sumner—afterwards Vice-President of the United States during one term of Gen. Grant's Presidency. Mr. Wilson was a self-made man, often spoken of as the "Natick Cobbler." He had been a shoemaker, and his home was still in Natick, Mass., and at that time I, too, had a house in a part of that town known as South Natick.

The village of South Natick is distinguished for being the scene of the labors of Eliot, the Apostle to the Indians. Whether any one of his red parishioners was ever able to read a chapter, verse, word or letter of the Bible he translated into their alleged language, is a matter of doubt in my mind, but he surely did make an impression upon these children of the woods, and they gathered around him; and indications that many of them, dying, received from him the rites of Christian burial, were plainly shown, in 1866, by numerous headstones of slate, bearing unpronounceable names, all more or less disarranged by encroachments of the highway, as well as of a dooryard fence and sundry flower beds and borders such as are inseparable from the New England garden. It cannot be that the intelligence of the Old Bay State will allow such a relic, such a memento of the early day, to entirely disappear from the ken of man by sheer neglect of ordinary care and precaution. South Natick is also the very same quaint old village referred to in Mrs. Stowe's story of "Old Town Folks." It was here that lived the easygoing Sam Lawson, whose lack of energy must clear him from any suspicion of being the progenitor of that Mr. Lawson who at the present time seems to be beyond question Massachusetts' most active and ingenious citizen.

I fell into conversation with the Senator, and being a townsman was a recommendation for me. We came to be on very friendly terms, and when night approached and a sleeping car was taken on, as it was found that the Senator had failed to secure sleeping accommodations, while I had been so extravagant as to preempt a whole section, I was glad to offer to divide, and he equally so to avail himself of my offer. I was not much used to sleeping cars at that time, and my little experience had led me to prefer the upper berth. The Senator insisted that I should have the choice of quarters, and desiring to be civil and exhibit due respect I considerately took the lower berth and allowed the heavy and much older man to climb into the upper one by the aid of the porter and a step ladder. I really thought the Senator treated me next morning with an additional regard.

Trains did not run as fast then as they do now, and it was late in the afternoon of the next day before we reached New York, down by the way of the Hudson River, arriving at some point, at present quite unknown to me, over on the west side, and from which we made our way, each carrying a portmanteau, to the New York Central Railroad station, then situated where the Madison Square Garden now is, at the corner of Fourth avenue and 27th street. We were too late. The train was pulling out. As that operation was performed by horse power there was some confusion about where each car was to go. Someone suggested that if we should hurry up—I think it was hump ourselves that he said —we might still make the train at the 34th street tunnel, or thereabouts, and this we attempted to do; but were too late at 34th street, and when we arrived at the upper opening of the tunnel, at 41st street, we saw the train gliding gracefully away, quite beyond our reach. The Senator and I parted company there, but not until he had explained that, on account of unexpected delays, he found himself almost out of money and, as I was a townsman of his, he would venture to ask for the loan of ten dollars, which I was very glad to grant; and my partner and office boys were much impressed two or three days later when the Senator found his way up our two flights of dark stairs, to the little back office, and repaid his loan with civil words of thanks. Not being a politician myself and the Senator not being an advertiser it was never my fortune to improve the acquaintance thus begun, but as I grew older, and learned to know more about traveling, I have always regretted that I did not let Mr. Wilson have that lower berth.

FOURTEENTH PAPER

The business of securing a list of the newspapers in existence began to seem a pressing one. There was a New England Business Directory that contained a moderately accurate list. A still better catalogue of the papers issued in New Hampshire and Vermont was also available, but beyond these, so far as we were concerned, all was chaos. The Niles and Pettengill agencies had lists, compiled during long dealings had by themselves and their predecessor, Mr. Palmer; but to ask a sight of such a list would be about as brash as to expect to be favored with a catalogue of their customers and the scale of charges made for services.

One of the best lines of business early developed was the advertisements of publishers for local agents to canvass for so-called subscription books, which were publications of pretentious appearance that were withheld from the trade, and therefore only to be had by subscription through an agent. These books were printed on thick paper, showily bound, padded to fill out a requisite number of pages, were generally sold for $3.00 or $3.50; and upon each sale the agent was allowed a profit of 40 per cent. The occupants of the farm houses of the country seemed to hunger for these showy volumes. The prices of produce were high, paper money was plenty, and an active canvasser of good address often made enough money in a season to furnish a capital on which he, too, could become a publisher and eventually make a fortune all his own. The "History of Methodism," "Beyond the Mississippi," the "Field, Dungeon and Escape," and Mark Twain's "Innocents Abroad" were good specimens of the literature thus disseminated. Some of the subscription books reached editions of a quarter of a million copies or more, and yielded a substantial competence for their enterprising publishers. The only time the writer ever had a personal conference with Mark Twain was at the office of one of these publishing houses. Mr. Clemens was then almost unknown to fame, possibly best known by his tale of the "Jumping Frog of Calaveras." I remember him as a rather youthful, sandy complexioned person, not appearing to be particularly impressed with his surroundings at the moment, but very much in earnest in a resolve to ascertain whether or no, in the City of Hartford, such a much needed staple as a bottle of Bass's ale could be procured. But that was later.

It so chanced that a book publishing firm doing business in Hartford, composed of two young men who had themselves been successful canvassers, was bringing out a book that it was thought could be sold advantageously in the Canadian provinces of New Brunswick, Nova Scotia and Prince Edward Island. This firm, Messrs. Scranton & Burr, had patronized our combination of New England papers to the extent of a hundred dollars. We had been paid, and looked upon them as prospective producers of future profits for our enterprise ; so one day, when an application came for a catalogue of papers and prices for a month's advertising in the papers of the regions named above, it deserved and received immediate attention, although neither Dodd nor I had ever seen a paper or a rate card from that region ; and, so far as we knew then or know now, no catalogue of the papers published there was in existence. There was one gleam of hope, however. Our solicitor, Fox, came from Nova Scotia. He was a printer by trade. He remembered the names of several home papers, but, better than that, he knew that for some unaccountable reason the provinces produced an oversupply of journeymen printers, and there was scarcely a printing office in Boston that did not number among its employees one or more of these "blue nose" craftsmen. I never knew why a man from Nova Scotia was called a "blue nose," but he always was so called—in Boston.

Fox started out with pencil and pad. Any man whom he had ever seen or heard of was, to Fox, an intimate friend. No-admittance signs did not deter him. He visited nearly every printing office in town, learned what men were there from the Eastern provinces, what papers they could recall, whether issued daily, weekly or semi-weekly, and about how large was the population of the place where published. When the names were written down they made quite a long list. The size of the town where issued might give some idea of the relative importance of the paper; the advertising rates in Canadian provinces were likely to be less than for papers in similar localities in Maine or Vermont; there might be some risk of having to pay to some of the papers a greater sum than the price estimated for the service, but we needed experience and this was an opportunity to get it.

The list was written out, a price set down against the name of each paper, and the estimate forwarded within twenty-four hours after the application had been received, and it amounted to a considerable sum; something over $200, as I remember. We hardly knew whether to be glad or sorry when, by return mail, the order came to go ahead; and go ahead we did, and much correspondence there was. Letters came back postmarked "No such paper published;" letters came from the Mirimichi *Lumberman,* successor to the *Forester* of that place, now merged in the first-named. Some wanted a higher price for their service and some desired the money in advance, or a better understanding of the probabilities of getting it eventually, before proceeding with the work. On the whole, however, the papers were eager enough, the prices offered, based on the war-inflated figures of the American papers, proved tempting; but, better than all, the call for agents met with responses and the people seemed to be in want of that particular book. The advertising brought results, and the publishers made money out of the enterprise.

It was a long time before we were able to render our bill, with a revised and corrected list of the papers; and the revised list varied so much from the estimate that one would hardly be certain that there was ever any connection between the two. It was explained by Fox, that the printers, from whose memories the original list had been compiled, had in most cases not been home in from five to fifteen years; in fact, rarely went home, or expected ever to go again, and there was naturally some change in newspaper offices going on all the time. Horace and I were anxious about that bill. We made it out with care, said not a word in explanation, believing that there would be quite time enough for that before it would be paid. It so happened, as I have said, that the advertising had produced results. The sending in of the bill having been delayed, it chanced to come at a time when the publishers were squaring up accounts and counting the profits. They were well satisfied. A check in full settlement came by return mail, with no questions asked, and the incident was closed. I often talked over the case afterward with Messrs. Scranton & Burr. They had been pleased with the service rendered and, as for discrepancies between the estimate and the bill, no thought of comparing the two had entered the head of either.

It was evident, however, that our young advertising agency must in some way acquire a list of newspapers. We began thereupon to prosecute inquiries on that head in every direction. Whenever a paper was quoted in another paper we made a note of the name and added it to our list. If an advertiser had a list of papers he had used, and submitted it to us for an estimate, that also served to enrich our collection of names. Something might also be done by going over the exchange lists of friendly newspapers. After a long time we compiled little leaflets containing the names of all the papers that we knew anything about, in each separate State, and, submitting these to the papers mentioned, asked each to erase those that had ceased to exist and add any that they knew that had failed to obtain mention; promising as a remuneration for the service that a free copy of a corrected list should be sent as soon as a revision was completed. Of these State catalogues a good many copies were sold to inquiring advertisers at 25 cents apiece ; and each contained an announcement of the superior facilities, possessed by our youngest of advertising agencies, to aid every advertiser in placing his newspaper patronage at lower rates and on better conditions than anybody else had ever been able to offer. The younger, the less experienced the agent, the greater his confidence in his ability to do better service than can be had elsewhere. That was true then, and just as true now.

I may mention one circumstance as further illustrating the scarcity of information about the names of newspapers: We were assured by a partner of the Chicago agency of Cook, Coburn & Mack that they had believed there was an opening for a successful agency in the field of which Cincinnati would serve as a central point of operations, and had determined to avail themselves of the opportunity, but finally gave up the idea on account of the apparent impossibility of obtaining a catalogue of the papers issued in Ohio, Kentucky, Indiana and Western Pennsylvania. They afterwards did gain sufficient knowledge to encourage them to carry out their first intention.

FIFTEENTH PAPER

The business went on pretty well. The first year's operations vindicated the accuracy of the calculations that had preceded entering upon the enterprise. Mr. Evans regretted that he came into the business too late, for no longer could an advertising agent count upon the clean 25 per cent profit that had been possible in Palmer's time. Our total operations for the first twelve months figured up a gross sum between twenty-seven and twenty-eight thousand dollars, and at the end of the year we had paid our office expenses, salaries, printing, rent, postage and whatever items were incidental to the business, and beyond these the books showed that the estimated net profit of ten thousand dollars had not only been realized, but was actually exceeded by two or three hundred dollars.

In the first year after surrendering the salaried position I had held for seven years my half of the earnings of the Agency I had established amounted to a larger sum than the total of the seven years' salary added together; and yet I have always been of the opinion that I did not stay too long in the office where my earnings were so moderate, for there was a value in the experience I gained, in the knowledge of men and methods I acquired, in the acquaintances I made among men who might be useful to me in after life, that was worth to me far more than the money paid me for wages, and I have ever regarded it as a mistake when a young man has left a position where his earnings would permit him to exist to take another in an office where, although he might have an increase of salary, his opportunities for acquiring business knowledge and training would be less. No man is likely to be a conspicuous success, from a business point of view, so long as he works for somebody else for a weekly stipend; but so long as he has to do this the fewer changes he makes the better it will be for him.

On one other point I would like to speak to young men in salaried positions who will read these words. Do not forget that business is buying to advantage and selling at a profit. You must be worth to your employer more than he pays you, or there is no profit to him upon his investment in you. If you are worth to him a very great deal more than he pays you he will know it and others will see it. By and by some one will try to take you away by offering a higher price. In that case it is likely that your present employer will advance the figure, but it is often much better to stay where they know you and your worth than to go to another place where you may fall short of meeting expectations. No salary is likely to permit of very great savings; expenses increase as income increases; but the value of knowledge gained may be something enormous, and available at a moment when least expected. The reputation of staying long in one place is a valuable asset for a clerk. The man who has been in ten places in ten years, and can refer confidently to each and all of them, is not on the high road to success. If you are a business man and want an assistant you will do well to steer clear of the man whose experience is so varied and who is always so eager to find a better place that he does not leave himself time to quite fill the one he at present occupies.

A good proportion of our business came from New York. As the list of New England papers could be managed so well why not have a similar list in the great State of New York? I consulted advertisers on the subject; some thought favorably of the proposed expansion, others believed it would be best to let well enough alone. I made a trip to New York City to look over the ground in person. Among the firms who had favored us with an occasional order were the publishing houses of D. Appleton & Co. and Fowler & Wells, the first a great firm of booksellers, the other the headquarters of Phrenology, the *Phrenological Journal* and the myriad publications issued by the prolific Professor Fowler.

At the office of the Appletons I talked with Mr. George S. Appleton, a man who had the most forbidding countenance and the crossest, curtest manner of any business man I had ever been brought in contact with. He said he had used our New England list once or twice, but did not think much of it; very likely might never use it any more; advised me to stop where we stood; did not believe a New York list would succeed as well, and, for his part, saw no likelihood of ever having any use for it. Mr. Wells was a pleasant-faced man, well advanced in years. He thought the idea ingenious and good; advised me to push it forward, and assured me that his firm would surely make frequent use of the facilities it would enable us to offer. It was eventually decided that we would inaugurate the New York list, so we made the contracts, issued our catalogue and proposals, and among the first orders received for the first month was one from D. Appleton & Co., and it is a fact that from that day to the end of the chapter no order ever came from Fowler & Wells.

It is my observation that every young man will have, in starting out upon a business career, about the experience I have indicated in the case of the two firms mentioned. He will obtain less assistance, less patronage, than he has allowed himself to expect from his friends and those whom he has reason to think he will be able to influence, but if he pushes forward and works industriously he will receive unexpected aid and valuable patronage from unexpected sources and from entire strangers. In after years I once found myself compelled to take a seat in a railway carriage at a White Mountain resort with him of forbidding countenance, the George S. Appleton referred to above. We fell into conversation, the talk was of business matters, methods, perplexities and successes. For twelve full hours our journey proceeded, as we sat and talked, and I have ever since liked to think of the day and the man. I found him cultivated, genial, interesting, and helpful to such a degree that I thought, that night, and have thought ever since, that rarely, if ever, had chance brought me in contact with a man in every way so charming, and it seemed to me in every way so excellent. It was a lesson to me, and from that time I have never allowed myself to believe a man lacking in lovable qualities merely because on the occasion of a first or even a second meeting he had seemed to me to be so.

Of course, there were difficulties and worries. Whoever has conducted an increasing business, on a small capital, has learned that such a condition entails a certainty of being short of funds. We were always prompt with our remittances, and never hesitated to borrow of A to pay B, even though B might be in no hurry for the money; in fact, quite willing to wait. This practice of prompt payment soon gave our firm the reputation of being better off than we were. Oftentimes there was an anxious need of a few hundred dollars when there was no place in sight from which it could be obtained. Then, too, there would be days when no business came in, and we knew that it *must* be had, or the outcome would be fatal to us.

How many, many times have I called on a hesitating advertiser, exhibited his proof, given him a day or a week to consider, and finally been disappointed. I particularly remember a Boston man who had invented a method of tightening the frame of a buck saw, that was, he thought, a vast improvement over the old plan of twisting a rope with a stick. He had some sale for his device, and believed it would eventually revolutionize the wood-sawing business. We talked by the hour; I might almost say by the day. I went to his place of business, and he came to mine. The service he had in mind would cost $125.00. There came a day when his inch and a quarter of copy was needed to fill my 20 inches of space in my 100 New England papers. I would have to pay for the space whether I used it or not. The order might be said to be one that would be all velvet if it came. The ad. was in type, waiting for a final O. K. and order to send it out, when the man came in, out of breath from ascending those two flights of stairs too rapidly. He had decided not to authorize the work, because he was in fact very busy, and he believed the enormous amount of publicity we were to give him for his $125.00 would bring in so many orders that his workshop would be glutted and general embarrassment ensue. I was grievously disappointed, and as a final argument told him if he would give me the order and the money then, I would engage to give him back every cent of the price if he should be able to show that, after the advertising had been done, he had ever had a single order from it or, in fact, heard from it at all except in the way of being solicited by other agents to order it inserted in other papers. My offer created surprise in the man's mind, but he did not give me the order, and it is not my recollection that he ever became well known as a successful advertiser.

One day we had a veritable bombshell in our camp, and it came from the hand of John Moore, our new solicitor in New York City. He had found at the office of an advertiser, of whom he had hoped to make a customer, a list of Illinois and Wisconsin weeklies for which advertisements would be taken at not more than 50 cents per paper per month, while our price was a dollar; and more remarkable still, the advertiser might insert his matter for a single week without paying more than 12 cents a paper. Evidently here was something with which, paper for paper, we could not compete. Not knowing anything about these Illinois and Wisconsin papers we were, as a matter of course, perfectly confident that our papers were of a much higher grade, and therefore, in the matter of quality, we were ahead. Still we could not do the work, by the single week, in even the poorest of the papers on our list at the price mentioned, without having to pay to the papers more money than we should receive. We could not understand it at all and the matter gave us a great deal of trouble for some days; but finally the explanation came from the very source that had sent the bomb. In the office of another advertiser Moore found that an order had been given for the mysterious Western combination, and copies of the papers containing the advertisement had been received, and, in fact, were there on the table and open for examination. This Moore proceeded to make, and his practical printer's eye immediately discovered that the advertisement was on the inside of all the papers, that the papers were uniform in length and number of columns, and more wonderful still, the type in each was identical with that in all the others, and the reading matter the same. That there was a ."nigger in the wood pile" was evident, but of what sort and for what purpose he was put there was still a mystery. We all understand this well enough to-day. That was the beginning of what is known among newspaper men and advertisers as the "patent insides," a scheme first introduced by Mr. A. J. Aikens at the office of the Milwaukee *Evening Wisconsin,* later taken up and most intelligently pushed into notice by the late A. N. Kellogg, of Chicago. The system has had many changes and enlargements of plan. It did not come much into competition with my hundred paper lists for several years, but it did eventually, after a considerable period, have an important share among the influences that eventually drove our system out of business. At the present day (1905) no less than eight thousand papers are printed on the now so-called co-operative plan, and the enterprise has, I am confident, created at least two millionaires. Its possibilities are still great, and it might not be unwise for Mr. Rogers, of Standard Oil, to look into them, when his present engagement with the copper output and Mr. Lawson of Boston shall have ceased to occupy his attention.

SIXTEENTH PAPER

There was at this time in Boston a learned barber, William Bogle by name. He had a store in front of his workroom, and in it perfumery and cosmetics were sold. The place had a conspicuous position on the east side of Washington street, perhaps half way between Milk and Summer streets, and here Mr. Bogle also dispensed a hair dressing, known as Hyperion Fluid. The barber was, as I have said, a scholarly man. The fact is testified to by records that show him to have been an active member, and at one time president, of a Boston literary club, known a: the Burns Society. His manner was dignity personified. I e was courteous, but very susceptible to annoyances; and under favoring conditions irascible. Nothing would sooner excite his scholarly criticism than the mispronunciation of a word; more particularly if that word, as was not infrequently the case, happened to be his own name. Horace Dodd used to tell of a wag who had met the barber at the literary club, and learned something of his peculiarities; who one day made his way to the shop where a conversation took place about as follows:

"Good morning, Mr. Bog-le."

"Good morning, sir. My name is Bo-gle, not Bog-le."

"I beg your pardon. I called to get a bottle of your Hyper-iron Fluid."

The package was wrapped in paper, as is proper, and presented to the customer with the remark:

"The pronunciation of the name of this dressing is Hyperion—not Hyper-iron. One dollar, please."

"Oh! Beg pardon again," said the man; and paying the price, and taking his purchase in hand, he bowed himself out with the parting words:

"Good morning, Mr. Bog-le."

Everybody in Boston knew the self-opinionated, self-important, little hairdresser and wigmaker; short of stature, neat in dress, his hair always curled, precise of speech; suggesting an ancestry perhaps half French, a quarter Scotch, and the remainder indefinable—without better information; and everybody could, therefore, appreciate, when considered in the light of a practical joke, how successful the hectoring call might have been.

On the southwest corner of Washington and Bromfield streets, not very far from opposite Mr. Bogle's emporium, that was distinguished by a wax bust in the window of a man wearing a lovely wig; a firm of fashionable tailors did business, the partners being a Mr. Tuttle and a Mr. Call; and the name on the sign board, and on the wide silver strips that embellished all shop windows in those days, read CALL & TUTTLE. It is hard to tell why this sign should attract so much attention, but it is doubtful if any man who lived in Boston, or even visited Boston in the sixties of the last century, will fail to assert, if asked about this sign, that he remembers it very well; and there seemed to be something really funny in the true story, that once, when in Boston, the humorist, John Phoenix, entered the store, asserted that he had frequently noticed the invitation, didn't know just what it meant, but could not stand out any longer, and now, whatever it might be, had acted upon it, had called, and would like to "Tuttle."

As we approached the end of our second year, it appeared that it would show a moderate advance upon the net earnings of the first. It had already became evident that advertising men more generally abounded in New York, than in Boston. I had also observed that a New York man could make up his mind more quickly, either that he would or would not; and as a consequence business could there be done more rapidly. Mr. Dodd was a Bostonian, and could hardly be expected to thrive beyond sight of the dome of the State House; and beside that, we had too good a local clientele to be neglected or thrown away. And then there was the *Dial*, which had grown to be a property worth a good deal more than it had cost, and it was a Boston institution pure and simple. It came finally to be understood that after the closing of the books at the end of the second year our firm would be dissolved. Mr. Dodd would keep the Boston office, and do business as an advertising agent in his own name. He would keep the *Dial,* at a valuation. Wesley Barber would remain with him, and I would go to New York, taking with me the firm name, and the books of account. The bookkeeper, Pierce, and the assistant, Frank Newton, would accompany me. Not all of our profits had been real-

HORACE DODD.

ized in cash. The books showed accounts of considerable value, and for these my partner was willing to accept my notes, payable at dates agreed upon, coming due at convenient intervals, running through the next six months.

After this had been arranged, that uncle of Mr. Dodd's, who had put up for him the original capital of $1,000 he had brought into the business two years before, suggested to him, and very properly I think, that I was going among strangers, and likely to find conditions different from those I had become used to ; and recommended his nephew to offer substantial inducements, if I would, and could, arrange to discount those notes and get them out of the way. My old father had about this time, by the sale of a piece of real estate, become possessed of ready money to about the amount I should be owing to Mr. Dodd. It constituted his entire fortune, although not more than $8,000 in amount. He reminded me of that fact, and that he was neither young, nor in good health; and told me, if I thought it safe to do so, to take the money, pay off the obligation to Mr. Dodd, and account to him for the loan when conditions would admit. Few persons, perhaps, have occasion to realize the immense satisfaction I had in paying back to the old gentleman, during the first year, the entire sum he had advanced; but the payment did not make me feel any less proud that he had been willing to trust me to the extent he did; and that I had had the confidence to accept the loan on the conditions which existed, and had been fortunate enough to repay it, and be free of the risk and obligation, and all, too, in a shorter time than had been expected.

John Moore had made the acquaintance of some men who did a business that I never quite understood, in an office in the New York Times Building, at No. 41 Park Row, for which they had a lease with a year to run from May 1, 1867. The office had been hired when rents were lower, and the lease was worth a premium. The rent paid to the *Times* was $1,200 a year, the premium demanded was $500, which Moore said was reasonable. He had a friend, a New Hampshire lawyer, settled in New York, Royal S. Crane, by name, who passed upon the legality of the lease transfer, and when I settled with him for his services, he had said: "Oh! It's a small matter; give me $20.00." In Boston I would have expected to pay about $3.00 for the service, and the easy manner at which $20.00 seemed to be arrived at rather took my breath away. Moore thought it all right, however, and it occurred to me that if the scale of charges in New York was likely to stand in about that ratio to that I was used to in Boston I would have to make an effort to get on to the revised system *tout de suite*. A little later this attorney did some advertising through our office and although it, too, was a small matter, we did the best we could to even up that $20.00 fee.

The time for taking possession of the Park Row office was fixed for April 1st. On the evening of March 31st (1867), therefore, my wife and I took the evening train for Fall River, and next morning arrived at the foot of Murray street on a gorgeous steamboat that seemed to be controlled by James Fisk and Jay Gould, and had the portraits of the two gentlemen, handsomely framed, placed by the gangway, where they attracted considerable attention, and some one mentioned what had been said of them by the famous stuttering Wall Street man, Mr. Travers, that "There ought to be a picture of C-h-rist c-r-rucified hanging between them."

It had been my fortune to see Jim Fisk when he had the famous peddler's outfit, with which he used to travel over northern New Hampshire and Vermont, he having succeeded to his father, who had built up a profitable business in that line. It was no ordinary peddler's outfit, however. There were four black horses, a colored driver with white gloves, most resplendent brass mountings for harness, and shining varnish for the warehouse on wheels. Fisk came to Boston afterward, and for a time had a connection with the firm of Jordan, Marsh & Co., then a store of his own, then he came to New York, and was prominent in the stock market for a time. Finally his experiences culminated in Black Friday, and in the end getting himself shot by Edward S. Stokes; who, after being convicted and sentenced to death, afterwards secured a new trial, was acquitted, and had an active business life in New York City for many years; the principal incident of which, to the outside public, seemed to be the establishment of the gorgeous bar room at the Hoffman House.

It is surprising how many stories became current that were attributed to Fisk. Some woman in his peddler days defamed his father. He had lied to her about a yard of ninepenny calico, so she asserted, but Fisk did not think the old man would tell a lie for twelve and a half cents, although—

possibly—"he might tell eight for a dollar." He refused to subscribe for the erection of a fence about the cemetery at Brattleboro, which was the home of the Fisks, on the ground that none was needed, because no one that was out of it wanted to get in, and none of those who were in *could* get out. It was he, also, who gave rise to the phrase: "Gone where the woodbine twineth," as applied to securities that had been pledged; that is "spouted" in the vernacular of the Street. As the Virginia Creeper, miscalled Woodbine, commonly grew over the waterspout, on New England farm houses, the expression, in Fisk's active fancy, seemed appropriate. I recall two well looking ladies, evidently friends of Fisk's, who resided at the St. James Hotel, and were spoken of, behind their backs, as "Erie common" and "Erie preferred," Fisk, at that time, being in control of the Erie railroad.

In later years Mr. J. Henry French, the dramatic publisher and theatrical manager, grew to very much resemble Fisk in personal appearance, and I recall one stroke of genius on Henry's part that seemed to me worthy of a financier. He controlled the libretto of a certain opera troupe, that would be on sale wherever a performance was given, and sought advertisements for the blank pages, covers, etc., as is common enough; but, instead of assuming to print a specified number of hundreds or thousands, and charging a round price for the service, he said nothing about the size of the edition, but bargained with advertisers for a fixed price for each performance where the libretto was used. A piano man or a dealer in furs, or diamonds, might pay $25 a night for one hundred nights, or a total of $2,500 for an edition which, if plainly stated to him, would have seemed over-priced at $250 or even $125. Henry was a boy then, and he did very well with his libretto; in fact, though a man of marked ability, he never showed more knowledge of high finance than in this effort of his youth.

Arriving at the foot of Murray street, on the morning of April 1, 1867, my wife and I walked up the street to City Hall Park and gazed with pride at the new sign, already in

place, over an entrance to the Times Building, then called the
New, although it has since been torn down and replaced by
the elegant structure which has recently had new stories
added until it approaches something near to the original
height of the Tower of Babel, although still falling a good
deal short of that still more wonderful structure, the still
newer Times Building, situated at Broadway and 42nd
street.

I recall one incident of the final parting from Boston that
caused considerable comment at the time among those interested. The firm was to be dissolved, some would come
away, and some remain. The pleasant associations of one or
two years were to end. Mr. Dodd, who had a keen sense of
humor, sought a confidential interview with Pierce, the
bookkeeper, stated the case to him, suggested the advisability of taking some steps to mark the occasion; possibly by a
supper at Parker's, or something of that sort. Pierce listened
intently, was fully in accord with the idea, and willing, more
than willing, to do his share. "How much, Pierce," asked
Dodd, "would you subscribe toward paying the expense of
the entertainment?" To this inquiry, Pierce, with enthusiastic generosity and interest, forgetful, perhaps, at the moment of the moderate figure that represented his salary,
responded, "I'll give three dollars." Dodd was more than
gratified; he was delighted, and said to Pierce, clapping him
heartily on the shoulder, "I think that will be all we shall
need to pay for the whole thing!" The celebration, as a
matter of fact, never did take place.

SEVENTEENTH PAPER

While the Agency was situated in Boston, the visitors at the office were mainly New England men. This was especially the case so far as the statement has reference to visitors connected with the advertising department of newspapers. One day, however, there appeared two exceptions in the persons of Mr. Jenness J. Richardson, connected with the *Democrat* issued at Davenport, and a certain Mr. Barnhart, representing the *Journal* at Muscatine, Iowa. Both these gentlemen are living to-day (1905), prosperous specimens of the best examples of the men of the Middle West, Mr. Barnhart being a member of the type founding firm of Barnhart Brothers & Spindler and Mr. Richardson a retired business man, a leading capitalist of that Davenport which, in Napoleonic phrase, he loved so well. He was at this time a rather raw-boned specimen of athletic manhood, who impressed people at first sight as being from the rural districts. In time I came to believe that he cultivated the manner and succeeded in making it profitable. No advertiser, big or little, failed to receive a visit from him. A rebuff rolled off him like water from a duck's back. He was in no hurry, he could wait, would much rather wait than call again. If the order was a small one he preferred it to none. If the man had no money there was no objection to taking payment in goods. Half cash and half goods would do very well indeed. He would be glad to make a hundred dollars, but would not turn down an opportunity to make only a single cent. It used to be said that if there was a stove in the office that Richardson could stand by and warm his mittened hands, holding them up one on each side of the stove pipe, no one was ever able under such conditions to refuse him the order for the precise space, position, price and terms of payment suggested by this most ingenious canvasser that ever came from the banks of the Mississippi.

In the years that followed it became a liberal education for any younger advertising man to be allowed to accompany Mr. Richardson on his peregrinations through the East. The only trouble was that not one of them could ever get through with half the list of visits that Richardson seemed to manage with apparent ease. If the train was half an hour late and there was in sight from the railway station the announcement of a liniment, or a rat poison, or anything whatever that was or could be advertised, Jenness never

J. J. RICHARDSON.

wasted that half hour, and the chances were more than even that before the train arrived he would be back in the station, with an order in his pocket, and an electrotype of the advertisement to be used, added to the half hundred weight more or less of similar hardware already packed away among the shirts and collars in the extra comprehensive grip that was as much his constant companion as the umbrella has been for the last ten or fifteen years to that modern model special agent, Mr. N. M. Sheffield, of New York.

There was one well-known advertiser, who placed his

contracts mainly through the Pettengill Agency, and had a
reputation for being so much of a bear that it was rare that
any canvasser, representing a paper, ever ventured into his
presence a second time.   I am speaking of the late Dr. J. H.
Schenck, who once had his name, and that of his Mandrake
Pills, painted on about everything that rose above the surface of the ground between New York and Philadelphia
that had a smooth side that could be seen from the railroad.
It was the doctor's practice to journey from city to city,
engage handsome rooms at a good hotel, or other desirable
quarters, and there the sick, in answer to his advertisements,
would flock in numbers for a free consultation; from which
each was likely to learn that the Doctor's Pulmonic Syrup
and Mandrake Pills were practically all that were required to
bring the bloom of health to the faded cheek.   The Doctor's
face was about as well known then as that of Mr. Douglas,
the shoe man and recent Democratic Governor of Republican
Massachusetts, is to-day; for the Doctor also, in his time,
had his portrait appearing in nearly every newspaper published at the East.   It was to the office of this famous man
that our friend from Davenport made his way on one of his
initial searches after advertising patronage.   The Doctor
was busy and Richardson had to wait his time—in later years
he was generally just awkward enough to blunder in ahead
of everybody else and get his contract signed before it
dawned on him that he was in anybody's way.   There was a
stove and a stove pipe in this instance, and while warming
his mittened hands he had an opportunity to note the un-
ceremonious and energetic manner in which each applicant
for an advertising order was dismissed.   When his turn
came, at length, it was not an advertisement he wanted at all.
He had heard of Dr. Schenck, and had seen his picture.   He
knew that nothing he could put in his paper would gratify
or be likely to benefit his readers so much as to afford them
an opportunity to see the portrait of that celebrated man; and
his object in calling was to borrow, if he could, one of the
electrotypes; which would enable him to present that famous
countenance to the people of Iowa, reinforced, if the Doctor

would permit, with a few facts concerning his birth, lineage and wonderful cures. He was not dismissed. The picture was produced, the needed facts given, and finally he was asked what his terms would be for the insertion of a quarter column advertisement, and, when the price was mentioned the Doctor, in his kindliest voice, said to his manager, close at hand: "Give the boy a contract." Further than that, he took the "boy" home with him that afternoon on his steam yacht, and rarely after that did Richardson visit Philadelphia, while Dr. Schenck lived, without having either to accept or decline a repetition of that visit. I do not think the Schenck advertisements were ever absent from his pages, until the time came that they disappeared altogether from the newspapers of the country.

On another occasion our friend had hired a livery team to enable him to drive a few miles into the country to seek the patronage of an old Quaker who also had a most valuable medicine. When he arrived the Doctor had himself gone to the city and would be likely to be met on his return. It was raining fearfully, the roads were muddy, a protecting oil-cloth-mud-and-rain-screen came nearly up to the eyes, but did not prevent the detection and recognition of the returning "physician" who was then and there accosted, told of the advantages to be had by advertising in the Davenport *Democrat,* and finally induced to give an order—verbal authority in this case being accepted.

Richardson's coming was one of the events of the season. Spring and Autumn he came, always, as years progressed, followed by a shoal of imitators with whom he was on most friendly terms, and to whom he gave valuable tips *after* he had himself booked an order, and now and then after he had satisfied himself that no one could book an order. In the last named class of cases he liked to meet the canvasser again and learn the particulars of the interview, but I do not remember ever hearing of a case where another man succeeded after Richardson had failed.

I never saw him angry, or even appear to be annoyed. There was a humor about him, so unpretentious and simple, and yet so subtle, that, while it would generally be effective at the moment, the full substance of it would not perhaps be fully realized before the next day. If arguments were advanced that had a bearing contrary to his purpose they were occasionally punctured by a question that, if answered, was certain to destroy the objection; but even so, no comment on the result would follow. If the argument seemed to have so much of foundation as not to be assailed in such case it did not seem to have been heard at all, and the next word, from the man from Davenport, would be precisely what it would have been if no argument had been urged. His manner, if not bashful, was at least not lacking in a flattering deference, and if it led him to push in ahead of others who were really before him it always seemed as though his errand was so short, so unimportant, and so easily disposed of that everybody would be glad to have it attended to and out of the way so that a clear deck for others to operate on might remain.

He had the greatest possible patience with those who were curious to know the extent of the *Democrat's* circulation. "Everybody takes it. We make the best paper we know how to make. Our press is one of the largest of the So-and-So pattern and we print all we can get onto it." I rarely knew him to be much more definite and, so far as the editor of Rowell's Newspaper Directory was concerned, that desperate inquisitor never found it advisable to waste much time in attempting to glean information. There was a sufficient willingness to talk, but considerable difficulty about keeping to the subject.

Possibly no less conspicuous as a canvasser than Richardson ever became, and antedating him in the time of his first appearance, was Col. W. S. Lingle, of Lafayette, Indiana. It was amazing how ignorant the advertiser of that day was about the geography of what was called *the West.* Everything west of Buffalo was "the West" and the man who attempted to realize that the center of the United States is fifty miles west of Omaha could not be found. To hear Mr. Lingle talk one might conclude that Indiana was practically all there was to the West, and Lafayette was the heart of Indiana, and his paper, the *Journal,* was read by everybody and influenced the thought of all. Naturally Richardson often crossed Mr. Lingle's tracks and at times had to answer whether, in his opinion, Lingle's Lafayette *Journal* did or did not practically cover and reach all the best people of the West ; and when he realized that his own paper was issued five hundred miles nearer the Pacific than Lingle's was, and that no one living within a hundred miles of Davenport had ever heard of the Lafayette *Journal,* he was almost tempted to regret that his controlling policy was one of never speaking ill of any other paper. To such an inquirer Richardson was once known to respond : "Over what you people at the East know as the West, that is over the territory between Buffalo and Illinois, I presume all Mr. Lingle asserts may be substantially true ; but beyond the Mississippi, among the Rocky Mountains, on the Pacific Coast and in the Sandwich Islands my paper circulates two copies to his one."

There were two Richardson Brothers. Jenness was the younger. D. N., the older, was the editor ; Jenness, the business manager, the advertising manager, in fact pretty much everything but editor. The relations of the two were as lovely as those of the Cheeryble Brothers, famous in the story of Nicholas Nickleby. D. N. made no claims to pre-eminence or superior knowledge, but Jenness always appeared to think him a fountain of wisdom. He always went to him for advice, but was never known to get any. Everybody but Jenness thought the younger brother was the whole thing, and D. N. seemed to be somewhat of that opinion, too, but Jenness always asserted that the facts were quite the other way. D. N. had a large family and J. J. a small one, but each took from the office what money was needed and no account between them was kept. If a piece of property was bought, Jenness selected it and bargained for it, and when purchased they owned it together. If it was bank stock, or a trust company, as years progressed, Jenness made the terms of subscription, but it was D. N., and not he, that sat on the board of directors. They both became men of prime importance as time went by. They were originally Vermont boys, who had learned the printer's trade, and gone West to grow up with the country. Being prudent, their earnings were allowed to accumulate in the hands of their employer, until he one day announced that he was bankrupt; but if the two wanted the paper in payment of the about $800 he owed them for wages, they might have it and be quite welcome; and that was the way they chanced to become publishers.

Jenness was not a particularly well-dressed man, and his clothes were not always brushed with so much scrupulousness as might be possible; furthermore, it used to be dusty riding over the prairie. On one occasion he had a characteristic experience. He had a yearly pass over the Chicago & Rock Island Railroad, and, to the not well-trained eyes of a strange conductor, did not seem to be the sort of man likely to be entitled to possess so important a thing as a yearly pass. Railroad men have a way of placing at a disadvantage those who, it is thought, may be trying to impose upon them, and this one asked with some sternness, "Is your name J. J. Richardson?" To which the passenger—really more than six feet tall, clad in the linen duster of that day, sitting on the small of his back at the time, as was rather a custom of his, with his feet on the heavy portmanteau in front, loaded down with advertising orders and electrotypes as usual—after a considerable hesitation, asked with a drawl which he used at times when he saw he was misunderstood: "If I show you my photograph do you think you can recognize me?" The conversation was not prolonged.

I have said that the Richardsons came from Vermont. They never seemed to lose their interest in the State of the Green Mountains, and rarely a Summer passed without a visit to the scenes that the memory of youthful days recalled. They could not fail to note the difference in the ways of the sedate New England village, that decreased every decade instead of adding to its population, when compared with towns of Iowa and Illinois that doubled the number of residents in a twelve-month sometimes. "Did you notice any improvements going on when you were at Danville this year?" I once ventured to ask of Jenness, and he replied with considerable promptness that this year, for once, he had noticed such; and, being led to specify, reported that the very day he arrived his attention was directed to the conspicuous fact that since his last year's visit Deacon Blank had repainted his wagon.

It was on a visit to Richardson that I first had the experience of crossing the Mississippi on a dark night in a small boat. It was at the Davenport fair grounds where I, at the age of thirty-three, for the first time in my life, saw a horse-trot; and it was there, and at that time, that I became acquainted with the only A. Frank Richardson, also a Vermont boy, who had gone to Iowa to join his relatives. Frank was at this time supposed to be paying attentions to a young miss of the city, but was so reticent about it that her identity was not known. He had applied for two circus tickets for the show then in town, and his uncle liked to tell how gracefully Frank responded to his statement that this particular show demanded to have in advance the name of every individual entitled to be a user of a press ticket, and that Frank thereupon wrote down his own name and that of the favored lady, after which the uncle, having secured the valuable paper and inspected it, handed over the tickets to the blushing applicant. I think I never saw so many house flies, or such fat and lazy ones, as filled the dining room at the Burtis House, the principal hotel in the Davenport of 1871, but there were no flies on the Richardsons.

There was an experience, connected with my first visit to Davenport, that never fails to come to mind when I recall the pleasant occasion. Employed on the editorial force of the *Democrat* was a certain Scotchman who claimed to have come from the same part of that country that had produced James Gordon Bennett, the founder of the New York *Herald,* and he said it was told of the future journalist that, on leaving home by sailing vessel, as was a common method of travel then, the vessel was delayed by storms, mystified by fogs, and lost her reckoning. The compass was out of order and the captain in despair; whereupon the young emigrant, taking something from his coat collar and laying it upon the chart, asked of the mariner, "Do you know what that is?" And the captain said, "It's a louse!" said to be pronounced *loose*. "It is," said Bennett, "and it's a Scotch loose, and you can bet your life it'll go Sooth." The points of compass being thus adjusted, the vessel and the emigrant duly came to port. My unfortunate proclivity of forgetting names led me to be oblivious of that of the narrator of this bit of journalistic history; consequently, in attempting to speak of him afterwards to other members of the force, I was led to designate him as "the Scotch louse." Unfortunately, the name seemed to commend itself to his associates and to stick, and, although I esteemed the man and always took an interest in him, we never seemed to become close friends, and I finally lost sight of him.

Jenness does not come to New York seeking advertising patronage any more. He does not need to, for he has been for a number of years one of the wealthiest men in Iowa, and D. N., his brother—good man that he was—is no longer spared to be with us on earth. Some years before he died, however, he took a vacation tour around the world and wrote one of the most charming books of travel that it has been the good fortune of the writer to come across. Dozens of times I have taken that volume in hand to read to a friend the description it contains of that dream in marble, the Taj Mahal, for I am satisfied that no other person ever dealt with the subject so truthfully, so poetically, so beautifully.

EIGHTEENTH PAPER

The first domicile sought in New York was at the St. Denis Hotel, then as now situated at the corner of Broadway and Eleventh street. I recall that early experience with the European plan hotel. On the bill of fare one might read: Porterhouse steak $1.25. In the beginning it was not desirable to pay too strict attention to economy, and "two porterhouse steaks", was the order given to the waiter, whose look of wonder was transferred to our own countenances when the huge platter came with the two steaks, each somewhat approaching the size of a buffalo robe.

It is always interesting to find people with inquiring minds, whose knowledge is less than one's own, and to such I like to relate that not much more than half a century ago, at North Cambridge, Mass., not far beyond the Harvard College region, there existed a celebrated road house, whose landlord was named Porter, and his hostelry called Porter's. Here numerous good things might be enjoyed by the lovers of fast horses, who were the principal patrons who stopped to be refreshed at the bar, or to have a dinner or a supper, whichever they might choose to designate it; and it was here that the choice cut of steak, with the sirloin on one side, the tenderloin on the other, and a narrow strip of bone dividing the two, was better served than any other cut ever was elsewhere, and became first celebrated there, then in Boston, and now wherever Americans congregate, and everywhere known as the porterhouse steak. Not many people, aside from old Bostonians who once had horsey tastes, are aware of the fact here stated. More are acquainted with the companion fact that at Moon's road house, on the lake near the City of the Springs, first came into notice the delicious crisp, fried potato slices that can now be bought, out of a barrel, at grocery stores throughout the Union, and known everywhere as Saratoga chips.

The St. Denis, with its European plan, was too expensive for permanent occupancy, and shortly a boarding-house was discovered, on the east side of University Place, between Eighth street and Ninth. It was a delightful old double house, was No. 17, with wide halls and large rooms, and had once been the home of a certain Judge Roosevelt, a progenitor, as I understood, of most of the Roosevelts of to-day. Here for seven years, longer than it had ever before been my fortune to dwell under one roof, I found a comfortable home; and many a doubting smile have I noted on the faces of the New Hampshire friends of my youth when I told them about the peculiarities of the great city, and mentioned that during all those seven years, I not only never knew who lived next door, nor did I, during all that time, ever see any person enter or leave that house, or ever notice a face at the window. The old place in after years was the home of the Café Martin, which became so well known and prosperous that when Delmonico's moved further up the avenue, The Martin took its place, at the corner of Fifth avenue and 25th street, and is now one of the institutions of New York.

Among the boarders at No. 17 University Place were the family of a certain Mr. Eastman, who had obtained certain land warrants, issued, I think, as rewards to soldiers who had taken part in the war of extermination against the Creek and Seminole Indians, under General Jackson; and covering vast tracts of pine forests in central Georgia. Before he and I had ceased to dwell there he had disposed of these land titles to a member of the family of Mr. William E. Dodge, the well-known New York merchant, and these holdings now have a place on the map of Georgia as Dodge County, with the township of Eastman as its capital.

Here also lived for several years that excellent woman, Miss Lydia F. Wadleigh, celebrated for her long and efficient service as Principal of the famous Twelfth street school for girls, and afterwards as Vice-principal of the New York Normal College, which was in fact a development of the earlier institution named. The present Wadleigh High

School in West 114th street was so named in remembrance of her. Hundreds of the best informed and best principled mothers of prominent people in New York City recall with reverence, and almost adoration, the teachings and influence of this noble New Hampshire woman. She was, perhaps, twenty years my senior, but there grew up a warm friendship between us which lasted till her death, which occurred may be as much as twenty years ago. She was a close connection of the celebrated Pillsbury family of Minneapolis, who are thought, by some, to manufacture most of the flour consumed by civilized people throughout the globe, and certainly all that is of highest grade and finest quality. She had another cousin, of her own name, Bainbridge Wadleigh, who had achieved a certain fame in the Granite State, while a member of the Legislature, by talking something like twelve hours against time, until it should be possible for a certain belated train to arrive bringing a missing legislator whose vote was needed to secure a majority of one for a Republican Governor; the people having failed to elect, and thereby thrown the choice into the Legislature. I happened to be at Concord, the State Capital, on an occasion when there was a deadlock in the Republican caucus over the nomination of a United States Senator. Wadleigh was not a candidate, but after many votes with no prospect of a choice some one made a speech mentioning Wadleigh's services of the year before. He was popular and had no enemies. The next ballot showed a few votes for him, and then the caucus was stampeded and everybody was for him. It was near midnight, but I thought the news worth telegraphing to my friend. Her cousin was elected next day and made an excellent Senator. Senator Hoar gives him a fine send-off in his charming autobiography, but his cousin, the school teacher, though respecting and sincerely attached to him, could never see that there was anything in such a commonplace occurrence to warrant me in sending the message, and awakening a house at midnight, to read a telegram—when there was nobody dead after all.

After Kent came on from Boston to join me, he also

boarded at the same house, and, as we were people of steady habits, and the lady he "respected" lived in Harlem, he was locked out now and then and had no scruple at all about the amount of noise he made on the door before he aroused some one to admit him. And it was from here that several of his friends went out with him for a mild celebration on the evening before his marriage. My recollection is that we were entirely decorous about the festivities we engaged in, but the only detail I can now distinctly recall is our going into a place called Swift's Oyster Bay, situated at the corner of Eighth street and Broadway, where we had half a dozen raw all around, and Kent's classmate from Norwich University, the present Col. Dudley F. Phelps, so long and favorably known to the merchants of New York for valuable services at the Custom House, sought out Mr. Swift, a large man of conservative pattern, and asked him whether he would feel above shaking hands with us—all around. He kindly acquiesced, and the celebration was then at an end.

Kent and I used to walk to and from the office, morning and evening. From eight a. m. to six p. m. seemed all too short for the work we found to do. There were no tram cars then, no subway, no elevated railway. How New Yorkers ever succeeded in getting up and down town in those days I cannot now conceive, although all of it we saw, at the time, and part of it we individually were.

Nelson Chesman, a schoolmate from my New Hampshire town, two years younger than I, and a lifelong friend; now and for many years known as a successful and prosperous advertising agent of St. Louis, Chicago and New York, came with me and took charge of the List System. A little later he became the first editor of Rowell's American Newspaper Directory. Our so-called List System contracts with the papers permitted us to use extra space above a full column at a proportionate price per inch. Occasionally the copy would overrun the space specified in the order by a line or two, and if the extra twelfth, sixth or quarter was not specified and paid for there was certain to be vigorous kicks coming from a hundred or two of the nearly a thousand papers under contract, and these protests had to be answered. Sometimes the price of the extra space would amount to no more than a cent or two, and the small fraction called for an endless amount of working out sums in fractions. I wonder if it was Chesman who helped us out by discovering that in cases of such fractional over-measure the whole difficulty could be solved by wetting the paper upon which the copy was printed. When it dried the extra quarter of an inch would shrink out of the copy. After making this discovery we adopted the plan; if the over-plus was a quarter of an inch or less we shrunk it out. If over a quarter we paid for an extra half inch. Sometimes this discovery of the beneficial effect of moisture was worth from $50 to $100 a month to the office.

The advertising agents of the City of New York in the spring of the year 1867 were S. M. Pettengill & Co.; Peaslee & Co., a concern consisting, as it appeared, solely of one man, Mr. L. F. Shattuck; John Hooper & Co., Mr. Hooper having some claim to be considered the oldest, that is the longest established agent then doing business in the city; L. P. Fontaine & Co., with a reputation for being slow pay; Mather & Abbott, who could discount Fontaine's record two to one; W. W. Sharpe, successor to the old firm of Joy, Coe & Co., and younger and not the least active Carlton & Smith, whose trade was mainly with religious papers. Doubtless there were other men in the business, some of them doing very well, but not making themselves conspicuous. One such, as I now recall, was Mr. Lawrence Burke, whose operations were almost entirely with the city papers. He was always a well-dressed man, always a dignified gentleman in his manner, always attending to his own business, and letting that of others alone. The last time I talked with Lawrence Burke was in the Dennett restaurant in Beekman street, about three years ago. We were speaking of James H. Bates, once Mr. Pettengill's partner, later of the firms of Bates & Locke and Bates & Morse. I asked Burke which was older, he or Bates, and he in reply said "Why I am old enough to be Bates's father." I thereupon stated that I happened to know that

Mr. Bates was at that time in his seventy-sixth year. To this Mr. Burke made no reply and the conversation seemed to lose interest. A little later, thinking he would have an interesting story to tell, I requested the editor of *Printers' Ink* to look up Mr. Burke, have him interviewed, and obtain and publish his picture. An attempt was made to do this, but the man could not be found, no one remembered seeing him lately, his name did not appear in the city directory, and the impression was forced upon me that I should look no more upon his well-groomed figure and handsome, dignified countenance. In this I was mistaken, for last Autumn (November, 1904) while spending a few weeks at Saratoga, I was one day walking on Broadway, with my wife, when I saw Mr. Burke close at hand and about to pass. Our eyes met with a half recognition, and we passed on; since which I have not ceased to regret that I did not make the slight effort needed to learn what facts and conditions had induced him to absent himself from New York, where so much of his life had been spent.

NINETEENTH PAPER

In 1867 the firm of S. M. Pettengill & Co. was the best known of all the advertising agents then doing business. There were two partners, Mr. Pettengill and Mr. James H. Bates. Bates had a one-third interest in the profits and, by their co-partnership papers, it was stipulated that in case of a dissolution the good will of the business, the firm name, and the books, would belong wholly to Mr. Pettengill. Mr. Bates, if he were living, would be 79 years old in 1905 and Mr. Pettengill three years older. The former died in 1902 and Pettengill about 1893. Their agency being the best known of any then, or at any previous time, in existence, advertisers found that the papers would accept the Pettengill contracts without question or delay, if the price was right, and that there was an advantage on that account in dealing`through them. The firm had numerous customers who came to them year after year. Among these were Robert Bonner, Jeremiah Curtis & Son, owners of Mrs. Winslow's Soothing Syrup, Dr. J. H. Schenck, who had his name and the words Mandrake Pills painted almost as freely as Hood's Sarsaparilla was in later years. Still the Pettengill business did not in 1867 exceed in volume the sum of $400,-000 per annum.

Mr. L. F. Shattuck was said to do business under the name of Peaslee & Co. because, it was alleged, he had left behind him in Ohio some obligations that might be a source of trouble for him. He had published a paper in the Buckeye State, and through that means it had come about that he had at one time been of service to an Ohio politician, Salmon P. Chase by name. Previous to the Civil War the firm of Peaslee & Co. had been by no means prominent, and its credit was not considered very firmly established. It used to be said that there really was a Mr. Peaslee in the office, but his position was rather that of a clerk than a principal.

Those who are old enough may remember that at the beginning of the Civil War, in 1861, the government was unprepared, and found itself sadly in need of money. Interest was paid at a rate as high as seven and three-tenths per cent per annum. Finally, when bonds were put on the market by the hundred millions, an enterprising young banker, once from Ohio, but then of Philadelphia—Jay Cooke & Co. was the firm name—came prominently to the front as a government agent for placing the securities. The bonds had to be advertised. The contract promised to be a large one. Mr. Bates of the Pettengill Agency had his eyes on it, and had actually gone so far as to prepare copy, and even send out some advertisements for insertion, when there came a call upon him to visit Mr. Cooke in Philadelphia; and there he was told that Mr. Chase, Secretary of the Treasury, had sent for Mr. Cooke, and had said to him that Mr. Shattuck was his friend, and that he, Chase, particularly desired that such advertising as had to be done should be sent out through Mr. Shattuck's agency. Probably no one of the parties had any idea of what the thing would amount to. The fiscal agent had no disposition to quarrel with the Secretary, who was his superior. He did what he could for Bates, but the business from that time forward went out through Mr. Shattuck's office. It was a great order. Prices did not cut much of a figure in placing it. Mr. Cooke said to Mr. Shattuck, "If a publisher has enterprise enough to ask for the advertisement give it to him." In some instances, as would be the case now, there was difficulty about the allowance to Mr. Shattuck of the usual agent's commission, that being then, almost universally, a quarter of the gross amount; but the Secretary stood by his protégé, and if the paper did not choose to allow the commission, Mr. Shattuck withheld the order. As the question of a high or a low price did not enter very much into the calculation, so long as the figures on the rate card were not exceeded, there was little real difficulty about any papers eventually securing the order, Shattuck getting his commission, and the public being favored with a sight of the announcement. Of course, a liberal advertise-

ment order made an editor shy about criticising any methods
of the Secretary, the President, or the fiscal agent; and without doubt the advertising order served as a subsidy in some
cases and caused editors to be just as friendly as they could
possibly see it in their way to be. It is not intended to be
inferred that there was any cheating or dishonesty on the
part of any one concerned. Nothing of the sort has ever
been suggested. It was a big order, it was relied upon to
produce quick results, it did all that was expected of it;
repeat orders came quickly and often, and when the war was
ended everybody was satisfied—more than satisfied with Mr.
Chase, Mr. Cooke and Mr. Shattuck; and so great had
grown Mr. Shattuck's reputation, that a little later, he had in
hand the enormous contract for placing the securities of the
Union Pacific Railroad, on terms that seemed not only to
assure him a full commission on every advertisement he
placed, but additional pay for all clerical work performed,
and a liberal commission as well on every bond that was sold.
The results of these two orders were so pleasing to Mr. Shattuck that he had little disposition to resume the humdrum
work of preparing competing estimates for patent medicine
houses and "such small deer;" and it came about quite
naturally that he, in possession of a million or two of savings, bought a place at Lenox, lived the life of a country
gentleman, sought and obtained entrance for himself and
family into the exclusive society of New York that main-
tains connections with the Berkshires and Newport.

Mr. Shattuck was the first of the New York agents who
did me the honor of looking me up and calling on me in my
new office, up one flight, front, at No. 40 Park Row, shortly
after my removal from Boston. I had never seen him before. He was a large, fine-looking man, handsomely, even
elegantly, dressed after the Shakespearian invocation:

> Costly thy habit as thy purse can buy,
> But not express'd in fancy.

He had evidently availed himself of a leisure moment, after
partaking of a midday luncheon at the restaurant of Crook,
Fox & Nash — then so well patronized — situated on the

first floor of the Times Building, directly under my office. While I looked at the card he handed to me, my eye dropped, and took in a handsome gold watch chain, crossing his rather broad waistcoat, and noted there a small deposit, a portion of a boiled egg that had evidently played a part in the midday refection. It is one of the absurdities of life that so trifling a matter should have any attention at all, but it is nevertheless true that from that day to this I never think of Mr. Shattuck without seeing the watch chain and the blemish of the egg spot. The good man died many years ago, the most successful of all the advertising agents that had had an existence in America; and the one, who, more than any other, escaped unkindly criticism. He could give an order to whoever asked for it. If the price could be defended by the rate card he was authorized to pay it; if it seemed excessive even to the newspaper man he might even up things by a notice of the bonds offered for sale or by a favorable influence exerted in some other way.

Mr. Shattuck did some business as a banker after he had ceased to be an advertising agent, but it is my impression that he did not add to his wealth in that way. He seemed finally to take kindly to his Lenox home, and a visit to the South in the winter, and it used to be my good fortune to meet him, two or three times a year, at the Union League Club, where he was pretty certain to drop in when passing through or sojourning in the city for a few days. Mr. Shattuck's advertising business, what there was left of it, reverted to Mr. E. N. Erickson, a capable man of unexceptionable character and standing, and he in turn having passed away is succeeded by his son Julius, who now conducts an agency at 21 Park Row under his father's name.

Of John Hooper it has already been said there were grounds for considering him the oldest advertising agent in New York. He had begun as a canvasser for the *Tribune;* was led into putting advertisements into other papers to accommodate a customer; would pay the bill, take a receipt, carry the bill to his principal, collect it and the transaction would be closed—no bookkeeping, no bother, no open account—and the commission on the order was a help. Sometimes a settlement in full might be delayed a little, but his customers were good. If the memorandum bills accumulated, it was still possible to care for them; and other agents used to say of Hooper, rather derisively, that he carried his office in his hat. He was slow of speech, slow of motion; as honest as the day was long; and, curiously, too, as time progressed, it was noted that he was never in any hurry about being paid, provided the customer was good and the busi-

E. D. WAYRE,
For thirty-five years bookkeeper for
George P. Rowell.

ness still being advertised. After a time he needed an office, and, like those farmers who find a wife cheaper than a hired girl, he took a partner instead of hiring a bookkeeper. By and by, however, he outgrew all of that, and needed bookkeeper, estimate clerk, checkers and office boys. His partner was Mr. George William Wayre. Mr. Wayre was an older brother of that Mr. E. D. Wayre with whom those who have had dealings with the advertising agency of Geo. P. Rowell & Co. may remember, as always since the year 1871, to be found at the bookkeeper's desk. He is the bookkeeper for the Printers' Ink Publishing Company at the present time (1905). Mr. Hooper's residence, until near the end of his life, was in Dutch street, which it might puzzle the New Yorker of to-day to find, although it is still plainly in evidence at some point between Nassau, Beekman, John and Gold streets.

From his system of being a slow collector, where the parties were considered good, Mr. Hooper was sometimes led into assuming rather serious risks; and it came about at one period that the firm of Colwell, Shaw & Williard, who man-

GEORGE W. WAYRE.

ufactured a patented tin-lined lead pipe, had become so much in his debt that he was finally, for his own protection, led to assume a proprietary interest in their enterprise, and eventually the lead business became of so much more importance than the advertising agency that he was induced to drop the latter, and in the year 1870 I was approached with a suggestion that I buy the good will of the concern, take over such customers as could be delivered, assume the office occupied by the Hooper company, and in general succeed to the business of the oldest advertising agency in New York. The price asked for the good will was $10,000; the business was clean, the office the best in the Times Building, corresponding nearly with that occupied until quite recently by J. Walter Thompson's agency, for the last score of years, or thereabouts. I am confident I got the purchase price back within the first year, but Mr. Hooper continued to turn over small orders to us to the end of his life. As a lead merchant he was no more conspicuous than as an advertising agent, and only those who knew him well failed to be amazed to find when he finally passed away that he had left a property worth very close to the sum—enormous under the circumstances—of five million dollars.

JOHN HOOPER.

The partner, Mr. Wayre, was an Englishman, and had ever a longing to return, with the competence he had earned, to the home of his youth. It was a mistake. He missed the occupation that had become so familiar to him; his health was not as good as it had been; and he died before very long. His American-born children, with their mother, did not lose much time in getting back to American soil, whereby they doubtless exhibited better sense than they had inherited from the father.

L. P. Fontaine & Co. and Mather & Abbott were advertising agents of the class that the newspapers used to take

very kindly to. They could not be counted on to pay a bill
when it became due, but they often did pay, in whole or in
part, and the unexpected experience had in it a spice of
variety very pleasing to the average newspaper man. In
answer to a charge that an order had been accepted from
Mather & Abbott at a price that would not have been satisfactory had the order came from the Rowell Agency it used
to be explained sometimes about like this: "You know that
concern is rather poor pay, we may never get anything for
what they owe us, and for that reason we are willing to
make the charge light because, if we never collect it, the loss
will not be of so much consequence." After I had been
some time in New York Mr. Fontaine came to me one day
for advice. His statement showed assets—so and so, and
liabilities—so and so. There was not very much difference
between the two sums, but the assets overbalanced the other
to a moderate extent. I was rather surprised at this outcome, under the circumstances, and said to Mr. Fontaine,
"You are solvent. You can pay all you owe." "I know
that," was his response, "but it will take all I have." He
failed a little later, and disappeared, but as the papers were
not paid I have always felt that he had something left over
for a rainy day.

Of W. W. Sharpe no one seemed to know much beyond
that he did a fair business, kept his agreements, minded his
own affairs and had very little to do with others. I think I
knew about as much about him in 1867 as I do now (in
1905), and yet, I am told, he has all this time done business
and still does so within a stone's throw of my office. I have
no recollection of ever having seen him.

John Moore said that in his walks about town, in pursuit
of advertising orders, he crossed the tracks of Carlton &
Smith more frequently than he did those of any other
agency. Carlton was a step-son of that Dr. Carlton who
was long at the head of that great publishing house the
Methodist Book Concern. The business was mainly with
the religious press, and largely with the Methodist division
of it. Mr. Smith retired from the firm before very long, and

Carlton moved his office into the Times Building near me. We became fast friends and that friendship terminated only with his life. He died in the summer of 1902.

Carlton extended his lines to take in the monthly magazines, then becoming of importance, and he had in his employ a young man named Thompson, given name J. Walter, to whom he paid a salary of $15 a week, and thought it rather munificent. Carlton was a bookworm. He knew all about books and publishers, and would rather spend six hours in trying to resurrect, for a friend, some scarce volume, worth possibly twenty cents, because not wanted by many people, rather than devote half as much time to securing an advertising order which might just as likely produce a profit of $100. I had once had an opportunity to engage this same clerk, Thompson, to work for me, but, after a talk with him, concluded he would be too easily discouraged for an advertising man. Carlton wanted to sell his business, and one day his assistant professed himself willing and able to pay the price. Carlton became a bookseller and the firm of J. Walter Thompson Co. started out, and became, in an almost incredibly short time, a greater house than Carlton had ever dreamed of, and one that, from that day to this, has had no set-backs, and about which no one hears anything but good words. Mr. Thompson, since the decease of the late Mr. James H. Bates, is, without any manner of doubt, the richest advertising agent doing business in the City of New York.

TWENTIETH PAPER

I think it was in the month of June, 1867, that the New York State Editorial Association held its annual convention at Penn Yan. A Mr. Cleveland, editor of one of the village papers, was President of the Association that year. He had the further distinction of being a brother of the wife of that celebrated journalist, Mr. Horace Greeley of the *Tribune*. Mr. Wirt Sikes, a literary man, it was announced, would read a poem. I came to know Mr. Sikes somewhat in after years, but upon what his literary fame rested then or rests now I am not able to specify. The only time I can recall having read about him, in connection with literature, was, I think, in the New York *Tribune,* wherein certain literary characters were reviewed in grades and classes, beginning with—I don't remember whom, Thackeray perhaps, and descending, as the editor expressed it, "down to Wirt Sikes." He was also the husband of Olive Logan, of whom I really ought to be better informed that I am, for I frequently met her. She was an actress, an authoress, or an elocutionist ; and I seem to never be able to ascertain which, or to what extent. She and Mr. Sikes were alike in one respect, they were both deaf ; but after all they hardly had so much to do with this newspaper convention, which was the first I ever attended, to warrant such extended reference to them, although it was there that I first came into a knowledge of their existence. Being new to New York, and, to a regrettable degree, unacquainted with its newspaper men, it seemed a wise thing to do to go to Penn Yan, and see them all in a bunch. The idea that it was a convention of newspaper men, held for discussing their own affairs, and that I was not a newspaper man, and had not been invited to be present, did not occur to me. When on the ground, however, it was noticeable that no very cordial reception was extended; still, as my principal competitor, Mr. S. M. Pettengill, was there, and a certain other agent from New York City as well, Peter K. Deyo by name, not to mention a press manufacturer or two, an ink salesman and two or three others who sought dealings with the newspapers, I did not feel specially out of place.

At the meetings, however, after Mr. Sikes's poem had had attention, and the business of the convention began, I learned that publishers had troubles of their own. and that

S. M. PETTENGILL.

among these advertising agents were accorded a position among the principal, if not the chiefest of them all. It seemed, from statements there made, that the agents were unmitigated bears on prices, that they always demanded the lowest prices, and the greatest amount of service, and, when a column had once been sold to one of them for $15 or $20 a year, because it at the time happened to be so much extra space on the newspaper man's hands, and compelled him to do an extra amount of typesetting to fill it, it was very hard to make that agent understand, if he happened to want a second column a month or a year later, that the price must be $100, and that no lower figure could be considered. At a certain point, my eminent competitor, Mr. Pettengill, arose and, in his mild-mannered way, berated the publishers for their lack of business methods, and took special exception to the practice, of which many of them were guilty, of selling to Mr. Rowell, an advertising agent then present, a column of space at a yearly rate, and allowing him to peddle it out to monthly users of an inch, more or less, at less than half the price the publisher would demand of the advertiser, according to his rate card, and much worse than that, at less than half the price the same publisher would demand from him, Pettengill, if he, instead of Rowell, should happen to send the same card of an inch or thereabouts to appear for a single month. One or two men with whom I had contracts, and who were well enough satisfied with them, rose to say to Mr. Pettengill that he, too, might have the same privileges if he would make a similar contract; but to do that would be to admit that there was some merit in my so-called List System, and this he could not very well do, because he had been pooh-poohing it to his advertising patrons ever since he first heard of it; and it was a fact, of which he did not then speak, that he, too, had tried the same plan in his earlier years, and had fallen down on it, mainly because he did not insist that every advertiser who availed himself of it should use his combination in its entirety, and because he did not send his copy and changes, with the clock-like precision that I had deemed requisite, and which was, in fact, the salvation of my scheme.

Later Mr. Deyo had some words to address to the convention. He supported Mr. Pettengill. He had been an agent once, but left his office at the call of his country to take the captaincy of a military company, and had gone to the war; but now the war was over, he needed an income from business, and would again be an advertising agent; and, as he had no office, nor much capital, and his old customers had formed new connections, he now wanted things made just as easy for him as possible, and he deprecated the idea that Pettengill's established credit, or Mr. Rowell's new-fangled scheme of buying by the column and selling by the inch, should be allowed to give either any advantage that should keep him from stepping back into the position he said he had, or thought he had, occupied before the South Carolinians had so impudently fired on Fort Sumter. I do not remember whether I had opportunity or occasion to say anything. What the others said had been good enough for me. My great competitor had publicly admitted that he had to charge a customer twice as much as I did for the same service, and asserted that even then I made a larger profit on the transaction than he did.

I wrote out a statement of Mr. Pettengill's remarks, as I remembered them, and having space to spare in a good many of the papers that were represented at the convention, I filled that space with a condensation of what Mr. Pettengill had said. No one would need to be told that, as I was not a stenographer, Mr. Pettengill was not likely to agree as to the strict accuracy of my report, and it came about that he was led to address a protest on the subject to some of the papers that had carried my announcement. Whereupon the vigorous editor of the Jamestown *Journal* espoused his cause with much enthusiasm, and came out with what the said editor, who had been present at and was about the most active man in the convention, said was what Mr. Pettengill really did say. Many a man has had reason to assert that he could deal well enough with his enemies if God would only preserve him from his friends. This Jamestown man proceeded to set the thing right in his paper, but he had no stenographer's report to guide him any more than I had. I do not think his report was quite so accurate as my own, but when the *Journal's* account came to hand that part of Pettengill's remarks that reproached the papers for allowing me to get so great an advantage over him was stated even more strongly than I had put it. This the *Journal* man was quite willing to do, because his own skirts were clear, he having refused to consider a contract I had offered to make with him. I bought and distributed

1,000 copies of the Jamestown *Journal,* and also issued a
new circular, and had a new advertisement, and they were
quite effective. I had never seen Mr. Pettengill before we
met at the convention. I was twenty-eight years old, he
forty-three. He was essentially an amiable man, furthermore, he quickly realized that his words, spoken in convention, had not been as well considered as they might have
been; consequently, when we met outside, he did not deem
it advisable to magnify my importance by making me out
too much of a competitor. On my part I was so well satisfied with all that had occurred, that my inclination was to
laugh at Mr. Pettengill, rather than argue with him, and
after the first day of the convention, but before my circular
and advertisement had appeared, we became rather friendly
than otherwise.

He had never been in my office, but something occurred
at the time of issuing my second circular that made it seem
advisable to submit a proof to him before sending it out; so
with that proof in hand I went personally to his place of
business, in the old World Building, standing where the
Potter Building now is, at the corner of Park Row and
Beekman street. Mr. Pettengill was not in, but his junior
partner, Mr. Bates, was, and to him I exhibited the proof.
Bates was twelve years my senior. I had never seen him
before. He looked at me through his gold-bowed spectacles, glanced at the proof, made some deprecatory remark
not at all calculated to please me—no one could make such
a remark more effectively than Bates could—and I came
away. It will be seen that my acquaintance with these two
men began in a business squabble—I sometimes say in a
row. Curiously it so happened that the acquaintance thus
begun continued, improved, ripened into friendship and
lasted until the termination of the life of each of them. They
were not at all alike. Pettengill came from Connecticut and
had in him some touch of the Puritan. Bates was a native
of Vermont, but his family moved to Michigan while he
was a child, and he was broadened by the wider life of the
Middle West. Pettengill was a leading member of Plymouth

Church, and a warm friend and ardent admirer of Mr. Beecher, although he did enjoy stating, when speaking of the unfortunate scandal that troubled the preacher's later days, that he, Pettengill, was in accord with the verdict of the Long Island farmer who commended the jury that had stood three for conviction and nine for acquittal, on the ground that, in his opinion, Mr. Beecher was three-quarters innocent.

Bates also lived in Brooklyn most of his life, but took

JAMES H. BATES.

more stock in Theodore Tilton than he did in Mr. Beecher. Each had a keen sense of humor, but Pettengill rarely made a brilliant success when he attempted a joke, or a pun, or to tell a funny story; while Bates under no circumstances ever failed to make what he had to say a little more sparkling, or witty, than anybody else ever could. I do not believe they were ever companionable. Pettengill had the lion's share of the earnings of the firm, while there were those who believed that Bates brought most grist to the mill. There came a period when there was serious friction between the two, and I at the time was very intimate with both. I would meet Pettengill at luncheon, and spend an evening with Bates, at his rooms, or mine. Both acquired a habit of telling me their personal grievances, each, I rather think, knowing that the other did so. By and by they separated. By the terms of the agreement under which they did business this left nothing for Bates to do but to step out. The books and the firm name belonged to Pettengill, and yet Bates was entitled to have an accounting and to be paid a proper share of the profits that had accrued. Here was a chance for a disagreement, and it did not fail to arise. No settlement being arrived at, Bates finally put his claim into the hands of an attorney, and proceedings to compel a settlement were gotten under way.

At this time I had the experience of being called on to act as an arbitrator. It was Pettengill who asked me to attempt it. Bates, when I spoke to him, said I had better let it alone, but I did not. I had numerous talks with each, not attempting to go into the merits of the case, but hoping to arrive at an adjustment based on the views they respectively held. Pettengill admitted that something was due to Bates, but could not say how much. Bates insisted that he must be paid, but I did not at first learn how much he demanded. The thing hung along for some time. Finally I induced Bates to name a definite and exact sum for which he would give a receipt in full. When he had done so I, with more or less difficulty, induced Pettengill to tell me how much money he would pay for a receipt in full, and a discontinuance of the action. When he finally was brought to fix his mind on a definite sum he seemed pretty determined that he would not, in any event, pay any more. Bates, on his part, had been equally decided that the figure he had named should not be reduced a single penny.

It was when this much progress had been made that two things became very plain to me. First, that each pretty well understood the merits of the matter, and that each was in essentials a fair man. The most unexpected thing about it all, however, was that the amount Bates demanded, and than which he would accept no less, and the sum that Pettengill would pay, and never a cent more, was the same sum precisely. The question arises then, why any need of law suit or arbitration? The reason was to be looked for in the fact that the strained relations that existed between them made it impossible for either to be quite frank with the other. Consequently, they could not get together. I by no means felt on solid ground when I had gotten thus far. I dared not play an open hand. "What sort of a receipt do you want from Bates," I asked of Pettengill, and he gave me a form, which when shown to Bates he would not sign. He, however, made out a form of his own, which he would sign, and that was taken to Pettengill for his acquiescence and, as the difference was not material, he waived his objection to it. It made no mention of the amount to be paid. I then asked Mr. Pettengill to give me a check for the amount he had specified, promising either to bring him the receipt or return him his check; but he said he had not so much money in hand. "Very well," I said, "you have an account across the street at the Nassau Bank, and have dealt there for twenty years or more. Just go over, while I wait; tell them you are going to overdraw your account, that the check may not be used, but if it is you will come in and arrange with them to make it good." He did this, came promptly back, and gave me the check. Whereupon I went again to Bates, then doing business on the other corner of Beekman street and Park Row, not a hundred feet away, and asked him to sign the receipt, made in the form he had agreed to, promising either to bring the money or return his receipt, and have done with the matter. This he did, but I did not give him the check until I had gone again to Pettengill, submitted the receipt for his approval, and received the same. I then went back to Bates and gave him the check, which he received rather grimly, for he was a bit impatient about the whole transaction.

A little later Mr. Pettengill sent me an appreciative letter and a framed engraving, both of which I have to-day and value very much. A few months later Mr. Bates sent me the handsomest and most symmetrical set of the antlers of the Black-Tailed Deer that I have ever seen anywhere, but he wrote me no note of thanks, and it was not till some years afterwards that he said to me one day that he really did send those deer horns as an acknowledgment of my services as arbitrator. In after years the two old partners became wholly reconciled, and, when finally Mr. Pettengill retired from business, it was to Mr. Bates that he turned over such customers as he could influence and all that intangible thing known as good will, that is often of very great value. Mr. Bates in this way became successor to the firm in which he had been a partner through many of the best years of his life.

I have gotten a long way from the convention at Penn Yan. Its outcome was so satisfactory that when, next year, another was announced, to be held at Watkins on Seneca Lake, I determined to go once more. Here the advertising agents were dealt with more mildly, and I made many acquaintances among the publishers and some friends, who remained such for years and years. I am speaking of the year 1868. Now and then I read the name of some one of those whom I met at Watkins, or see their faces or portraits; and, although I am sorry to note that the hair is whitened or departed, I do not fail to recall features that I learned to know, and indications of character that I learned to recognize and respect more than a generation ago. Among them I like to recall Mr. A. C. Kessinger of the Rome *Sentinel* and Mr. A. O. Bunnell of the Dansville *Advertiser*. I could go on and specify perhaps a dozen others, but most have passed on to that land where it is supposed that all things will be known and where, consequently, there will be no need for advertising or newspapers.

There was one circumstance that occurred while at Watkins that goes to show how carefully every one should avoid even the appearance of evil. It so happened that for that particular year I, like Rip Van Winkle, had sworn off. I neither drank nor smoked, but one evening at Watkins was made memorable by a delightful reception given by the citizens to the publishers attending the convention, at the house of Mr. L. M. Gano, the President of the Association and publisher of the Watkins *Express*. It seemed that a firm of wine growers, having vineyards there, had sent down an unreasonably generous number of cases of an American champagne of their production. The foaming fluid flowed as freely as apollinaris was said to do at Mr. Wanamaker's receptions when he was in Mr. Harrison's Cabinet, and I was constantly urged to join this one and that one in a toast. Becoming tired of excuses I ventured to remove some dried grasses from a sort of celery-glass-fashioned vase that stood on the mantel, and had the thing, which held nearly a quart, filled up with wine to the very edge of its scalloped brim, after which I walked about and made a pretence of quaffing with every one who hazarded a suggestion to that effect. I did not taste a drop of wine that night, but not for twenty years did I cease to come now and then across someone who had been present on the occasion at Watkins, and to be congratulated upon my apparently healthy appearance, and to listen to the suggestion that the speaker had then had some anxiety about me on account of what he saw of my habits and condition as exhibited at Mr. Gano's reception.

TWENTY-FIRST PAPER

Mention has been made of the difficulty in obtaining lists of the newspapers published. In pursuance of efforts to awaken interest in the matter, as well as to provide a medium of communication with persons likely to be interested, and with advertisers generally; we had, while in Boston, started a little periodical called the *Advertiser's Gazette*. It was in connection with that publication that attention began to be directed to some queer rulings and usages of the Postoffice Department. The arrangement for issuing the *Advertiser's Gazette*, had with a Boston printer, was so satisfactory that it did not seem desirable to disturb it; but as the office of publication was now announced to be New York the Postoffice Department could not allow a New York publication to be mailed from Boston. The same question crops up nowadays (1905) on occasion, as in the case of the *American Agriculturist*, purporting to be published in New York, but really printed and mailed in Springfield, Mass., the influence of Mr. Herbert Myrick, the apostle of beet sugar, being able to secure a privilege that might be refused to a concern without a pull. It is not easy to see what connection there can be between beet sugar and the Postoffice Department, but no one man can expect to see everything.

In our case the *Advertiser's Gazette* had to be sent by express from Boston to New York, that it might be mailed from the city where it purported to be published. The Boston printer had been in the habit of sending to the Boston Postoffice for such mail sacks as he required for delivering the papers to be mailed, and when he began to express the papers to New York, he continued the same practice, and the bags would thus go into the Postoffice at New York instead of Boston. In transit from the printer to the Postoffice the sacks or bags were in charge of an express company; while by the previous method they were intrusted to a truckman. This went on without comment for a time, but finally the eye of a Postoffice inspector lighted upon the U. S. gunny sacks, in transit as express matter, and we had prompt notice that such use of the bags was contrary to regulations, and, if persisted in, would entail certain penalties. We thereupon contracted for a sufficient number of bags or sacks, to be made at our own expense, and arranged to use these in place of those which the department had previously furnished. This worked all right so far as the express company was concerned, but as soon as these bags, belonging to us, and stamped with our name, went into the New York Postoffice they promptly received the great U. S. brand and went into the general stock, and we were never able to get a sight of one of them again or to obtain any assurance that there would be any more satisfactory outcome should we procure more bags, and so on indefinitely.

We had in our employ at this time an office boy who was subject to epileptic fits. He was a little gentleman, quiet, industrious, anxious to please; furthermore, he was the son of a widowed mother, who had once been well to do, but was now in such reduced circumstances that the boy's small earnings were so much of an object to her that we hesitated about parting with the unfortunate youth, although his occasional attacks upset the office very much, and grated so hard upon my own nerves, that it was usually noted that when one hack was called to take Herbert to his mother another was brought into requisition to carry me to my own apartments, where it required the rest of the day to free my mind from the nervous shock which the horrid scuffle and fall were certain to produce. The loyal and faithful Herbert took the incident of the mail bags much to heart. He considered the Postoffice a headquarters of sin, and on some subjects his ideas were rather sound. Every day it was his duty to superintend the receipt of several of these great sacks from the New York Postoffice, containing the newspaper mail for the agency, which had become very large. There was a spare room, used for storage purposes, and not often visited by any but the boy or the janitor, and to this Herbert carried the mail bags that were received from day to day, letting them accumulate, until we should get even for our own bags that the Postoffice had appropriated and failed to account for. This had been going on for an indefinite period before my attention was brought to the condition of affairs, and then I think the accumulation of bags was not a pound short of a couple of tons in weight. It was a question what to do with them, but there was no difficulty about it. A truckman took the collection to the Postoffice, and they were received as though such consignments were an everyday affair. Poor Herbert left us shortly after this, there having opened for him an opportunity to go to sea as a cabin boy—a course thought likely to improve his health. We learned afterwards that during one of his attacks he fell out of a boat and was drowned. Thus does God temper the wind to the shorn lamb.

There was still more trouble about mailing the *Advertiser's Gazette* as there was likely to be then and now about mailing anything as second-class matter, as every publisher in the land knows full well. It had seemed to us advisable, for some purpose, to add to the mailing list the names of all the druggists in the United States, numbering many thousands; not one of whom, perhaps, had ever subscribed for the paper or thought of doing so. This the New York postmaster could not permit. It was contrary to regulations.

Now it had so happened that during my Boston experiences I had been brought into relations with an eminent abolitionist named George L. Stearns; and Mr. Stearns, shortly after the close of the war, determined to devote a portion of his great wealth to the publication of a newspaper, to be widely distributed throughout the Southern States, that should fill the reconstructed South chock full of the sort of information needed by it, and thereby benefit that region and all mankind as well. As he was willing and able to assume all the expense, he took no pains to secure subscribers, contenting himself with the names and post-office addresses of the people he wished to favor or influence. The edition printed counted fully 300,000 copies weekly, and, as it was thought to have a value as an advertising medium, and as Mr. Stearns did not wish to be bothered with that sort of detail, my name was given place in the paper as advertising manager; and, curiously enough, as it seemed, there did not appear any other name as publisher or manager; consequently, many of the recipients of Mr. Stearns' favor, in their ignorance, thought me the whole thing, and many, and emphatic, were the letters I received, and numerous, and often odorous, were the copies of the paper that were returned to me in connection with these letters. There was evidence that the people to whom the paper was sent not only had not subscribed, but, further than that, did not want the paper. The name of the publication was *The Right of Way*. It was not continued, I think, more than a year, but it did go through the Postoffice without being stamped.

I told the New York postmaster all about this, but it did not go for much. He held up my *Advertiser's Gazette;* and I took occasion to commission Mr. Kent to visit the office of the Postmaster-General in Washington. He was listened to. His facts were not disputed. Some curiosity was exhibited as to how he happened to know so much, but he came back with a duplicate in his pocket of a letter to the New York postmaster that told him the *Advertiser's Gazette* must be mailed to the druggists as we had desired. The New York postmaster said it was all wrong, and I guess it was; but the *Advertiser's Gazette* was mailed in spite of all that.

It is this irregularity and uncertainty about postoffice usages that has made so much trouble for business men and publishers for now these many years. The department makes all sorts of rules; in making them the say so of a $1,200 clerk sometimes has more weight than the opinion of the less well informed Postmaster-General. Conditions vary, politics and political influence enter in and so do ill-nature, pique, ignorance and forgetfulness. The ill-considered rule made to-day is found faulty to-morrow, and is rescinded next day; or, if not rescinded, is disregarded or overlooked until some one hunts it up for a new application a little later. A great deal would be accomplished toward doing away with the difficulties that arise if every decision or regulation and, more than all, the repeal of each decision or regulation having to do with the mailing of printed or other matter might be given out as news or printed for distribution, so that he who wishes to learn what conditions do exist would have some facilities afforded him for obtaining the information he requires. No one would be more benefited, and scarcely any one so much surprised, as postoffice officials themselves would be, could they see, in cold type, a collection of the decisions they have enacted, retracted, re-enacted and forgotten during the last forty years. As things are managed now, and have been managed, it is almost impossible for a publisher to learn in advance what he may or may not do, and almost fatal to ask any question, because it is so much easier to say no or to evade the point than it is to examine the case and decide upon its merits. Then the decisions are so funny. The *Century Magazine* is sold to subscribers for $4 a year and *McClure's* for $1 a year. If the *Century* should wish to reduce its price to $1 a year there would be no objection, but if it offered to give people a *temporary* privilege of buying it at $2 a year the Postoffice Department would exclude it from the mails on the ground that it was being sold at a nominal price. If a publisher of Augusta, Georgia, should undertake to do what has been permitted to publishers in Augusta, Maine, he would find himself brought to a standstill in short order. One explanation of the wonderful variety of postoffice decisions that are made from time to time may be found in the fact that the average term of a Postmaster-General is less than eighteen months. Notwithstanding all this I am firmly of the opinion that both the world at large and "Our Postoffice" in particular actually grow better as they grow older.

TWENTY-SECOND PAPER

It was in the year 1869 that the first volume of Rowell's American Newspaper Directory appeared. It was modeled pretty closely after Mitchell's Directory of the Newspapers of Great Britain, but with two important differences. Mitchell's was sold for an English shilling, while ours was priced at five dollars. Mitchell's did not attempt to give any information about the circulation of the papers described, while with ours the rating of circulation was a feature considered of prime importance. It was a new thing, however. It had never been attempted before. I was often told that it would not be allowed in England, and it is a fact that it has not yet been attempted in any country but America; and an effort made in London, about two years ago to bring out a directory on the plan so long in use by us was promptly squelched by the Courts.

So far as the success of our Advertising Agency was concerned the publication of the Directory was probably a mistake. The book placed at everybody's disposal as complete a list of papers as we ourselves possessed, and although it was copyrighted, that would not prevent others from extracting from it all the information they had use for, thereby being enabled to publish a competing book at little expense, depending upon ours for all information needed except in cases where, for private purposes, it became desirable to convey other and different information. There is not sufficient sale for such a book to defray the cost of its production, and the publisher of one, like the publisher of a newspaper, must rely for his profit, if he makes one, upon the advertising patronage he is able to secure.

Our book carried a great deal of advertising, taken always upon the condition that the charge for it should stand on the books of the advertising agency until balanced by advertisements inserted upon our order "at cash rates less the usual agent's commission." There is and was, in many cases, a great difference between the rate a publisher might be induced to accept for cash and that printed on his rate card; and sometimes a publisher, oblivious of the fact that there stood a charge against him for an advertisement in the Directory, would accept and commence upon carrying out a pretty heavy contract at perhaps not so much as half his schedule rate, and would be too disgusted for anything to have the bill for the Directory advertising resurrected at a time when he had counted on fingering a considerable sum in ready money. An instance is recalled of a visit from a business-like looking man who came from a Maryland town, was the owner and operator there of a stone quarry, but had loaned money to the publisher of the local paper, and finally had to take possession of it. He had not found the books in good order, but there was an account against the Rowell Agency for about $150 and the foreman had told him that it was O. K. As he was coming to New York he decided to collect the account in person. It looked all right, but there were counter charges. The paper had bought a keg of ink on one or two occasions, there was a charge of $10 for "Riley's Indispensable," which was a recipe for a dryer to be added to inks in certain conditions, there was the agent's commission of twenty-five per cent, which to the quarryman was an entirely new idea, and finally there was a charge of $75 for a page advertisement in the Directory. Figuring it all out and, he being new to the business, taking pains to exhibit the orders and the original charges, there was found to be due to him the sum of $1.18 for which a check was given, payable, as was the practice, "to the order of the publisher of" the paper. He looked everything over, asked an intelligent question here and there, found no fault, but as he deposited the check with his roll and replaced the strap on the leathern pocket-book he had extracted from his pantaloons, he remarked with an expression that seemed to indicate he was learning much about the publishing business, "It wasn't a very heavy transaction after all, was it?"

The method of paying for advertisements in the Directory, as indicated above, was grossly unfair. A charge against the New York *Herald* for $75 was as good as $75 in the cash drawer, while a similar charge against the quarterly *Chariot of Wisdom and Love,* published at Singer's Grove or Battle Creek, might remain on the books for years before any one should be found to give even as much as a five dollar bill for a hundred dollar advertisement in the magazine which, with the commission deducted, would just settle the account. The comparative worthlessness of these charges was demonstrated about a dozen years ago when several juniors of the establishment became the managers of the Advertising Agency, and it was thought better that these charges, payable in swap advertising, should not pass over to them. It was decided to use up all the space of the sort then on hand by introducing to public favor a new proprietary medicine called Ripans Tabules. The total amount of advertising required to balance the exchange accounts then on the books amounted to something in excess of $125,000. An effort had been made to sell the space to some one of half a dozen owners of proprietary articles, at twenty cents on the dollar, but it was not successful. At the end of fifteen months, when the books were balanced and the advertising all done, the total sales of Ripans Tabules, at wholesale and retail, had reached the very moderate figure of $976.48. Comparatively worthless, from a money point of view, as a large majority of these accounts were, there would always be among them a considerable percentage of such as were worth dollar for dollar.

The charge was frequently made and reiterated, that whether a paper advertised in the Directory or did not advertise in it, made all the difference in the world, with the question whether that paper would be accorded, in the Directory, a high circulation rating or a low one. Although there was never a shadow of foundation for these charges, there is no doubt at all that the publication of them did lead a great many newspapers to advertise in the book who would not have done so otherwise. The edition for 1891 contained no less than 1,221 solid pages of advertising for which the charge for no single page was less than $75, and went even as high as double that sum when the page was subdivided among many.   It was mainly from these accounts that the balance arose that was devoted to the introduction of Ripans Tabules, as before stated.   Concerning the value of these advertisements a Texas editor once wrote that he "would as soon think of advertising on the under side of a coffin lid," and he was about right.   No one saw the ad. save by the merest chance, unless he looked it up in the index; and it is not thought that people are very much given to examining indexes for the purpose of regaling themselves with the sight of any particular advertisement. That edition of 1891 made nearly every other advertising agency crazy, and most of them, thereafter, issued directories, mainly for the purpose of accommodating the overwhelming willingness on the part of newspaper publishers to place announcements anywhere, provided they could be paid for by swapping space.

It is often noted that the heart of a mother goes out most strongly toward the child that has made her most trouble.   Perhaps the same sort of feeling explains why it is that the writer of these lines has always taken more interest in the Directory than in any other enterprise with which he has had anything to do.   It has made him no friends, for being conducted in absolute good faith there was nothing that could be offered on the score of friendship that would not have to be accorded just as freely to the bitterest enemy.   This has often been a point that a newspaper man, considering himself an intimate friend, has found it difficult to understand.   On the other hand, the book created for its originator so many enemies that for many years it seemed wise for him to steer clear of newspaper offices when on traveling expeditions, for profit or pleasure, unless some representative of the office looked him up at the hotel and exhibited signs of amity.

When a publisher, whom I do not know personally, comes into my office, I generally turn to the Directory.   If his circulation rating is given there in Arabic figures I know the man is friendly; if, on the other hand, the rating is by letters, and particularly if it has the so-called "Z" attachment, that indicates that the paper finds it impolitic or impossible to make a circulation statement that will hold water, or a "Y" that means that the publisher finds it better to make no statement at all, or the double question mark, meaning that the rating is unsatisfactory, but facts to warrant a better rating cannot be got at, or the plus and minus signs, indicating that two statements of circulation received from the office, covering the same period, give different figures, or the double exclamation marks that indicate that there is something about the paper that the advertiser ought to know before he spends much money in it, or the double daggers that indicate that the publisher is a kicker from whom little information can be extracted, or the white pyramids that indicate that the paper may be dead, or the black spheres that indicate that the paper says it ought to have a higher rating, but is shy about furnishing facts to warrant the accordance of such a claim, or the so-called doubt marks that, not to put too fine a point upon it, indicate that the publisher has been putting out circulation statements that were false, and got caught at it; then things are likely to be different. If any one of these conditions show up there is cause to believe that the visitor has no love for me or my book. Still he may be a new man, or a junior, who, like the lamented Spenlow, has always been overawed by the wicked Jorkins, but is now asserting his independence, and determined from this on to be my friend and help to make the book as perfect in fact as the advertisers of the country so persistently seem to think it is now.

One cause, perhaps, for the decline of charges of blackmail made against the Directory has been the practice, pursued for the past ten years, of continuing and repeating each year's rating, year after year; a practice that shows that one paper always tells its circulation and tells it straight, another always tells it but never tells it straight,, another never tells at all, while still others change from one of the three classes to another and back again. There is probably not a prominent lawyer in the United States who has been in practice thirty years without being consulted on the subject of a suit for libel against the Rowell Directory. Yet the book has been issued for thirty-six years, and although hundreds of libel suits have been threatened, and are still threatened, one or more almost every week, yet never has one made so much progress as to make it necessary to go to Court to defend, or even to put in an answer to a complaint.

There are occasional instances of a marked change of attitude on the part of a newspaper editor toward the Directory. Not long ago I was surprised as well as pleased to note certain manifestations of good will on the part of a publisher whom I had thought, in the language of the day, "had it in for me." "I thought you were my enemy," said I. "So I was," was his answer. "I wanted you to credit me with 4,000 circulation when I was printing only 3,800 copies, and 'got hot under the collar' because you wouldn't do it, but I learned to see the matter more clearly after a while, and at present I believe that the method you pursued has had a good deal to do with making my fortune."

Since the practice of inserting advertisements to be paid for by swaps of space has been discontinued, the advertising patronage accorded to our Directory has been very much curtailed, and this is still further the case since it has been deemed expedient to refrain from soliciting patronage from any but papers of a high grade of advertising value. So straight-laced has the publisher been about never selling anything to one man that another might not have, that he was absurd enough at one time to refuse a check for $5,000 from the sons of Robert Bonner for inserting forty-two very innocent words about the New York *Ledger*, which they desired to have follow the catalogue description. A little later he was inserting just such "Publishers' Announcements" on terms that would have caused the notice to be acceptable for $7 that was declined at $5,000.

Experience has demonstrated that a large sale for a

book like the Directory can never be had. It was offered experimentally one year for fifty cents a volume, the price the year before and the year after being $5, and yet the sale of the 50 cent edition was no larger than at the higher price, while after the subscription price was advanced a few years ago to $10 a volume, the cash sales have actually been a little larger than ever at a lower subscription price.

TWENTY-THIRD PAPER

Which were the principal newspapers in those days? In New York City (1868) the newsboy's cry was *Herald! Times! Tribune!* Each sold for four cents a copy. Mr. Dana had not yet assumed editorial charge of the *Sun.* In the evening there were the *Post,* William Cullen Bryant, editor, and the *Express,* Erastus Brooks, editor, and Ben Woods' evening *News,* that every poor man read. The edition of the weekly *Tribune* was very large. Sometimes every subscriber to it got a strawberry plant or a picture of Horace Greeley as a premium, and advertisers paid $2 a line. In those days *Harper's Weekly* was of more importance to an advertiser than any other single paper and, for a position on the last page, the cost was $4 a line. *Harper's Bazar* was for that time what *Vogue,* the *Delineator* and the *Ladies' Home Journal* consolidated would be for to-day. The *Clipper* was the theatrical and sporting paper. On Sundays the *Herald* and the *Mercury* had the field pretty much to themselves; the last named being a good deal of a yellow journal—not exactly a home paper where there were daughters in the family. Not every one knows that the *World,* when established, was intended to be a religious daily. That is the fact; but it could not be made to go. *Vanity Fair,* Artemus Ward's attempt at a comic or satirical paper, had poked fun at in a paragraph that I recall. This was it: "Cheap Living: Buy the New York *World* and get board (bored) for only one cent." *Vanity Fair* was dead in 1868 and had no successor. *Puck, Judge* and *Life* had not been born. The *Scientific American* was, perhaps, as important then as it is now. It was originally a sort of house organ for the patent agency of Munn & Co. Few papers have exerted an equal influence for good. How thankful we ought to be that the Postoffice Department did not kill it. The *Iron Age* was without doubt the best example of a class journal. It may be that there are none any better in 1905. It, too, was a house organ in the beginning.

The Albany *Journal* and Utica *Herald* were important dailies of the interior of the State. The first named, Thurlow Weed's paper, had a great weekly circulation, not less, it was said, than thirty or forty thousand. The other was then edited by a political friend or henchman of Roscoe Conkling, and his name is now familiar to everybody who has a United States silver certificate in his pocket, whereon he may read "Ellis H. Roberts, Treasurer of the United States." Mr. Roberts was a terror to advertising agents, for if they put an advertisement in his paper the rate would have to be met to the last penny, and on that account they also all had a great deal of respect for him.

In Rochester, beside the daily *Union and Advertiser,* there was published the *Rural New Yorker,* owned and edited by Daniel D. Tompkins Moore, who achieved a great success in his time. No other paper of its class, except the *American Agriculturist,* was so widely or so favorably known. Mr. Moore was one day surprised by an offer of $125,000 for a half interest in his paper, from Messrs. Pettengill & Bates, the advertising agents. He did not accept, but it set him to thinking, and he thereupon moved his publication office to New York City, and made the mistake of his life. In Rochester he had been prominent—Mayor of the city and much beside. I remember with what pride he used to sometimes exhibit the handsome gold badge that had been presented to him while he held the office of Mayor. In New York he was well received, but did not cut anywhere near so much ice as he had in the Flour City. I recall a men's reception that Mr. Moore gave at his house in Fifth avenue at the northeast corner of Forty-first street, on which occasion there was speech making, and a dignitary from Rochester got into rather deep water by attempting a pun upon the name of Moore. What he had in mind to say was that the man gained by New York City had been lost to Rochester, but what he did finally succeed in saying was, first, that New York had gained more than Rochester had lost, and then that Rochester had lost more than New York had gained. Probably the second form about expressed the facts. Moore had been a great man in Rochester. Here there were many as great, and some greater. His income, princely for Rochester, was nothing particularly notable in New York. His expenses increased, while his capacity for work and his consequent earnings did not. Finally he failed and died a very poor man. His paper passed into other and less skillful hands, and not very long ago the writer of this was given an opportunity to own it, out and out, by merely assuming an obligation to a paper dealer that amounted to barely one-fifth of the sum that Pettengill & Co. had been willing to pay for a half interest. If it was bad luck for Moore that he had not accepted that offer it was equally bad luck for the Pettengill people, for, after it had been declined, they proceeded to launch upon the sea of publicity a weekly of their own, called *Hearth and Home*, and which, before they got through with it, had eaten into their resources to an amount little if any short of $300,000, of which sum Mr. Bates, who owned but a third of the advertising agency, stood in for a full half, he having asserted and maintained a right to an equal interest in the newer enterprise.

Hearth and Home was finally acquired by Orange Judd, who had made a success of the *American Agriculturist*, and after ruining him, passed along to the Goodsell Brothers who, as representatives of some Canadian capitalists, were printing in New York an illustrated daily called the *Graphic*, of which the new purchase was to be a side issue, in the way of a weekly edition. Somehow the Canadians seemed to get cold feet very soon after acquiring the new property, and it, with its daily side partner, eventually passed out of existence. *Hearth and Home* was a good paper. I never could understand why it did not succeed. It was conducted on a liberal plan by men who were experts in advertising, and by others who were successful as publishers; but it proved a veritable old man of the sea to everyone who ever attempted to carry it on his shoulders.

His publishing experience was a sad one for Bates, but in after life, when he had recouped his losses and had the consciousness of a competence put aside that would keep the wolf from his door forever and ever, and even longer, he used to like to tell of his experience in transferring his burden to the shoulders of the unfortunate Mr. Judd, who was then in the heyday of his prosperity with his *American Agriculturist*. Mr. Judd was not at his office the day Bates determined to do business with him. He was at a rural summer resort somewhere in Connecticut and to that place Bates proceeded, but Mr. Judd was not at the hotel; he had gone a-fishing at a pond a mile away, and to that pond proceeded Mr. Bates, and there, in a boat, near a bridge, anchored in water six feet deep, the great agriculturist was engaged in catching perch, chubs and now and then a bull-head, and passing the hour with much contemplative satisfaction. Bates climbed out of the wagon and sat down on the overhanging planks of the bridge, within twenty feet of the Waltonian, and awaited recognition, which was not delayed. "What are you here for?" asked Judd. "I came here to sell *Hearth and Home* to you," responded Bates without circumlocution. There was a short pause while the boatman's boy removed a chub from the hook and re-baited it with a portion of a clam. The sportsman inspected the lure with approval, spat on it, as is the custom with fresh-water fishermen in New England, and dropping it over the side of the boat, looked again at the man on the bridge and, removing his straw hat, using it for a fan, he said, "You have found that it takes something more than money to make a newspaper!" And then, tapping his forehead a little to the left of the space over his left eye, added sententiously, "It takes brains!" Bates did not contest the point. Whatever it required he had become conscious that he possessed it not. He had sought that bridge with the purpose of unloading his burden on Mr. Judd, and when he arose from the planks on which he had sat he had succeeded; had freed himself from a nightmare, and the fisherman had secured something that eventually proved to him about as fatal as would probably have been the result could he then and there have hooked the veritable sea serpent.

In Buffalo there was no better paper than the *Commercial;* in Cleveland the *Herald* was first, the *Leader* second and *Plain Dealer* third, it having failed to sustain its circulation after the impetus gained as the medium through which the early literary efforts of Artemus Ward went out to the world.

In Detroit the best paper was the *Tribune,* in Chicago, too, it was the *Tribune* that stood first, although the *Times* was a close second, and, in the mere matter of copies sold, very likely stood number one. Under Wilbur F. Story, the Chicago *Times* was the equal of any yellow journal in existence to-day. It had as many interesting qualities as may be found in the New York *Journal* and *Town Topics* combined. I recall a charming woman at the West, the mother of a growing family, who never failed to have the Chicago *Times* at hand, but at whose breakfast table, in after years, I missed the Sunday edition. "I thought you always had the *Times,*" I said. "Yes," answered she with a shrug of the shoulders, "I thought it very amusing for a long time, but when it got around to dishing up the doings of my own daughters it did not seem so funny as it used to, and I don't take it any more." West of Buffalo the paper was everywhere. Among other things, it was noted for the scare heads of its new columns; a good specimen of which I recall, introducing an account of the hanging of a man who had given evidence before the day of execution that he had repented his evil life and felt assured that, like the dying thief, he would find rest and forgiveness. "Jerked to Jesus" was the caption of the story.

In St. Paul Mr. Driscoll's paper, the *Pioneer* had first place and also control of the Minneapolis field. Minneapolis did not count for much just then. In Milwaukee the *Evening Wisconsin* and *Morning Sentinel* were then, as now, both good papers. In Omaha the *Republican* was not of much account, but there was nothing better there. In St. Louis, as has been said, the Republican *Democrat* and the Democratic *Republican* were about the whole thing; although that still conspicuous American citizen, Mr. Stilson Hutchins, owned and controlled a paper called the *Times,* and was said to have as much influence with the police department as Boss Butler has ever exercised in recent years. Mr. Hutchins has been prominent at the National capital in recent years. He is reported to have asserted that twice in his life he had made a fool of himself in connection with a newspaper; once when he sold the Washington *Post* and again when he bought the *Times* of the same city; the last named is now the property of Mr. Frank A. Munsey, the originator of the ten cent magazine and bears so much evidence of prosperity that it would not seem strange if Mr. Hutchins should revise his statement of the second case of foolishness in his history and so designate the sale instead of the purchase of the *Times.* Mr. Hutchins successfully exploited the Mergenthaler type-setting machine, is very rich and to some extent prominent in Washington society. "I see your wife's back from Paris," said a gentleman to him one day. "I know you could see it a hell of a ways," he replied, "but I didn't think you could see it that far."

In Indianapolis the *Journal* was a pretty good paper, and the *Sentinel* then, as now, claimed more than it could seem to back up. Whoever had much to do in those days with the capital of Indiana was generally thankful when he had gotten through and could come away. How well I remember the Bates House and recall a characteristic incident that illustrated or emphasized some of my own experiences there. A favorite son of Indiana, so the story ran, lay ill at the Bates House. Delirium tremens was what's the matter. An attached friend was in attendance—for before now Billy had done as much for the Colonel and would again. When the Doctor went away that night he said to the watcher, "I think Billy is going to do well now. Do you sleep on the lounge there?" "Yes." "Well, if he wakes and complains of seeing things, give him one of these powders." Next morning when the Doctor came the Colonel made his report. "Billy did first-rate until about five o'clock this morning, when I was wakened by hearing him exclaim in an excited voice 'I see bugs on the wall!' I got up to give him the powder, but before doing so took a look at the place where his eyes seemed to be fastened, and bi-god, I saw 'em, too! and I took the first powder myself."

In Virginia the Richmond *Dispatch* was the paper, in South Carolina the Charleston *Courier,* in Georgia the Savannah *News,* in Alabama the Mobile *Register,* in Louisiana the New Orleans *Picayune* and the *Times.* In Texas the Galveston *News* was the whole thing, as it and its twin, the Dallas *News,* have pretty nearly succeeded in being ever since. In Tennessee it was the Memphis *Avalanche.*

It has come about that old-fashioned personal journalism has lingered longer in Kentucky than anywhere else. What Mr. Greeley was to the *Tribune,* Mr. Bennett to the *Herald,* Thurlow Weed to the Albany *Journal,* Samuel Bowles to the Springfield *Republican,* Murat Halstead to the Cincinnati *Commercial* or Charles A. Dana to the New York *Sun,* that was George D. Prentice to the old Louisville *Journal,* and that Henry Watterson has been and still is to the Louisville *Courier-Journal.* Henry to-day is the last living specimen, the last leaf on the tree, the last drop in the well, the very, very last rose of summer. When he is called hence no other representative of the old-time personal journalism will survive.

It was in a little paper published by my firm, called the *Newspaper Reporter*—which, by the way, was so exact a prototype of *Printers' Ink* that if they were seen together now no one could, at a first glance, very readily tell them apart—that the young man acting as editor, asked my permission one day to write up and publish his opinion of the, to his mind, most promising young journalist then in America. He wished to prepare a historical sketch occupying several pages. Having permission to go ahead he thereupon caused to be printed a first-rate account of Henry Watterson, the best and most complete that had then appeared. The little paper had a good many interested readers, and it came about that the article was largely copied, and we had occasion to know that the young blue grass editor appreciated and was pleased with it. Many years after I was one day introduced to Henry Watterson on the street in Louisville, at about three o'clock of the afternoon. When I left him it fell little short of being three in the morning, and if Mr. Watterson had been one-half as full of appreciation of the original as I was of other things when we parted I should say that when Lord Bacon asserted that reading made a full man he was quite right as to the effect of that article in the *Newspaper Reporter* upon the rising journalist of the West. I cannot refrain from mentioning here that the young editor of the *Newspaper Reporter,* just referred to, is now the New York sanitary engineer, Mr. Charles F. Wingate, who, when he is unable to personally banish bad sanitary conditions, never fails to enlist public interest by writing letters to the newspapers on the subject. Mr. Watterson, like his predecessor, Mr. Prentice, has been very much before the American public and, without doubt, is a man of marked individuality and brilliant ability.

Col. Dick Bright, of Indianapolis, while in Washington at one time, looking after an appointment as Sergeant-at-Arms of the United States Senate—which, by the way, he secured—gave me an estimate of the comparative merit of different members of the Watterson family that impressed me as having some probable foundation. "Henry and his father are both in Washington," said the Colonel, "for the old gentleman wants an appointment in the gift of the House of Representatives, and Henry means to help him get it. Henry and his father," continued the Colonel, "constitute a mutual admiration society of two. The old man thinks Henry is the greatest man that the Almighty ever created, and Henry thinks the old man is the best." Then after a moment's pause the Colonel added for himself, "And I think Henry is nearer right than the old man is."

After Mr. Prentice of the Louisville *Journal* had died Mr. W. N. Haldeman, who had long controlled the *Courier,* the competing paper, succeeded in consolidating the two, it being, I think, the first instance of what is generally designated as the hyphenated journal; and the Louisville *Courier-Journal* became, and has remained the most important and most influential newspaper of Kentucky, or, for that matter, of the Southern States. The Galveston and Dallas *News* combination, however, has made a great deal more money. Colonel Belo, when he died a few years ago, left an estate of more than three million dollars.

In Cincinnati the leading papers were the *Commercial*, Murat Halstead, editor; the *Gazette*, controlled by the good Deacon Richard Smith, who had an alleged wicked partner with whom Mr. Dana of the New York *Sun* long had fun, persistently speaking of him as the piratical Kidd or Kydd. There was also the *Enquirer*, published by the father of the present John McLean, the *Dollar Weekly*, having a wide circulation and published in connection with the daily *Times*. Mr. Halstead of the *Commercial* used to assert that every Ohio Democrat took the *Enquirer* and every Republican the *Gazette*, because they all knew what each would say; but that all Democrats and all Republicans took the *Commercial*, because they did not know what in hell it would say.

In California there were three papers of prime importance. The Sacramento *Union* stood first, because before the days of railroads it was twelve hours nearer the mines than San Francisco was. Next in importance came the *Morning Call* of San Francisco, with the *Evening Bulletin* a close second. The *Chronicle* had not then been born, and the *Examiner* had not been thought of. Some people thought the *Alta California* an important paper, but it was not—not very.

In Portland, Oregon, the *Oregonian*, the great paper of that region to-day, had already pre-empted the ground, under the management of Mr. Pittock, its founder; as modest, as persistent, as meek in appearance, and as firm in insistence, as any man in the newspaper world. In connection with this Mr. Pittock I would say a word of a younger brother of his who was born, flourished and died in Pittsburg, Penn., where he had failed as a newsdealer before he was thirteen years old, had made a success of the *Sunday Leader* before he was eighteen, and finally established the daily *Leader,* in which enterprise, though it was successful, he was overweighted and died before he had much more than reached manhood's years. Under conditions and circumstances wholly favorable, I think, Johnny Pittock had in him the making of a great newspaper man. The most influential paper of Pittsburg at that time, as it is to-day, was the *Dispatch,* then presided over by an able man who had the misfortune to be conspicuous by the necessity or advisability of wearing a wooden nose. Not everybody liked Dan O'Neill, but no one thought it wise to take liberties with him. One day a review had been planned of a visiting regiment to arrive from Philadelphia. The Mayor would deliver a speech of welcome. It had been written out, set in type at the office of the *Dispatch,* and only awaited delivery, when a telegram, at the last moment, announced that, for good and sufficient reasons that are not now recalled, the regiment would not arrive. O'Neill and the Mayor talked the matter over at the city hall and the newspaper man spoke warmly of the excellence of His Honor's address and how the people would enjoy it. "But I make no address," said the Mayor. "The people will read it just the same," said the newspaper man, "it is all in type and we'll print it all right." "O'Neill," said the Mayor, "I wouldn't have that speech printed for a thousand dollars." "Now you are talking business," answered Dan.

Pittsburg is in many respects a remarkable town. It was in this neighborhood that a boy telegraph operator named Andrew Carnegie learned how, and put his learning into operation, by acquiring a greater fortune than any other human being has ever tried to give away. I am told that within a circle of fifty miles from the Pittsburg city hall there are more people to-day (1905) than exist in any other circumference of one hundred miles diameter on the continent, and, if existing plans of annexation are carried out, the city will soon rank third in population, standing below Chicago but above Philadelphia.

From a Pittsburg newsboy I once learned a lesson worth being taught by that Chicago savant, who instructs in business building—by mail. It was on a sort of cross country road, running north toward Buffalo, and it did seem as though the hour of arrival would never, never come. "I've made a study of it," said the boy. "If you've got any high-priced things to sell you must take them around first; if you don't you won't sell 'em. I've tried it over and over, and I know what I'm talking about. After you have sold a passenger a copy of *Leslie's Weekly,* a pint of peanuts—and one apple—you might just as well keep away from that man."

It must not be neglected to state that Mr. John W. Forney used at this time to speak approvingly of "My two papers—both daily," referring to the Washington *Chronicle* and the *Press* of Philadelphia. There was also in Philadelphia the *Inquirer,* spelled with an I. Mr. Tony Drexel had bought the *Ledger* for his friend, George W. Childs, who changed it from a losing business into one paying a profit of a thousand dollars a day, so people said, by simply changing the price at which it was sold, that is increasing it from one cent to two cents. The *Ledger* was the one paper of Philadelphia while Mr. Childs lived, and is still, perhaps, the most effective want ad medium of the City of Brotherly Love.

The Baltimore *Sun* was, comparatively, a much more prominent paper in 1868 than it is in 1905. It and the Philadelphia *Ledger* and the New York *Herald,* composed the trio of prominent journals that would allow no commission to advertising agents. The *Sun* was the last one of the three to change front on the position taken on this point. It now has a New York special agent.

In Boston the *Journal* and *Herald* were most conspicuous papers, and I would not forget to mention the Springfield, Mass., *Republican,* the Worcester *Spy,* the Providence

R. I., *Journal,* the Hartford *Courant* and the Brooklyn *Eagle.*

The religious papers were then of vastly greater account than they are to-day, and prominent among them were, in New York, the *Observer,* the *Evangelist,* the *Examiner,* the *Christian Advocate,* and more assertive than any, and carrying more advertising, at a higher price, than all combined, was Mr. Henry C. Bowen's *Independent.* In Boston there were *Zion's Herald,* the *Watchman and Reflector,* and the *Congregationalist.* Mr. Hamilton W. Mabie's recent assertion that a Boston religious weekly, in its effort to keep up with the times, changed its name from the *Fireside Companion* to the *Christian Register* is an impious misstatement. It was the *Register* in 1821—before there was such a thing as a hot air furnace in Boston. Of the magazines *Harper's* was the only one of very much account. That sort of publication was not then considered to be at all worth the consideration of advertisers. *Harper's* not only did not seek advertisements, but actually refused to take them. I ought not to forget, however, in connection with magazines, that Philadelphia was exceptional, for there were issued three of large circulation that had been known since the youth of the oldest inhabitant. They were *Arthur's Home Magazine, Peterson's Magazine* and *Godey's Ladies' Book.* All of them are now dead, but *Godey's,* like King Charles II, was an "unconscionable long time dying."

Speaking of magazines reminds me finally of a Boston periodical, long published by Moses A. Dow. It was a weekly having a sort of an arabesque decorated heading that I am confident thousands of people remember, and was named the *Waverley Magazine.* It sold on newsstands for 10 cents a copy, charged a dollar a line for advertisements, was said to never pay anything for contributions, and to be filled with the effusions of romantic misses and young men, ambitious of literary fame, from the various schools and seminaries of the country. Mr. Dow was a very plain, quiet man. He got out his periodical as cheaply as he could, although always on paper of a good quality. He had been a compositor in a printing office until he conceived the idea of the *Waverley,* and attracted little attention, until late in life he built a great hotel in Charlestown, where he lived, costing several hundred thousand dollars, and it thereupon transpired that he was and had long been the heaviest taxpayer in the City of Bunker Hill. The *Waverley Magazine* is still published, but its old heading has been modernized, and it is no longer a fortune builder.

Mr. George W. Childs, of Philadelphia, before he acquired the *Ledger,* had owned a somewhat famous paper called the *Home Weekly.* Advertisements in it cost 50 cents a line, paid for in advance—no commission to agents. The paper was sold to a man named Nunes, whom I afterwards met as United States Consul at Matanzas, Cuba, and when it ceased publication one day, although still getting 50 cents a line for advertising, it transpired that the entire edition printed fell short of 2,500 copies.

TWENTY-FOURTH PAPER

The memories of the early experiences with the advertising agency cluster and concentrate around the year 1868. In that year the writer had attained to the mature age of thirty, and after it had come to an end he was so little informed upon the ways of the world as to believe that because the government had passed a law authorizing the collection of a tax on incomes, it was on that account incumbent on him to respond to the requirements set forth and actually to put in his report, and be prepared to pay that tax. Figuring it out was easy enough. Admitting that the capital in the business, which apparently increased day by day, was as great on the last as on the first day of the year, it was evident that whatever money had been withdrawn from office earnings within the twelve months was income. It appeared to figure up a respectable sum, somewhat exceeding $54,000, and upon that sum the government would exact something more than $2,500 as an income tax. It was as bad business policy to hand in a report, as it generally proves to be for an incoming passenger on an ocean steamship to fill out the declaration of what goods are in his trunks upon which duties ought to be paid. It would have been cheaper to allow the officials to make their own estimates and arrive at their own conclusions.

I hardly believe that my neighbors, including my landlord, Mr. George Jones of the New York *Times,* would have thought it likely that I was doing much more than earning office expenses. Mr. Jones often told me, in after years, that he kept a pretty close watch on the rent account for some time, for he did not believe, in the face of the competition I would have to meet, I would succeed in gaining a permanent foothold; but as the rent was payable monthly and always seemed to be handed in one day before it was due, without any call from a collector, he, after a time, be-

gan to acquire confidence, and became quite willing to allow
our firm, then consisting of Mr. Charles N. Kent and myself, to take on office after office, as other tenants went out,
and we required more room. While we remained in the
Times Building we gradually increased our floor space until, at the time we moved in 1877, we were paying a rent
of $11,500 a year, and had actually given Mr. Jones, in this
way, considerably more than twice as much money as the
purchase of No. 10 Spruce street involved, with its 17,500
feet of floor space, in fee simple.

It was not until well into the third or fourth year that I
ever had time to appreciate the risks I had actually run in
coming to New York, with so small a capital and with
scarcely any acquaintance. I bought a safe of Herring &
Co. The firm was willing to sell one to be paid for in advertising, as it might be wanted, in papers of their own selection, but as the price was $1,300 the manager seemed to
be only taking a proper precaution when he asked for such
references as would make it seem probable that he would
get his advertising when he called for it. That matter of
references was an embarrassing one. We had done some
business for dozens of New York advertisers, but that involved trusting them, not being trusted by them. We had
accounts with several of the New York papers, but they
were small and collected monthly; and each publisher felt
about as Mr. Jones did, and would be quite in sympathy
with the same man. Every one was more in need of information than prepared to give it out in my behalf. I had had
an account at the Broadway Bank before coming from Boston, but had at that time been led to think that the only
function of a bank official was to appear to be somewhat in
doubt and say nothing very much to the point. It is my
recollection that the safe man, Mr. Farrell, who is still living and a director in the Lincoln Bank, had decided to let
me have the safe, when it occurred to me to tell him if he
would knock off $300 from the price I would give him a
check for the remaining $1,000 that very minute. He ac-
cepted the proposal with so much alacrity that I was led to

think then, and have never ceased to think since, that had I suggested an $800 reduction, and offered a check for $500, I would still have become possessed of that great iron cabinet that continues to this hour (1905) to inclose and protect the books of the Advertising Agency, and for which, in case of closing out the business, it is not, in my opinion, probable that the receiver would ever realize so much as $125. Transactions in safes were so peculiar thirty or forty years ago that the sign DANGER, always exhibited on the street when a safe is in sight, has ever seemed to me to be singularly appropriate. This is in no sense a criticism of Mr. Farrell or Herring & Co., for my treatment by them was very considerate, and they allowed me to have my own way in the whole transaction.

By and by the newspapers printed a list of the people who paid an income tax, and the amount thereof, and in my case, for a wonder, my name was spelled correctly, the initials were my own, and the figures absolutely accurate. Few people, who have not had a similar experience, can realize how that publication enhanced my personal importance at that boarding house in University Place. The managers were two maiden sisters, the Misses Stryker, or I think I may say that the elder, Miss Katherine Stryker, was the manager and the younger her companion, dependent and pride. Miss Helen must have been a beautiful girl, in her youth, and there was always about her an air of mystery and melancholy that won upon the sympathies of those who looked upon her on the rare occasions when she allowed herself to be seen. I and my small family became the star boarders; had a private table in one corner of the dining room, quite separate and apart from the long one at which all the other boarders sat; and, although the cost was increased, I was never quite certain that I liked the new arrangement, for there is a great deal of fun and friendliness to be found in the associations of a boarding house, and the peculiarities of the inmates and their conversation —their pride, their hopes, their ambitions—have in them much of human interest.

One good lady had a distinct formula, always used in ordering her breakfast. "Delia," she would say to the waitress, "I—want a—very—small—piece—of—beefsteak, v-e-r-y rare, and v—e—r—y tender, tell Miss Stryker." And another boarder, who sat opposite, commenting on this daily formula, used in after years to relate that Delia would go out, and after being gone half an hour, return "with a piece of gristle about as big as my two hands."

There was a gentleman of Southern birth and breeding; a lawyer, an educated man. He it was who first directed my attention to the delightful humor of two books, not now very often seen: "Georgia Scenes" and "Flush Times in Alabama." This good man had evidently not been used to boarding houses, for he always passed a dish before helping himself, and as no dish ever came back, or if it did, came back empty, he gradually grew serious and thin. We all eat too much, however, and I am not certain that the man did not live longer than he would if his manners had been less considerate. In after years this same good man, who lingered on after I had gone away, came to me to say that the old house had been given up, that the two old sisters were as poor as they were deserving—and that meant very poor indeed—that they seemed to have no friends to lend a helping hand, and that he, personally, had charged himself with the duty of finding out a respectable, comfortable old ladies' home, where they might be permanently cared for, if only a certain specified moderate sum might be raised to cover a stipulated admission fee. It was one of the sweetest pleasures afforded by a moderate prosperity that I was able to respond to his suggestion in a manner that made it unnecessary for him to present the case in other quarters; and, although I do not now recall the name of the institution, and never visited it, I did feel complimented to receive its annual reports so long as the good ladies lived, and to note that my own name was given a place among the very respectable list of gentlemen that constituted the board of managers.

There was living at this boarding house a beautiful woman, in appearance much what Mrs. Patrick Campbell is to-day. Her husband, a gentleman of old-fashioned, graceful manners, was a descendant, and bore the name of a famous Virginia family. In the privacy of their room, with the intimacy that grows with every-day acquaintance, occasion was once taken to speak of the luxuriant beauty of the lady's hair, whereupon she produced what I think was the longest umbrella box it was ever my fortune to see, and, opening it, exhibited material out of which a considerable switch might be manufactured, and explained, that for years, at her toilet, it had been her practice to straighten out and preserve every hair that parted company with its neighbors. These good people disappeared from my view for many years; but once, while in Washington, having occasion to visit the State Department to obtain a passport for use on a proposed visit to foreign countries, I was surprised, and pleased, to find the gentleman who would attend to my requirements, was no other than my old friend of University Place. Having obtained the address, I proposed to pay my respects to his good lady. Not being particularly familiar with Washington localities I remember going out of a side door of the hotel where I was stopping and engaging a coupe, ordering the driver, for some reason I hardly know what, to come around to the front entrance for me a little later. There was a peculiar expression on the face of the man when I gave him the address to which he was to take me; but I took my seat and he departed, stopping a minute later before a house that stood within twenty feet of the place where his cab had been standing at the time I engaged him. I then understood the smile I had previously observed. While in conversation with the lady inquiry was made as to the ultimate fate of that wonderful umbrella box of former years and she thereupon, while asserting that her hair had lost something of its luxuriance, directed my attention to a very beautiful coil, which she assured me was the satisfactory result of her years of painstaking saving.

There is one other memory, connected with the life in the University Place house, that often comes to mind. Confinement to a desk had made it advisable for me to seek some out of door entertainment; and an old friend from my New Hampshire home sold me a small, young, rather ugly, strawberry roan mare, that developed not only a most charming disposition, but an unexpected capacity for speed; and many a delightful surprise she gave me on Harlem Lane, and out beyond McComb's Dam Bridge, on the road to the Jerome Park of those days. Few horses were encountered that, in a short brush, she would not get ahead of; but I remember distinctly an old clergyman, as I thought, who rode in a top buggy, driving a single horse, whom, under no circumstances, could I ever get by. On one occasion I made up my mind to find out, if possible, who the old gentleman was, so, taking pains to keep him within sight, I followed towards the city, over the bridge, past the road houses, and through the park. In the park he appeared to receive respectful attention from every policeman, although I thought he was driving a little faster than the law permitted. Shortly I heard a policeman address him as Commodore, and then it flashed upon me that his face was familiar enough through lithographs and other pictures, and that this was no other than Commodore Vanderbilt. In thinking of the matter to-day it would seem that this must have been very, very long ago, for in the morning paper I read of this and that Mr. Vanderbilt, who overspeeds his automobile, or does some other things of almost equal importance in social circles, or is a cause of anxiety to Mr. Jerome, and I take occasion to reflect that the person mentioned is not a son, nor a grandson, but a great-grandson of the old gentleman with the benevolent face who always drove such an excellent horse.

My strawberry roan, Maggie, fell a victim to that curse of willing horseflesh, navicular disease, making her lame in her forefeet, and she had to be sent back to her old home among the Granite hills. I was led to make a present of her to my father, on a suggestion from him that I might do worse, but the old gentleman, with customary New England thrift, immediately sold her out of the family, and when I heard of that I expected to see her no more. Fully twenty years afterwards, however, a letter came to me, saying that old Maggie was still alive, and existing under the ownership of an unpromising man, who was not kind to her, nor to anything else connected with him, and that the mare could be bought for five or ten dollars, a sum that my

GEO. P. ROWELL, JAMES H. BATES AND THE STRAWBERRY
ROAN MARE IN 1872.

friend believed I would be willing to contribute for the purpose; and he said that he, on his part, would take her to his own stable, see that she had at least one night of comfortable shelter with plenty to eat, and promised that the next morning she should be shot and put out of danger of further ill-treatment. The next morning, however, my friend reported that the old darling looked so bright and cheerful, and seemed so lively that he concluded to keep her until I should see her and decide upon what should be done. This led to her being sent to a farm I owned, not far away, and there for a year or more she did considerable service. During that time I had a visit from the literary artist, Mr. Clifton Johnson, who was then preparing his book, "Sketches of New England Life," and in it he placed a picture of a scene in a New England sugar orchard, in which there appeared a representation of old Maggie in harness, with a mate of twice her size, engaged in the work of hauling sap from the trees to the evaporator in the sugar house. I value the picture very much. The picture shown here was taken at Lancaster, N. H., in 1872, a year after the mare had returned to her native hills, and at a time when Mr. Bates was spending a little time in the White Mountains on a vacation trip. Maggie was finally transferred, in trust, to the father of my farm superintendent, who liked to have a horse at his command, but had not too much money to invest in the purchase of one, and there she did more good service, for another year or two, although I heard from the superintendent that the old gentleman was a little afraid of her, she was so spirited. She finally died and her joys and troubles are now at an end.

TWENTY-FIFTH PAPER

The List System—the idea of contracting for a column of space to be sold out by the inch, or by the line, at a fixed price, based upon the alliterative proposal that had taken so well at first—an inch of space inserted a month in one hundred papers for $100—had begun in New England and been extended to New York State. Then there was what was called a Western State combination covering Ohio, Indiana and Illinois; a Middle State List, having papers in New Jersey, Pennsylvania, Delaware and Maryland; a Northwestern combination, taking in Michigan, Wisconsin, Minnesota, Iowa, Missouri and Kansas; a Southern List, taking in all the States south of Mason and Dixon's Line; and, finally, there was a Pacific Coast List, started and conducted in our name, but managed in San Francisco by Mr. J. F. Place, a New Hampshire newspaper man who had noted the progress of the work in New England and thought there might be millions in it. The man in charge of the List System after the removal to New York was my old schoolmate and friend from childhood days, Nelson Chesman, well known of later years, and at the present time, as conducting a successful advertising agency of his own.

There soon began to be a great deal of trouble about keeping each List down to the limit of one hundred; then, too, there were some of the localities, notably California, where a hundred was a larger List than could be obtained. Some papers would always be remiss about performance, consequently to make sure of having the full complement to exhibit to an advertiser, as vouchers, it was always necessary to contract with a few extra papers, while, if the number of papers was not specified with so much definiteness, the patron would not be so exacting as to the last one or two required to complete the tale. So it came about that while the geographical subdivisions were maintained the uniformity of the number of papers on each List and the like uniformity of price was not kept up, and by and by some Lists had twice as many papers as another one did and cost two or three times as much.

No good thing goes on very long without having imitators: There was a certain man named Page, who, buying beechwood by the log, transformed it into wooden poster type, salable at such an advance over the cordwood price as to make it seem as though every dollar that came to his hand was ninety-nine and three-eighths per cent profit. He had an active agent in New York in that Mr. J. G. Cooley, who, at a later day, established a successful paper in Norwich, Connecticut, existing to-day as the weekly of the Norwich *Evening Record,* and still known as *Cooley's Weekly.* Mr. Cooley, too, still lives (1905), though long an invalid and shut in.

Mr. Cooley was also a sort of a representative of a certain firm of typefounders, who were always in a chronic state of being short of money, and he, with their aid, or they with his, took advantage of a combination or boycott existing among the typefounders of the country whereby nobody who was not a typefounder was allowed to sell type. Mr. Cooley discovered that every popular face of body type could be duplicated by an electrotyping process—that I, being no mechanic, do not at all understand—and the product, notwithstanding the charge that it lacked something of the perfection of the original, found a ready sale.

I recall a circular issued by Mr. Cooley, in which he dealt with some assertions emanating from Bruce, Conner, Farmer, Little & Co. and other typefounders, to the effect that his practice was but little short of thievery. No attempt on his part was made to deny the charge, but he quoted an alleged conversation between two colored chicken thieves. "Sambo, is this right?" inquired the one highest up on the roost. "That am a great moral question," answered Sambo after a moment's reflection—"Please to pass down that other pullet."

In the pursuit of his legitimate business, as above, our

old friend Cooley soon found he could sell more type to the newspapers than he could induce the publishers thereof to pay him for. By and by the idea opened before his vision that he could buy space on the same plan that the Rowell concern had brought into public notice, and, if he paid in wood type, could cut the Rowell price in half and still have a profit. He thereupon started in to make contracts, taking any paper that was to be had, and at this time he also took as partner that Mr. Dauchy, so well and favorably known as the head for more than thirty years of the very respectable advertising agency of Dauchy & Co., and the two became advertising agents by self-appointment—as is always the method—paying all bills in wood type and conducting their operations under the name of Cooley & Dauchy.

The new concern took no particular pains to choose papers. All were fish that came to their type net, and soon we had a rather lively competition on our hands. When we said that our papers were better, Cooley said, "Well, ours are more in number." If we claimed that we secured a special position, as we did in most cases, Cooley responded that he bought the best space there was in the paper, which, as it meant positively nothing, seemed to be entirely satisfactory to everybody. If said our list was worth more than his, he responded that perhaps it might not be, but it ought to be, for we asked a higher price than he did, which was true. He was also much aided by a trade association with a young firm of advertising agents just getting into business in Philadelphia, who were destined, eventually, to carry the business further and do it better than anybody else had done in this country or the world. I am speaking of N. W. Ayer & Son of Philadelphia.

After a time the Cooley & Dauchy opposition, in connection with the growth of the Lists of papers printed on the co-operative plan, made it impossible for us to always fill our columns on profitable terms in all of the more than a thousand dailies and weeklies with which we had contracts. In consequence of this difficulty the wording of the contracts was gradually changed, to provide for a column rate without agreeing to fill a column; and gradually the business secured on the plan became so limited that at last a time came when the day to send out copy was at hand and there was not so much as a single inch of matter ready to be sent; but even then the price per inch continued to prevail with a majority of the papers, and did prevail for years and years, and does still prevail in many cases where the publisher has ever forgotten how such a rate originated. But Cooley & Dauchy, and afterwards Dauchy & Co., could beat us even at that, for we paid the price in cash and they paid in wood type at from two to four hundred per cent profit, although to some dailies and papers of more than ordinary importance they would, on occasion, sell Lindsay's electrotyped fonts, all of which was legitimate and proper enough, being in precise accordance with the agreements the papers had entered into with them; and, after all, these arrangements were no more unbusinesslike than the agreements they had with us, that enabled us to accept an advertisement for a dollar for insertion in this paper and that, and get it inserted for 37 cents on our yearly column contract, while other advertising agents, who neither had a yearly contract nor were agents for wood type, would be called upon to pay sometimes as much as $2.50 gross, for precisely the same service.

As has been said before, advertising space may, from some points of observation and under some conditions, be worth to the paper absolutely less than nothing. Observation shows, however, that those publishers only are permanently successful who consider their space as worth all they ask for it, and uniformly refuse to let it go unless they get the price named on the rate card. Just what price to demand when making up a rate card is a puzzle to every man who struggles with the question for the first time. Mr. M. H. Mallory, publisher and owner of that excellent organ of the Episcopal denomination, the New York *Churchman,* was once heard to assert that advertising space in a newspaper is somewhat like a lady's favors, which are valued very much as she values them herself. When I have quoted him on the point, however, it has been urged that he is a single man, and never having bought any favors, and so far as known never having had any, he is not competent to act as appraiser. Still, for all that, there is a shadow of truth and justice in what Mr. Mallory has asserted.

TWENTY-SIXTH PAPER

One day there came an application for information concerning the cost of inserting a small advertisement in all the best papers throughout the country. It was from Augusta, Maine. The name of the applicant was not in the rate books of the mercantile agencies and was not known to us. It was the sort of inquiry that comes into every advertising agency with much frequency, and usually means about as much as if a boy should ask, at the country store, how they sold raisins, and on being told the price, and asked if he wanted some, should answer, "No, only I thought I'd like to know what they would cost if I did." To prepare ourselves to answer such an inquiry, as fully as it would be done if it came from a customer known to be in earnest and intending to do business, would take the time of a competent man a good many hours, and the service would cost the office as much as forty or fifty dollars. The answer to such an inquiry has been carefully worked out in many an advertising agency, and after due delay, a follow-up system has revealed a man no more interested than the boy who would investigate the raisin market, and the inquirer from the agency might be told that it was an oversight that no acknowledgment had been sent of the receipt of the information; but, as matter of fact, the letter had not been read yet; and the inquiry was really only made to decide a bet— or something of that sort.

The particular application before us seemed to be in the handwriting of a very old man. It was easy to tell, however, what the advertisement would cost in the between one and two thousand papers in which we controlled space of the so-called "List System." This was done, the price named being $1,800. By return mail came the reply, "That may be all very well as far as it goes, but I want what I said I wanted when I wrote my first letter." So far as could be judged by the advertisement proposed to be used the business was not one to warrant any considerable outlay, and so far as we could learn, at short notice, the applicant was an unknown man whose responsibility was not established, if indeed he had any. Still something had to be done, so a letter was dispatched saying that the matter was of sufficient importance to warrant a personal interview; and if the inquirer could not come to our office for that purpose, he would, in any event, wish to use the papers upon which prices had already been quoted; and if a check for $1,800 should be forwarded as an evidence of good faith, and that business and not curiosity was in mind, we would on receipt of the check dispatch a competent man to deal with the inquirer at his own place of business. By return mail came the check on a Boston bank, with few or no words accompanying it; and the necessity for going to Augusta was apparent.

It was in mid-winter, a great storm was in progress, but it seemed too bad to waste more time after so many delays, and with my warmest overcoat, a fur cap and a great pair of boots—of which I was very proud—I started out that evening, stopped over in Boston to learn if the check was sure enough good, and, finding that it was, proceeded to Portland, and to Augusta, at which point I arrived in time for breakfast at the hotel, after which I waded through the deep snow, to find my impatient client. He had a room up one flight of stairs, in a barn-like loft—the chambers of what appeared to be a block of stores. The room was warm and comfortable enough from the influence of a great stove that stood in the center. In various positions, conveniently arranged for light and warmth, half a dozen girls were busy at tables, apparently assorting letters, addressing envelopes, or making up packages of the postal currency then in general use. All were busy. An alcove in one corner of the room was boarded off like a coal bin and appeared to be filled with waste paper, consisting of opened letters and torn envelopes. In the darkest corner of the room there sat at a desk a youth of considerable more than ordinary height and breadth of figure, but apparently not more than eighteen years of age; and he was very busy, and his manner was rather stern and somewhat impatient. We soon got down to business, however, and he told me something of his life and his plans. He was a Maine boy—his family were poor. His first recollections of Augusta had to do with the time, during the Civil War, when soldiers were in camp there, and he, as a small boy from the region beyond, had found among these a market for all the berries he could pick, or could control from the gleanings of less business-like companions.

Growing older, he had become interested in advertisements that he saw in the newspapers, wherein it was made to appear that certain people had things to sell and wanted agents to aid them. He had become agent for more than one, and found that there actually were possibilities of earning money; but before long he arrived at the conclusion that more money than was made by the agents was undoubtedly made out of the agents by the principals; the men who inserted the advertisements. So, after a time, he had experimented with one scheme and another, inserted advertisements on his own account, had dealt with agents to some extent, and got enough out of it all to pay his advertising bills and make a living beside. The last did not cost much. What he was aiming at was not so much to get money to spend as to build up a business, and the scheme interested him as it developed. Lately he had hit upon something that promised to go. He had a recipe for making a washing compound. Every farmer's wife, every poor man's wife, did her own washing. This compound made washing easier. The ingredients could be had at any drug store, and were inexpensive. Whoever bought the recipe and tried it pronounced it a good thing. The recipe could be expressed in forty words. It was about the equivalent of a six line nonpareil paragraph in a newspaper. Printed on small slips of the size of a postal card the recipes could be prepared for a dollar a thousand or even less. If they could be sold for a dollar each the profit would be tremendous, and even if sold in large lots at ten cents each, a hundred, costing no more than a dime, might produce a ten dollar bill. Of course, the secret of the recipe was his stock in trade. The buyer of a copy could commit its words to memory in five minutes, and would forever after be a perennial fountain from which unlimited numbers of the recipe could be taken, or he could invoke the services of a printer; but our friend knew how to get around all that. Whoever bought a recipe, or became an agent, received with the invoice a printed statement which plainly said in effect, "You solemnly promise and agree not to divulge or make known the formula and to exact the same promise from every one to whom you sell the valuable secret."

All this goes to show that there is an unsuspected amount of honesty and good faith in the world. The advertisement this young man would insert called for agents to sell the recipe for making the washing compound. The price at which it was to be sold was one dollar, but the buyer, after testing its excellence, might become an agent for the sale of the recipe to others and might buy in quantities, at graduated rates, and appoint and deal with sub-agents on his or her own account. Five recipes could be had for $2, ten for $3, twenty-five for $5, a hundred for $10, a thousand for $25. An effort would be made to give every agent such exclusive territory as the amount of his purchase would warrant, and if by any error it so chanced that territory assigned to one conflicted with the rights of an agent previously appointed, then an equitable adjustment of the matter would be made by assigning to the agent who complained such additional territory as he might specify, always provided the amount of his purchases showed him to be an active and efficient canvasser.

The scheme had been tried locally sufficient to show that there was something in it, and now it was to be applied to the whole country, and there was no time to spare. "But the man who buys can print his own recipes when he wants a new supply," I said. "No," was the answer; "he agrees not to do so." "You say in a printed slip that he so agrees, but do you wait for him to acquiesce in that, and if so how is the contract worded and what is the penalty?" "There is no contract and no penalty. Most people are honest and intend to act in good faith. It is surprising how little trouble there is on that score. There are instances of bad faith, of course, and one man got the recipe published in a local newspaper, but it did not seem to do any particular harm." "Do you file the letters you receive?" "You see the file over there in that bin." "But you could never find any particular letter there." "No, we don't try to. If a correspondent has any grievance we take his word for it and do the best we can to make him satisfied. If he says he did not get his last lot of recipes we send him some more. If he claims that somebody else is working his territory we ask him to specify a new territory that we may assign to him to make good. We do keep a record of the names and of the date and amount of transactions had with each."

I did not think the scheme would work, but the young man without being at all uncivil made it plain to me that I did not have to have an opinion on the subject. That came within his province. What he wanted me to do was to put out the advertising—and do it quick.

I went back to the hotel, had a fire built in the stove in my chilly room, took my copy of Rowell's American Newspaper Directory, edition of 1869, and with a pencil, put down an estimated price for the required service, going through the book from Maine to Texas, taking the weekly papers of largest issue. Then I secured a sufficient quantity of foolscap and copied off the names and the prices, this to be left with the advertiser, the book to be taken back to New York for use in sending out the copy and as a record of the list agreed upon. When all was done it was night, but the youthful advertiser worked evenings as well as mornings. He asked a few intelligent questions, queried a price here and there, noted the total, and in half an hour agreed to the whole; and again expressed regret that so much time had been wasted in getting started. I already had $1,800 of his money. I must receive $3,200 more, preliminary to sending out the orders, and it must be agreed that one week from that day $500 more should be sent to me, and $500 every recurring Thursday for twelve weeks; at which time the advertising would be practically completed, the amount of the order being $11,000, with a possible balance or advance to be adjusted when a final settlement was arrived at. There were no objection to the terms, but the bank was not open at night. I would wait over till morning, being pretty tired anyway. In the morning he left me at his desk while he went to the bank. He returned in less than ten minutes, with a cashier's check on Boston for $3,200, and I came away with the conviction that if the $500 weekly remittances did not come I could stop the advertising without incurring any actual loss, and a deep feeling that, however unwilling, I had been made the instrument of bringing to an inglorious end the Agents Wanted campaign of this one time dealer in berries about the military camps at Augusta. I was confident that the transaction would ruin him, and, as an advertiser, I should never hear from him any more.

We sent out the orders and the advertising began. The weekly remittances never failed to be in our office at least twenty-four hours before the day named in the agreement, and always came by express, the package always being one of those old-fashioned boxes that had contained that choice example of confectionery that the youth of New England in my time always spoke of as loz-en-gers. The remittances were sure to be in the postal currency that was at that time in vogue, varying in amount from five to fifty cents; and a torn, defaced, dirty lot of stuff it was, that we were puzzled to know what to do with, until some one suggested that the bank would take it on deposit and verify the accuracy of the count. I was very glad at that time that I was not the receiving teller at the Broadway Bank.

Well, the transaction came to an end; was closed up, and I was glad that my youthful friend at Augusta had apparently come out of it better than I had expected he would;

but I certainly did not count on his repeating the experiment. One day in the September following, however, he came into the office, looking cheerful and well dressed, and wanted to know at what price I would contract to insert an 18 line advertisement for three months in every paper in America. I had a habit, at that time, of giving a price offhand whenever a very complicated estimate was asked for, especially if it was not very likely to mean real business. I answered, promptly, six dollars a paper, and he, almost as promptly, that I might go ahead. We estimated that the total number of papers printed then counted five thousand, thus, at $6 each, the bill would amount to $30,000. He was to give me $10,000 down and $1,000 a week for twenty weeks. He gave me a draft for the advance payment and received his receipt therefor; then he asked me what discount I would allow if he would pay the other $20,000 then and there. I said five per cent. He responded that that was good enough and proceeded to give me a new draft for $19,000 more, in full settlement. I found later that for several weeks he had been making investigations through newspaper men and the other agencies, and knew so well what he had in hand that he would just as cheerfully have paid me quite a number of thousands of dollars more than I had demanded of him.

I never knew whether I made or lost money on that contract. I do know, however, that it cost more than $10,000 to settle with the papers of New York City alone. There was a little comfort in the circumstance that, in the nearly two thousand papers then printed on the co-operative plan, the cost to me would not be much more than fifty cents a paper. It was the only contract that I ever knew George Jones of the New York *Times* to accept at a cut from his rate card. I went to him, saying, "Mr. Jones, here is an advertising order with a check for $500. It is for your daily, Sunday and weekly issues. The price I get for the service is only $18 and I want you to tell Theodore, the advertising clerk, to accept the order without going into the figures." Mr. Jones looked at it a moment, said, "Mr.

Rowell, you know I don't like that sort of thing"—hesitated, shrugged his shoulders, said, "Well!" handed the order to Theodore, who stood by, and I came away.

This man, of whom I have said so much, was Mr. E. C. Allen, and he it was who founded the great system of what is called Mail-Order Journals, that has done more than any other class of publications, or any other thing that passes under his supervision, to make the Third Assistant Postmaster-General at Washington unhappy.

The law does not allow a publication to be sold at a nominal price, but Augusta issues a monthly that circulates

E. C. ALLEN.

a million and a quarter copies regularly and is sold at 25 cents a year. It does not admit as second-class matter any paper that has been established primarily for advertising purposes. Yet Augusta issues dozens that were established for that purpose and no other. It does not permit sample copies to be mailed repeatedly to the same list of names, but the Augusta publishers do that constantly. It so happens that the Congressmen from Maine, in both Senate and House, are, and have long been, men of more than average ability and influence. Augusta is the capital of the State. The prosperity of its publishing interest is something the people are proud of. Mr. Allen told me more than once that the managers of the party had suggested that he be the next Governor, but he said he was too busy. Among his successors one has been Mayor of Augusta over and over again, another has been Governor and was highly esteemed as such. I have recently read the following paragraph in a Maine paper: "Governor Hill is erecting at Augusta the finest private residence in the State. The best architects, builders and decorators are being employed in its construction and when it is completed it will certainly attract the attention of lovers of fine architecture throughout the country. At the present time the Governor and his family occupy the residence of the late James G. Blaine." Governor Hill is son-in-law of that Mr. Vickery, who was one of Mr. Allen's earliest imitators and the two comprise the firm of Vickery & Hill, of Augusta, Maine, who stand in the very front as publishers of mail-order journals.

In Mr. Blaine's time a nephew of his had a good place in the Allen business, and, on the whole, the postoffice has generally found it advisable to deal gently with infringements of what they call the law whenever they happen to originate in Augusta. And they do this the more willingly because no two postoffice officials have ever yet been found who could agree just what is and what is not permitted under the law concerning the carriage of second-class mail matter.

Incidentally, Mr. Allen may be said to have been the original cause of the ten cent magazine, for Mr. Frank A. Munsey was a Maine boy and in his youth acquired ideas from his familiar acquaintance with Mr. Allen and his methods.

In addition to his publishing and a great mail-order business in many lines, Mr. Allen issued and sold unknown quantities of lithographed pictures, chromos and steel engravings. I rarely go into houses in a remote district, whether in Florida or Alaska, without seeing the small engraving of the boatman and his living freight; the boy and girl, children in the bow, looking forward, with merry faces; the youth and maid on the next seat, looking at each other;

then the young man and his wife, sober with thought and care; and, last of all the old couple, looking backward to the shore they have left and will never see again. Mr. Allen told me at one time, before the sale was at its height, that he had already disposed of one million seven hundred and fifty thousand copies of this picture. Having the plate of a fine steel engraving he could make electrotypes of it indefinitely, preserving the original from wear, and could issue untold thousands of copies, the last just as perfect as the first one; and he could produce copies of engravings usually sold for $20 at a cost to him for paper, ink and mechanical work of no more than ten cents.

First and last he paid me, perhaps, as much as $100,-000 for advertising; but when he had his print shop under way and a catalogue of his pictures ready for distribution he had no further need of my services, because there were so many papers ready to sell him all the space he wanted, to be paid for in pictures that he could afford to let them have at bargain prices, and still get the service for less than a tenth of the cost to him that it would be to me.

He is not living now. He died while still under forty—a millionaire. He never married. His fortune went to a sister, who shortly after married the manager of the publishing business, and they left it to others more eager to make money than they had occasion to be.

Mr. Allen once told me that in deciding what picture to press for sale, and secure a run on, he did not care for the opinion of any art critic or connoisseur. His customers were the common people. He would display his drawings, on the floor, or on the walls of a great vacant room; and, from time to time, would have the young people in his employ, mainly girls, in groups of half a dozen or more, come in to look them over. He would note which ones or which particular one was most generally admired, and when he had no doubt on the point, that one, or the two or three that appeared to be favorites, would be made the leaders whether their excellence did or did not appeal to him or to the artists he employed.

TWENTY-SEVENTH PAPER

In the Spring of the year 1871 I realized several new conditions, one of which was that on the 4th of July I should be thirty-three years old. I had been in business six years, commencing with no capital, and could see that I now had assets in hand to an amount somewhat exceeding the, to my mind, magnificent sum of one hundred thousand dollars. I remembered that at the time I left the New Hampshire farm, fifteen years before, it had been my ambition to acquire a fortune of $10,000 and return and be a sort of farmer capitalist, the envy of all my neighbors. I did not then think it desirable to dress better than others, probably $25 a year would provide for that item. To my mind cowhide boots were more serviceable than those made of calfskin, and therefore more desirable. I remember particularly that I did not approve of boots being blacked, except it might be for Sunday or on the occasion of going to a party; but I thought they should be greased—possibly almost every second day. I could go back now with much more than the $10,000 originally aimed at, but it appeared that even before that sum had been put aside, one five times as great had been set up in its place, and before that second goal had been reached it had begun to appear that the limit would have to be again multiplied by at least another five before the legitimate interest on the capital would equal the scale of expenditure, already reached, for what are known as living expenses.

But there were danger signals ahead. I did not sleep. There was an unpromising flush upon the upper part of my cheeks, and an annoying cough. Work had been carried on under too much pressure. It was time to call a halt. During those six years there had scarcely been a waking moment when the thought was not on the business. In the stage or tram car, at the table, walking on the street or sitting in church, the mind was rarely engaged in consideration of any of its corporal surroundings, but was dealing with a possible form to be given to a new circular, or may be, an argument that might induce a fat contract from this patron or that. I hardly knew what went on in the world outside of the routine connected with my office. Time could not be spared to go to a railway station to meet a friend or see one depart. The office must be reached by eight o'clock, twenty minutes was time enough for luncheon and it would be six o'clock before it seemed possible to go to dinner, and it was fortunate if the evening was not devoted to completing the day's work. During those years two relatives, both dear to me, had died and, as I was not in attendance when the last obsequies were performed, I seemed hardly to take cognizance of their going or to realize that they had gone; and even now, a generation later, as I read their names and the dates of their departing engraved on a granite shaft, I seem to remember them as I had known them and to think of their stepping out as having taken place, without notice, at a moment when I happened to be thinking of something else or looking another way.

It might be that I had stamina enough to continue that sort of a life for another six years, and it was possible in that time I might accumulate money enough to make me absolutely rich in very truth; so much that it would require only a small percentage of my gains to erect a really gorgeous monument over my grave, which I should probably have caused to be prematurely opened to receive me. There was something delightful about a business success, and to one of my moderate views what I had accomplished seemed actually brilliant. Yet, to have a play hour now and then, without feeling that something was neglected; to see so much of relatives and friends as would not permit more of them to pass away before I realized that there was even danger of losing them; to take so much of recreation as would, perhaps, so quiet the nerves that sleep would come when the couch was sought at night; all these seemed on the whole to be rather worth while than otherwise, and one

day I made a resolve that I would that season take a four
months' vacation, leaving the office absolutely to be managed by my partner and the clerks and, further than that,
I would from that time forth take an equally liberal allowance of rest until I should some day find that I could no
longer afford it.

I often feel inclined to smile when I hear old men talk
of the value of age and experience. They have their value
doubtless, but to my mind the age of ability for doing things
is the early thirties. Is there not a significance in the fact
that the great work our Savior came to perform was done,
and he gone again from earth, before he had completed his
thirty-third year of sojourn in the sight of men? It is probably the reputation that men early acquire for character,
enterprise and wisdom, that pushes them into places where
they afterwards have opportunity—that was not open to
them while younger—to do great and notable things. That
the ability to do them is greater after thirty-three than it
was before that age I do not believe. Alexander died at
twenty-eight, Napoleon did no more brilliant things after
thirty-three than he had done before. At thirty-three I do
not think his good sense would have allowed the march on
Moscow. Lafayette was even under twenty when he
brought his valuable services to Washington. De Tocqueville
was not far from thirty when he wrote his great work,
"Democracy in America." Lord Byron had done his best
work before the age of thirty-three; he died before he was
thirty-eight. William Pitt was Prime Minister of England
at the age of twenty-four. Can any one doubt that if Andrew Carnegie or Pierpont Morgan were seeking a manager
of even their own great affairs they would give the prefer-
ence to one like what they themselves were thirty-five years
ago rather than to one more like what they know themselves
to be to-day? Be the fact what it may, at the age of thirty-
three I had brought about, in a business way, about all that
it was ever permitted me to accomplish. What came afterwards followed from Mr. Kent's industry and the impetus
the business had already gained. My advertising agency

was more widely known than any other had ever been, and my own name so familiar to the public that I could scarcely mention it in a shop, or write it on a hotel register, that the inquiry was not immediate, "Are you the advertising agent?" At Harrigan & Hart's variety theater, which was as well known then as Weber & Field's is now, they had a picture of the Times Building, as a background, and our enormous sign, that crossed the entire front towards Franklin Square, stared the audience in the face with a persistency that delighted every one of our clerks who had money enough to buy a ticket; and this valuable advertising never cost us a penny. It may be that I looked younger than I was, for it was a common occurrence to have people who came to see me on business seem momentarily embarrassed or annoyed, and explain that they would wait to see my father.

It is a fact that from the time the four months' vacation out of every year was inaugurated our business ceased to make material progress. Mr. Kent, my associate, was an insatiable worker, but never attempted to originate new methods. His capacity for doing work himself led to a failure on his part to raise up about him men who were so well trained as to be competent to take his place when absent for an hour or a day. He was a most discouraging man to a young assistant—he could do so much work and do it so well. I have known him to go to a correspondence clerk, talk a moment about the possibility of clearing his desk of accumulations that had been permitted, listen to an assertion that it would take till midnight, or all day tomorrow, and then seen him assign the clerk some other matter, that would perhaps require an hour or two, and when that was completed, turn over to him his entire accumulation with everything answered, every estimate made and nothing left for the young man to do until something new presented itself. It was a great quality, that capacity for work, and Kent had it to a wonderful degree. In some lines of business it might have been our salvation, but I believe he and I would be richer men to-day had it been less highly developed in him. He was a good manager, an excellent, conservative business man. Had he been able to assign to others a larger share of the actual detail work and thus allowed himself more leisure he would have had about him a better corps of assistants, and found more time to devote to his personal relations with customers and others who might from time to time be so situated as to vastly appreciate a larger share of attention at his hands. I am not criticising him, only stating a conviction—God knows our connection was ever a blessing to me. He was my partner for more than thirty years, my friend from boyhood and, though not in recent years associated with me, I never think of him without affectionate and respectful regard.

It was not a very long time after the purchase of the John Hooper Advertising Agency, and entering upon the resolve to have a four months' vacation every year, that I made an attempt to introduce, in a restricted way, the profit sharing system with employees. I owned three-fourths of the business, Mr. Kent one-fourth. There were five men in the office who were in positions where it seemed possible they might become more useful, if greater possibilities of reward were open to them. These men were George H. Pierce, the bookkeeper; John A. Moore, the solicitor of advertisements; Nelson Chesman, editor of the Newspaper Directory; Theodore P. Roberts, the estimate clerk; and Elbridge Blaisdell, at that time manager of the List System. I proposed that each should continue to draw the salary he was at the time receiving, and that whenever profits were withdrawn from the business it should be in sums of $2,000 or in multiples of that sum, and that of the profits so drawn each of these men should receive one-twentieth or five per cent, the whole to be charged up to me, thus reducing my share of the earnings from three-fourths to one-half. Kent, with characteristic fairness, requested that his share be taxed in the proper proportion, but this I did not allow. The scheme was talked over, everybody liked it and no one but myself stood to lose anything. A letter was written to each of the five setting forth the new conditions, and on the last day of the year, preceding the inauguration of the arrangement, the office paid for a sumptuous dinner, for the seven of us, at Delmonico's, then situated at the corner of Fourteenth street and Fifth avenue. Speeches were made and the future seemed full of promise.

In actual operation the plan did not work well. Moore and Chesman always had done their level best and could do no better. Pierce and Blaisdell had never been quite satisfactory, and after the change, that almost made partners of them, they seemed to take kindly to that common idea that prevails in the business world that when something is added to the salary there should be a corresponding addition to privileges allowed, as well as a considerable reduction in the hours of labor. The year that followed the arrangement was not a very profitable one. The plan was continued; but for one reason or another the participants dropped out. Blaisdell went to be advertising manager for the Humphreys' Specific Medicine Company, and was responsible for the change of their motto to "The Mild Power Cures," instead of the original "The Mild Power Subdues," and was never able to see any incongruity in the altered phrase. Chesman had an ambition to conduct an advertising agency of his own and went to St. Louis for that purpose, establishing there the firm of Rowell & Chesman, in which I was for some years associated with him. Roberts was tempted by a high salary to go with the then rather new agency of Bates & Locke; and Bates used to relate that he did first rate for a little time, till one day when he seemed to have a visit from about everybody in my office, each one of whom exhibited a new $1,000 greenback; and that always after that Roberts seemed discouraged. The explanation was that there was a $20,000 division of profits made shortly after Roberts left, whereby each of the beneficiaries under the five per cent arrangement received a thousand dollars, but Roberts, by going away, had terminated his right to participate. Finally Pierce went to Maine, to be for some years with Mr. E. C. Allen, the founder of the publishing business of Augusta; Moore died and the division of profits scheme came to an end. So far as I could see it was at no time quite satisfactory to any one who participated in it, and it cost me a good many thousand dollars, for which I received no compensation whatever.

Mr. Chesman is still living (1905), being the head of the well-known and reliable advertising agency of Nelson Chesman & Co., with branch offices in several cities; Blaisdell died a few years after going to Dr. Humphreys; Pierce at a later day returned to Boston and died in the service of J. Wesley Barber, who had been his fellow clerk in the Congress street office in 1866.

Roberts was a well-spring of information about newspapers and advertising rates. He had the whole story in his head, and was a lightning calculator. It was useless to look at a rate card if Roberts was around, for he could give the information needed much sooner than the rate card could be consulted, and he was accurate. Furthermore he knew which publishers were influenced by their rate cards and which were superior to any such implement for impairing their right to do what they chose. He wrote a handsome hand, had a fluent command of language, both in speaking and writing, and was well liked by everybody. He could secure the attention of a negligent publisher if need be. To one such, who was remiss about sending vouchers, he once closed up a long letter with the sentence: "And finally, my dear sir, permit me to say that it would be easier for a camel to ride into the Kingdom of Heaven on a velocipede than for any one to find a late copy of your paper in the City of New York."

Roberts and Pierce had both married, while in my employ, the wives being sisters, belonging to a family originally from one of the Southern States. Roberts had became rather dissatisfied with his position, and possibly had acquired the opinion that the office could not get along without him. When any man has that impression, in any position, it is time for him to control the business or to get out. If he did have the idea suggested he was not alone in it, for I am satisfied it was concurred in by quite a number of people both in and out of the office. It was on that account mainly that I was more than willing to allow him to go, and told my friend Bates that I not only would not stand in the way of his accepting the handsome salary Bates proposed to give, but that I would have no feeling against Bates for taking my best man from me. And so he went, and there was curiosity in the office and out of it to see whom we should select to fill his place.. I was well aware that there was no man alive who could fully fill it to the satisfaction of everybody, but I kept my own counsel and a few days later, when Roberts came into the office, I asked him if he would like to meet his successor. I could see by his expression, more than by his answer, that that was just exactly what he would very much like to do. I took him, therefore, to the place where his desk had stood so long, where he now saw no desk at all, but a bookcase, filled with office Directories and that sort of literature. We never did have a successor to Roberts, and notwithstanding his very valuable qualities, were almost able to say, when he had been three months away, that we did not particularly miss him. He came with me again, some years later, but did not remain many months. I always like to meet and talk with him. He is now, and has been for some years, established in Chicago, where he is recognized and has a very good standing as an advertising agent, having the placing of all or most of the advertising put out by the great mail-order house of Sears, Roebuck & Co.

TWENTY-EIGHTH PAPER

Reference has been made to village papers with the inside or outside uniform with perhaps dozens of other papers issued in towns near by or distant. Fully one-half of what are known as country weeklies now avail themselves of the economy of this method of production. The paper is bought with one side ready printed, and the fact that dozens or hundreds of other papers are presenting the same letterpress does no harm, for each paper appeals to a separate set of readers, who neither know nor care what appears in a paper in another village near by or far away. The system was first put into practical operation during the Civil War by Mr. Andrew Jackson Aikens, then as now (1905) business manager and part owner of the Milwaukee *Evening Wisconsin*. Mr. Aikens was a Vermont boy, having learned his trade as a printer in Woodstock, that most refined and charming example, that can be found in the Green Mountain State or any other, of what a New England village may be at its best. Here while yet a boy, he had known instances when a neighboring paper had overcome the difficulty of a pied form or broken press by availing itself of the facilities of its Woodstock contemporary until the home trouble was overcome. Remembering this, Mr. Aikens brought his experience into practical use one time when Wisconsin printers were leaving the case and shooting stick for the army and real shooting irons. Two papers had applied to the Wisconsin job office to be helped out, and Mr. Aikens having seen a form made up for one, out of the type then standing in the composing room that had already been used in printing the weekly edition of the *Wisconsin*, conceived that there was no real need of making any change in the matter when he set about filling the order for the other paper, the two happening to be of the same size. No complaint or protest having come in and the service being continued from week to week, Mr. Aikens caught on to the idea that more work of the same sort might be had for the job office, and he issued a circular to such Wisconsin weeklies as were situated at convenient railroad points, telling what could be done and naming a price for the service.

There would not have been very much profit in the work had not the idea occurred to Mr. Aikens that, as the papers he was serving were all issued at points tributary to Mil-

1865   1890
ANDREW JACKSON AIKENS.

waukee, if Milwaukee merchants should care to advertise in them he would be in a position to place the advertising on most favorable terms, inasmuch as all the papers were printed from the same form, and on that account the advertisement, although appearing from two dozen offices, more or less, would have to be set in type but once and that once in Mr. Aikens' own office. It was war time, trade was brisk, paper money plenty. The price Mr. Aikens demanded seemed absurdly low and he procured without difficulty cards and announcements that nearly filled a column, and these, for which he did not propose to allow the real publisher any money consideration, served to increase his profits, make him more willing to extend his service and eventually tended to cheapen the price he demanded from the papers for that service.

There was a profit in the work. One of the first to discover the possibilities of the system was Mr. Ansel N. Kellogg of Baraboo, who had had some experience with the plan on a paper he was publishing there. He moved to Chicago, took hold of the enterprise in an intelligent way, and laid the foundations for a great business and a substantial fortune. Mr. Aikens, whose idea it was that Mr. Kellogg was utilizing, was not slow to note, that if the business was to spread and acquire importance Chicago was a much better point than Milwaukee; and soon he, too, had a place of business in the larger city. Fortunately he and Mr. Kellogg had the good sense to act in unison, and nothing like a ruinous competition ever grew up between them. The actual source of profit was in the space retained for advertisements, for which the newspaper man received nothing beyond a concession on the price paid for his partly printed sheets; and now the entire country was appealed to for advertising patronage, and with success. The advertising idea was new, novel and therefore patentable, as Mr. Aikens learned at a later date. He also learned that whatever value it may have had, he had thrown it away by allowing it to be publicly used without protest.

Mr. Aikens and I had become acquainted, in a business way, and he often spoke with me about the advisability of starting the ready print scheme in New York, and I had not discouraged the idea. Finally, however, I became rather unwilling to have anything to do with it, on the ground that I did not wish to divert the money that would be needed from my already established business, which was doing very well. At that time I had dealings with one Samuel French, a printer, whose plant was situated on Park Row, where the great St. Paul Building now stands. He did such

printing as I had to be done, and issued the *Advertisers'*
Gazette for me. Mr. Aikens had some talk with him about
his plans. French had the presses and the type and would
like more work. Mr. Aikens rather laughed at the idea of
my hesitating on account of the capital required, and said if
we put in $500 apiece the earnings would take care of all
future needs. French was willing, and he could supply
office room free of charge, so we paid $1,500 into the treas-
ury, and launched the enterprise that eventually became
known as the New York Newspaper Union. Aikens was
right, no more money was needed the first year, and during
the second each of us received a dividend of $2,500.

About this time two things happened. Mr. French had
long been a sufferer from asthma. Every year he would
have to go to England, where he could breathe. While in
this city he never went to bed, but sat out his nights in an
arm chair. He was also owner of certain dramatic rights
and plays, conducting a small business in Nassau street as
a dramatic publisher. This had brought him into relations
with Thomas Lacy, the dramatic publisher of London, and
Lacy was old, and wished to sell out his business, and
French knew enough about it to make him anxious to buy.
He did buy, and a very fortunate transaction for him it
proved. But French was not rich. He needed all his resources to meet the five thousand pounds he was to pay
Lacy. Among other assets he counted his one-third share
in the New York Newspaper Union, and Aikens and I
agreed to give him $5,000 for it, each to give a six months'
note for $2,500, and each to endorse the note given by the
other. It was our idea that the business would pay the
notes and thus do away with any need of putting our hands
into our pockets to pay out any money.

French was a good deal of a speculator. At the time of
one of his visits abroad he had acquired a patent for the
manufacture of a water gas, and on his return, became interested in a chromatic press that would print a picture in
colors. He had these two enterprises on hand at about this
time and had lost fully $25,000 in experimenting with his

press; but sold his gas patent to Henry Clews & Co., at a profit of an equal sum, so those two enterprises took care of each other. What he received on the notes we gave him, and about $20,000 that he realized from the sale of his printing office, was all the money he had. He was then fully fifty years old, and was leaving his country to do practically a new business in another. Yet it turned out well, and he was always able to live in London like a capitalist. In after years the idea of the chromatic press proved of substantial value, and the patent for the water gas turned out to be of no earthly account. So impossible is it to always forecast the future. It is no uncommon thing for an old man to trace his successes to some apparent failure that he has encountered, or his ruin to a matter wherein he had supposed he had achieved the victory of his life.

Mr. French had one other curious experience. I have said he suffered from asthma. He was living then at No. 9 Park avenue, in a house afterward occupied by Whitelaw Reid when he was a bachelor. Mr. Reid understood telegraphing to some extent and had a private wire to the Tribune office. I thought it very enterprising. No one dreamed of the telephone then. While making his arrangements to move his family and household goods to London Mr. French sought a temporary lodgment in a boarding house in Thirty-second street, and from the moment he entered that house his asthma left him and staid away while he remained. Many years afterwards he came again to New York, and his old enemy immediately took possession of him. He sought the boarding house, but it had passed into other hands. In his extremity he obtained an interview with the lady then residing there, and she kindly allowed him to bring his trunks and, strange to say, he was again free from the scourge that had oppressed him, and remained free so long as he staid in that house.

The other circumstances to which I referred as happening in connection with the New York Newspaper Union enterprise, was the return to New York of Mr. William E. Cramer, Mr. Aikens' partner, from an extended tour abroad.

Mr. Cramer, who is still living (1905), was then in the early fifties, had bad eyesight and was very, very deaf. You had to talk with him through a tube, and he managed it beautifully. He could tell what you had in mind before you had spoken a quarter of the well chosen words you had intended to regale him with, and would shut you off effectively by pulling the tube out of his ear, thus reducing himself to a condition in which he could hear nothing, and then would ask a new question, the answer to which would be served the same way just as soon as he could see the direction it was going to take. I remember that he flattered me very much by pausing from time to time, looking at me as intently as his poor eyes would permit, then would tap me on the forehead with the fingers of his left hand and say, in a contemplative manner, "Good head, good head!" I recalled that subtle flattery for some years with pride and pleasure, but one day I chanced to be near him in his Milwaukee office, with an opened door between us; he was interviewing a stranger, with eyes grown still poorer, and the same old speaking tube. Finally I noted a pause, and through a crack of the door, saw the old gentleman put his left hand to the forehead of his visitor, and say in a contemplative manner, "Good head, good head!" I told Aikens of this, and he laughed and said, "Why he does that to almost everybody. He does it to me almost every time I have a talk with him." Then Aikens said—there is a touch of vanity about Aikens, I have none!—"He don't say it unless he thinks the man really has a good head." Well, while Mr. Cramer had been abroad, his income had been accumulating. He had money that sought investment. Aikens told him about our New York Newspaper Union enterprise, and the old gentleman gave me a check for $10,000 for my share of it, paid the $2,500 note and let me out, with $12,000 profit, on an enterprise in which my total investment had been but $500, and to the management of which I had never devoted so much as twenty-four hours.

There came a time after some years that I again became interested in the affairs of the New York Newspaper Union.

A brother and a son of the Mr. James H. Beals under whose immediate personal supervision I was during my seven years' service in the office of the old Boston *Post,* were in New York with eyes open for a business opportunity for the younger man, who was then conducting a newspaper enterprise in Richmond, Va., and not wholly satisfied with the outlook there. Mr. Aikens had become tired of devoting so much of his attention to a business conducted so far from his home in Milwaukee, and was willing to part with his interest. Mr. Cramer, too, would sell out to oblige. It took $50,000 to obtain the rights, and supply deficiencies ; and I subscribed for a one-fifth share. With considerable hesitation, I also bought twelve $100 shares for a near relation of my own who had recently been left a widow, with scant resources beyond a $10,000 life insurance policy which her husband had been so thoughtful as to procure. A man who had been for some years connected with the office, having begun with me working at a desk and soliciting advertising orders by mail for the lists of co-operative papers, at a weekly salary of $20, came about this time into possession of something like $10,000, and was willing to invest it in the venture. As time went on the new manager, Mr. James H. Beals, Jr., developed an unusual aptness in the conduct of affairs, placed everything upon a solid substantial basis, contented himself with paying moderate dividends to the stockholders, and went on without attracting attention from the outside world.

Not long afterwards Col. C. C. Messervey, who had long served Mr. Aikens in an editorial capacity at the office of the *Evening Wisconsin,* and had early been sent on to act as editor of the New York Newspaper Union combination of papers, was led to join with other parties and start an opposition business along the same lines. It chanced that at one time a difference arose between Col. Messervey and the younger Beals, that might have afforded possible grounds for a law suit ; but in talking the matter over, they one day arrived at an agreement to have the question in dispute decided by referees. In attempting to agree upon the referees to be chosen Col. Messervey mentioned my name, whereupon Mr. Beals told him that he would be satisfied to leave the case to my decision without calling in any other person; but asked Messervey if he was aware that I was a director and fifth owner in the company of which he, Beals, was the manager. To this the Colonel responded that he did not care about that; for, from his experience and knowledge of me, he believed I would as soon decide against myself as for myself. So it was settled and the parties came to me, stated the case from their different standpoints and I, not knowing anything about the preceding discussion of my fitness, decided that Beals was wrong. A few days later Mr. Beals told me the circumstances of my appointment, and I do not hesitate to say that I have rarely or never received a compliment that I appreciated more. Furthermore, I believe I can say, with absolute good faith, that Col. Messervey did not overrate my disposition to be fair, and that I never did decide a case in my own favor when I thought another man's rights were thereby encroached. Mr. Beals and the Colonel afterwards got along so well that they arrived at a business understanding whereby they compared notes from time to time, acted in unison in the conduct of the business, and eventually, after Col. Messervey died, Beals acquired the control of his company also; but continued it at the old stand, in the old name, and, I think, still so continues it.

It must give occasion now and then for a quiet smile when a publisher, who has long bought his supply of ready printed sheets from one of these concerns, decides that the other may give a better service or offer better terms, or when such a publisher, getting behind in his remittances, responds to a dun with a threat to take his patronage over to the opposition. Be that as it may, Mr. Beals has developed a wonderful faculty for conducting the business smoothly, satisfying everybody and keeping such close control that no opposition house has seen a way to get itself established. I parted with my stock long ago. Three-quarters of it went to the new manager, at par, because he seemed to want it. For the other $2,500 Mr. Kent afterwards gave me $13,000 and I know that I let him have it too cheap. The lady for whom I, with so much hesitation, invested a small sum in this enterprise has not failed any year during the past twenty to get as much as $1,000 annually, in the way of dividends on the original outlay of $1,200, and the gentleman of whom I have spoken, who put in $10,000, gave up a clerical position a few years later, where he had been earning a modest $2,000 a year, and, being a man of quiet tastes and no family but a wife, has lived ever since in a style of simple elegance and quite unconsciously, I think, has impressed most of those who come in contact with him socially, or upon his travels, that he is a millionaire at the very least.

Mr. Kellogg early developed a habit of saying, or thinking, that the class of papers that bought their ready prints of him, were in some vague way better than those that bought of Mr. Aikens or of any other of the numerous companies that sprang up. He gave a certain glamour of reality to his claim, by being specially careful about the style and quality of the printed matter he issued for the purpose of inviting and influencing advertising patronage. Since his death his representatives have kept up and even intensified this feature. As a matter of fact I do not suppose there is any material difference in the average quality of the papers, or see how there very well can be. Every company engaged in the business takes on every paper that applies. The editions are rarely less than four quires, or one hundred copies, and sometimes run to many thousands. The papers, however, are nearly all of the sort having "JKL" circulation ratings in Rowell's American Newspaper Directory; that is, not claiming to issue so many as 1,000 copies. The largest circulations will generally be found in locations where populations are most dense. Little villages everywhere are ambitious to have a local paper. In thinly settled counties there is a considerable amount of legal advertising sure to go to the first paper established therein. If a young man has learned to set type, and has saved a hundred dollars, he can get trusted for a press and small outfit, order a hundred copies of paper—printed on one side—and next week, behold there is a new newspaper born, a new job office established; and who shall say that both will not grow and eventually make the fortune of the enterprising founder. Within the past half century, or a little more, a compositor of this sort came out of Poughkeepsie and established a paper in Brooklyn that he called the *Eagle,* and that paper lives to-day and earns for its stockholders a net profit of not much if any less than a thousand dollars a day for all the seven days of every week.

As these so-called co-operative papers increased in number they have aroused, first and last, all manner of opposition; and the publishers who have used them have been subject to much opprobrium. Once the Postoffice authorities were invoked to declare that such sheets were not newspapers. "If not newspapers," said Senator Matt Carpenter of Wisconsin, who appeared for Mr. Aikens and his partners before the Congressional Committee on Postoffices, "What t'ell are they?" And the question was too hard for the opposition to answer. It was contended, however, that the law required a paper to be mailed where it was published, and these papers, half printed in one place and completed in another, were not really published anywhere; but too many country editors had control of little papers of the sort objected to for the Postoffice people to be willing to incur their ill will. Newspaper conventions resolved against the "patent insides," but sometimes it was found that a majority of those present were either victims to the habit or thinking of taking it on.

In the beginning only the insides of the papers were printed, but as the presswork was much better than could be turned out in the local offices, there soon arose a demand for "patent outsides" and this was met, and proved so great a hit that pretty soon it was outsides and not insides that were generally demanded. To the argument that no self-respecting publisher would allow an outsider to edit his paper for him, without showing in advance what matter was to go in, it was easy to answer that almost every publisher, who was not himself the editor, did trust some one to that extent. To the claim that the system produced inferior papers it was easy to obtain testimonials from readers that the paper under the new method was better than it had been previously. To the assertion that only poor papers adopted the plan, it was possible to induce the libeller to name the best paper in half a dozen towns and then confound him by showing that a majority of those he had named had already adopted the plan he objected to.

The plan has made such progress that more than half the local village and country town papers have adopted it. Advertisers contract, at a central office, for combinations numbering fifty to five hundred or several thousands. The total number printed on the plan to-day exceeds eight thousand. One electrotype answers for the job, one man takes pay for the whole. The price per paper charged for advertising is so small that no individual paper, no matter how insignificant, cares to attempt to compete with it. Many advertisers assert that advertising in them does not pay; and many others declare that the local paper is, par excellence, the best advertising medium in the world. Probably the country weekly cannot nowadays compete, in value and economy of service, with the greatest daily papers and the best magazines, but the man who would use the county papers at all makes a decided mistake if he does not use the Co-operative Lists first, as far as they go.

Mr. Aikens is still living (1905), being about seventy-six years of age. A more unselfish man never drew breath. I am indebted to him for numerous enjoyable experiences. He has shown me how to take the small-mouthed black bass off Sugar Loaf at Green Lake, Wisconsin, to shoot red head, blue bill, teal and canvas-back from a blind in Lake Puckaway near by, and chickens on the prairies of Iowa, and snipe and plover now and then, and I should not be quite fair if I omitted to mention squirrels, gray, fox and black—that perhaps afforded more pleasure than rapid flying birds, because they would wait and give another chance if I missed the first time—as I often did. We are both too old to go hunting any more, but a little contemplative trout or bass fishing may be held in reserve for us even yet. *Quien sabe.* Mr. William E. Cramer is also living, being now in his eighty-eighth year. The co-operative interests of the house have, in more recent years, been under the management of Mr. John F. Cramer—a nephew of William E.—who is still a very young man. I remember very well the first time he ever came into my office—a very young man indeed, with black hair, bright eyes, handsome face and figure, well dressed and amiable. He wore a gold watch chain with a peculiar globular ornament that I so much admired that I had a chain made as much like John's as possible, and gave it to Kent for a birthday present or to mark some other auspicious occasion. That was only thirty-eight years ago, and John is just as old now as he was then, and not a day older; and he is about the only man I ever see of late years who tells me a new story—one that I have not heard before. It is not probable that I could name any newspaper office, other than the *Evening Wisconsin,* where three proprietors, now living, were the three proprietors when I began business in 1865, and have been the proprietors all the intermediate time with no other partners in the interval.*

Mr. Kellogg died several years ago. He was never of a robust habit, and was very frail for some years before he passed away. He was quite deaf, but an excellent business man, not deficient in a sense of humor; and I well remember a gleam in his eye when he at one time told me he was thinking of buying a saddle horse—the doctor had recommended out-of-door exercise, and some one had assured him that "the outside of a horse was good for the inside of a man." He also saw a covert reference to the business to which his life was devoted in the paragraph—sold by a joke-smith—that quoted a Kentucky editor as printing on his first page the sentence: "For the evil effects of intemperance see our inside." If I had had as much faith in Mr.

* Since this paragraph was written Mr. William E. Cramer has passed over to the majority, leaving a fragrant memory of a life abounding in wise foresight and kindly acts.

Aikens' ideas of the possibilities of his plan for co-operative printing that he had and events have justified, we would both of us have been millionaires years ago—and may be not half as useful citizens as we are to-day.

TWENTY-NINTH PAPER

Early in the year 1876 there came a personal letter from Gen. Joseph R. Hawley, afterwards for many years United States Senator from Connecticut, who was President of the Philadelphia Centennial Commission, as well as an owner, in whole or in part, of the Hartford *Courant;* suggesting the advisability of attempting a newspaper exhibition on the Centennial grounds. It would require a good deal of space, and consideration of the subject led to the conclusion that a separate building would be requisite. For such a structure, in a favorable situation by the shore of the pretty artificial lake that beautified the grounds, a concession was granted, and we undertook to make the exhibition. The plan contemplated a space or pigeon hole for each separate publication, with ample room for attendants and visitors, desks for newspaper correspondents and others, retiring rooms for tired sightseers, chairs, lounges, a plentiful supply of stationery, and whatever else appeared requisite to make the place attractive and comfortable. An architect was engaged to prepare plans and specifications for a building covering 46 feet by 67 of ground space; the main floor being all in one room, arranged with spaces on both sides for the disposal of the papers and the accommodation of attendants. In the center great tables were in position whereon might be displayed files of leading dailies, making them readily accessible for all comers. The central portion of the structure was open to the roof, producing an airy effect very desirable in the hot summer months during which the exhibition would be held. There were wide galleries around the four sides, approached by flights of stairs in the corners; and these galleries furnished well-lighted and well-ventilated space for a considerable number of desks, for the free use of newspaper correspondents and others. There were also several small retiring rooms which, with toilet conveniences near at hand, proved grateful retreats for tired women sightseers on many occasions.

I had in my employ at this time a man whom I had first known as an advertiser. He owned or controlled a proprietary medicine, in the advertising of which a certain caution had been introduced that appeared in practice to bring about results quite the opposite of what purported to be aimed at. The conclusion that his advertisements must be withdrawn, and not renewed, had been finally arrived at; and the advertising was the principal detail of business that occupied his time, because a proprietary article, made always after a fixed formula, and put up in a manner that has become established by usage, falls naturally under the management of assistants that are not necessarily of a highly paid class, and the matter of sales is still more simple, on account of the distribution being entirely through jobbers, who buy only what they require to supply the trade and expect to pay for their purchases exactly in accordance with the terms of a price list. For these reasons, a proprietary article that is no longer pushed into prominence, and is being milked for all the profit there may remain in it, requires little attention beyond taking charge of the cash that comes in. This man, therefore, surprised me one day by appearing at my office and saying, "I want you to make a place for me, if you can. I am without very much experience in the details of ordinary business and I want to learn and I want occupation; I will try to do a man's work, but expect to begin with a boy's pay, for I can manage to live as I do at present, even if I have no salary." I had taken him at his word, set him at work doing those things that usually are assigned to the youngest members of the office force. He proved to be something of a treasure, was always on hand during office hours, never made any complaints or offered any excuses, was more careful than any other person I ever knew to do things always in the exact way it was understood that they should be done; was so reliable and dependable that he gradually rose from one position to another, and was eventually admitted to a partnership, with the approval and by the advice of Mr. Kent, acquiring a one-sixth interest, Mr. Kent's proportion being at the time increased to one-third.

This man, Mr. Oscar G. Moses, was associated with me until his death in 1900. He was not a Hebrew, although on account of his name I, for a good many years, supposed him to be one. I have no race prejudices, but one day, speaking of the matter with him, I mentioned that I supposed, of course, he was a Jew; and he thereupon assured me that Jews were never farmers, and his ancestors had been agriculturists in Connecticut since the original conquest of that territory from the Pequots. Mr. Moses married a Miss Lee. When they had a son, in the attempt to compliment both father and mother, they called him Oscar Lee, and as the father was familiarly spoken to as Oscar it came about that the boy was addressed as Lee, and wrote his name O. Lee Moses. When he became a man and had a seat on one of the Stock Exchanges and a transaction was announced in the name of O. Lee Moses, his brother brokers would almost worry the life out of him by shouting out in chorus, "Holy Moses!" A gentleman whom they met at a summer resort and whose most conspicuous feature was a thin specimen of the Roman variety, once said to Lee's mother, "Madame, with your name and my nose, what a business we could do in Chatham street." It was to Mr. Moses that the duty and responsibility of conducting the newspaper exhibition on the Centennial grounds in Philadelphia were committed. He went there with half a dozen assistants, some taken from the home office and others selected from among local applicants, and very faithfully he attended to it all. Every day I would receive a long letter from him, telling me what he proposed to do next, how he would do it, and the reason for doing it, and he would await approval before proceeding. His plans were always well considered and his reasons excellent. I do not recall that I ever saw occasion to criticise one of them, but his excessive caution made delays. I finally instructed him to submit no more plans for approval, but to go ahead and manage everything as he thought best and write me daily, not what he wished to do, but what he actually had done. This worked first rate and there arose no occasion at any time to regret the trust I had placed in him.

The newspapers responded with commendable alacrity to the request that a six months subscription for a copy of each edition issued should be contributed to the enterprise; and I do not recall that there was a single refusal to comply with the suggestion, although there were not wanting examples among publishers of men who did not particularly like our firm, because they had, or thought they had, a grievance against us on the point of some under-statement of their circulation in the Newspaper Directory we published or, what was just about as bad—possibly worse—the over-statement of the issues of a competitor.

Just what is meant by circulation and how it should be ascertained, measured and expressed, is not fully understood and agreed upon even at this day, and in 1876 the views on the subject were not anything like being so well settled as they are now. The small paper, printed on a hand press, knew how many quires were generally wet down. If the supply was purchased from one of the ready print houses, both parties knew, of course, how many quires the weekly package contained, but even then they had difficulty in understanding that four quires counted only ninety-six sheets and ninety-six did not make a hundred; and failed equally to understand that a ream of four hundred and eighty sheets did not produce five hundred papers. In neither case was any allowance thought of for spoiled copies, and much less of such as remained unsold. The daily paper generally thought of its circulation as properly measured by the edition pulled off on some recent, or not very recent, occasion, when there had been a special edition printed that counted more copies than had ever been issued before. "What is the circulation?" was, however, even then beginning to be a vital question, and any under-estimate made in a directory was resented with considerable more energy and emphasis than it is at the present time.

The number of papers printed in the United States in the year 1876, as shown by the Directory of that year, was eight thousand one hundred and twenty-nine. Of course, some new ones were started after the Directory appeared and a smaller number of those already established would die. The Directory had to be the basis for the arrangement of the papers for exhibition purposes, but it was too bulky, and too expensive, to serve for a catalogue; consequently a smaller volume was prepared—bound in paper covers—that enumerated the 8,129 papers, and designated each by a number that corresponded to that borne by the pigeon hole where the copies would be kept for ready accessibility when called for. Of course, the Alabama papers were designated by the small figures, beginning with number one, and those of Vermont, Virginia and so on would have the higher figures.

One day a Rhode Island publisher, who was proud of having a circulation of exceeding 8,000 copies, came into possession of one of our catalogues in which his paper was designated as number 7,777, or something like that, and expended a rather liberal sum in telegraphing to our firm, denouncing the error as an outrage, and letting it be known in pretty plain language just what we might expect to have done to us if the injury was not rectified at once and a handsome apology, given as wide publicity as the preceding defamatory under-statement had received. A carefully written letter explained the matter fully, but, I believe, that publisher continued, to his dying day, to think we had injured him.

I once heard of a man who, discussing a name on the visiting list, said to his wife, "You know perfectly well that I don't like that man." "Don't you think you are a little unreasonable?" asked the wife. "Your dislike arose because he did not answer a letter you wrote him, and you found afterwards that the letter was hung up all summer in the pocket of your overcoat, and was never sent to him at all." "Yes, I know that," was the rejoinder, "but it was so long before I found it out that I couldn't overlook his rudeness, and I never forgave him, and I don't believe I ever shall." There is a good deal of ill feeling in this world that is without any firmer foundation.

A dozen of more prominent papers favored our enterprise by a liberal advertising patronage, bestowed upon our exhibition catalogue; but on the whole, the papers of the country were not wholly pleased with the prominence we seemed likely to secure by means of the exhibition we were making, and it came about that the most liberal and appreciative notice that our enterprise received from any quarter, was given, in its largest type and on a conspicuous page, in the London *Times.* I took pains to secure a copy, had the page framed and it hung in my office at No. 10 Spruce street for nearly thirty years, occupying a position so elevated that no one could read the print without bringing into requisition the services of a stepladder. Of late, since *Printers' Ink* has severed its relations with the Advertising Agency, and not only moved into separate quarters of its own but dropped my name as proprietor, Mr. Editor and Publisher Zingg has appropriated the valued *Times* souvenir and given it a place in *his* office, where it still hangs so high that nobody can read its commendatory words without the aid of the stepladder, as in former years. If there are any who would like to know what the *Times* really said, they may read it here without climbing up on anything:

THE "TIMES," JULY 25, 1876.

AMERICAN JOURNALISM.

(From Our Special Correspondent.)

Philadelphia, July 10.

I have frequently had occasion to notice the big way in which the Americans do things, and I do not know that it would be easy to find an apter illustration of it than that furnished by the "Centennial Newspaper Building," in the Exhibition grounds. Here you may see any one or, if you like, all of the "8,129 newspapers published regularly in the United States." In England a man thinks it cheap if he is given his choice of a few score of newspapers for a penny, and as our penny is here practically represented, as a rule, by a five-cent or even a ten-cent piece (the smallest shoeblack, for instance, expects ten cents (5d.) for "shining" your boots), a man could scarcely grumble if asked, say a quarter-dollar, or one shilling, for the run of 8,000 papers. Need it be said that in the Centennial Building he can see them, one and all, for nothing? He is not only permitted as a favor to see them, but he is invited, nay pressed, to confer the favor of entering the building and calling for what paper he likes. As he passes the entrance his eye is caught by some such kindly and courteous invitation as "Come in and see a paper from your home." "Write your name in the register, give your card to the superintendent, and make yourself at home." The home into which he is thus cordially welcomed is, moreover, a very pleasant one. Without any pretensions to imposing architectural effect, it is simple, elegant and neat. Its length is 67 feet, its width 46 feet, its height 33 ft. It is admirably lighted and ventilated by long rows of windows and a large lantern roof. Open on all sides, it catches every breath of air that ventures in this weather to stir out, and on one side the air is cooled by passing over the lake, on the border of which the building is pleasantly situated. It is, in fact, altogether about as cool and agreeable a place—quite apart from its literary attractions—as a visitor to the exhibition could wish to be offered a chair in. He may at first wonder how, among 8,000 papers, among them such mighty sheets as the New York *Herald,* he is to get at the small, loved print of his home, thousands of miles away, it may be, over the Rocky Mountains. But the management is so simple that, by consulting the catalogue, or even without the aid of the catalogue, any one can find whatever paper he wants. They are pigeon-holed on shelves in the alphabetical order of their States or Territories and their towns, the names of which are clearly labeled on the shelves. Thus the newspapers of Abbeville, in Alabama, would be found on the first shelf, and those of Laramie City, in Wyoming, on the last. But anybody in difficulties has only to apply to one of the eight superintendents who, all "pineapples of politeness," are ready to execute his orders as if they bodily belonged to him. If he would like to take notes or write, he has, in two galleries, which run round the upper part of the building, his choice of some thirty desks, with pen, ink, and paper, all provided, of course, gratis; or, if he has ladies with him, or friends with whom he wants a perfectly private chat, there are at his disposal two or three private rooms comfortably fitted up. The visitor is, in fact, so spoilt that before he has been in the building five minutes he begins to feel himself injured because he cannot order at the usual prices of the establishment an iced "cocktail" and a bath.

It will not, I hope, detract from the merits of this pleasant home and refuge for the warm and wearied readers of newspapers to mention that it is an advertisement, since no attempt is made to disguise the fact. It is a fact which, however harmless in itself, is in America too often mixed up with lofty professions and motives, the juxtaposition with which makes it ludicrous, to say nothing worse. No subject seems to be considered too sacred or too sublime to be used as a stalking-horse by some enterprising advertiser. Even the original MS. of the Declaration of Independence, the Magna Charta of every American—above all, every Philadelphian—is exhibited in a patent safe—of course presented gratis—over which the names of the makers are so blazoned that they quite throw into the shade the modest signatures of Franklin and Jefferson; and in the exhibition a fountain with a cross, on which is written, "Ho, every one that thirsteth," supplies water—of course gratis—to all comers, but also supplies the name of the quarries from which the granite came. But the proprietors of the Centennial Newspaper Building are, avowedly, advertising agents, the largest, I believe, in all America—Messrs. G. P. Rowell & Co., of New York. Their enterprise will cost altogether about $20,000 or £4,000, including the building and the expenses of "running" it for six months. How much comes out of their pockets I cannot say, as they have been largely subsidized by some of the leading American papers. But they have the management of the enterprise, and will naturally get the lion's share of the glory. It will certainly make their names known all over America, in corners which it may never have reached before. For the Americans are newspaper readers to a man—almost to a child—nor, indeed, does one need to be an American to appreciate the opportunity of resting in a comfortable room, in order to read the latest news from one's home. I have seen quite young children in the building reading their papers as steadily and attentively as any of the adult voters around them.

At first the newspaper exhibition did not receive very much attention from the public; there was so much to see and the newspaper building bore no sign to indicate its character. Finally two great posters were prepared and placed one on each side of the broad entrance door, proclaiming in mammoth letters the invitation, "Come in and see a paper from home." These were effective. It was often amusing when a group of people, young and old, hailing from a remote region, would be led to ask for the little sheet printed at their county seat or nearest village, and to note the surprise and delight that would mantle the countenances of everyone when the paper was found to be actually forthcoming, could be taken in hand, read at the great table or even carried to one of the private rooms, and it was learned that for all this there was absolutely nothing to pay. The exhibition entailed a cost of not far from $20,000. As an advertisement, so far as we could see, it was a flat failure. I was never able to trace a single advertising contract as having been influenced by it; still the influences of advertising are indirect, often concealed, although very real. Notwithstanding the fact that I traced no order to the influence of this enterprise, it is a significant circumstance, that after paying all outgoes for that year the net earnings of the office were larger than for any other of the decade between 1871 and 1881, of which 1876 was the central period.

I had positive knowledge that the exhibition made some talk at distant points, for I was riding on a cross country railroad, in northern Iowa, in the chicken shooting season, of that Centennial year, and two countrymen occupied the seat in front of me. It was in the dusk of early evening, nothing to see inside the car, nothing to note on the prairies outside. My ear was attracted by the sound of my own name. One of the two men was returning from a visit to the Centennial Exhibition at Philadelphia, and was regaling his friend with an account of what he had seen; and at the moment was dealing with the wonders of my own exhibition. "There was a sign out," he related, "that said 'Come in and see a paper from home.' Every paper printed in the United States was there and almost everybody was there looking at them. It was a big building put up by Rowell & Son of New York. They do an immense business"—and so on and so on. I could not hear the whole but was greatly pleased that I had chanced upon what did come to my ear. The immensity of our business might be in part in the imagination of the narrator and the "Son" mentioned as a member of the firm has never materialized.

It was at the Centennial Exhibition that I first saw John Wanamaker, then a prominent clothing dealer in Philadelphia, under forty years of age, and conspicuous in the work of the Young Men's Christian Association and other good influences. Since then he has become the greatest retail merchant and the best newspaper advertiser that the world has ever produced.

One day when I visited our exhibition building the manager told me that a frequent visitor to the place looked so much like me that he had taken pains to find out where he came from and was anxious to have me see him. He took me over to the Arkansas State Building, where he had ascertained that the man was employed; and as I knew Dr. Lawrence, the Commissioner, I ventured to ask to be introduced to the man. He was of my own age—about thirty-eight—had my complexion, hair, height and weight, and wore a moustache and goatee as I did then. Dr. Lawrence

took a new look at me, said the resemblance was marked
and then added, "And his name is Rowell, too." The man
was called into the private office. He did not seem to take
any particular interest in me, or in resemblance in name or
person; had never heard of me; knew about the newspaper
exhibition building, but did not know whose exhibition it
was; had no acquaintance in New England, or the East;
and was born—in the Sandwich Islands. And that was all
I learned, but he was undeniably a white man, and a blonde.
Such are not indigenous to the Sandwich Islands; but I
did not solve the riddle. Within comparatively recent years
I have read of the death in those Islands of an old missionary by the name of Rowell who, it was related, had gone
there in the early days, having originally lived in New
Hampshire, where my own great-grandfather resided. I
possess a list of something more than seven hundred descendants of my respected progenitor just referred to, but
the missionary is not among them. Perhaps if I could
ascend the ancestral tree one other step I might discover
that there really was a kinship between me and the Arkan-
sas-Kanaka who seemed to be my double.*

I took pains to save three sets of sample copies of the
papers printed in that Centennial year. They were rather
hard to arrange with any system, and it was something of
a question what to do with them after they had been col-

---

*A letter from Honolulu dated August 8th, 1905, says: "I am writing you
thinking that you will be interested to hear that Mr. W. E. Rowell, your 'Arkansas Kanaka', is still living. He remembers you distinctly and recalls the
conversation he had with you at the Centennial Exhibition in Philadelphia. He
has, in his opinion, traced a distant relationship between you and himself."

Application to the family historian, Mr. Roland Rowell of Manchester, N.
H., reveals the fact that W. E. and G. P. Rowell are each seven generations
from one Valentine Rowell, who was a son of Thomas, the original English emigrant, the progenitor of the American branch of the family:

Wm. E. Rowell 9	George P. Rowell 9
George B. 8	Samuel 8
Joseph 7	Samuel 7
William 6	Samuel 6
William 5	John 5
Valentine 4	John 4
Thomas 3	Philip 3
Valentine 2	Valentine 2
Thomas 1	Thomas 1

lected and boxed up; but before the exhibition ended we were approached by two purchasers, and one set was understood to have been bought for the great Vatican collection, and a second went to Tasmania; just what they wanted of it there I cannot imagine. The third set, the most complete, I retained for some years, but it was so bulky, filled so many boxes that were always so much in the way, that I often wished somebody would steal the whole collection. That could hardly be done, however, because there was so much of it, it was so heavy and so unmanageable. I was speaking of this incubus one day to Mr. Ainsworth R. Spofford, so long in charge of the Congressional Library at Washington, and he assured me the Government would be glad to accept the collection as a donation. I took great pleasure in shipping the papers over to him, just as soon as I got back to New York. This was before the new library building was constructed. I often wonder what was done with the assortment. It is undoubtedly valuable, and will grow more so as years pass, but how to arrange them in any way so that any specific one could be referred to as wanted, was something that I could never determine. It is a complete set, containing one copy of every newspaper and periodical published regularly in the United States of America throughout the year 1876. If one should think of binding so many thousands of periodicals, one large like the *Iron Age* and another of liliputian dimensions like the *Philistine,* he would find it more difficult than the traditional Chinese puzzle, said to have mystified the omnipotent Philadelphia lawyer. A hundred years earlier the task would have been comparatively simple; for one of the souvenirs of the newspaper exhibition, given to all who would take it, was a complete American Newspaper Directory for the year 1776, cataloguing a total of thirty-seven papers.

On one occasion, during the Centennial Exhibition, I was spending a night at the Continental Hotel. My partner, Mr. Kent, was there, too, and also Mr. S. M. Pettengill. We dined together, and there was a suggestion made that we visit some place of amusement, I think it was mine, and that I offered to supply the tickets. A question arising as to which theater we would patronize I recalled to mind a certain rather lively variety show something on the order familiar to New Yorkers who frequented the place in Thirty-fourth street, so long kept by Messrs. Koster & Bial. Mr. Pettengill always had a sanctimonious countenance, and I did not know much about his taste in theatrical matters, so I said to him, "I know a place I would visit, but I would not be willing to have it said that I took you there. I'll show you where it is, and if you feel like buying the tickets I think Kent will go with you and I know I will." I hardly expected Kent to fully appprove of the place, but it would do no harm to try it on him. The plan was adopted. Pettengill bought the tickets. The show was broader than I had expected, and I tried to get the two to come away before the last act, and thereby avoid the crush coming out, but, being there—and never likely to come again—they seemed inclined to see it through. Neither one said much about the performance, and I was rather sorry on the whole that I had taken them there, but soon forgot all about it. A month later, however, Kent was at the Continental and detained over night again, and to pass the evening thought for once he would be real devilish and go to the same variety show. He told me about it on his return, how he went alone, bought his ticket, entered the place, took his seat, and who should he find, in the very next seat to his, but Mr. Pettengill. He also had gone alone.

THIRTIETH PAPER

It was sometime during the year 1878, not very long after the removal of our office from the Times Building, into quarters of our own at No. 10 Spruce street, where we have ever since remained, that I for some reason thought it advisable to issue a small pamphlet wherein was set forth my view of the principles and conditions under which the business in which we were engaged existed and was conducted. I have recently come across a copy of that leaflet, and although it is not likely to possess any thrilling interest for anybody, yet as it doubtless is a more painstaking, thoughtful and thorough effort to deal with the subject than has been attempted by any other person it may as such be deserving of space among these papers.

The title page bears the words, suitably displayed, as follows:

AN ADVERTISING AGENCY.

A STATEMENT INTENDED TO MAKE PLAIN THE NATURE AND METHODS OF THE BUSINESS, AND THE CHANGES NECESSITATED BY THE LAPSE OF TIME AND OTHER CIRCUMSTANCES.

The position in the business occupied by our firm at that time was doubtless stated with clearness and accuracy in a short editorial that appeared in the issue of the New York *Times* for June 14, 1875, which is here reproduced:

Ten years ago Messrs. Geo. P. Rowell & Co. established their advertising agency in New York City. Five years ago they absorbed the business conducted by Mr. John Hooper, who was the first to go into this kind of enterprise. Now they have the satisfaction of controlling the most extensive and complete advertising connection which has ever been secured, one which would be hardly possible in any other country but this. They have succeeded in working down a complex business into so thoroughly a systematic method that no change in the newspaper system of America can escape notice, while the widest information upon all topics interesting to advertisers is placed readily at the disposal of the public.

The letterpress of the leaflet is reproduced below. It is set in smaller type as a notification to the reader that it tells nothing new, and may be safely skipped by all save those who would care to know what was my idea, thirty years ago, of what an up-to-date advertising agency ought to be:

The business of conducting an establishment such as ours for the reception of Advertisements for Newspapers, is of comparatively recent origin, and the principles upon which it should be conducted are not as fully settled or understood as in other and older lines.

Newspaper Advertising Agents were originally authorized to make rates for the papers, and the prices fixed by them were understood to be binding upon the Publisher represented.

The Agent arranged witl publishers for authority to represent them, and the commission to be allowed was a matter of bargain, but, by usage, came to be fixed at an established percentage.

As Newspapers increased, the Agencies assumed to represent the new ones without previous agreement, and this arrangement was satisfactory to the Publishers.

The public appreciated the convenience of these Agencies, and they increased in number. Clerks in existing agencies, observing the methods upon which the business was conducted, established new Agencies of their own and assumed an authority equal to that claimed and enjoyed by their former employers.

Other persons without previous training or experience, established themselves in the business and assumed the rights and privileges which custom had authorized.

In the early days, the Agent assumed no responsibility. He paid over money to Publishers after he had collected it. If he never collected, he never paid.

Observing a tendency toward abuses, an Agent desirous of ingratiating himself with the proprietors of the Newspapers which he represented, set up the principle that the commission should cover a guarantee of payment.

This rule was, as a matter of course, popular with the Publishers, and finally became the usage.

In dealing with an Advertiser, the Agent furnished a list of papers and the prices which should be paid to each for the advertisement.

The multiplication of agencies brought about a competition which resulted in such reduction of rates that the Publishers were sometimes compelled, for self-protection, to repudiate contracts.

This action becoming more common, Agents were led into the practice of promising to the Advertiser that the prices named should be accepted. Consequently, in cases where the Publisher insisted upon an advance, the Agent's profit would be, to that extent, reduced.

For the purpose of creating a fund to meet such contingencies, without trenching upon the commission, a practice grew up, among the Agencies, of offering to each paper a lower gross price than that at which the Advertiser had bargained.

The surplus thus created was sometimes more than was needed, and the excess formed an additional profit for the Agent, beyond his commission.

It is easy to perceive how strong the temptation became to make the profit as large as possible. The principle of getting from the Advertiser all he could be induced to pay, and offering to the Publisher as little as he would consent to accept, became established. A merciless cutting of rates to the papers was the result, until Publishers were forced to repudiate any right on the part of an Advertising Agent to fix prices which should be binding upon them.

During the busy times of our civil war there came into existence a class of Agencies which undertook to secure advertising patronage at the best prices to be obtained, and promised to pay papers whatever they demanded—often largely in excess of the amount received—the result being the final bankruptcy of the Agency conducting its business in this manner.

We have shown that the Advertising Agencies were appreciated as a convenience to the public. To such an extent has this been true, that those which have been conducted under judicious management and whose dealings have been equitable, have reaped fair rewards for their labor; but it has become apparent that, whatever may have been the relation when Agencies were first established, at the present time they do not represent the newspaper in the way in which an agent is generally understood to represent a principal. The Advertising Agent is sufficiently authorized to accept advertisements for a newspaper at the Publisher's schedule price, but his experience teaches him that on any but small orders the advertiser must get rates below the schedule rates, or the cost of his advertising will more than absorb the profits of the business advertised. It is of importance to the Agent that the investment of his advertising customers shall be a remunerative one. If the advertiser is induced to trust $5,000 to be expended, and the investment brings a return of no more than $2,500, he is not likely to repeat the experiment; while, if the Agent secures for the money so much publicity that the result is a return of $10,000, leaving an excess of $5,000 above the cost of the advertising, then the advertiser is in good spirits and likely to consider a proposal to make a new venture, possibly risking many times as much as on the former occasion. But when the advertisement comes to be offered to the Publisher at a price below his schedule rate, he claims the right to reject it. He does not admit that any action of the Agent can bind him; and the arrangement for the advertisement, whether it shall or shall not appear, becomes a matter to be adjusted between the Publisher and the Agent precisely as between two principals, except that it is tolerably well understood that, upon the price finally fixed, the Agent will be allowed the usual commission.

The system upon which Advertising Agencies used to be conducted (and still are by some establishments) led to extensive canvassing for patronage. Advertisers were besought to allow the applicant to put in a bid or estimate.

It came to be the practice of persons who were in the habit of spending considerable sums for advertising, to prepare specifications, and submit them to all of the known advertising agencies, with a promise of awarding the contract to the lowest bidder. As the system became understood by publishers, they were not slow to perceive that the successful bidder had allowed himself to become so bound by the stipulations of his contract with the advertiser, that if he (the publisher) stood firmly for an excessive price, the agents would be obliged to acquiesce in his terms.

Forty Years an Advertising Agent

It is probable that few agents were ever held strictly to the literal promises of such contracts, but, on the whole, they were carried out substantially as made. New, inexperienced and irresponsible men solicited the privilege of submitting estimates, and in some cases without any previous acquaintance with publishers, contracted to insert advertisements in papers they had never seen, at prices which an agent having experience would regard as impossible; losses were the result, but not having capital to begin with the agent did not lose, and by obtaining credit from the publishers and ceasing to deal with such as declined to trust, he sometimes remained in business for years, failing completely at last and then abandoning the business.

The publishers of the country submitted to a series of losses until the grievance became very great. It is not now so easy for persons to obtain credit as advertising agents without possessing some basis of financial responsibility.

Our Newspaper Advertising Bureau, No. 10 Spruce St., New York, is an establishment intended to facilitate the convenient and systematic placing of advertisements in newspapers. It is conducted upon the principles which we conceive to be the right ones for securing the best results to the advertiser, the publisher, and ourselves.

We undertake to represent American newspapers—not only the newspapers of the city of New York and of all other American cities, Religious, Agricultural, and other class newspapers—but also the small country journals. We receive regularly and keep on file the newspapers of every description throughout the land, whether issued daily, weekly, or monthly.

We confine our transactions to newspapers, and do not accept or undertake the management of other classes of advertising, such as books, signboards, posters, or job printing.

It is our hope that by adhering to one branch of advertising we may make ourselves master of it.

We also restrict our dealings to newspapers published within the geographical limits of the United States and Dominion of Canada, with the single exception of allowing our name to appear as agents in New York for the *Levant Herald,* published at Constantinople.

We have a system of filing newspapers by an arrangement of shelving and partitions, separate space being accorded to each, and labeled with the printed name of the paper it is intended to accommodate, by means of which arrangement a stranger can find any paper he wishes to examine with something like the readiness with which he would a word in a dictionary, a name in a directory, or a book in a literary catalogue.

Our firm undertakes to maintain an established credit with every newspaper office, and to have at hand a schedule of charges adopted by the publisher of each for advertising space in its columns; to be able to quote those rates to an advertiser who wishes to insert an advertisement in one or several, and to procure the prompt insertion of the advertisement without any extra charge for the service rendered; which service consists of quoting the price, printing or writing as many duplicates of the advertisement as may be required to furnish one to each paper to be used; forwarding the copy for insertion at our own expense for postage or messenger service; examining the papers to see that the advertisement appears, when, and in the manner it ought to; checking each subsequent issue of the advertisement, in each paper, in a book kept for the purpose, at all times subject to the inspection of the advertiser, and marking plainly in each paper the advertisement as it appears; so that when the advertiser comes (or sends) for the purpose of having the files examined (to see that the service for which his money pays has been actually rendered), the eye may light promptly upon his announcement, without the labor of searching a whole paper or page.

If errors or omissions occur, it is our duty to notify publishers, at our own expense for labor, postage or messenger, and to see to it that the publisher of the paper actually does the specified service for which the advertiser contracted.

As before explained, we are paid for the service rendered the advertiser and for the expense of keeping up our establishment by a commission from the newspaper upon the price of the advertisements furnished by us.

For instance, a five-line advertisement to appear in the New York *Daily Times,* the schedule price of which is 20 cents a line, makes a charge of one dollar. We charge the advertiser one dollar, and, when sending the order, the paper is instructed to charge us the same amount; but when we pay the bill, a rebate or commission of 10 per cent is allowed to us as "Advertising Agents."

If the charge, instead of one dollar, should be a larger sum, our profit or commission would still be 10 per cent; so that upon a one-hundred-dollar advertisement we should make ten dollars, and fifty upon one amounting to five hundred.

The commission allowed varies with different papers, and, in most cases, is more liberal to us than that fixed by the New York *Times.* Sometimes advertising orders are very large, otherwise it would not be possible to maintain our establishment with the considerable expenses necessary for making its appointments complete.

Although a good proportion of our orders are for small amounts, varying from one dollar to fifty, it not infrequently happens that single advertisements are sent us which cost a thousand and sometimes many thousand dollars.

Advertisers sometimes inquire whether if, dealing direct with the publishers of newspapers, they would not be able to obtain the allowance or commission. Our observation teaches us that if the amount of their patronage is large they will generally be able to obtain concession from the rates. Nearly every publisher of a newspaper, in fact almost any man of business, likes to come in direct contact with his customers, and holds out inducements to that end, but the real object is pretty universally admitted to be, the attainment of a larger percentage of profit; and it has been the result of our experience and investigations that the most honorable publishers make no pretense of allowing an "agent's" commission to an advertiser doing his own business, and that those who are willing to make such a concession generally get a better net price than they would expect if the order came through our hands.

The conclusion we arrive at is that advertisers who have small orders, amounting to a few dollars in each paper (although possibly footing up hundreds in the aggregate), cannot obtain any material concession from first class newspapers, and that those advertisers who have large advertisements, amounting to considerable sums in individual publications, are apt to learn that where they obtain the concession of the agent's commission, WE are able to secure a still lower net price for them and at the same time retain our own profit intact. For instance, a paper charging $100 for a specified advertisement, might gladly allow a concession, called an agent's commission of $25, getting a net price of $75, while we should not think of allowing our customer to pay the paper in question more than $40, and from that sum should exact from the publisher the regular allowance for our commission.

This is a subject upon which an advertiser soon comes to have a decided opinion, and it is something in favor of the soundness of our conclusions that so many who make a point of getting the best service at the smallest cost, deal largely with our house or similar establishments. It may as well be stated here that although unwilling to promise an advertiser a concession from our commission or to admit a right on his part to ask it, yet in point of fact such a concession is exceedingly common. Many papers allow a commission of 25 per cent, which is a larger profit than we consider ourselves entitled to, except on trivial orders or such as involve unusual attention to detail. It often happens in this way. Example: We have named $12 as the price for an advertisement in a certain newspaper without any reference to the publisher's schedule, which we are aware demands much more; with 25 per cent off the cost to us is $9 net, giving a profit of $3. Now, if the publisher returns the order and demands $20 for the required service, it is evident that we cannot comply. The commission upon $20 is $5, making the net cost to us $15, which is $3 more than we are to receive. If we believe the publisher likely to consent to a compromise we can with safety to ourselves offer $15 gross, the commission upon that sum being $3.75 makes the net cost to us $11.25, while the advertiser pays $12, a profit of 75c., which, although too small standing by itself, is, if the advertiser is entirely responsible, more satisfactory than it would be to ask for an advance or to omit the paper from the contract.

The efforts which have been made by our firm to print and spread abroad information concerning the quality and character of newspapers and their circulations, and the persistent advertising of our business, which it has been our policy to maintain, has brought, and continues to bring us, applications of a miscellaneous class (largely from persons who are entirely unknown to us), so that to answer all, fully and in detail, by special letters and estimates for each applicant, would, while resulting in no adequate profit to ourselves, leave us little time to attend to anything else. We have therefore prepared circulars which contain the information generally sought.

We have entered upon contracts with selected newspapers throughout most of the States, whereby we insert small advertisements, which are to appear for a short period, at rates decidedly favorable to the advertiser.

These combinations, known as Geo. P. Rowell & Co.'s select lists of local newspapers, we conduct as proprietors, extending to establishments similar to our own the privilege of taking orders for them, and receiving a commission approximating that allowed by publishers for a similar amount of patronage. The rates for these combinations of newspapers are plainly printed and rarely varied from, but are freely quoted in writing for any inquirer, and these quotations are the only estimate issued from our office which GUARANTEE insertion in a combination of newspapers at any marked reduction from publishers' shedule rates.

There are other similar (although lower-priced) lists, conducted by different establishments, more or less like our own, for which we solicit advertisements and quote terms supposed to be as favorable to our patrons as can elsewhere be obtained.

Whenever an advertiser expects to pay the rates of the newspaper he intends using, we guarantee prompt insertions, and for small advertisements, to appear for a short period only, in a limited list of high-priced journals, customers expect to pay the rates fixed by the publishers' schedule.

The practice of remitting to the advertiser a portion of the commission on small orders brings with it a tendency to permit remissness on the part of publishers in rendering the full number of insertions contracted for, crowding the space or in some of various ways to make good the remitted portion of the commission. It is doubtless true that orders so taken are often faithfully carried out, but first-class service cannot be afforded, and therefore ought not to be promised. Take a case in point. A 100 line advertisement inserted in the N. Y. *Daily Times* costs $20, upon which the commission is $2. Ten per cent is as small a profit as will pay for the transaction of a business involving so much attention. But there are those who would remit one-half of the commission and take the order for $19, or possibly, in a competition, and to make certain of a first order, which may lead to other and more profitable transactions, would make even a greater concession. This sort of competition is managed to best advantage by canvassers or those agents who have light expenses, because not assuming the cost of maintaining an office or checking the insertion of advertisements.

An advertiser having extended dealings finds it prudent to place his interests in charge of persons having the required facilities combined with experience and responsibility. The practice of seeking business which must be done without profit, for the sake of establishing a name for cheap service, and the hope that a profit may be realized after the confidence of the advertiser has been secured, is one which never recommended itself to us. But, notwithstanding all the above, we do not expect any patrons of ours to pay us more money than would elsewhere obtain the same service.

Nothing is more quickly affected by stagnation of business than space in the advertising columns of newspapers. It is unlike other kinds of merchandise. The grocer who owns a barrel of sugar will have it in stock to-morrow if he does not sell to-day; and although the price of sugar may decline, it will be worth something, and there is a possibility that the price may advance.

How is it with a man who has a column of space to dispose of? His newspaper goes to press to-day! If he does not sell his space it is lost, and worse than lost, for if an advertiser does not pay for an advertisement to fill it, the printer *must be paid* for the necessary type-setting required for filling it with reading matter. Consequently, in the majority of newspapers, except for the small announcements which come as a matter of course, and the local patronage which is compelled to come from the necessities of the case, the price of advertising depends largely upon the question, "How much can we get?"

Publishers become expert, and can tell better than would be imagined how much an advertiser will pay. The vender of a patent medicine who has sold to a village druggist $100 worth of goods on a promise to advertise a column a year in the village paper, will find the price of that column held with greater firmness if the village editor happens to have heard of the transaction.

So, also, when half a dozen advertising agencies have applied to a publisher for a special price for a specified advertisement, he assumes that one or the other of them will contract for and promise the use of his paper, and that all that remains for him to do will be to fix a price and hold to it firmly, believing that the successful bidder will be compelled to come to his terms.

For a ten-line reading notice in an ordinary country weekly one dollar is charged; few print any lower rate than ten cents a line for reading matter, which would make a year's insertion cost $52—at schedule rates—while ninety-five out of every hundred publishers would accept the order at from $3 to $8, but there would be one or two in every hundred who, without being worth intrinsically any more than the others, would insist upon the full charge. Consideration of these facts made it apparent that we should best serve all interests by never undertaking to sell newspaper space of which we had not previously become possessed or obtained a reliable quotation.

When a newspaper publisher has much less advertising than he is in the habit of thinking his paper should carry, he is not likely to refuse even a low offer for a desirable advertisement. The publisher of a country weekly, who asks $100 per annum for a column, having a couple of columns to spare, will be likely to sell one at a low rate to a responsible purchaser; possibly as little as $40 would be accepted; but after the contract is closed, if another advertiser applies for a column, he will be likely to have to pay a higher rate; and if two or three come along, the paper becomes so crowded that the last applicant will be refused a column even at $100, on the ground that some space must be reserved for transient customers.

So also a paper which has promised special positions to two or three advertisers ceases to have desirable positions to offer, and demands a high price from a new applicant, while a neighboring journal, which may be better or quite as good, not happening to have made any such contract, is entirely free, and may grant the place asked, without an increased charge.

What we strive to make plain is, that so many things influence the price of an advertisement, that if compelled to promise an advertiser in advance exactly what we will do, we are obliged to charge an extra price to cover contingencies. We have often procured advertising for $20 which we should not have been willing to promise for $50.

Advertising costs a large amount of money. No advertiser can afford to pay publishers' schedule rates for an extensive line of advertising. The question becomes, then, What is the method which will obtain the largest possible amount of newspaper publicity for the smallest investment of capital? When an advertiser who is a patron of our agency applies to us for an estimate, we carry out against the name of each paper upon his list the price which we recommend him to offer. If he is not anxious about particular papers and is willing to omit any which will not contract at a low rate, considering its circulation, position and influence, the prices will be lower than they would be if he were more desirous of using all or nearly all the papers on the list. Sometimes an advertiser wishes to reach the people of a certain State and is willing to invest not to exceed an amount of money which he names. In that case we should make a complete list of all the newspapers issued in that State, and against each affix a price which will be UNDOUBTEDLY a low one for the service demanded.

It is not expected that all will accept. Sometimes the price is made so low, that it is not believed that more than one-fourth, or one-third, will consent to do the work at the figures named. Frequently the result is surprising, especially if the proposals happen to be forwarded when advertising business is slack. After all have been heard from, it is customary to review the correspondence, *in company with the advertiser,* and then reasonable proposals from publishers at important points who have not accepted the original propositions can be considered and acted upon.

Estimates of this sort are subject to revision by the advertiser who brings to bear upon them any knowledge which his experience with his own advertising has given him; and if we seem to him to have marked too high a price for any paper he notes the case and the figures are reconsidered. All correspondence received by either the advertiser or ourselves, having bearing upon the advertising under consideration, is open to inspection of both parties.

In fixing the prices which shall be offered each paper, good judgment is needed. An advertisement which would cost at schedule rates in the Chicago *Times* $5,000, would amount to no more than $300 in the Peoria *Transcript,* for the same number of insertions; often when all in a State are used, the best bargains are among the papers to which the largest amount of money is paid.

The undoubted truth of this statement sometimes leads advertisers into the error of supposing that a newspaper must be valuable because it charges a high price, or that no price can be actually too high for a really good paper.

In fixing the value of advertising space in any particular journal, the first question to be considered is the number of copies issued; next, the character or quality of the circulation.

A well-printed paper is worth more than one badly printed; an influential journal carries more weight than one without reputation.

So also a paper which habitually charges high prices for its advertising thereby makes its columns exclusive, and will have fewer and, as a rule, a better class of advertisements, and is worth something more on that account.

The value of all these considerations is recognized, but exactly *how* much each one is to be considered becomes a question of judgment.

One other point. No matter how valuable any newspaper may be, no advertiser wants to pay for the mention of his announcement in its columns any more than the lowest price which can be made to secure the service required. If it can be had for $20 he will not willingly pay $25, even if he considers it actually worth $40.

It has been urged against our system of business that by it the advertiser never knows what his advertising is going to cost; but we have not been able to see the force of this reasoning. The advertiser is not in our hands, but in his own. He goes into no paper except at a price which both he and ourselves consider a low or a fair one. We are both interested that no publisher shall compel a payment above the value of his circulation and influence. He knows as well how much the advertisement is to cost, as he would if doing the business himself, direct with the publishers. He knows what each paper will cost if it accepts the work at the price offered, and that no paper will receive any larger price until he, the advertiser, has considered the reasons therefor and decided that they are good.

Whenever we are doing the advertising for any individual, or firm, we consider them entitled to our best services. If they suggest a paper which we know to be not the best for their purpose, we say so and give the reasons. We often expend a good deal of time for very small advertisers, much more than the profits on their patronage would warrant; but as they entrust to us what they have to disburse, and influence in our direction the patronage of their friends and acquaintances, we are content.

The man who applies to many agencies cannot always tell to his satisfaction which actually does offer the best inducements, while the feeling which he brings about is not calculated to secure the best service of any. Almost every advertiser of prominence who has an established financial rating, makes his advertising contracts through the same advertising agency from year to year.

It is a matter of prime importance to us, for the purpose of maintaining our influence with publishers, that it shall come to be understood among them that our statements about the adverising to be done, or not to be done, are to be relied upon, and to this end our dealing with our advertising patrons must be upon a basis of mutual confidence and respect.

By a system of competing estimates, the interests of the agent and advertiser are antagonistic. They stand to each other in the relation of buyer and seller. Our relation is that of a skilled assistant to the buyer; we act as counsel for him; we give him the advantage of any knowledge which we possess to enable him to procure for his money the most service which that money will buy.

We have shown that formerly the agent represented the newspaper and was subject to instructions issued from the publisher. In contracting with an advertiser, he strove for the best price to be obtained, his duty being owed to the newspaper which accepted his contract, protected him with his customer, released him from obligations if the advertiser proved financially unsound, and allowed him his commission on all payments received. In those days there were no such things as newspaper directories or printed reports of newspaper circulations. Now things are changed.

The commission is still allowed to the agent by the publisher, but so freely and with such slight question, to so large a number, that rival agents in every city urge a conflicting authority to represent every newspaper of importance, and the most successful one finds his profit not in a commission from schedule rates, but in his knowledge of the lowest price which a publisher will be likely to accept, in his confidential relation with advertisers who entrust their patronage to his management, and in an established credit which makes his orders as current as bank-notes among the newspaper offices.

His strength or weakness depends so largely upon his relations to his advertising customers that the advertising agent of to-day may be said to work fully and wholly for the advertiser, having no concern about his standing with publishers beyond a reputation for systematic methods of business and the prompt settlement of accounts. He makes his money out of the advertiser, and owes service to the advertiser, and to him alone. The publisher is responsible to the advertising agent, and the agent to his advertising patron. The advertiser could, with entire propriety, pay the agent for his services, but the practice of allowing a commission is so thoroughly established among publishers that its propriety is never questioned,

The real strength of the agent lies in his ability to obtain the greatest concession from publishers' rates.

To know what newspapers must have $100 for a one-hundred-dollar advertisement, and what one will take the same for $50, $30, or $10, is the most useful and profitable portion of the stock in trade of the successful advertising agency.

We promise those advertisers who entrust their advertising patronage to our management that we will not allow them to be charged in any instance any more than the publishers' schedule rates; that we will procure for them the acceptance of any advantageous offer made to them definitely by any newspaper publisher, advertising agent, or canvasser of responsibility. Although we are unwilling to do work without a profit, and never offer to do so, yet in conformity with the promise made above, we sometimes find it advisable. Competitors anxious to gain a hearing and secure attention, occasionally make offers which it would advance the true interests of our customers to accept. In such cases we hold ourselves bound to secure the bargain offered.

These bargains are sometimes based upon some actual advantage possessed by the person making the offer, and in carrying out the agreement we might employ the very person who made the proposal. In that case the interests of our patron are as fully protected, and we have the satisfaction of retaining the supervision of his expenditures, and knowing that they are such as we would recommend.

If in this way we at times become possessed of information which is of service to us, we presume no one would be otherwise than pleased to have been a means of advantage or profit. It is our intention to *deserve* the good will of those who do business with us.

We promise that the placing of patronage with us shall never result to the pecuniary disadvantage of the advertiser.

Applicants for our services should note the instructions given below, as by so doing delay and correspondence will often be saved.

A copy of the advertisement to be used is the first requisite.

Nothing tells so well the object which the advertiser desires to accomplish.

If it is not possible to prepare the copy for exhibition when negotiations are commenced, it is well to select from some newspaper a similar advertisement, and all figures and estimates can then be made for that as though it were the copy actually to be used.

Some newspapers insert no medical advertisements; some object to such as seem to promise the public more than it would seem possible to give for the consideration asked; some exclude announcements which leave the reader in doubt concerning the object or business of the advertiser; many decline to place before their readers the prospectuses of other newspapers. In certain States the laws forbid the publication of any scheme which partakes of the character of a lottery or gift enterprise.

So also many papers have special rates for certain classes of advertisements; as, for instance, amusements and legal advertisements are often charged at an advanced price, while New Books and Railroad or Steamship Time Tables are in many prominent journals advertised at a discount from 25 to 50 per cent from the schedule fixed for other kinds of business.

The space which an advertisement is to occupy should be designated if the advertiser is particular upon that point.

This should be in inches or lines, and if in lines, the kind of type should be specified (Agate or Nonpareil). The term "square" should never be used in this connection, its meaning is too indefinite.

If the advertisement requires no special display, the space may be ordered to be "as small as possible."

If only a head line or one display line is wished to be made prominent that statement is sufficiently definite.

If definite instructions are not given at the time of sending copy, we consider that it is left to our own judgment and act accordingly.

When printed copy is furnished, in the absence of instructions to the contrary, it is taken as indicating the display desired.

When an advertiser is content to leave the matter of display to our own judgment it is generally best for all parties, but in contracts of importance it is our custom to have sample advertisements printed and approved before forwarding for publication. For this service it is not our practice to make any charge.

After the advertisement has been determined upon the next matter of importance is the names of the newspapers to be used.

The list should designate whether daily or weekly issues are wanted, or both, and whether, in dailies, the advertisement shall appear once, twice, thrice, or six times a week, or include a Sunday edition, if one is issued in connection with the paper under consideration.

When the advertiser is competent to do so, he usually makes his list without aid from us. When not posted about newspapers, it is a general practice to write out a list of towns and submit it to us; after which we write against each town or city the paper or papers which we recommend as best calculated to serve the interest of our patrons.

Sometimes our patrons are unable to name the papers which they ought to use. They wish to reach a class or section. For such it is our duty to make known the publications likely to accomplish the object which they have in view.

Persons who have had little experience as advertisers often have a pretty clear understanding of what they would like to do, but are entirely ignorant of the probable cost.

We have made out for such a person a plan of advertising calling for an investment of $5,000, and on submitting it for approval, found our customer dismayed at the magnitude of the expense, he not having contemplated an expenditure exceeding $200 or $300. In such a case labor would have been saved if at the commencement of the negotiation the question had been asked: "How much money are you prepared to devote to this advertising?"

We work with the advertiser and for the advertiser precisely as an expert whose services were obtained to aid him at his own office would do—precisely as the advertiser would do his own business, did he possess our facilities, knowledge and experience.

It is hoped that those who read the foregoing with so much care as to be able to comprehend the system which we adopt, will recognize and acknowledge the cogency of reasoning which has recommended the methods we announce. To such we promise that whatever advertising contract is entrusted to us shall receive our best consideration and attention. If we are not always willing to consider propositions from advertisers who do not understand or approve of our system of procedure, we ask that no one will believe us to be less anxious than we ought to be to secure patronage. To entertain proposals to transact business in any other way would be to disregard the teachings of thirteen years of our experience; to abandon a system which we have found to be the one upon which we can best maintain dignity in our correspondence with publishers, and one which has retained longest and satisfied best those patrons who have dealt most largely with us. No sum, to be invested by an advertiser, is so small that we do not desire to have its management entrusted to us; neither is the patronage of any advertiser so important that we can afford to undertake it, if by doing so we must abandon the principles which we conceive to be the only ones proper for the correct conduct of our affairs. The advertiser who has an estimate from a good and responsible Advertising Agency can hardly be supposed to need our services. We do work in the best and most thorough manner; no house has better credit or standing in newspaper offices; but to have it said that, had we not taken the advertisement in question another Agency would have forwarded it at higher price, does not improve or add to our popularity. It is better that no other Agency have any concern in the affair.

If the advertiser has an estimate from an Agency which is neither honest, solvent or capable, or lacking in either particular, we are tolerably certain not to be able to promise so much, and *performance* is a matter which cannot be weighed until after the contract has been issued. That we decline submitting estimates when competition is invited, must not be construed as indicating any lack of eagerness to secure patronage, but attributed to the feeling, on our part, that such a course will best subserve all the interests involved.

THIRTY-FIRST PAPER

I should think it was during the closing days of the year 1879, that at the annual banquet of the New England Society I was introduced by my old friend, Hon. Horace Russell, to a man then prominent in the leather trade, which at that time and ever since, has been congested in the swamp at the foot of Spruce street where my office has so long been situated. This gentleman invited me a day or two later to dine with him at the rather newly organized Hide and Leather Club, occupying chambers in the building at the northeast corner of Ferry and Gold streets. The place was so convenient for a luncheon club, and the company so congenial, that I afterwards sought and was accorded a membership; and, following invitations from me to partake of hospitalities there, three other men, more or less associated with my own line of business, eventually became members; and we, with six or seven others, commonly occupied a table in an inner room that would conveniently accommodate a dozen diners; and here, from day to day, I am confident we ate more hearty luncheons than were good for us, and lingered longer than we should have done over cigars, coffee and other things.

At the age of forty, and beyond that, one hardly expects to form friendships that shall have anything like the permanence and sincerity of those made in youth or manhood's early bloom, but something pretty near to that was, in two or three instances at least, a result of the daily meetings at the Hide and Leather Club. It is out of existence now. It was too beautiful to last. William Palen, the first president, known to the leather trade everywhere, always sat at the head of the table in that little inner room. He was then a man of fully sixty years. My friend already referred to, Mr. Charles H. Isham, had the place, one or two seats removed, at Palen's left; opposite him it became the usage for the seat to be occupied by Isaac W. England, then the publisher of the New York *Sun;* at England's right sat my old friend William D. Wilson, founder of the Printing Ink Company that still bears his name and is known to many readers of *Printers' Ink* as the fountain head from which the alleged Printers Ink Jonson—who sells ink everywhere and pays the freight, but always in-

GEO. P. ROWELL.   CHAS. H. ISHAM.   W. D. WILSON.
WM. PALEN.   I. W. ENGLAND.   J. H. BATES.

sists upon fingering the cash before letting go of the goods —actually draws his supplies. The seat between Isham and Palen gradually became recognized as pre-empted for James H. Bates, the advertising agent; he, with Wilson, England and myself, constituting the outside element of the Club; all the rest being in the leather trade; if we do not further except Isaac H. Bailey, at that time the owner and publisher of the *Shoe and Leather Reporter.* I often sat at

the foot of the table, opposite Mr. Palen. Of the vacant
seats a good portion were likely to be filled by guests, although M. H. Moody, whose office was with Mr. Isham;
Mr. Barnes, who took no pride in the circumstance that he
was a brother-in-law of Ex-Mayor A. Oakey Hall; G. B.
Horton of the firm of Horton Brothers, tanners; Mr. Nelson, associated with Mr. Palen; and Mark and Oliver, of
the prominent firm of Hoyt Brothers; were more or less
constant in their attendance. Moody, Nelson, Isham and
the writer still remain (in 1905), but all the others have
passed away. England went first, Wilson not much later,
Bates not till 1902 and Mr. Palen—at the ripe age of 86—
during the latter part of 1904. Of the six members who
went one day, nearly a quarter of a century ago, to a photographer, who stood them up like a group of schoolboys,
only two survive, Mr. Isham and the writer; and to a recent
proposal to draw lots to determine who should go next the
elder man responded in a manner that indicated he thought
there was a screw loose in the Presbyterianism of the proposition.

It was at the table of the Hide and Leather Club that I
saw the celebrated Tom Reed for the first time; and it was
there that I saw General Grant for the last time. Reed was
a friend of Bailey's, both hailing from Maine. Bailey was
a wit; but brusque and sometimes merciless in the use he
made of his ability to say bright things. One day Mr. Palen
was late, Bailey took his seat, but apologized when Palen
came in. Palen said, with a trace of sarcasm, "Physically
it is well filled." "Intellectually it never has been," was
the laconic rejoinder. The year Bailey was President of
the New England Society President Grant attended, and
Lieutenant General W. T. Sherman was there also. In his
introductory remarks, as master of ceremonies, Mr. Bailey
said, "You will notice that we have not with us to-night any
member of either house of Congress. The President is
here and the General of our armies"—pause—"We had to
draw the line—somewhere!" Notwithstanding the facility
with which Bailey usually arose to an occasion it was won-

derful with what apparent lack of effort Reed could and did cap Bailey's rather cruel sallies; and how thoroughly each sentence seemed so effective as to leave no possible further word to be said.

It was at this table that Judge Noah Davis mentioned one day a retort made to him by some one who was before him, while on the bench, and to whom he had felt obliged to say, "You are no gentleman," to which remark the other retorted with a deprecating grimace, "You are no judge!"

Mr. England was an uncut diamond. Those who knew him well found him gentle as a woman and with a heart as full of kindness. When he departed this life, and I knew that I should see his face no more, I realized that never before had I been called upon to part with one whose association and friendship I should miss so much. He went trout fishing with me once at the Rangeley Lakes. There was quite a party of us and I feared, from what I then knew of his usual manner, that he would not prove an amiable companion among our little group, most of whom had been in camp together on numerous other occasions. We found him the quietest and gentlest of the lot; and he took me seriously to task one day for thoughtless, needless cruelty, because I attempted to shoot a flying swallow. It would seem a difficult feat to perform but in truth is not particularly so. I missed that one, however, and tried no more while my mentor was by. He was impressed by the quiet of the wood, by the lake expanse, the effect of moonlight on the forest at evening, by the simple noonday repast in some secluded nook by the lake side or near running water; and said to me one day, thoughtfully, "I am glad I came. It is a new experience to me, and leads to introspection; and when I go home I think I shall speak less frequently with impatience or annoyance to the wife and the little ones."

Mr. Wilson was a lovable man, a warm-hearted Irishman. He always stated things strongly. With him men were of two classes. Every one he knew was either a prince or a dirty dog. The princes predominated more than ten to one. His strong way of sizing things up led a member to cast discredit on his veracity one day. It was a man who did not know him well. Whereupon another member asserted that he should never call Wilson's general truthfulness in question, although he might be, perhaps, denominated an "evangelical prevaricator"—seeming to intend a covert reference to Wilson's ever earnest advocacy of the tenets of the Methodist Church, of which he was a sincerely devoted adherent, and his ever ready defense of which from even the mildest criticism was of a type that was pronounced as well as devotional. It was a privilege to know Wilson in his home. As a host he was ideal. In business he would do everything possible to be done to retain the good will and confidence of a customer. He was a good sportsman, a delightful companion in camp, on the trail or in a boat; an ardent and enthusiastic caster of the fly, to lure the wily trout or bass. No one had a more cheery greeting, a more hearty hand-shake, or was more earnest and constant in adherence and loyalty to friends. It is nearly twenty years now since we buried him in the pretty cemetery at Roslyn, Long Island, where he rests only a few yards away from his old neighbor, William Cullen Bryant, the poet, so long editor of the New York *Evening Post,* which in those days was always printed with Wilson's Ink.

After Mr. Wilson died it was the wish of his widow to go again to that Emerald Isle that had been the land of their youth, and it was largely with a desire to help the good lady to accomplish her desire that I was led to purchase a controlling interest in the stock of his company, and to become, for a time at least, a manufacturer of printing inks. I never could bring myself to approve the long credits and still more objectionable methods that seemed to prevail in that trade, some of which led to giving over to the pressman or buyer a considerable percentage of the price paid for inks; and I determined to try an experiment one time to see whether it were or were not actually possible to induce people to buy inks and pay promptly for them, and judge them by quality instead of favor to a salesman, or on account of money accommodations furnished by the ink manufacturer. It was with this object in view that I inaugurated the series of advertisements that have run in *Printers' Ink* for the last dozen years or more, latterly in the trademark name of Printers Ink Jonson. At first the name was William Johnston, he being the foreman of my printing office, and expected to manage the correspondence, receiving a small extra compensation therefor. After a time it became evident that a valuable trademark name was being created, upon which its creators could have no legal claim, and that could be carried over to a competing house, under certain possible conditions easy to conceive; and so we changed the name one day in the advertisements, and "Printers Ink Jonson" became famous as an ink dealer, while plain William Johnston remained foreman of a printing office which he now personally owns and has called for some years "The Printers' Ink Press." In the beginning I wrote all the Johnston advertisements, and they proved to be readable, attracted attention, and brought business. Whoever would buy must send the cash with the order. The seller paid the freight. If the goods were not found as represented they could be sent back and the seller paid the freight again and sent back the whole sum that had been paid. It worked very well and has tended to revolutionize the ink trade· News ink, that used to sell all the way from four cents to twenty-five, now go at a very nearly uniform rate of four cents, and of vermilion, that at one time was retailed at thirty-two dollars an ounce, my successors in the ink trade now sell a collapsible tube containing four ounces for the more moderate charge of fifty cents for the package and contents, the price including carriage to the point of delivery, whether to Hoboken or Hawaii. I gave up writing the Johnston ads after a time, and since then they have been the work of Mr. Daniel F. Barry, the present secretary of the W. D. Wilson Printing Ink Co., who, before he took up the work, had not, I think, ever had so much as a thought of writing an advertisement.

With changes that are inevitable—with the departure of

three or four of the inner circle by death—the Hide and
Leather Club, after a few years, disintegrated, but I am
confident that none who sat by that table in the inner room
can ever fail to recall with pleasure many an hour spent
there that might have been more profitably devoted to business. I am further confident that if I had tried to keep up
the same sort of mid-day luncheons I, too, should before
this time have been called to an eternal rest. The ten cent
luncheon at Dennett's restaurant, that includes a bowl of
milk and seven soda crackers, is, I think, much better calculated to prolong life than all the luxuries of the season,
washed down with fluids no matter how delectable. Think
of the late Roswell P. Flower dying in the comparative
youth of the fifties, of an acute indigestion, and then look
at Russell Sage, consider his daily glass of milk and piece
of pie, and his hale and hearty age of eighty-nine in this
year of our Lord 1905. It may be a question, however,
whether it is not more blessed to be one person, and be
dead, than another and live on and on indefinitely.

Before leaving the Hide and Leather Club to oblivion I
feel impelled to refer again to the man who happened to be
the means of my connection with it, although he was neither
printer, advertising expert, nor dealer in leather. I refer to
Hon. Horace Russell, who introduced me to Charles H.
Isham at a dinner of the New England Society and out of
which all the experiences at the Club were an outgrowth. I
had known Judge Russell long years before, and long before he was a judge, although he is a much younger man
than I am, and we had even been through that supreme
test of acquaintance—we had been a-fishing together. In
fact it was from talks around a camp fire that I was first
particularly impressed that in the ordinary words of common conversation, and in a wholly unconscious manner, he
made use of more quotable phrases and apothegms, that one
would think of afterwards, than any other man I have ever
known. He possessed, he possesses—for he is still with us
—one other personal charm. If there is a handsomer man
to be seen in New York I can truly assert that I am not in

the habit of meeting him. I was once, in Russell's presence, trying to explain to a clergyman, who afterwards became a bishop, the nature of the business of an advertising agent, and was not succeeding very well in convincing my hearer that such a calling was at all necessary, when the judge injected a sentence that seemed to dispose of the subject effectually. "The man who does his own advertising," said the judge, "is the same sort as the one who taps his own boots and cuts his own hair." It may tend to explain the breeziness of the expression if it be stated that it was delivered on a sandy beach of a little bay, on the western portion of Lake Superior, just at sunset one evening, while the audience reclined upon their stomachs around a miniature camp fire that served to discourage mosquitoes, no-seeuns and black flies.

THIRTY-SECOND PAPER

Among the guests who came frequently to the midday repasts at the Hide and Leather Club, was David R. Locke, better known as Nasby. He was associated with Mr. Bates in the conduct of the advertising agency, the firm name being Bates & Locke. Just what good Locke did the agency I could never learn. He surely was not a safe counselor for an advertiser, after getting beyond advising him to use the Toledo *Blade*—which generally belonged to Nasby as much as half of the time, if not more.

He seemed to make some effort to cultivate, in his own person, an approach in appearance to what a reader would expect to find in an incarnation of his *nom de plume,* Petroleum V. Nasby of Confedrit Cross Roads, Kentucky; and he was more than moderately successful in his effort. His clothes never seemed to be new, nor fashionable, nor tidy. He generally wore a stove pipe hat; but it was not frequently ironed, nor even brushed. He talked much of drinking, and was willing to do his share, if occasion presented; although it was noted that he was commonly the tempted one and rarely the person to offer to set 'em up. If there was ever a man more keen in retort, or more absolute in his power to make a rejoinder that left nothing whatever that the opponent could answer back, Locke was the man. I wonder how many stories of his and about him I have listened to; and I can hardly recall one that will not make me laugh, even when I am not in good spirits. He told one day of that superlatively handsome man, Col. Nicholas Smith, who had married one of the Greeley girls, and with whom he had spent an hour at the Lotus Club the evening preceding and talked about the potent influence of manly beauty. The Colonel had admitted that in his case it was a constant annoyance; so much so that he did not dare to dress as well as he would like to, because, when he was really well dressed, the women pursued him so. "What rot!" exclaimed Bates, in disgust at so much egotism. "You don't know what you are talking about," responded Locke, and proceeded to assert that for the very reason given by Smith, and no other, he, Locke, had for years had his trousers cut so as to make him look bowlegged.

He and Bates owned the first successful typewriter; the one that later became the Remington. Locke used to say that the time would come that the typewriter would be in as general use as the sewing machine. That seemed preposterous then, but does not seem so much so now. They had a warehouse and show rooms on Broadway; but were in advance of the market and finally parted with their rights—and possibly with a great opportunity to make thousands. One day Bates visited the warerooms. They were Locke's special province, but Locke was not there. The bookkeeper thought he might be in the saloon around the corner; and there he was looked for, and discovered—sitting by a small cast iron fountain in the back yard that cast up a gimlet sized stream of croton that dripped down and gave a little life to a few thirsty straggling plants. On a table, at his side, was a mug of beer; in his hand the extinguished stub of a Pittsburg stogie; with feet elevated to the fountain basin; with soiled paper collar—broken from the fastener—for the day was warm and there was perspiration if no cravat. The visitor was welcomed with warm good fellowship, and bade to sit, and before he could open the subject that was in his mind, was called upon to listen to views already thought out under the soothing influence of the tiny fountain. "I've been thinking it over, Bates," said Locke, "and I know why we don't succeed. It's our men! I can see it! The trouble is, bi-god, we are not represented by gentlemen!"

Mr. Lincoln admired the Nasby Letters; they afforded him recreation from the cares that oppressed him; the scholarly Charles Sumner found in them something to admire; they made the great circulation of the Toledo

Blade, and were the foundation of a substantial prosperity for the writer of them. Locke had many friends who, at first acquaintance, would be inclined to lionize him; and he would submit, in a queer, rather amused way, to a good deal of that sort of thing; and if champagne and cigars took part there was no objection to them—none whatever. On one occasion he determined to make some return for entertainment and hospitality bestowed on him. He opened his heart and decided to give a dinner to a dozen choice spirits, talked about it a good deal, consulted bon vivants about an appropriate bill of fare, and the most desirable house of entertainment where the occasion should be celebrated. It might be slightly Bohemian in its character; it would be all the better for a spice of that, but was to be the real thing, and done up in good shape. Sieghortner's famous restaurant in Lafayette Place was at length decided on as just about what was wanted. The invitations had been informal, but at the hour appointed about a dozen guests assembled. The host was a little late—but he came. No room had been provided, but the restaurant was equal to the demands of even such a sudden call, and soon the party were seated around a table covered with a bare cloth, and the host had before him a voluminous bill of fare. After looking at it for some moments, he laid it down and addressing his guests said, "Well, boys, what'll you have." Some one, rising to the ludicrousness of the situation, suggested an oyster stew. There was hesitation, but the host had no suggestions to help on a decision; and, after a moment or two, another man pronounced in favor of the form of refection that had been suggested, and soon all fell into line, and the party thereupon demolished twelve oyster stews; and with a mug of beer and some cigars, of which Nasby had a pocket full—such as they were—the "dinner" came to an end.

He was one day conversing with Mr. Gano, partner of Murat Halstead, then conducting the Cincinnati *Commercial.* The daily *Commercial* was the most important paper in Ohio at that time, but its weekly was of no particular account; and probably did not print more than one or two thousand copies; while the weekly Toledo *Blade* had more than a hundred thousand paid in advance subscribers on its list. Mr. Gano criticised the quality of paper used for the *Blade*—said it looked dirty. Locke did not deny this, but thought the common people liked it. "Why!" said he, "every time I have a day to spare, and want a little recreation, I go over to the Maumee, a little above where our paper mill stands, and spend a whole afternoon throwing turf and mud into the river." Gano did not appear to see his way open for any comment on this, and Locke, after a pause, continued, "Gano, you use a handsome white paper for your weekly. "Yes," said Gano, "we try to give as good as there is to be had." "By the way," continued Locke, "how many copies of it do you print?"

He used to tell that he thought of buying a farm just outside of Toledo for a brother, but that the brother's wife objected, on account of the remoteness of the situation. She thought it ridiculous for them to try to live "where they would have to drive four or five miles every time they wanted an egg or a pint of milk." And he used to relate, sympathetically, the story of the good woman of Connecticut, who, church woman as she was, hated to die when the time came that die she must. Being comforted with visions of heaven, the great white throne, the gates of pearl, the golden streets, all of which she appreciated to the full, she still repined, because, in spite of them, she said she knew she would miss there a good many of her Hartford privileges.

Some one used to report the proceedings of a convivial evening, when, at an unexpected moment, although not an early hour, Locke seemed to be overcome with sudden grief, rested his head on his folded arms upon the table before him, and sobbed and sobbed. "What is it, Locke?" asked a friend. "What is the matter, old boy?" "Excuse me, gentlemen," said the stricken one, "it will pass over." "You are among friends," said another, "let us share your grief, speak up, let us know; we will comfort you." The kind

words were not without effect, and after a momentary recurring of hesitation the company learned that the grief
that had overcome their companion had arisen from his
thoughts having been directed to the sad circumstance that
he had—a drunken brother.

It was in Rome, at the Hotel Costanzi, in the early
months of 1883 that Locke used to come in every evening
to have a cup of coffee, a cigar and a teaspoonful of "fin
champagne" in company with half a dozen Americans to
whom I had introduced him. He dressed in his usual manner, and talk'd likewise. "I met so-and-so on the Corso to-
day," said he, "and he told me I ought to be a temperance
lecturer; and I said I had not the requisite qualifications,
for I was not a reformed drunkard. To that he replied,
'All you've got to do is to reform.'" The speech had not
annoyed him. The remembrance of it seemed to amuse him.
His mind dwelt upon it, and he referred to it every day,
and thought perhaps he would write a temperance lecture.
Well, he actually did do so; and delivered it, and many
others, on the platform, where he was always popular, and
by means of which he had earned a good deal of money. I
do not know whether he "reformed," as he called it, or
whether he needed to, for he made a great deal more of a
pretence of drinking than he did of the actual demonstra-
tion of it.

Bates used to relate that one morning when he went to
his office about eleven o'clock, as was his practice, he found
Locke asleep on the lounge opposite his desk and was somewhat annoyed by his heavy breathing. Soon, however, the
sleeper awoke, wiped his eyes with his knuckles, sat up,
looked at his partner and said, "Bates, would you like to
see a man that's drunker than I am?" Bates was incensed,
but answered mildly, "I wouldn't say, Locke, that I would,
but I will say that I seldom have." Whereupon Locke
arose, walked slowly to the office door, opened it, turned
around, and said, "Bates, you get somebody to introduce
you to me—in—an—hour!" And then he went out and was
seen no more that day.

I recall one day, at the Club, Mr. England was so late that his coming was despaired of. Finally, when the coffee and cigar stage had been reached, he came in, looking flushed, annoyed and generally disgusted. "What has happened to you?" was the general inquiry. "We had given you up." "I'm all right," he responded, "and started to come here three-quarters of an hour ago, but at the corner of Spruce street and William Locke came out of Bonner's *Ledger* office and got hold of me by the button, and I have just this minute been able to get away from him, and all he had to say was to tell me over and over again, that if I didn't quit drinking whiskey would get me." And to calm his nerves England took a little Scotch with his water.

At one time I had in my employ a highly educated and accomplished man who had been brought up in the lap of luxury, taught to expect all the good things of earth to be subject to his order, and then, on account of financial reverses that came to his family, found himself under the necessity of earning his daily bread. He was a gentleman through and through, but owing perhaps to the misfortunes that had come to him, and perhaps in part to a congenital tendency to a delicate condition of health, he had acquired a habit of taking some drug that tended to upset his nerves and unfit him for work. Not knowing what it was, it was hinted to him rather gently, now and then, that his illness was to be attributed to whiskey. He did not admit this, and in after years, I knew it was not the case, but he was conscious that there was a cause that he did not wish to reveal, and the hints that had been conveyed tended to make him unhappy. He was genuinely attached to me, and really wished to stand well in my opinion, and on that account tried to avoid any appearance that should confirm the suspicions I had expressed. He was acting as editor of that early predecessor of *Printers' Ink,* the *Newspaper Reporter and Advertisers' Gazette,* and sat at a desk so near to mine that he could see and hear whatever went on in my direction. One day I had a call from Mr. Locke, who had nothing unusual or specially to be noted in his appearance; but my man—his name was Waldron—was in a highly wrought condition that day and saw, I think, more than could be seen; leastwise, next morning, just as I was about to leave the office to attend a meeting of the directors of a small bank, to whose board I had recently been elected, Waldron handed me a letter, beautifully written in his copy-plate hand, covering sixteen full pages of half-note size, referring to the warnings I had given him, regretting the need of any such, and saying that what I had said had been very forcibly brought home to him the day before, by observing the ravages the vice I had suspected him of were already making in Mr. Locke, as he had had full opportunity to observe during his prolonged visit to me of the day before. He overstated the case to such a degree that it seemed to me rather· ludicrous than worth any particular attention. I read a part of the communication at my desk, but discovering it was merely one of those vagaries that would lead to nowhere I started out on my errand, with my letter in my hand, and continued to peruse it as I walked slowly from my office in the Times Building across the City Hall Park towards the bank, which was situated at the corner of Thomas street and Broadway. As I arrived about at the point in the Park where the subway entrances are now situated I saw Nasby approaching. There remained no more than two or three pages unread and I could see that they were not going to lead anywhere, so I folded the sheets and greeting the approaching victim said, "Look here, Locke, this letter seems to me to be more intended for your benefit than mine," gave it to him and passed along. For as much as two years after that Locke did not seem to like me very well—and yet he was by no means a thin-skinned man. He forgave it all afterwards—apparently—but never spoke of it.

He was a newspaper publisher, and as such it would have been singular if he did not have or take. occasion to feel incensed at the circulation rating now and then accorded to the Toledo *Blade* in the Newspaper Directory that I published. He told me once that he had in his safe an opinion for which he had paid $50 to Lawyer Waite of Toledo, not long before General Grant had appointed him Chief-Justice of the United States Supreme Court; the gist of which was that he could recover whatever damage he could show as resulting from an inaccurate rating, but would have to show that the rating was inaccurate, and to what extent, and that he had on that account lost business profits in such and such cases, specified and to such and such amounts, also specified. "Now you can see, Rowell," said he, with the utmost good nature, "if I showed that I was actually damaged I should have to prove that advertisers took stock in your old book; and the more damage I established the greater the advertisement it would be for you. I did not see anything in it for me, for I had always asserted that no one was influenced by the book; and if that had been the case, of course, I couldn't get any damages."

At a time when he was less incensed concerning the ratings in the Rowell Directory than he had formerly been he came into the office one day, smoking a three-fer cigar, sat down by me, took up the Directory, put his feet upon my desk, so near to my countenance that I found it advisable to sit back in my chair, and proceeded to examine the book, turning from page to page to note what figures were accorded to various papers about which he knew something. Our plan of obtaining statements at that time required a publisher to tell how many copies he printed of the first issue for the present month, the last month, and the month preceding the last; the three sets of figures being added and divided by three were then taken to be the circulation. If we suppose that a publisher of a country weekly reported that the respective issues called for were 800, 850 and 800, the sum, when divided by three, would show a circulation of 817. But at that time no one went very closely into tens and units; and Mr. Locke closed his examination with the remark addressed to me, "Rowell, there is one thing about that book that I admire;" and he rose to go. "I'm glad you find anything to commend," I said, and then asked, "What is the particular feature, Locke, that you admire?"

to which he responded, "It's the god-damned exactness of it."

What was meant by circulation was not as well understood in those days as it is now when it seems to be established as properly represented by the average number of complete and perfect copies printed during the period of a full year that has passed. Then it was always given in round figures—generally prefaced by the word about. The country paper that printed regularly as many as 600 copies, and on some memorable occasion disposed of nearly twice as many, and hoped to do as well on some future occasion would feel justified in asserting that its circulation was "about a thousand;" and an equally indefinite method was in favor with those papers that issued larger editions. Sixty thousand copies would constitute a pretty good claim for "about a hundred thousand," and so on.

At the Lotus Club one night a party of gentlemen were conversing over their cigars. One of them was Mr. Street, of the old firm of Street & Smith, publishers of *Street and Smith's Weekly,* a story paper of the servant girl grade, that had perhaps a greater sale than any other weekly published at that time. Locke was also of the party, and the comparative prosperity of newspapers, past and present, being spoken of, Locke asked Street what circulation his weekly had acquired, and was told that it was about 300,000 copies. There was no comment, but a few moments later Street said, "Mr. Locke, you issue a paper that is widely read the Toledo *Blade.* What circulation has it?" Locke said he was very glad to be asked that question at that particular time, because he was in a position to answer it definitely; that he always had weekly reports of the condition of affairs at the office, and one such had come to hand that morning—and producing a pocket-book and looking at a paper it contained, but upon which no one saw any writing or figures, he continued—"My bookkeeper tells me that the edition is falling off a little, and they are now printing only 529,227 copies." This statement, like that made by Street, passed without audible comment, although there were one or two cases of drooping of the eyelids, among the hearers. Pretty soon Street threw his cigar stub into the cuspidor, and withdrew, Locke remaining, everyone smoking. The retreating figure was hardly out of ear-shot before Locke, looking after it, gave expression to his feelings by uttering the words: "What a liar *Street* is!"

I ought not to dismiss Nasby without quoting his favorite motto, which was:

A ROLLING STONE IS THE NOBLEST WORK OF GOD;
AND AN HONEST MAN GATHERS NO MOSS.

He used to relate, that in his lecture tours, which were a source of considerable profit to him, he in the beginning had found that it was expected he would hold an informal reception after the lecture, and later have a session and big talk with the members of the local committee. At these it appeared that something additional was expected from the speaker, and he was at times at a loss to know just what to do or say—but finally, after a time, he prepared three sets of stories, with twelve stories in each set, one set suited for lyceums or literary societies, another for occasions political, and the third, altogether different from the second, to be used after Y. M. C. A. gatherings. When the time arrived he looked at his envelope, refreshed his memory by consulting the memoranda of the twelve that would fit the present occasion, and when they had been retailed the services were deemed complete. He drew a picture, true to the life, of the average small western town of those days. "Two rows of one-story houses, facing a street about a mile long—lost in the prairie at both ends—plank sidewalks pretty much the whole length—a mud hole in the middle of the roadway about half as long as the village, and thirteen signs in sight, on every one of which you could read 'Lager Beer.'"

Mr. Locke died in 1887. Contemporary with him there was an almost equally noted journalistic character known as "Brick" Pomeroy. His real name was Mark M. Pomeroy, and he first came into notice as the editor of a Copperhead Newspaper at LaCrosse, Wisconsin. The first time I ever saw him he wore, as a scarfpin, a miniature doorplate, bearing the word BRICK, in Gothic letters. Later he moved to New York, issued a daily, as well as a weekly; was for a time almost as conspicuous as Mr. Hearst has been in later days, and had the proud distinction of owning and publishing the weekly paper having a larger circulation than any other in the United States. Later he discontinued the daily and toned down the weekly to make it almost respectable; but his readers would not stand for that, and after a time it died a natural death.

THIRTY-THIRD PAPER

I have made reference to the circumstance that I was at one time a director of a small State bank. It had come about in this way. While I lived in Boston I was called upon one day by a cousin, a year or two my senior, who was a storekeeper in East St. Johnsbury, Vermont. We made arrangements to go to a theater that evening, and he brought with him two men, also from Vermont, one being a Mr. Hibbard, a junior partner of the well-known firm of wholesale drug and medicine dealers, Messrs. Geo. C. Goodwin & Co.; the other a man in some way connected with the drug and medicine trade, hailing from Waterbury, Vermont, and named John F. Henry. We were all of about the same age, possibly Henry may have been the senior by a year or two. He was a typical example of the New England Yankee—tall and lean, of a light sandy complexion, and a manner giving evidence of considerable shrewdness. It was a pleasant evening and I felt that I had made two not undesirable additions to my rather small list of acquaintances, and possibly thought myself not of the least consequence of any of the four of us. In this I was mistaken, for each of the other three was in reality a good deal better situated than I was in the way of a start in business life. I was probably earning a salary of $16 a week at the time. Henry had done some business with a peddler's outfit, and I think I felt a little sorry for him.

Soon after I came to New York, however, Henry made his appearance there and had a connection with the great medicine warehouse of Demas Barnes & Co., then the leading institution in that line in the United States. Barnes owned a great many trade-marks, a half interest in Plantation Bitters and was about that time launching Castoria on the sea of public favor. Pretty soon Henry told me he was a partner in the concern, and before I had gotten over my surprise at that he had bought Barnes out and the firm became John F. Henry & Co. The mercantile agencies rated him A1—a million and over—he was talked of for Mayor of Brooklyn, seemed to have his own way if he went to Albany about any matter before the Legislature, was listened to when he talked before the New York Chamber of Commerce, after the gray-beards had gotten over their surprise that any one under sixty should venture to speak at all, and was very much in evidence everywhere—still retaining his rather lanky and countryfied air, but competent to meet all comers, and needing no one to aid him in his efforts to take care of himself.

Henry had come in contact with a Mr. Joseph U. Orvis, a man who had had much to do with banks and banking, and who had in mind establishing a new bank with a capital of $250,000. It was already well under way when Henry proposed that I should buy some stock, and suggested that if I took a considerable interest I might have a place on the board of directors. I put my name down for $10,000 and was made a director. The board was made up somewhat on the plan adopted for the New Hampshire Legislature, where the idea seems to prevail that it is a good school and can hardly have too many members. I rather think our board numbered as many as two dozen in all, and among them were several men of first-class consequence—including in this category, without doubt, Mr. Henry and the writer. Of those that gathered about that table in the directors' room I believe that save the Hon. Stewart L. Woodford—former Lieut.-Governor of New York and United States Minister to Spain—and myself no others are now living.

Our most solid and influential member was Mr. Edward Clark, owner of at least one-half the stock of the Singer Manufacturing Company. Perhaps the director who was most active in promoting the progress of the institution was Mr. Henry. The one who was most listened to was Mr. Inslee A. Hopper, elected to the board by Mr. Clark's suggestion. I was the youngest member and Hopper the next younger. The main secret of his preponderating weight was that he was supposed to voice Mr. Clark's ideas, and Mr. Clark, who owned about a third of all the shares, rarely spoke at all. He was that Mr. Clark who founded the great Clark estate, of which New Yorkers hear a good deal, which at his death amounted to thirty million dollars, and at the present time is thought to run up above a hundred millions. Isaac N. Singer, the original owner of the famous Singer Sewing Machine, was not living at this time. Mr. Clark controlled the affairs of the great Sewing Machine Company, but Mr. Hopper, young as he was—scarcely more than thirty—had for some years been its president.

Isaac N. Singer was a Yankee of Connecticut origin. He used to travel about the country with a horse and a covered wagon, in which he carried and from which he sold wood type, and delivered it to printing offices for use in the preparation of poster and other work that required the sort of display seen nowadays in Mr. Hearst's newspapers, when it is desired to direct attention to murders and similar enterprises. He had obtained the sewing machine patent in the way of a swap or small speculation, and being a man of resources and tireless energy not only made more progress in introducing his particular sewing machine than any one before him had ever done, and also got into more lawsuits, in that and other connections, than falls to the common lot of man. Mr. Clark was his attorney, and there came a time when there seemed to be due to him for services rendered the considerable sum represented by the figures 10,-000 following a dollar mark, and in settlement of that claim Singer gave him a half interest in the business.

I was going over to Washington one day, and it chanced that in the parlor car Mr. Hopper had the chair next to me. Having nothing better to do we talked to each other. "How did you, so young a man, happen to get yourself made president of the Singer Manufacturing Company?" I asked. "I'll tell you about that," he said. "You know I have held the office for some years. I was bookkeeper for the old concern, and one day Mr. Singer came to my desk and said, 'Hopper, are you married?' I said no, and asked why he made the inquiry. 'I'll tell you why,' said he. 'We are going to incorporate this business, and Clark won't let me be president—and I swear I won't let him. We ought to have a married man. You are pretty young, but I think if you were married we would make you president. Don't you know some nice girl that you would like to marry?' I did know such a girl, but my circumstances were not such as to warrant me in assuming extra obligations, and I had never hinted of the matter to her; but that evening I went to see her and told her the whole story. She was nice about it, and agreed to help me out. We were married within two weeks. I was made president. They fixed my salary at $25,000—that's what all the directors receive—and I have held the place ever since."

I think Mr. Clark must have been fond of Mr. Orvis. He gave a dinner one night in honor of the directors of the Security Bank. This was at his residence in 23d street, not far from where Dutton's book store is now situated. Other gentlemen were present. It was the finest entertainment I had ever seen. There was some speechmaking, and one gentleman, with a playful facetiousness, told a story of early experiences when he first came to New York as a boy. He, with a companion, was walking through Chatham street to their boarding house in Cliff street, when, not far from Printing House Square, they saw, in a window, a sign in white letters cut on red glass, illuminated by a gas jet behind it, that read HOT MINCE PIES, and the two thought, as it was late and cold, a hot mince pie would be about the right thing to go to bed on; so they made up the price—25 cents—between them, and with the pie wrapped in butcher's paper, under the arm of one, they sought the privacy of their attic room, produced their knives and prepared to regale themselves, when the operator, whose best blade was the one known as the pen knife, was amazed to find he had broken the steel in his effort to divide the treasure—the pie was frozen stiff. Next day they went in company, hot—

unlike the pie—with anger, and energetically remonstrated with the Hebrew who had fooled them so. They gave expression to their views; he listened with some apparent interest, but when they gave him a chance to speak, reminded them that he had not told them that the pie was hot, but—pointing to the sign—continued, "That's the *name* of 'em." The gentleman then referred to our bank and its designation, "The Security" and hoped that, unlike the pie the name would in fact be found to represent an actual condition. We all hoped so, too, and probably thought so, but that speech, at a later period more than once recurred to my mind.

Mr. Orvis had a good knowledge of banking. It was said that he had been the responsible head in starting not only the Ninth National, but also the great Park Bank, but for one reason or another had seceded from each. I guess he was something like what a Western man once called the brilliant Frank Hatton—"A hell of a commencer"—for after a time there was dissatisfaction with our president in our own board. We had decided that the capital was too small, and we would double it, and I, to show my good will and faith, put up another $10,000 for more stock and this made me the largest holder next to Mr. Clark—the gap between him and me was pretty wide, however. Finally there was a disposition to induce Mr. Orvis to resign. To this I was opposed. I stood by him. The matter was held a considerable time in abeyance, but one day I had a visit from Mr. John Mack, another director—perhaps his principal claim to fame may consist of the fact that he was the father-in-law of the great Tammany orator, Bourke Cockran—who told me that Mr. Orvis must go; that a large majority of the directors were pledged to vote that way; that he had felt as I did, but had changed his mind, and I must, too. It would make no difference in the result, but it would be better to have the action unanimous and avoid any appearance of a disagreement. I acquiesced, reluctantly; but knowing that Mr. Orvis counted me as a supporter, insisted that I would go to him at once and tell him how things stood—and how I stood. Mr. Orvis' reception of me and my story made a strong impression on me. He had been pretty strenuous in his objection to being ousted, and pretty energetic in his language at times, but he listened to me calmly, with an unruffled countenance; thanked me for my frankness, found no word of fault with me or anybody else, and seemed in an altogether pleasant and placid state of mind. This was so different from what I had expected that, although it gratified me to see it, I could not refrain from remarking upon his calmness and apparent unconcern; whereupon he said—quite pleasantly—"It is my impression that you will find that people always *submit to the inevitable* without any fuss."

The bank did no better under a new head; in fact did worse; dividends were passed; we on the inside could see that the capital was impaired; we seemed to go from bad to worse. There began to be talk of this measure and that —consolidation with some other bank and I know not what beside. As I was the youngest member of the board, my voice had never been raised at the meetings, but I had begun to think less than formerly of the wisdom of some who spoke oftenest and most influenced the conduct of the concern. Finally some one made a suggestion that seemed to me specially objectionable; and, blushing, I arose to express some views of my own. Mr. Clark had taken the presidency temporarily, to give the concern the benefit of his name and reputation for wealth; he sat at the head of the table, and to him I addressed what I had to say. "We had gone on year after year, we had made no money, every change had been for the worse, no step seemed to advance us in any direction other than down hill; we who were present represented a large percentage of the stockholders —a majority—we knew there were assets sufficient to pay the depositors in full; let us do that then while we can and let the stockholders stand the loss that they cannot avoid; let us wind up the institution ourselves and wipe our hands of it."

To the right and left of me I could see only disapproval.

In Mr. Clark's face I could read nothing. Mr. Hopper sat by my side and rose to speak as I sat down. I could not guess what would be the tone of his remarks, but he surprised me. He commended what I had said; commended the course I had mapped out, and moved that Mr. Rowell's suggestions be adopted and carried out; that the work be done by a committee of the board, and that Mr. Rowell be chairman of that committee. His earnestness seemed to impress Mr. Clark. Some remarks were made from each hand, beginning in a rather sarcastic strain, commenting upon the unexpected prominence the youthful member of the board had stepped into, and suggesting one or two other courses. Mr. Clark said a few words that carried much weight, and it was voted that the plan should be carried out precisely as I had suggested, by a committee to be appointed by the president. Mr. Clark thereupon appointed me and Mr. Hopper—I to act as chairman. Mr. Hopper then arose and said if he was to serve he wished to have Mr. Clark also added to the committee, so that he might be available as an adviser, and on account of the confidence his name would inspire. This was so ordered, and the meeting adjourned; but before any one had left the table, Mr. Hopper said to Mr. Clark, with a half laugh in his voice—like a big boy asking of a father a favor that he was confident would be granted—"Mr. Clark, I want you, now, to go down to the Chemical Bank and tell them to let us have all the money we want—if we do want any." Mr. Clark smiled, a peculiar but not unpleasant smile; his eyes were seen to glisten through his gold-bowed glasses; and he went out and did just what Mr. Hopper had suggested that he should; and the first information the public had of any trouble in our little bank was a printed notice to the depositors requesting them to draw their checks for the balances standing to their credit. And, would you believe it? they were so slow about doing this, and we realized upon our resources so promptly, that we never had to avail ourselves of Mr. Clark's backing to the extent of a single cent.

I closed up the affairs of the concern, paid the depositors in full, and eventually gave the stockholders about thirty cents on a dollar; but before the final dividends were paid a broker in Wall street had succeeded in buying up practically all the stock at a percentage below its actual value, and as I took it off his hands I found, when the affair was closed, I, personally, was protected from any actual loss on my $20,000 investment. The stockholders who did not sell never made any complaint, and as I charged nothing at all for my services and gave them every cent that came in, it is not probable that any one ever thought of being other than well satisfied. I can see no reason why they should. This was my only experience in banking.

THIRTY-FOURTH PAPER

Among the things I attempted during the time of my most ardent ambition to make my advertising agency complete in every respect, was the establishment of a printers' warehouse department from which the newspapers, to whom we should become indebted for advertising space might order the goods they needed, and generally obtained from typefounders, pressmen, inkmakers and others. The plan did not work as well as one might have supposed it would. The trouble arose partly from an impression that seemed to be strongly intrenched in the mind of the newspaper man, as a rule, that because he knew our firm well enough to be willing to trust us for a $10 ad, we, on that account, must know him well enough and be equally willing to trust him for a $50 paper cutter, or a $500 Gordon press, upon which our profit would be no more than $5 or $25 respectively. Perhaps that difficulty might have been overcome; but it gave rise to another complication. The publisher who bought wood type of Mr. Cooley, and agreed to buy more wood type to balance any charges he might have against Mr. Cooley for advertising, seemed to imbibe from that transaction the impression that we had also sought his patronage for articles sold on a closer margin of profit than that afforded by wood type, and had also made an agreement to let the bill stand until we should have sent advertising orders to an amount sufficient to balance it.

There was still another difficulty. The country paper that would carry a standing column of electrotyped matter for a gross price of $25 would, when indebted to us, become decidedly insistent that the price of the column we desired was not $25, but $80 or $100 or $125, and, in a correspondence that might ensue, it was not always easy to answer the statement "We paid you what you asked for the paper cutter or imposing stone, why should you not pay me what I ask for my advertising space?" The man knew the answer as well as we did, but somehow correspondence on the subject never seemed to lead out in a way that was satisfactory to either. Of course there were things that could be sold to publishers on their own terms, but these were not standard. I will mention one example of transactions in an article of this description.

The Chicago Advertising Agency of Cook, Coburn & Co. communicated with us at one time on the subject of selling to publishers, who should also happen to be job printers—as nearly every publisher of a country weekly is —a recipe for making a dryer, that had the attractive name of Riley's Indispensable. When that was used the ink would not smooch. There need be no delay before packing up and delivering the job. Their agency had been approached in the same way, had issued a circular to papers they were dealing with in their territory, and had sold so many of the recipes, and the buyers were so well satisfied that they were confident we, with our broader connection, could dispose of a very large number. The recipe was printed on a card, was to be sold for $10, the buyer being understood to promise to keep the secret and not give it away. It was the same plan that Mr. E. C. Allen had found to work so well in selling his recipe for making a washing compound. For each recipe sold we were to pay $2.50. We sent the circular to every paper to which we were indebted for as much as $2.50 and a considerable number of orders came in, upon no one of which could we possibly incur any loss. Later we were favored with a right to buy other copies of the recipe at $1 each, and issued a new proposal to all papers to which we were indebted for as much as $1, and sold a larger number than before. Next there came an offer to sell us a perpetual right to print the cards ourselves for the payment of a gross sum of $100. We thereupon communicated with the hundred or two printers who had bought the recipe of us and learned from their replies that they were pretty generally satisfied with the transaction. One facetious editor, noticing that Balsam Copaiba was one of the ingredients, wrote to say that he had formerly been familiar with a preparation that he presumed was substantially the same thing, although he had used it for an entirely different purpose. He, as well as others, was satisfied with his purchase of the recipe. We paid the $100 for the perpetual right, issued a new circular to all of the about 5,000 papers then published, and within thirty days had fully 500 orders in hand, thereby creating a credit of $10 for us on the books of the papers in question, a total of $5,000, and all for an outlay of not much beyond the $100 paid for the right. Other orders came in from time to time. Now and then an ill-natured man, who had a grievance, or thought he had, would print the recipe in his columns, and make remarks about it, but that did not seem to do any harm. Still the trade came to an end in time, and at this day I have no copy of the recipe nor any knowledge of any of the ingredients beyond the one of which a correspondent had spoken so highly.

The typefounders of the time had a combination among themselves and would allow no commissions to us on any sales of type, and I went to England and perfected arrangements there whereby I might import type; but the profit was confined to a much smaller percentage than that realized on the Riley's Indispensable, and the inconvenient delays in getting sorts, when wanted, prevented the English type from becoming popular either with us or with the printers to whom we sold it.

Eventually I sold out the printers' warehouse branch of our trade to Mr. R. H. C. Valentine, who had managed it for us for some years. He had no money to buy with, but we trusted him, and he, eventually, paid us in full, although, before he died, I think some other people who sold things to him did not come out as well as we did. We also sold to Mr. Valentine our weekly paper, the *American Newspaper Reporter and Advertisers' Gazette*. He immediately changed the sub-head to *Printers' Gazette,* and after numerous changes of make-up and character it finally ceased publication and disappeared, to be resurrected years later in the form of little *Printers' Ink*.

While we sold merchandise to printers we had rather extensive dealings in ink, sold mainly to country papers who generally bought in 25-pound kegs. There were two standard qualities, the best being sold at 25 cents a pound, the other grade at 20 cents, making the price of a keg $6.25 and $5 respectively. The cost to us was $2 for the best grade and $1.80 for the other. We sold hundreds of kegs of the stuff. I remember contracting for 2,000 kegs at one time. There would be twenty sales of the dearer sort to one of the lower priced, and, as it complicated matters somewhat to keep the two kinds separate, as the kegs looked exactly alike on the outside, there came a time when we ceased to put in any of the second grade. Thereafter, when a man ordered the 20 cent sort, he got the same as he would if he had ordered the 25 cent sort. I once read in a paper, edited by an embryo humorist, the statement that "Printers' ink is a sticky compound and many printers have got stuck with it." The indications, so far as my observation has extended, all go to show that the printer who gets stuck with ink generally has a hand in it himself.

The differing ideas that prevail in printing offices about the comparative qualities of inks is one of the most curious things in life. There is, or used to be, a sale for black inks at as high a rate as $10 a pound, but there never was a black ink made that would not afford a profit to the maker at 25 cents a pound, if selling and delivery expenses could be eliminated. Our inks sold at 25 cents a pound gave universal satisfaction, while those who bought the same goods at 20 cents a pound were less likely to be satisfied. The complaints about the quality of the 20 cent goods outnumbered those about that of the 25 cent sort more than two to one, although the sales of the 25 cent sort outnumbered those of the other as much as twenty to one. Whenever a kick came we took back the ink, sent another lot just like it and rarely heard any further complaint. Inks cost somewhat more to make to-day than they did twenty-five years ago; but in the advertisements of Printers Ink Jonson that appear weekly in the pages of *Printers' Ink* at the present time the same grade of goods that we sold for 25 cents or 20 cents, as the buyer preferred, is now offered at 6 cents, and probably costs 3 to make, with cost of keg to be added. My old friend Wilson used to feel first rate when he took my order for a thousand kegs, for which he would collect $2,000 from me, which I now know would make him fully $1,000 richer than he was the day before. But if the keg cost him $1, me $2, and the printer $5 or $6.25, as he preferred, I did not seem to occupy the position of least advantage among the three of us.

Before Mr. Valentine went out of business he had a contract, for a considerable time, to supply the printing ink used by the *Delineator,* and took his pay in advertising space in that publication. Of so little account was the advertising considered that it became hard to get an advertisement inserted there without hunting up Valentine and bargaining with him. So far as I know he may have obtained the entire franchise for advertising in the *Delineator* merely to pay for its ink supply. Under better management to-day the advertising patronage of that magazine now produces money enough to pay Mr. Roosevelt's yearly salary out of the proceeds of any single month of the entire year.

The United States Postal Laws say that a paper issued primarily for advertising purposes must be regarded as a circular, and have postage paid on it as such, and may not enjoy the mailing facilities and postage rates accorded to a periodical. The *Delineator* was established for the purpose of advertising the Butterick Paper Patterns and with no other view. Its contents, from cover to cover, long consisted solely of pictures of garments and announcements of the prices at which the patterns could be had, yet, bare as it was of other features, it early found more than a hundred thousand women who were glad to pay the subscription price in advance for it, and, although the question puzzled the clerks in the Department at Washington who dealt with such things, if they ever excluded it from the mails, it was not for long. Under recent more intelligent management the magazine now has other excellent features of a magazine for women, and instead of a hundred thousand circulation, is making rapid strides toward the million mark. It already gets six dollars a line for its advertising space.

THIRTY-FIFTH PAPER

In the sixties and early seventies many names of cities, prominent now, had a strange sound to the ear. Omaha suggested an Indian tribe, Seattle—perhaps it did not exist, certainly I heard no word of it during a six weeks' stay on the Columbia in 1873: but before that time I was told about

Denver—told a good deal about it—in letters from a most enthusiastic journalist, already settled there. He sent me maps that made the place look like an enormous spider with a multitude of legs, every one of which represented a rail-road—projected. Whether there really was one completed

road that would take a passenger there I do not know. This man's name was O. J. Goldrick, and his paper the *Rocky Mountain Herald*. He sent me his photograph, showing a slight, wiry, middle-aged man, wearing a black suit, a black tie, a boiled shirt, a black moustache, and hair as black as only a photograph or a hair dye can make it.

About this time Mr. John Taylor Johnston of New York City, who was the first president of the Metropolitan Museum of Art, owned a picture by Turner called "The Slave Ship." It may be there was no other genuine example of this great artist in America at that time. Most of the canvas was black paint, but in the center there was color of flame, toned here and there by splashes of the yolk of an egg; and, by being shown now and then in exhibitions of the fine arts, I was familiar with it; but connected it in no way with my Colorado correspondent, until one day a man came into my office, the very counterpart of the picture I had kept in my desk, save that the hair and moustache were not black at all but flaming in the colors and shades of the burning ship. On speaking with him he developed a brogue, not, of course, to be detected in his letters; and, on the whole, he was a quite remarkable specimen of an amiable Irishman of the sort we acquire the habit of speaking of as wild. It was through him that I had heard of Denver for the first time, and he had all the enthusiasm that has grown to be inseparable from every person who lives for so much as a week in that wonderful city. While there in 1882 a newspaper paragraph directed attention to a block of stores situated on ———— street, begun last Monday—the paper stated—would not be completed before Saturday—but in the meantime had all been let. In 1890 I was there again, and talked with the elder of the Lawrence Brothers, who had long owned and published the Ohio *Farmer*. His home was in Cleveland, but he had gone to Denver to recruit a damaged lung, and, as everybody else seemed to do, had become fascinated with the place. "I suppose," said I to Lawrence, "you expect to live to see this city have 500,000 people, do you not?" "I don't know about that," said he, "but I am perfectly certain it will have a million in less than five years."

Mr. Goldrick is now hardly remembered by anybody in Denver, and what became of him I do not know, but of the picture, to parts of which I have compared his hair and beard, I recall something further. There was a time when the stock of Jersey Central declined from 180 to 8 and Mr. Johnston, who was interested in it, sold his fine art collection at public auction. It was a notable sale, and among those who attended was Mr. Fred B. McGuire, Director of the Corcoran Gallery at Washington. By his side sat a man of advanced years, a large man, with bushy hair and eyebrows, and a heavy cane with a hole through it, embellished with a cord and tassel; and when the "Slave Ship" was at last knocked down at $10,000, and the name of the buyer announced, the old man seemed to become crazy with pleasurable excitement. He bravoed, pounded the floor with his heavy cane, stamped his feet, and could hardly contain himself, and his exhibition of feeling excited Mr. McGuire's surprise to such an extent that he ventured to ask the old gentleman what it was that excited his enthusiasm to such an unusual degree. Whereupon the older man, looking around, broke into a laugh and as soon as he could command his voice said, "Why, the damned thing's going to Boston!"

Walking up Broadway one evening many years ago I came to a store I had not previously observed, and noted that it was devoted to the sale of preparations put forth by the Boston house of Joseph Burnett & Co., proprietors of Burnett's Kaliston, Burnett's Flavoring Extracts, Burnett's Cocoaine, Dr. Jonas Whitcomb's Asthma Remedy, and so on. As Dr. Burnett was something of an advertiser I was interested in this new enterprise of his, and stepped inside the place to investigate. The venture being new, business was not brisk—I hardly think it ever did become brisk in that store—and I found the man in charge quite at leisure and willing to talk. He was of about my own age, of a rather reserved manner, but he had opinions, and was not inclined to keep them in the background, even for the sake of making a conversation go more smoothly. We came pretty near to getting into an altercation; I do not remember what about, but it was certainly nothing of any particular consequence. The man knew all about me, when I told my name, but he also knew all about advertising and needed no points on the subject. He had been with Burnett for some years, and this new store was the carrying out of an idea that he had personally urged. Somehow we got so warm in our arguments that we were both quite out of temper when I came away, and it was all for so nearly no reason at all that I think we must have been—both of us—a little ashamed of it, for when we met again some months after the recognition was mutual and pleasant. We spoke of the former meeting, both laughed and were good friends from that hour and always remained so—in a measure.

This man was Lyman D. Morse, afterwards associated with James H. Bates under the firm name of Bates & Morse, and the founder of the present Lyman D. Morse Advertising Agency, which still does an excellent business at its offices in the Potter Building at No. 38 Park Row, numbering among its clients some of the best advertisers of the time.

I might mention that Dr. Burnett had the advertising idea, and all his efforts at publicity had about them indications of both efficiency and good taste. He failed more than once while comparatively young in business, but eventually acquired an ample competence, lived like a gentleman and associated with gentlemen. One of his sons married a daughter of James Russell Lowell, the poet, once our Minister to the Court of St. James. This son had rural tastes and he would be a farmer. He also had the advertising idea, and it was from his farm at Framingham, Massachusetts, that the delicious slim little sausages called the Deerfoot were first put upon the market. They may be had now in every State of the Union, and the trademark must be really valuable. Just think of being able to apply a trademark to a sausage.

Morse married a lady whose sister was the wife of

Frank T. Brown, son of that John I. Brown, who established the one time largely advertised Brown's Bronchial Troches. I am of the opinion that another sister was the wife of Jerry Curtis, son of Jeremiah Curtis who made a success of the Mrs. Winslow's Soothing Syrup trademark. In consequence of these connections Morse might be said to be in an atmosphere of advertising and he liked it, and had ideas of his own on the subject, and they were good ones.

LYMAN D. MORSE.

He succeeded better than any other man I have known in getting large advertising value out of small advertising space.

The Burnett advertisements and the Deerfoot notices have almost always been small, but particularly well placed. Mrs. Winslow's Soothing Syrup advertisements are always small, and the wording of them is rarely or never changed. The Brown's Troches advertisements were also small, and of the four referred to, they alone used anything like a cut or picture. I don't think, however, that Morse had much if anything to do with shaping the publicity of the Curtis or the Brown publicity. Burnett's he managed long, perhaps as long as he lived, and no man ever worked more faithfully, more tirelessly to get a low rate, an extra concession and a position that nobody else could secure. Time was no object. If a small concession was all that could be had that was better than nothing. No matter how good the terms that were offered Morse was never quite satisfied. He was always in earnest, never laughed. He had no sense of humor, but held the dollar very close to his eye.

Alfred Cowles, part owner and so long the business manager of the Chicago *Tribune*, used to tell a story of Morse. He had been in Chicago for a week or ten days, and came daily to the *Tribune* office to talk about rates and position for an advertisement he wished to place in its columns. Cowles was one of those brisk, brusque men who would make a decision off-hand and wait patiently enough while you talked as much as you liked; but when you were done his decision stood as stated in the beginning. Morse never wasted any time talking with subordinates. He would go to the fountain head, and daily he entered Mr. Cowles' private office, and daily he went over the figures of the contract he had in mind. "Won't you give me anything," said he, "no concession whatever?" and to this Cowles answered with a bit of cynicism in his laugh, "Morse, I don't know that I wouldn't give you a ticket to get you out of town." The order was finally given and Morse went away, and for several days Cowles had a rest. But one day, perhaps a week later, Morse came again. He would go to St. Louis in the morning and came now to ask Cowles if he was in earnest about what he said about giving him a railroad pass.

I came to have occasional dealings with Morse and to place some business for him, before he became associated with Mr. Bates. I never saw a man who so greatly appreciated commendation, praise—I may say flattery. He would wait for more of it—as a cat will to have her back stroked. I would not have thought him at all calculated to succeed as an advertising agent, but he really did first-rate, and Bates always had a high opinion of his abilities. The two were no more alike than chalk is like cheese.

THIRTY-SIXTH PAPER

Mention has been made of an early ambition to get back to the soil. That longing never left me; and in the year 1880, at the age of forty-two, I bought a farm in the same White Mountain region of the Granite State where my boyhood had been passed. For half a dozen years or thereabouts I was not seen at the office very much. New clerks failed to recognize me on the occasions of my rare appearances, and my partners commonly refrained from consulting me or telling me very much about what was going on. There were daily or weekly reports sent to me, but I had sense enough not to attempt to control a business that I did not give attention to. I diversified farming with a six months' tour of Europe, an expedition to the West Indies, Mexico and our Pacific States; devoted considerable time to trout and bass fishing—but never quite so much as was good for me—expended much energy and some money in improving the farm, concerning which I am able to say, that in spite of my early training, having been born and bred on a farm, I did not, during any single month of the more than twenty years that I experimented with Prospect Farm, succeed in getting enough income from it to pay the running expenses of that month. This seems more strange when it is stated that occasionally nearly the entire product for a year would be sold and turned into money at one time. Surely one might think that the month of the greatest sale would now and then provide for at least its own share of the yearly outgo, but no such case ever did happen. I introduced thoroughbred cattle, and at the county fair, came so near carrying off all the premiums offered that I aroused the energies of my brother farmers to such an extent that they elected me president of the Agricultural Society; and that seemed a death blow to its fortunes, for a year or two later the grounds were sold to an association of gentlemen, who had horse trots very much more on their minds than prize pumpkins or fat oxen.

I became a citizen of the town, voted there, and was even complimented by a nomination for Representative to the State Legislature. This was, on the whole, a rather sad experience. Old schoolmates crossed the street to avoid meeting me, fearing they would have to refuse a request to vote for me, and thereby become false to party affiliations. I had flattered myself that I was rather popular. The store-keeper where I traded was a schoolmate and friend; my farmer, who superintended my agricultural operations, seemed to think well of me; the gardener—of Irish origin— talked so pleasantly that I gave him a suit of clothes and a good overcoat; but not one of these favored me with a vote, although the gardener was loyal enough to leave town the day before election and thus avoided voting against me. On election morning I drove over the four miles of road that intervened between the farm and the town hall; was alone in the wagon, and overtook two neighbors—father and son —born Democrats, dyed in the wool, the older a man of perhaps not less than seventy years. I stopped and asked them to ride. There was a moment's pause before the old man spoke; then he said with some hesitation, but not without dignity, "Mr. Rowell, we are going to vote for you to-day, and there are some who will not expect that, nor like it. I think we had better walk, for if we should be seen riding into town with you it will cause talk and I think that would not be a good thing." If any other Democrat voted for me I never knew it. One neighbor, a Republican, wanted to vote for me, but thought he ought to get some consideration for it, but I could not see it that way. The fact is, as a politician, I was as green as grass, and my conduct in that campaign showed it.

A merchant in the village, prosperous, public-spirited and popular, was the Democratic candidate who opposed me. We had been acquaintances and friends from our youth, but he intended to win if possible, partly because that was the thing to do and more perhaps because at the preceding election he had seen himself defeated by a majority of one. It was reported that he contributed over $3,000 for printed matter and the legitimate purchase of votes in our innocent rural community, casting only about five hundred ballots. If this was so, I am certain he must have felt chagrined when the count at town meeting showed he had a majority so large that he could not have failed of election had he never turned a hand or expended a cent to influence the result.

I hunted up a lake that was a famous place for trout fishing, and got up a little club, in which some of my newspaper friends took an interest, and by buying the land all around the lake and on both sides of the inlet coming from mountain springs and the outlet, falling over cascades that pickerel could not ascend; and ending in a river where pickerel swarmed; I supposed, in the light of the advice of leading lawyers of the State that our little association actually had secured a trout preserve and controlled the fishing and a right to be let alone. And may be we did, for the case is still in litigation in the United States Courts, after about twenty years of continual struggle, that have exhausted the resources of the State judiciary, led to the enactment of no less than eight separate statute laws by the Legislature—each one intended to deprive us of the rights we thought we had acquired. All of these, in one way and another, have caused our little association to pay out four times more money for lawyers' fees than we ever did for real estate, camp furniture and fishing tackle.

There not being work enough about my farm and garden to occupy my spare time, I felt impelled to acquire control of one of the village newspapers, and show the rural editors of the United States just how a village paper really ought to be conducted. A price was agreed upon, the money paid over, and I thought I was in full possession; but after taking over the office, the former owner surprised me by asserting that unpaid subscriptions up to date of transfer belonged to him. I referred him to my lawyer, who had conducted the transaction for me, and he, with commendable loyalty to his nearer neighbor, and doubtless in accordance with actual right—though it did not seem so to me—decided the case against me.

I reduced the subscription price to a dollar a year, payable always in advance, made myself disliked by the leading and richest people in the town, who were also my best friends, by stopping their papers when their subscriptions expired; adopted a flat rate for advertising, so low that a small advertisement, inserted once, hardly brought in money enough to pay for handling the type, and figured up such a considerable sum, on a yearly contract, that nobody failed to be amazed. The advertising agents, who had the prices quoted to them for inserting electrotypes by the year, seemed to have their breaths taken away, and told their customers that a crank had got possession of that office and it would be better to scratch the paper off the list. We bought new type and introduced many improvements that nobody seemed to notice particularly, although the St. Johnsbury *Caledonian,* printed thirty miles away, did assert, in a paragraph one day, that I was "trying to run a nonpareil paper in a long primer town."

I was too proud and of too much importance to solicit local patronage. The storekeepers resented having their old time contracts superseded, or were glad to be free from importunities to renew them. They advertised but little. Occasionally I wrote a few lines, in my simple kindly manner, making reference to some village affair; possibly an individual; and was uniformly amazed to note that some people were thin-skinned and not at all disposed to submit to criticism from such an outsider as I was. One paragraph, which asserted that some people thought rum was sold at one of the drug stores, gave no offense at all to the one I had in mind, but made a good deal of hard feeling on the part of the owner of the other store. If a boy stole money out of a till and left town he was pretty certain to have been born near the schoolhouse that Nelson Chesman and I had attended in our youth; and his mother, perhaps, was that red-cheeked girl who wore her dark hair in such big braids. Anyhow it would not do to mention the affair in the paper and it even seemed hardly safe to make a six line reference to a six column account that appeared next day in the Boston *Globe,* of which a good many copies came into the village.

One day the foreman directed my attention to a two column electrotype, about five inches long, that had been sent in, direct, from an insurance company, and asked how much he should bill them for it. "You know the rates," said I. "It measures ten inches of column space; that makes 120 lines nonpareil; at 2 cents a line the price will be $2.40. What's the matter?" "Nothing," he said, "only that electrotype comes every year, and we have always received $12.50 for putting it in. They never ask the price." "Well, I can't help that," was my decision, "we charge two cents a line flat and as we will take no less neither can we receive any more." The bill was paid without comment, but next year the order went to the other paper that had an old time publisher, who knew enough to make hay on the few sunshiny occasions that turn up in the office of a village newspaper. That's mixed metaphor, but no one can fail to get the idea.

While in control of that office I had an opportunity to note how lean, how destitute of possible profit, were most of the proposals that came to hand through the mail. If the price was liberal the sender was unknown; or if known, was poor pay. If not known he would not often turn out on investigation to be worth knowing. If the soundness of the sender was beyond peradventure the price offered would be cut to the quick, while the conditions of insertion would be exacting and onerous. There were proposals to give fifty-two reading notices for subscription to an unknown magazine, or to insert three inches a year to pay for the *Scientific American* (that a mechanic in the town would take off our hands at half price) and all the thousand and one schemes and proposals that country papers had been writing me about and kicking about, charging them all to the evil influences of advertising agencies ever since I had elected myself to be an advertising agent a dozen or twenty years before. I had always talked to such publishers in a patronizing way, told them they held the remedy in their own hands, if they did not like a proposal they need not accept it, but that every proposal ought to have an answer, and so on and so on. All the experiences referred to and the alleged remedies for them as well are known to every one of the class of human beings whom Horace Greeley, in a moment of petulance, once denominated: "Those little creatures whom God for some inscrutable purpose has permitted to edit country newspapers." I was one of these now and could see for myself.

It would be all very well to conduct the business on iron-clad rules. Surely everybody ought to get the same treatment that was afforded to everybody else; but there was one difficulty to which I had not given sufficient thought. The country editor must live. The advertising agent and foreign advertiser may not admit this necessity, but if he does live he must generally make his paper bring in the money he pays for food, fuel and shelter. The man who sold out to me did this, and lived very well. He had between nine and ten hundred subscribers and those that did not pay in advance paid a higher price later—sometimes. He took the $12.50 from the insurance company and retained their respect. I cut the price to $2.40 and made them think that a paper that valued its columns no higher than that could not be worth continuing on the list of papers to which their advertisements should be sent. Had the company sought a yearly contract and placed the order with an agent who knew his business my predecessor would have received possibly as much as $30 gross, $22.50 net for fifty-two insertions, while the gross charge under my system would be $124.80 and the agent would have to pay it or keep out. If the company took the agent's advice it would stay out—and it ought to.

As I have said, my predecessor made a living out of the paper. I did not. I had many compliments on the first rate character of the paper I produced; some of the village people asserted that they were proud of it; but never did I get so many as 900 subscribers on the list. I think 844 was high water mark. My predecessor had a little larger mail list than I ever secured. When I had conducted the paper three years I found the net deficit, the amount the outgo had exceeded the income, was a little more than $6,000 or an average loss of a trifle over $2,000 a year. So I sold the material at public auction, sent postage stamps to the subscribers to pay back the balance due on subscriptions and the paper was dead—for as much as a week. My predecessor took it up again, made a fair income from the start, sold it out to other parties, at a profit on its cost to him, and it has gone on ever since, fully a score of years, showing so much prosperity as to indicate that the management is in no need of points from me.

Some people would think I might have learned a practical lesson in publishing from the experience I have narrated, but in spite of it all I not very long afterwards became responsible for a little weekly issued in New York City by the Charity Organization Society. I was a member of the executive committee, wanted the paper run in a certain way, and agreed if there was a deficit I would make it good. Well, *Charities* run me behind in twelve months as many dollars as the Lancaster *Gazette* did in three years, and I do not think my brother members of the executive committee understand to this day what it was that made me so firm in my determination to have nothing more to do with the publication after my time of guarantee had expired. It is still published and, judging by the look of it, I should think it a self-supporting enterprise. If it is so, it is equally certain that it was not I that made it so.

After both these unhappy experiences I conducted little *Printers' Ink* on pretty much the same plan and, since Editor Zingg has supplanted me in the control, I have still had influence enough to induce him to keep on with it, and in its case the plan works so well that there appears to be no present temptation to change it.

Probably not a very large number of people have ever devoted any particular thought to the subject, but the few who have know that at no time, and under no circumstances, has a newspaper publisher or editor been the leading man in the town where he lives. The person of greatest influence may be a shoemaker, a lumberman or a farmer, but never a newspaper man. Whenever a man who thinks himself of some local consequence, or really is so, undertakes to conduct a paper he burns his fingers every time and loses both money and prestige. There is a way of accomplishing the desired result, however, that is much more successful, and easier as well as cheaper. It is managed by lending money to the man who ostensibly owns and runs the paper. This works much better when applied to a paper already having a foothold than it does in an effort to establish a new enterprise, for new papers fail, as a rule, and before they come to the last gasp are certain to use up a lot of money; while an established paper, even a pretty poor one, can go on year after year with a small deficiency, or none at all; and the man who owns a mortgage on it will always have a greater power to influence its policy than he would if he stood before the world as the actual owner.

It has been told that after having had notice to go forth from the Garden, our progenitor, Adam, was so convinced of the error of his ways that he decided, if he could be allowed to remain, he would turn over a new leaf. I fear, however, I am not of so yielding a disposition, and if I should live again and be a publisher I should still strive to establish and maintain a flat rate for advertising. If I were a publisher of a paper in a small place I would surely devote myself—heart and soul—to encouraging and helping local interests, and although I would answer applications from foreign advertisers, would be civil in wording my replies, and always tell the number of dollars and cents that the service would cost, I would still get my price to the last cent every time. Whatever favors I had to bestow should go to the people who did business nearest my own office—my home patrons.

THIRTY-SEVENTH PAPER

After seven years of farming, more or less intense, there came a desire to be an advertising agent again—in fact, instead of only in name—and I began to be a more regular occupant of my desk at the office; although I by no means thought of surrendering the four months' vacations I had granted myself in the year 1871, and latterly extended to cover pretty nearly the whole twelve. I had kept a lodging place in the city, during all the frequent and long absences, and at the time of the great blizzard, in March, 1888, was snugly domiciled in the best suite of rooms the Union League Club afforded. Perhaps it was from the walls of those very rooms that I acquired the literary style shown in the construction of these reminiscences, for before I secured them they were long occupied by James R. Osgood, who had succeeded to Ticknor & Fields, the oldest and best of Boston's publishers of high grade literature; and after me, and interchangeably with me, domiciled General Horace Porter, until our country sent him to represent it in Paris, and to resurrect the body of Paul Jones; and after him came Frank A. Munsey, the founder of the first ten cent magazine. The last time I was privileged to occupy one of these rooms I found it regularly assigned to Col. Pope, who made bicycles famous, and is now exploiting automobiles. One of the rooms, in my time, looked on a little balcony; and by opening the French windows it was possible to set a chair out in the open air, and from it watch the life in Fifth Avenue, through the blue smoke of a cigar. I had retired to bed at midnight the night before the blizzard. It was raining and the air was close—so the French window was allowed to stand ajar like an opened door. When I awoke there was a snow drift across the room about two feet wide and in height like a wedge, thin at the farther end,

three feet thick by the window, but with the symmetry
vastly marred by bending over the bed, that stood in its
range, and carried at least a hundred pounds or half a dozen
bushels of the white crystals that covered the city. After
escalading the snowy ridge and getting into every-day wear
and outside of a breakfast, I hardly realized that anything
special had happened; and as the weather was certainly not
of the best I ordered a coupe to take me down town—just
as though coupes grew on bushes and could be had by
reaching out a hand—and it so happened, queer as it was,
that although men who were before, and those who came
after me, failed utterly, my demand was responded to, without the least delay, and I started for No. 10 Spruce street,
without realizing that anything very extraordinary had taken
place. Before getting there, however, I began to take notice,
and by the time of arrival had concluded I should be worse
than an idiot if I parted with that cabman and his comfortable vehicle before he should leave me again at the still more
comfortable lodging from which he had brought me. I gave
him a five dollar bill—to put in his pocket—told him to seek
shelter somewhere, feed his horse, and come for me at three
P. M. It was then about eleven in the morning. Well, at
three o'clock he came, returned me to the club house, in perfectly good order and condition, being no more than two
hours and a half in getting there, and it was not until some
days after, that I began to realize how lucky I had been. I
have never since seen a man who secured a ride both down
and uptown that fearful day; and our great man, Roscoe
Conkling, was by no means the only one who lost a life
through efforts to buffet the storm.

In establishing my advertising agency in New York I had
an ambition to make it in every way excellent and complete.
We would represent American newspapers—all of them.
We would have facilities for keeping a file of each, so that
any paper could be produced at a moment's notice, and advertisers could see their announcements, and watch the insertion of them, to any extent they pleased; and the rate
cards of every paper, kept up to date, should also be con-

veniently at hand. In those days papers counted on an income, possibly a profit, from the subscription list. Making paper out of spruce trees had not so demoralized the business as to make publishers more than willing to recognize any excuse that would warrant placing a name on the subscription list, without the shadow of a chance of ever being paid. We accomplished something pretty good in the way of keeping complete files, and eventually our efforts produced some result. Advertisers did not care particularly about the perfection of our files, for they relied upon our keeping a record of all insertions and being able to prove up the correctness of a bill; but everybody who had occasion to visit New York, from any point outside, learned by and by that he could see at our office a paper from his native burg; and would be given a chair, wherein he might sit, in the best lighted part of the room, and read at his leisure, with his feet on another chair. There was nothing to pay, and the service was not much, and, on the whole, he generally, or at least occasionally, seemed to think us a Puritanical one-horse concern, because, in the room that contained little beside thousands and tens of thousands of dry newspapers, arranged in racks that kept them in just such a position as would make them burn like tinder—almost like guncotton—we did not permit a visitor to enjoy his cigar while he sojourned there. Everybody who heard of a notice that concerned him, whether complimentary or libelous, came to us to see the paper, felt injured because he could not buy and carry it away; was slightly but not enormously grateful when allowed to clip the notice and take that with him, if it would not mutilate the paper to a ruinous degree.

Publishers who dealt with advertisers direct, and allowed them the agent's commission—because they were their own agents—sent those advertisers to us, to see such missing papers as were needed to be checked before a bill could be paid; and, if it so happened that the particular copy they had failed to receive—because the edition ran short that day—had also failed to come to us, they went away with the impression that our boasted complete files of all newspapers was a very faulty institution after all. We were a tremendous convenience to other advertising agents, who would come to us and see the papers they did not receive; and some of our friends, the editors of city papers, sent their youngest and most inexperienced employees to us, from time to time, with polite notes, asking the loan of this paper or that, that should be returned in an hour or two—and sometimes was and sometimes was not—and these did not fail to think small beer of us when the time came that—because such papers sometimes failed to come back—we adopted a rule that no paper from our files could be taken away from the office.

Trying to make our institution so complete involved extra expenses for room space and attendants; and, to some small extent, added a percentage to the cost of conducting the business, a fact that competitors, who attempted nothing of the sort, were not slow to mention to advertisers as going to show that they could afford to do business cheaper than we could; and as the best papers took pride in announcing that they treated all agents alike, and all papers seemed to be confirmed in a practice of allowing the agent's commission to everybody who said he was an agent, the practice among competing agents, some of whom kept neither files nor offices, of remitting to the advertiser some portion of the commission allowed by the papers soon got a foothold. To this practice I was opposed. It did not seem to me fair and right. May be it was only done in exceptional cases—possibly never unless it seemed advisable for the purpose of nailing an order. Once begun, however, the practice grew, and as it was always my theory that I should use the man who trusted me, and had confidence in me, just as well as I did the one who did neither, I finally concluded that I, too, must divide commissions; and I thereupon issued a circular, to all the customers we had, and to all whose names we knew, that we hoped to have, agreeing to remit five per cent from the regular commission upon all orders for advertising in the New York daily papers. The New York *Times,* in whose building our office was at the time, soon had one of our circulars brought to its notice as an argument for allowing the agent's commission to the advertiser direct; and George Jones, the proprietor—practically the proprietor—immediately changed the rate of commission allowed to agents from fifteen per cent to ten. He was the first to take that step. It afterwards became nearly universal among the papers of highest grade whose advertising columns were most sought at highest rates for space.

There was another idea that I entertained, and long thought to be a good one. It was my theory that when a newspaper had accepted my order, had carried it out in accordance with the agreement, and sent in a bill, with a view to obtaining payment for the service, the bill would then be due and payment should be made forthwith. I knew that not all agents agreed with me on this point; but my methods had mainly been studied out by myself and I was never given to acknowledging it a sufficient reason for doing a thing, or refraining from doing it, because others did or did not do it. I would borrow money to pay a bill that was due, even though the man to whom it was due said he was in no hurry. Let me say here, that in the matter of collections I never allowed any of our people to admit that we were in no hurry to be paid. If any customer ever said to me, of an account then due, that I could have the money any time I wanted it, he never failed to be told that it would be exceedingly useful that very day.

On one occasion, I saw, on the bookkeeper's desk, a very great pile of unpaid bills. While I was looking them over the bookkeeper came in. It was the luncheon hour, and he was a little late. May be I suspected he had supplemented the luncheon with a game of pool in the billiard-room then situated in the basement of the Times building. He was an adept with the cue, and I was not. He enjoyed the game immensely, and it did not cost him much, because it was the custom for the score to be paid by the defeated one, and Pierce did not often stand in that position. Perhaps I felt a bit ill-natured. I remonstrated with him on the accumulation of work before him in the shape of bills to be examined, approved and paid; and he, with a shade of triumph in his tone, administered a reply that was thought to be a sockdologer; and it was a pretty good effort in that direction. What he said was, "Mr. Rowell, there is not money enough in the bank to pay them." A little examination showed two things. It was true the balance was not enough to pay for them all, but it was sufficient for caring for half of them, and if the half had been paid the accumulation would not be so tremendous. I insisted, thereupon, that the work be taken in hand with earnestness, and it was: and it so happened that next day money enough came in to admit of clearing the deck; and there was a grand discussion of the whole subject between the bookkeeper and me. "It takes time to examine a bill." "Yes, but it takes no more time to examine one to-day than it will to examine the same one to-morrow, and if it is done to-day it will not have to be done to-morrow, and to-morrow will be open to attend to new bills that come in to-morrow."

But we did not always have money on hand to meet all obligations. Possibly if the matter was carefully looked into such occasions did not arise as often as might seem. At any rate, if no accumulations were ever permitted, except at times when we were short of money, then the accumulation would advertise that the stringency existed. Finally, we agreed that it should be the rule that every bill that came to the office before noon should be examined and paid before the office was closed that night, excepting only instances when the office should not be in possession of the funds necessary to carry out the plan adopted. I then went to the printing office and caused a sentence to be printed on white sheets of paper, in heavy gothic letters, reading as follows:

ALL BILLS RECEIVED BEFORE TWELVE O'CLOCK
WILL BE EXAMINED AND PAID TO-DAY.

Several of these strips, about a foot in length, were taken to the bookkeeper; and one of them was pasted in front of him, over the window labeled Cashier, and he was instructed to live up to what was printed there, whenever the funds on hand would permit; and when they would not permit, he was to cover the notice with a larger piece of white paper to be pinned over it—so, I told him, that every boy and man in the office might know, by the sign, that the concern was out of money. That sign remained in position a great many years, and was so generally lived up to that some newspapers grew to consider us a sort of savings bank, or safe deposit vault, that could always be counted on in an emergency.

I arrived at my office desk rather early one morning in

UBERT T. PETTINGILL.

the 80's, and had hardly taken a seat by my desk before I was approached by a tall man, who had in his hand one of those black varnished bags, with white stitches showing on it, such as commonly used to identify the countryman when he appeared in the streets of New York. My visitor also wore a long linen duster, then all out of fashion, and his head was surmounted by one of those white fur hats that people who are seventy years old or thereabouts may remember seeing on the heads of well-to-do men when they attended church, funerals, town meeting or went a-visiting.

The surface was fluffy, the fur stood out pretty straight, and if you blew upon it the impact of the breath would produce a sort of a rosette that was very pretty. My visitor put his bag down by my desk, and from a very great pocket-book, that was fastened by a long leather strap, that passed more than once around it, produced a quantity of paper— that had plainly protruded from each end before the thing was unstrapped—that proved to be a bill for advertising in his paper; and by actual measurement it was over fourteen

STEPHEN R. NILES.

feet long, and the sum of its charges amounted to a total of more than fourteen hundred dollars. His paper was one of a sort that we should think we were doing a pretty lively business with, if we sent it orders amounting to so much as a hundred dollars a year. I was familiar enough with the paper he purported to represent, but had never seen the man before. Leaving him and his belongings where they were I stepped to the bookkeeper's desk, and said, "Mr. Wayre, how does your account stand with the *Journal,* published at Horseheads, New York?" He looked up with a curious expression on his face and said, "About all I can tell you about it is that we seem to be doing business with it all the time, and we have never paid them a cent of money, or seen a bill from them, since I came with you in 1871."

I looked at the account on the ledger. It covered page after page—most of the items outlawed long ago—and going back to my waiting guest, said to him, "We can make neither head nor tail of an account like that, unless you choose to leave it with us for several days. If you wish to look at our ledger, and be paid in accordance with what appears there, we can probably fix you up while you wait." That seemed to him quite reasonable. He and the bookkeeper compared notes for a few moments. The man remarked that there didn't seem to be much difference, and a little later expressed some surprise that the amount to his credit was quite a good many dollars more than the footings of his bill. He wrote a receipt in full of all demands upon the ledger page, also receipted his mammoth paper document, and was given a check in satisfaction of his claim to date. When this had all been done, and he sat by my desk before taking his grip to depart, I said to him: "Tell me, please, why did you allow that account to run so long?" He replied that it was his experience that whenever he got any money he spent it; that he had long wanted a new press, of the kind then known as a Whitlock, costing about $1,200; that all the newspaper men said we paid all bills on presentation, and he decided to let the account run until it amounted to enough to buy the press; and, when at last it did, he concluded to come to New York himself and attend to the matter in person. I tried to impress upon him that although as a class advertising agents were little lower than the angels, yet he was putting more trust in them than existing conditions would warrant; that he was lucky in this case in getting all his money without delay or friction, but urged him never to let our account, or any other, run on in such a way. He seemed to see the point and the danger, and to recognize the reason for thankfulness in this case, promised he would not do so any more, went away, and I never saw him again.

I made mention of the circumstance that in the case just described at length the ledger showed a larger amount to be due than the bill called for. This is by no means an uncommon condition in an advertising agency, and it is not always by any means safe to attempt to make the needed correction. In some cases there is a conflict of interest in the office of a paper, and the unexpected collection of an overlooked item leads to an attempt to collect the same over again by some other person who claims to have had an intervening interest, and to be one to whom the money should be paid, while the man to whom it was paid had no right to receive it, but is irresponsible, will not pay it over—and so on and so on. I was much troubled by this condition when I first observed it and had a consultation on the subject with S. R. Niles and U. L. Pettingill of Boston, each of whom had had vastly more experience than I, and found that both had long before arrived at a conclusion that it would be time enough to pay a bill when it was presented for payment. The items that are overlooked amount to more than enough every year, with every agency doing a general business, to more than cover the bad debts made in conducting the business. I have no doubt that outlawed charges might be resurrected against my firm, that have never been presented and never will be, that would amount to a total a good deal in excess of $50,000.

THIRTY-EIGHTH PAPER

New conditions had arisen during the seven years when my absences from the office were so frequent and prolonged. Before that L. H. Crall and E. B. Mack were domiciled in New York as special agents for papers mainly in Chicago and Cincinnati. Now the woods were full of special agents, prominent among them being Mr. S. C. Beckwith and Mr. J. E. Van Doren. Now and then a so-called special was an actual representative of a single paper, notably in the case of the Chicago *News,* but usually the special agent represented several papers, from two to six, from five to twenty-five, and received a commission on the amount of business he sent. The special agent had some important advantages over the so-called general agent, such as our firm would be considered. The special was in direct daily communication with the few papers he represented. All advertisers within certain geographical limits were considered under his charge. Inquiries addressed direct to the office of the paper were sent to him, and the inquirer was referred to the special as the proper man to convey the information he desired. The special did not wait, however, for an application to be made to him, but promptly presented himself, or sent a representative, to interview the inquirer at his own domicile. If he took an order that was never paid for he did not stand the loss. The general agent, on the other hand, was supposed to guarantee payment on all orders he forwarded.

When the general agent talked with an advertiser who would spend $5,000 or $50,000 in a certain campaign he spread it out pretty thin, made it cover as many good papers as he could, cut the price as close as he dared, because the better he could make the investment pay his principal the more likely he would be to receive continued orders—year after year. The special agent, on the other hand, when he learned that the appropriation was to be $5,000 or $50,000, set himself the task of seeing how near he could come to capturing the entire appropriation for his own little list, or single paper; and, as it is true that a liberal advertisement in almost any paper is more likely to prove profitable than a small one the general outcome of the special agent's operations were not less satisfactory than those of the other, and it often came about, and does come about to-day, that a special agent representing a dozen papers or thereabouts gets more advertising for his little list than some general agent, well known and apparently prosperous, sends to all the papers that exist—for he pretends to represent them all. I know one man who received a salary of $12,000 a year for representing a single paper in New York City, and considered himself underpaid and surrendered his job on that account. As a matter of fact the amount of business he sent was such that the salary he received was by no means equivalent to what a general agent's commission would have been had he forwarded the same; and although the special representative guaranteed no account yet so careful was he about extending credits, and so good about making collections, that the total losses incurred did not amount to so much as a half of one per cent.

A large share of the best service a general agent can render a client consists of informing him about the papers that he ought to keep out of; but when he does this he is constantly liable to the charge that his advice is given because the commission that paper will allow him is small. The special agent is much better situated about giving this sort of advice. Of course, he will not recommend that any of his own papers be omitted—that would not be expected even if he thought they ought—but he can safely make up for restrictions in this direction by recommending the advertiser to keep out of practically all the papers that he does not represent. People who are expected to give disinterested advice are not wisely chosen from among those who are too near to the subject. It is said that an artist is never a safe adviser for a buyer of paintings. Mr. Whitelaw Reid and Mr. William R. Hearst probably both know that the *Herald* is the best want ad medium in America, but would any one suppose, in case these gentlemen were approached for advice about where to place a want ad, they would refrain from mentioning the *Tribune* and the *Journal?* although it is perhaps probable that neither would mention the other paper if a second one were to be chosen.

The special agent gets closer to his customer than the general agent does; goes to see him oftener, knows his peculiarities better and can humor them. He has no competition to fear, for if the order is to go to his paper at all it must go through him. He is headquarters. Advertisers have very little idea of what an advertisement is worth, and are always well satisfied when they are convinced—not that what they get is worth what they will pay for it, but that they did not pay any more than the smallest sum that would have secured it. Many an advertiser has patted himself on the back in congratulation for a specially low deal forced with much talk, and the canvasser has retired chuckling with the consciousness that he would have been glad of the order at half the price he is to receive.

In the days of my connection with the Boston *Post* I was sent to New York one day on a matter that illustrates what has been said above. A firm of steamship agents, Spofford, Tileston & Co. was I think the name, had written asking the cost of inserting a certain advertisement. Now the *Post* was a commercial paper, and steamship advertisements were right in its line. That particular one was specially wanted, but the *Post* had another object in life, and that was to earn an income for its owners, and the *Post* had three scales of rates that might be applied to such an advertisement as the one in hand. By one rate the space of eight lines could be inserted for $40 a year, by another, a charge of $80 would be proper, and by the third it might be possible to charge $156; and in an emergency the last rate might be shaded down to the second one, or pretty near it. The advertisement then before us if ordered in at the $40 rate would have been satisfactory and necessitated no visit to New York. It occupied the space of twenty lines, and at the lowest rate would cost $100; but any one who has been trained in the office of a daily newspaper of long ago—perhaps no such condition exists now—knows what a pity it would be to take an order for $100 for which the advertiser would just as cheerfully pay $390 or even $200; and it was my task to go to New York, with the letter in my hand, talk with the advertising manager, feel his pulse, and bring back the order at one price or another. He shied at the $390 price. Talk of newspaper values ensued, and the value of newspaper space, firmness of rates and what not and, finally, he gave me the order at one-third discount from the $390 rate, viz., at $260 net.

This very satisfactory transaction had not occupied more than twenty minutes' time, and I could not return to Boston until evening. I had in my pocket-book a large advertisement of a proprietary article, denominated Constitution Water, emanating from a firm—in Liberty street, I think it was—named Morgan & Allen. To that place I proceeded. It was about noon.. On asking for the advertising manager I was directed to Dr. Morgan, who was found in the middle of the floor showing a green porter how to fasten in the head of a barrel, that had just been filled with a miscellaneous order for goods, and the admiration his skill evoked from the porter, in connection with the tingling of the blood caused by his unwonted exercise, had put the good man in the best of humor. He was a kindly appearing man anyway—about fifty years of age. "We can't advertise in your paper," said he; "you charge too much." "The trouble is," was my reply, "not that we charge so much, but that you are not willing to pay a fair price." He seemed to pay no particular attention to what I said, but handed over to the porter the hatchet he had been handling, and I continued—with the advertisement in my hand: "At our full rates that advertisement would cost $800 for insertion for a year." "That's altogether too much," he said. "I don't know about that," I responded, "but if I should ask

you half that sum, you would still say the same thing."
"No, I wouldn't," said he. "Do you mean that if I will take
it at $400 you will pay $400?" was my next inquiry, and to
that he said, "Yes," and I said, "I'll take it just to meet
your views for this once." If the conversation had begun
in some other way I do not think I should have ventured to
ask more than $300 as a starter. When I reached the office
I really thought they ought to tack a couple of dollars to the
$16 a week salary I was then receiving, but they did not do
it until some time after.

To feel the advertiser's pulse is very important to the
man who would secure his patronage at paying rates. It is
also often necessary for the general agent to feel the pulse
of the newspaper man, to learn what sort of a price he will
or will not stand. I was once placing an eight inch electrotype for a paint warehouse. We wanted to make the money
go as far as we could and we sent the order to a Halifax
daily to be inserted a year for $40. It was accepted. A
little later we had a four-inch advertisement from Oliver
Ditson & Co., the great music publishers of the time, to go
to the same paper, and feeling that we had crowded the
mourners a little on the preceding order, we decided to offer
just as much for inserting the smaller advertisement as we
had paid the month before for twice the space. We did
this, but the order came promptly back and the price demanded was $120. Correspondence ensued. The case of
the paint ad was cited. "We know that very well," was the
response; "we had the space to spare and took the order,
although the price was low, but this ad we receive regularly, year after year. We get $120 for it. It is bad enough
to have you step in and intercept it, and demand a commission of twenty-five per cent, without trying to induce us to
take it at a gross price of precisely one-third of what we
have been getting, net, when it came to us direct from the
advertiser." And we had to yield.

It is quite important that a special agent shall be on
good terms with the publishers of the paper he represents.
The more friendly and intimate their relations become the

better for both, for they work together and can exchange confidences. The special agent is the only one acting in his field. With the general agent the case is quite different. He is one of many, and whatever terms are extended to him must in good faith be offered to every other general agent in the field, and if the general agent becomes a warm personal friend of the publisher that becomes a reason why he should not try to break his prices, while another general agent, who does not know this publisher, is under no such constraint and may offer a half or a quarter of his rates without any compunction.

A special agent represents but few publishers; so few that when one of them comes to town he can afford, if the publisher will allow it, to wine and dine him, and take him to the theater, and when he goes to the publisher's town he practically lives with him and they spend all their time reviewing the situation. Their interests are mutual. They are agreed that the thing to do is to get all the advertising that can be had, and at just as high a price as can be had. With the general agent all is different. He assumes to represent every periodical that is published. If he visits a town and calls on half the newspaper men, the other half, if they hear of it and esteem his patronage, feel neglected because he did not call on them also. On the other hand, if he travels a good deal, is active and successful, and gives publishers a chance to entertain him, they will put him under more obligations socially than he can ever repay. When he has visited a city of 20,000 people, and the manager of the prosperous newspaper—in which he is running two or three fairly good contracts—finds that the agent has leisure he seizes the opportunity to prove to him the growing consequence of the town and of his own paper; brings out a pair of horses; shows him the suburbs; takes him to the club, and later carries him home to tea with his wife and daughters; and at a cash outlay of perhaps no more than a dollar and a quarter has put the agent under an obligation that in New York it would cost $25 or more to return. Furthermore the agent may never go to that town again, but the resident publisher will go to New York this year, next year, and every year, world without end.

Some one, who has thought the subject over, has asserted that the general agent is a judge, the special agent an advocate whose business it is to sell space in his own paper and sell as much of it as he can, and that cases have been known where men who might have become good advertisers have been put practically out of business by following the special's advice. May be somebody else would have just as bad a story to tell about the effect of some advice given by a general agent

Things tend to set themselves right in the long run. The first thing the special agent generally does after his appointment, is to induce the publisher to issue a new rate card, putting up the prices to a point that will admit of giving the general agent the commission he expects, leave a satisfactory margin for the special, and eventually bring to the newspaper a somewhat larger net price than it received formerly, and it is the hope that the gross amount of business may be materially increased. The result, in the case of papers of first-class importance, has generally been satisfactory; but the specials have so increased in number that it is doubtful if any of them are now able to do very much for papers that are not of the highest grade, although dozens of such are represented. The special agents in New York City are, as a class, a bright, busy set of men. Among the most conspicuous are the S. C. Beckwith Special Agency, Mr. Dan A. Carroll, Mr. Emanuel Katz, Mr. C. J. Billson, J. E. Van Doren & Co., Smith & Thompson, La Coste & Maxwell, Leith & Stuart, and L. H. Crall & Son.

The influence of these active special agents has been sufficient to cause it to be pretty generally understood by this time that there are good papers enough published to exhaust any advertising appropriation no matter how large, and that there is no price low enough to make it wise for a general advertiser to attempt to use the poor papers. The good papers naturally tend to a uniform rate of charge and adhere to their schedules with so much firmness that the variation from rates that in old times made it fatal for a general agent ever to consult a rate card has practically passed away. The old conditions still exist with the small papers, but the advertisers who place business through reputable general agents no longer use the small papers to any extent, except such as would exert a valued influence in some specified localities, and in such cases even the managers of the small papers have learned that they in the long run get more actual money in a year when they hold to the rate card than they do when they allow their prices to be split into fractions.

THIRTY-NINTH PAPER

In the early days of advertising agencies I do not think the majority of papers had any price for advertising. They depended mainly upon subscriptions for a livelihood, and if anything came for an advertisement it was so much clear gain, whether the price was high or low. When papers had rate cards the agent was justified in charging in accordance, if the rate seemed reasonable; but when agents multiplied and competed with each other it soon became the thing to do to charge an advertiser as near to the prices named on a rate card as it seemed likely he could be induced to pay, and then cut the paper down to as near nothing as the paper could be induced to accept. From sixty to a hundred dollars a column a year was an average price in a country weekly, forty years ago, but an agent who could secure an order for five hundred such papers at $25 a column—taking them as they run, in a specified territory—would very likely double his money on the cost of placing in four hundred and seventy-five out of the lot, while the other twenty-five might cost him $125 each, without one of those that cost so much being of a higher value than the average of the others.

Publishers, after a time, began to catch on to the agent's scheme, and to assume that he had contracted for the use of their space, and would be obliged to deliver, no matter how much he had to pay for it, and it was not a cheerful thing for an agent to sit in a newspaper convention and hear some of these tell of the successes they had had, and what fools the other publishers were that they did not pursue the same tactics. If an advertiser had corresponded with the papers before giving the order to an agent he thereby made the order much more expensive to place, for a newspaper man, having named a price, felt to some extent in honor bound to maintain it.

There is an oft-told story of a circus man who visited the office of the only paper issued in the town where the show would presently arrive, to negotiate for advertising space. The price demanded seemed exorbitant, but the editor would take no less. Then a price was asked for half as much space, and for that as much money was insisted on as for the other—but an entire page could be had without paying any more. The circus man was mystified, but bought the page and issued his order on the show to pay the price; then he asked for an explanation and got it. The newspaper man had calculated on a show at this season, had borrowed money to tide him over a pressing need. The note would be due shortly. He had counted on the circus to pay it, and pay it it must. The price would be the same whether the space used was an inch or a page.

For many years my largest customer was P. H. Drake, the Plantation Bitters man. In those days a $50,000 contract was unheard of, but he gave me an order one day amounting to $46,000. On another occasion I was in his office, not expecting any business, when he showed me a small slip of paper, about two inches square, on which was written the names of twelve Pacific Coast newspapers, and exhibiting a great sheet of reading notices, intended to appear every other day in the daily editions and in every weekly issue, asked at what price I would insert the notices in the papers named. It was in the days when currency was at a discount, while the Pacific Coast journals had never gotten away from gold payments. The railroad had not then crossed the Continent, but would be completed very soon. The papers were high-priced and hard to deal with; but I said, off-hand, in reply to his question, "I'll place it for $9,000 gold." To which he responded, without a second's delay, "Go ahead." After a moment more he added, "Now, I don't want you to come around here in a couple of months and ask to be let off. I want you to do the advertising in every paper on that list." To this I responded that he need have no fear.

When I came to place the business I found there had

already been a good deal of correspondence with each paper, and each had named a price. An agent in San Francisco, a Mr. L. P. Fisher, whose office is still in existence, in 1905, then had pretty much the run of the business for the Pacific Coast, and he also had been experimenting with the order; and each paper knew what was coming, and not one intended to abate anything from the price that had been named. With considerable promptness I secured the service in nine of the twelve papers, and had an ultimatum from the other three at prices that seemed out of all reason. I had no disposition to shirk my responsibility, but thought I saw a way out; so I went to Mr. Drake and showed the nine acceptances. He inquired about the other three. "Those shall begin at once, by order by telegraph, unless you choose to avail yourself of a better thing which I have come to offer you. You are to pay me $750 a month in gold for the job. The work is started in nine papers. If you will give me a memorandum that the work is completed to your satisfaction in the other three and will pay the $9,000 as you agreed, I will leave the notices out of those three papers and give you, this minute, a gold check for $3,600." He thought for a moment, then said in a tone that indicated he was pleased, "I'll do it" and I gave him the check. Within three months the railroad was through; the Pacific Coast experienced a fall in prices, and I tried to get a new order for the three papers that had been dropped; but Mr. Drake did not seem to be interested. Finally I was able to offer him the service for $1,200 currency, or less than one-third the sum paid back to him, but he declined.

As further illustrating the different rates that may be named for a paper I recall one extreme case. A traveling representative for a Texas journal called on me, soliciting the Drake notices I was then giving out. He looked at the huge sheet of print, sat down and with a pencil made many figures. Finally he said, "It comes to a great deal of money." Being asked how much, he said, "It comes to $15,000." His tone seemed to indicate that the price might be shaded somewhat, but the figures were so preposterous that I thought it would be a good joke to send the man to interview my principal. He came back later in the day and surprised me by saying that he got the order. I dropped everything to listen to the details. It appeared he had accepted the work for $120, that at his rates, he had said, would amount to $15,000. The price he accepted was not far from a fair figure, but I lost $30, my commission on the order, by my effort to have a joke out of the matter. In business matters it rarely pays to attempt to be funny.

There were a few papers that became famous, among the general agents, for having schedules that would run up the price of a yearly order to most unexpected sums, and would abate no penny, relying upon what experience had taught them, that the agent had bound himself to deliver the service in their columns before negotiating with them for a price. The Utica, N. Y., *Herald,* the Cleveland, Ohio, *Herald,* and the Sacramento, Cal., *Union* were in this list; and I particularly remember one village paper in Western New York—the Leroy *Gazette*—having perhaps a circulation of eight hundred copies, that more than once got $100 from me for a service that better papers, in the same region, thought themselves well paid for at $30 or $25. It was this peculiar way of doing things that induced me, in the early seventies, to adopt what came to be known as the open contract plan which, when it was finally well digested, was expressed in a headline on all our estimates in these words:

THIS ESTIMATE DOES NOT GUARANTEE THAT ANY PAPER NAMED UPON IT WILL DO THE WORK AT THE PRICE NAMED.

The old plan worked well enough so far as profits on orders went, but it seemed hardly honest to charge $40 for a service in a paper that, although at its rates would amount to $75, yet in practice would commonly be secured at a gross price of possibly less than $25, while, on the other hand, it was exceedingly unpleasant to be mulcted $100 or more for a service for which we received less than $50, and which papers of equal value were generally willing to render for $20 or $25. By the plan we were inaugurating we should no longer expect to receive more than the gross price paid the paper. In practice we were led to waive some portion of our commission, sometimes all of it, rather than go to the advertiser to ask for an increased price—particularly as it was expected in such cases that the publisher's letter would be exhibited as a statement of the conditions that existed. This led finally to a general practice of dividing commissions, until at last the papers stepped in and simplified the matter by cutting the commission to a point where any further division made business undesirable. Some of them simplified the matter still further by arguing that when an advertiser placed his own advertising he became his own agent, and allowing him the agent's commission, for that reason.

Anybody with experience in canvassing for advertisements has had occasion to notice the peculiar fondness advertisers have for a discount from the price. Many an order has been landed at $100 because from that sum the paper would· remit the agent's commission, formerly 25 per cent, thus getting $75 net, while had $50 net been asked in the beginning, and insisted on, there would have been no chance of securing the patronage. It wasn't the price that nailed the order it was the discount.

Mr. E. B. Mack, one of the two original special agents in New York City, once made a contract with the managers of the B. T. Babbitt soaps based on this discount fascination. He would act as a general agent, place the business in any papers selected, charge the schedule rate, and make a specified large discount from the amount in every case. On the greatest papers he would have his labor for his pains, but great papers are comparatively few, and smaller ones were so numerous that on a $100,000 contract he stood to have $50,000 in profits. Before the bills were paid the advertiser was put wise by somebody; but Mack relied on his contract; the case went to the courts; Mack died before it came to a decision—what was the basis of the final compromise I never knew.

It was at one time a common practice with general advertisers to prepare two sorts of copy: a set of reading notices and a set of electrotypes of display space; and offer the work to publishers at what would be rather a low price for either the notices or the display space alone. No proposal for advertising was ever yet sent out at a figure so low that some paper would not be found to accept it. This is the reason why publishers are so often annoyed by what seem to them to be preposterous offers. In the case I have mentioned a few would accept the whole at the price named. By doing that they made sure of the order beyond peradventure. Such as did not accept would be asked to name a price for the notices separately and the electrotypes separately. We never could tell how the answers would come in. Some would run the notices free if the price for the electrotypes could be advanced somewhat; others would run the electrotypes free if the reading notices were figured a little closer to the price on the rate card; some would cut the price for the notices very low indeed, because they looked like reading matter, and demand a high, or at least a higher price for the cuts, while others wanted cuts, to fill up with, and wished to avoid the extra composition that the notices would entail. When the final round-up was made, one paper would have the order for both sorts of copy and others for whichever at their prices seemed most likely to be profitable. If a small paper insisted upon charging for notices by the line it would often demand as much as $100 for inserting what a brother publisher of perhaps a better paper, who charged only for the space occupied, would accept perhaps quite gladly for $10. Oftentimes it seemed that a paper was only interested in knowing how much money was to come and was practically indifferent about how much service was to be given for it. The story of the circus man is a case in point.

Newspaper men used to complain, in conventions and

elsewhere, of the unreasonable conditions that advertising agents impose along with their contracts; but every one of these unusual demands, if traced to its source, will be found to have originated with some advertiser who placed his own business. A Rochester, N. Y., manufacturer of fireproof safes, Warner by name, who bought a second-hand kidney remedy—which he vigorously pushed into notice as Warner's Safe Cure—was responsible for the beginning of the condition of mixing advertising with reading matter—until it is difficult to tell which is which—that now so universally prevails. The advertising agent never invents these schemes. He likes to have the conditions simple, so that the work will go smoothly, and the bill may be paid in full; but when the advertiser sees another advertiser enjoying this and that good thing, the agent, who wants to get and keep business, finds himself obliged to promise what others are securing. It used to be asserted of the late S. M. Pettengill that he would always make an attempt to procure whatever unreasonable thing an advertiser should specify. I heard a publisher say to him once, "I believe you would contract that I should put this ad on the top of the City Hall spire." He often seemed so incapable of understanding any difficulty in the way of carrying out a specification that the newspaper man would sometimes accede to it in sheer despair.

No advertising agent ever finds it prudent to take any publisher's word that he will not vary from his published rates. He may say it over and over again, but it is not safe to believe it until it has been proved by repeated trials that he really means what he says. It is a curious fact that the comparatively few papers that never break their rates are the ones who will go on writing courteously to that effect day after day, and year after year, with never any evidence of impatience. If a publisher writes in an exasperated tone on the subject, expressing the sort of feeling often described as "getting hot under the collar," the agent generally concludes that he did break his rates yesterday or probably will to-morrow. We kept for a long time a specimen letter at our office, wherein a publisher devoted four full pages to impressing upon us the necessity of paying according to his schedule, said the price would be the sum he named, "and not one d——d cent less" and added in a postscript, "Now what will you give?"

FORTIETH PAPER

Inasmuch as it has been made to appear that these papers are being read by a considerable number of office boys and clerks, as well as other young men who are interested in advertising as a profession, although may be not at present engaged in any business of which advertising forms a part; and inasmuch as it is from these that the advertising men of the future will have to be recruited, I am tempted to avail myself of the opportunity to preach a short sermon to that portion of my audience that is composed of young and inexperienced students of advertising, as indicated above. The youth who has a connection with an advertising agency, likes the business, thinks it has possibilities, and determines that one day he will have such a business of his own, should realize that his material progress will depend upon his acquaintance with the men who have advertising to place, and the degree to which he can deserve and win their confidence. The solicitor for advertising orders is often supposed to have a pretty rocky path before him, but his is the one place from which an upward step comes most natural and easy. The solicitor, or canvasser, touches the pulse of the advertising public, and learns much that the people in the office ought to know, but never have the opportunity. He meets men; comes in contact with them face to face, and on rather pleasant terms, if he understands his business and respects himself. There are few better positions from which to study human nature. Let the young man, then, seek every opportunity to come face to face with the advertising patrons of the office. Let him be glad when he is called upon to go on an errand that will bring him in contact with a customer or one who is sought or desired as a customer.

A young man who would do work as a canvasser for

advertisements should be neat and cleanly in his dress. I would not think it advisable to be too well attired. That the clothing appeared to be well brushed, well cared for, but inconspicuous, is better, I think, than to have it of a quality that is noticeably fine. Cleanliness and care in the matter of clothing indicate self-respect, while finery suggests vanity. The vain man, or youth, is intolerable to many plain substantial business men, and is not specially admired by anybody; but the quiet, self-respecting boy or man has an unobtrusive dignity, that places him in a position of advantage in every case where his personality is brought into notice.

As we understand the word, it will generally be found that the advertising canvasser will be better, and do better, without anything about him that can be properly designated as "style." If there must be a "style," however, let it be that of a plain, decently dressed, cleanly, respectful, young man who is working industriously to advance the interests of his employers, and is very much in earnest. If he is to succeed he should believe in the usefulness of his work.

In approaching a possible customer it should be your ambition, your hope, your determination, to state your case to him—if possible—so plainly that he cannot fail to comprehend the point you wish to impress upon him, thereby making it probable that the answer he gives to your application shall be framed with a full comprehension of the subject.

Do not be afraid—if you can help it. If you are afraid, pause a few moments outside and fill your lungs by taking several of the deepest, fullest breaths you are capable of inhaling. You are in business to earn a living. The line of business in which you are engaged is respectable. You are employed because those who pay you are of the opinion that there is a possibly profitable field open for your work. Remember that presidents, governors, senators, bankers, insurance magnates and newspaper owners are but men; that once they were young men, with their own way to make in the world—most likely—as is the case with yourself; that, other things being equal, each and every one of them would rather do you a favor than not, that half of them would—were such a thing possible—be glad to change places with you; for you that are young have a vastly great advantage over even successful men, who are not so.

Your success is not to be measured by what you accomplish to-day, or this week; but by the average outcome, considered day by day, and week by week. When you have approached a possible advertiser, obtained a hearing, stated your case, and failed to obtain the order, you have nothing to reproach yourself with. You have not wholly failed; in fact, you succeeded; but at the time there was no market for your wares. You were definite in your statements, respectful in your manner; there was nothing offensive in your appearance; the advertiser who denied you may even have felt sorry to refuse your request. You have left an opening by which you may go again.

Keep your health good, your conscience clean; have an objective point ahead and persevere. Be careful of your associates, seek the society of those whose ways of life commend themselves to you, and avoid those whose habits and principles are in any way such as you cannot approve.

If you have become a full-fledged canvasser you will not expect to secure every order you go after, but will be certain to go after every one you think you ought to secure; that is every one that you think the advertiser would do well to give you. That thought, that belief, will do much toward your success. If you really think the man's interest will be advanced by complying with your request, you will exert a hypnotic influence upon him that will bear fruit to a degree that will be almost surprising.

You are not to make a nuisance of yourself under any circumstances. You are not to force your presence upon a man when he is busy with a conference. It is not generally well to wait long for an audience, although if your name and business have been announced you must wait; but there is great advantage in a free field. When you are in the presence I would advise that no time be lost in presenting the case. Do it concisely, promptly, without circumlocution. "I called to ask your authority to do so-and-so. I think it will be profitable to you, and I know it will please me, and be of advantage to me if I receive the order."

There is something good in human nature that makes every man glad, rather than otherwise, to grant a favor which is asked of him, if the cost is not much, and especially if there is a possibility that a profit to him may result. And the man who has done you a favor once or twice, and finds himself no worse for it, has become your friend, will be interested in your progress, watch it with interest, and do all he can to advance it.

The deserving man, out of a job, often seems to find it hard to find a position that he may step into; but, believe me, those who have such positions in their gift find it still more difficult to place a hand upon a competent man to fill an important post that is about to become vacant. The more people you can impress with the fact that you are always to be relied upon the greater the probability that important positions and commissions will be entrusted to your care.

It once happened to me that, because I had planned to return to my office on a certain day, I felt obliged to insist that my wife and several guests should have breakfast before sunrise of a January morning, and ride eight miles to a railway station, while the thermometer marked 28 degrees below zero. To the protest that no particular need existed for going that day I said, "I do not know how many people may have made plans dependent upon mine, which have been announced, or to what extent they may be inconvenienced if I fail to do what is expected." And then I added, "It was my well-established habit of doing what I had planned, or promised to do, that enabled me to borrow a quarter of a million dollars one time without putting up a scrap of collateral. I would not like to throw away the reputation I seem to have established." I was recently conversing on this point with Hon. Chester B. Jordan, Ex-Governor of New Hampshire, a self-made man—whose boyhood was passed on a backwoods farm, and he said, with some warmth, "I have never in my life been able to accomplish anything of much account without having a plan marked out in advance and then sticking to that plan."

If you find yourself in the presence of a man who is ill-natured, worried, angry or dyspeptic, try to let him see that your business will not detain him long; try to realize that he has troubles of his own and to get out, if possible, with so good a grace that you may be recognized on another and more propitious occasion, and obtain your reward for the tact and forbearance you exhibited. If you obtain an interview under favorable circumstances, and state your case clearly and without loss of time, no man has occasion to find fault with you; and those who do are half ashamed of themselves for doing it, and if you conduct yourself with tact, will be ready on another occasion to do something in your favor, if only to redeem their own good opinion of themselves.

Having secured your interview go straight to the business in hand. I reiterate this charge to be direct. State the case as well as you can and accept the verdict—generally without argument. With a deprecating smile you may suggest that you fear you have failed to make the matter as attractive as you had wished, and that on some other pleasant day you will venture to renew the application, with a hope for better success. If you can keep good-natured and respectful you will frequently make valuable customers of those whose first greetings were anything but friendly—perhaps anything but civil. On one occasion a young man from my office reported an utter failure of his own. He had not succeeded in interesting the man he interviewed, and been dismissed rather cavalierly. Next day there came an order from the firm he had visited, with a request that credit for it be given "to that young man who called yesterday—and who was so good-natured."

The new advertiser ought always to be a small advertiser. It is well to bear that in mind. Great enterprises never start out full grown. It is a great thing for you when the advertiser, who will do some business with you, gets his interest really aroused and thinks of his advertising, day and night. With him you may spend much time. He will regard it as a favor. Take all the pains you can. Humor him all you can. He will develop ideas that will be useful to you as well as to him. He may be given credit even beyond the apparent limit of prudence; but if an advertiser develops a tendency to trust his advertising plans entirely to you, you should go slow; even restrain him if he seems inclined to go further than prudence dictates; for if he fails to succeed he will blame you and his words to others will not be to your advantage.

I have often thought that the day of the classified advertisement is yet in its infancy. There seems to be no limit to the power for usefulness possessed by inconspicuous, undisplayed, classified announcements that tell of actual needs. You may obtain anything you wish by advertising for it in the right medium, if you express your need in appropriate words. You may get rid of anything you do not want by employing the same method. If you wish board in a private family—polite, refined, and at a moderate price—and if you know of such a family, living next door, but do not feel justified in asking them to take you in, it may happen that if you put your advertisement in the paper that family reads you may hear from them by the next mail. When I have wanted to employ a man on hard terms, to do exacting work, I have for many years made a practice of stating all the conditions, with great precision and distinctness, in an advertisement, which was then placed where it would be most likely to be seen by the right parties. At a later day, in case of dissatisfaction, that advertisement could always be produced as specifying the conditions of the engagement—the exact terms of the contract. The classified advertisement can also be made to serve the purpose of an agent sent out to obtain information needed before entering upon a new enterprise.

I was in New Mexico on one occasion, spending a few days with a friend who had an enormous cattle ranch there, and the life charmed me very much. I thought I, too, would like to own a cattle ranch, and we went together to the nearest neighbor having a ranch, in a lovely valley, ten miles away, and who had expressed a wish to sell out his brand. I had a little talk with him and offered to take the outfit at the price he had put upon it; but he had changed his mind and wanted nearly twice as much. Having the matter very much at heart, but thinking that more knowledge on the subject than I then possessed might be of advantage, I prepared a list of from twelve to twenty papers, known to circulate among cattle men, and inserted in them such an advertisement as I thought calculated to bring out information likely to be useful to me. Every one who would answer the advertisement was requested to go somewhat at length into the advantages which his location offered over others, and to explain why, and to what extent, the claimed advantages were valuable.

The advertisement appeared but once, but in the course of a couple of months it brought a pile of letters two feet high, each one consisting of from two to twenty pages, and —would you believe it?—nearly half of them were written by bank cashiers and presidents in the Eastern and Central States. Each one told of advantages; why they were advantages; and why some so-called advantages were really disadvantages. On the whole, those letters were interesting reading. The ranch business was not overdone at that time; people did not generally want to sell, but sought to interest more capital so that they might go in still more largely; but when I had read all the letters, I believe if the man in New Mexico had sent one among them, offering me his brand and outfit, and valley of surpassing beauty, for half the sum I had offered him, I should not have considered it at all. The business was all right enough, but I became convinced by the correspondence that, like all other business, the man who would succeed in it would have to give it personal attention.

A little later an intimate friend of mine had it in mind that he wanted a country place—a farm. He thought

Berkshire County, Massachusetts, a good location, and at his request I inserted an advertisement in the papers published there. We happened to use in the advertisement an expression to the effect that he would like a place that was "capable of improvement" and it was remarkable, almost laughable, to what an extent it proved that every place that was for sale was "capable of improvement" and, from the number of replies that came, it seemed as though about every place in the county was for sale. The effect upon my friend was not so discouraging as in my own case quoted above. He was willing to pay from ten to twenty thousand dollars for a farm and would not particularly mind, if by the time he had experimented with its "capabilities of improvement," it should stand him in as much as forty or fifty thousand. He got the place he wanted for fifteen thousand dollars, and it is still capable of improvement, although he has expended upon it not much less than twenty times its original cost; all of which goes to prove that the power of small classified advertisements, for both good and evil, is something positively enormous. Valuable as the small advertisements may be to the public, they are even more so to the paper that secures them. The paper that has the most announcements of this class can generally be safely pronounced the best paper. It rarely happens that one publisher can secure them after the seal of public approval has been placed upon another paper. I never knew it to be successfully performed, save in one instance—the case of John R. McLean's Cincinnati *Enquirer,* which demolished the Cincinnati *Commercial's* want ad columns and practically expelled Murat Halstead from a field of his own choosing, and that, too, by pursuing tactics of his own adoption.

Speaking of small advertisements brings to mind a distinct recollection of an advertiser who always succeeded in confining his announcements to two lines. His name was A. J. Fullam and he sold pianos. One day he gave me an order to insert his two lines for a year in a specified list of papers at a cost of $2,600, the same to be paid for weekly. Wishing to get the matter off his mind, he sat down at a desk, took out a checkbook, with fifty-two checks each dated a week ahead of the last, and turned the whole lot over to the bookkeeper so as to have no more trouble with the matter. The checks were all good, and the piano man, too, I guess, for he always had and occupied a pew in Grace Church.

In the advertising business it is of first importance that the canvasser shall believe in the concern he represents—have faith in it. To him it should seem to be the best in its field, or of its class. If not most important on account of the amount of business it controls, may be it has a still greater virtue in the thoroughness of its method and the care and promptness which characterizes its service. Unless the canvasser can convince himself of the accuracy and honesty of his claim he will not succeed in convincing others—and he ought not to. Most canvassers do fail to convince themselves of the truth of the claims they put forth, and these always fail. A man who knows he is lying is never a convincing talker. He may achieve an occasional success, but it is never permanent.

As a general thing the advertiser cannot tell whether a particular advertisement pays him or does not. The most he knows, as a rule, is that when he advertises most he does most business, and makes most money; and when he saves on his advertising his net profits at the end of the year are less than they were in the other years when he thought perhaps he was wasting money in advertising. I recall one year when I thought too much money had been spent in pushing business and decided to cut the promotion expenses in two, and succeeded; but the net surplus—the real profit—made next year, was less than when the department of promotion had not been strangled by economy.

Most reasons for not advertising set up by advertisers, to the canvasser, are urged not because the advertiser believes in them, but to hear what will be said in rebuttal. It is, of course, true that not every advertisement produces profitable results, although no one can tell when a good advertisement has ceased to bear fruit. The advertising agency of Geo. P. Rowell & Co. is doing business to-day for a man who first came to it after reading an announcement printed in the New York *Times* in the year 1871. Early in my business career I used to make persistent efforts to get business from the old firm of wholesale druggists, Messrs. Tarrant & Co., but not a bit of encouragement could I get for half a dozen years. Then there came an order and another, and for a dozen years the firm was one of the best customers we had.

It is, of course, true that not every advertiser, who tries an advertising experiment in one class of papers, will also use those of another class, still there is something to be learned by a discussion of the subject, if he will allow you the time. The talk may result to mutual advantage at a later period—if not at the time. The magazine bears no fruit until next month, but the daily paper produces its crop to-morrow.

The man who has not had sufficient results from his advertisements knows that his announcements have not been what they should be. It is to be noted everywhere that the men who advertise most get the largest profit out of it, and are likely to exceed all others in their advertising efforts next year. The ledgers of every successful newspaper will verify this statement.

The way to treat an advertiser is to be always civil, respectful, considerate. Flattery is out of place, although when you know of some act of his, or some quality of his goods that excite your admiration, you do right to mention it. The man who misses an opportunity to commend, where commendation is due, commits a serious fault. It is always a duty to say pleasant truths when there is an opportunity; either at home or in business. Your own self-respect will not allow you to jolly a patron you care for, and his respect for you will not be increased by cigars or drinks which you contribute. If any treating is to be done the advertiser is the man to do it—not the canvasser.

It would be my idea that a decided "No" should always be taken as an answer, although under favorable circumstances it might still be permitted to tell the reasons that had made you think the service offered might be profitably made use of. I would suppose the man who said "No," quite decidedly, would be quite as receptive of arguments in print as any other person, and such a man might be approached later with a deprecating smile and tentatively inquired of whether his ideas had not undergone a change.

On the matter of excuses from clerks or others for the non-performance of something that others have a right to expect to be performed, I have always held decided opinions. Sometimes it has seemed that he was most unpardonable who presented the best excuse. At the Sphinx Club one night, Mr. Edward W. Filene, an enterprising and painstaking department store owner of Boston, had something to say on this subject that appealed to me. "We have a motto at our store," said he, "that reads, 'The better the excuse the worse the reason,'" and he went on to say that if there was a good excuse it ought to have been foreseen if the matter had been thought over in advance; and the better the excuse the more plainly it ought to have been foreseen. By the young men in subordinate positions who are paying me the compliment of reading these papers, and I know that many such are doing so, I hope that these few words on the excuse habit will not be overlooked. The boy or young man who does things when he might have produced a good excuse for not doing is the one who will get his salary advanced soonest and oftenest, that will get a place in the firm when a new partner is admitted. If he wishes to marry his employer's daughter his having been free from the excuse habit will be a recommendation for him. He will be twice the man without the habit that he ever can be while he gives way to it. I read a witticism recently dealing with this matter, and there was a good deal of reality in it. "Is that the best excuse you can put up," said the wife, "for not coming home until two o'clock this morning?" "Yes, dear," was the answer. "If you're not satisfied with that I shall have to tell you the truth." Whenever a defection is unforeseeable and actually unavoidable no excuse is needed or expected, it explains itself.

In conclusion, I wish to say a word to such as have in mind cutting loose from past connections and starting out on an independent career. In such case you will find that you cannot rely very much on any assistance that will come from family or friends. You may count on strangers with much more confidence, there are so many more of them. You must work out your own salvation. Advice will not commonly help you much. It is well to listen to all the counsel available, but if you do not act on your own judgment you will not succeed. Hundreds of times during my long life I have been consulted by young men who wanted advice about whether they had better do this or had better do that. I have commonly said in such a case, "Now, young man, it don't make a continental's difference what you do, provided you do it. Go ahead. Do what you think is the right thing and you will succeed."

Again, I have added, "You came to me because you thought I have succeeded, did you not?" "Yes," would be the reply. Whereupon I would conclude, "Let me tell you then that if I could have gone to somebody, as you have come to me, and stated the case, and could have been told of a quarter of the difficulties I have had to meet with, you could not have kicked me into the business. Still, I succeeded very well. The difficulties arose one at a time and I overcame them, and every other young man of stamina will, as a general thing, do the same."

FORTY-FIRST PAPER

Every man who has to do with newspapers has occasion to wonder now and then what that intangible thing is that is spoken of as The Associated Press. In the beginning a New York paper made a practice of sending a man down the harbor to intercept vessels arriving from distant ports, with a view of giving the news a little earlier than it would appear in the columns of a competitor. As the advance information so obtained proved to be valuable, the other papers had to do the same thing, but to avoid duplication of service one messenger gave his news to all the others and they divided the cost. By and by papers in other cities wished the service, and were allowed to share in it, paying a reasonable portion of the expense incurred, and then other sorts of news were gathered by the Association, and now all sorts of news is dealt with; the Association has representatives at important—and unimportant—points the world over, and the right to participate is not accorded to every applicant, but has become a privilege worth tens or hundreds of thousands of dollars to the particular journals that have acquired a membership.

When one hears that Mr. Ochs, of the New York *Times,* has bought the Philadelphia *Times,* the conclusion is natural that he wants to own a Philadelphia daily. When he later consummated the purchase of the Philadelphia *Ledger,* and consolidated the two, men wondered why he wanted both, and what there was for him in the consolidation, for the two papers were scarcely more alike than the New York *Post* and *News,* and no one would expect that either would increase in circulation by combination with the other. Soon Mr. Ochs, who had named his properties the Philadelphia *Ledger and Times*—the *Ledger* in prominent and *Times* in small type—dropped the sub-head, and the *Times* had ceased to exist. Then one began to hear that other Philadelphia dailies had paid $50,000 apiece to Mr. Ochs, in consideration of his action, and that the explanation was, that by chipping in $350,000, more or less, they had extinguished one Associated Press franchise, and thereby reduced by one the number of papers with which they would in future be called upon to compete. It is possible that if the *Times* franchise had been kept alive the enterprising Mr. Hearst might buy it some day, and his entrance upon a journalistic field has not always been particularly enjoyed by the publishers of papers that are more staid in their manner and make-up and may be less enjoyed than Mr. Hearst's journals are by the lower million of the populace.

The same condition outlined for Philadelphia exists everywhere else, and many a man or association has given up the idea of starting a new paper because of the impossibility of securing the Associated Press franchise; and many a moribund paper is kept alive, and finally sold for what seems a fabulous price, merely because it happens to possess the right to receive the news gathered from every part of the world and forwarded by the agents of the Associated Press. Once it was the New York Associated Press. Now the local destination is eliminated; but Chicago appears to be in control. Frank B. Noyes, of the *Record-Herald,* is President; Melville E. Stone, founder of the Chicago *News,* is the active manager. What Victor F. Lawson, owner of the *News,* has to do with it I do not know, but some people seem to think that what he says goes. There is in New York City a certain Mr. Murphy, who holds no office, but is the chief or leader of a political society, and many people assert that he exercises a greater control over the city's affairs than Mayor McClellan or Senator Depew. Possibly Mr. Lawson is the Murphy of the Associated Press—but if he is he might not see his way clear to admit it.

While New York was at the helm seven daily papers of the city held the franchises; consequently four of them would constitute a ruling majority. I suppose it would not be denied that it was once the ambition of a financier to control those four votes, and that to put Whitclaw Reid in funds to buy a control of the *Tribune* was a first step in that direction. Mr. Reid had not at that time became the son-in-law of a multi-millionaire. Later the control of the *World* was gained, then of the *Express;* and Jay Gould sought George Jones and offered two million dollars for the *Times,* and when that was declined pressed him to name a price; but Jones refused to discuss the matter or consent to another interview. "If you had the *Times,*" he said, "I should not sleep at night." "I should not do with it anything very different," was the comment—but nothing came of it. Isaac W. England attended the Associated Press meetings, and voted for the *Sun;* but Mr. Dana was the *Sun,* and one day he instructed England how he should vote. England—with a touch of independence—said to him, "Go yourself to the meeting and do your own voting." And Dana went, and from that day, and for a long time afterward, the previously existing war between the *Sun* and the *Tribune* seemed to have come to an end, and derisive remarks about the *"Tribune* tall tower" ceased to appear in the illuminator that still shines for us all. New York was the central force that controlled the news for the papers of America, and who could command four votes in the New York board might possibly color news dispatches, if that should ever seem to be a good thing to do. I am not suggesting that any one has ever made use of an improper power over the Associated Press; but if any one would and could that he would be in a position of considerable influence must be quite apparent.

Outside of our Associated Press the greatest news gathering machine in the world is called Reuters, with headquarters in London; and much of the foreign news appearing in American papers is filtered through Reuters in the coming. Reuters is an English enterprise, and in *Scribner's Magazine* for August, 1905, there appeared a twelve page argument going to show that much of the sympathy for

Japan in the war with Russia, so universally prevalent in America, was a result of the coloring of the news service that reaches us through English influence and manipulation. It is a subject well calculated to engage the attention of thoughtful minds.

There are other news associations, but the Associated Press is the giant among pigmies. One day a few years ago Mr. Laffan, of the New York *Sun,* overturned things, and seemed in a single day to have knocked off numerous millions from the value of newspaper franchises; but the Associated Press recovered, and although it carries the scar, it is doubtless much stronger to-day than it ever was before.

I do not understand all the intricacies of the system. So far as I can see no one does, or if there is a man capable of telling the whole story he has no thought of making the attempt. If it were told it could not be condensed into a few pages of *Printers' Ink*—it would require a book bigger than the revised version of King James's Bible.

I have not been so fortunate as to wholly escape newspaper abuse, always arising, I think, from dissatisfaction with circulation ratings that were printed in the Newspaper Directory issued by me. As a rule such things rolled off me like water from a duck's back; for I had a clear conscience and could never bring myself to care particularly what people said about me so long as I had the personal consciousness of being clean and straight. In one instance, however, several of my friends felt so much incensed at what was printed about me that they insisted something ought to be done about it; and I took the case to a lawyer; paid him a retainer of $500; and papers were served to inaugurate a libel suit, the damages being placed at $50,000. It will generally be noted, I think, that whenever people are injured by the publication of a libel the measure of the injury is expressed by the figures $50,000. I had been called a liar and a blackmailer or something mild like that. The paper was an influential one. Its editor was a power in politics. Law suits take time in coming to a head, and mine met with numerous delays. Before long the partner of my attorney was a candidate for election to represent New York in the United States Senate, and at my club I saw him and the editor dining together, now and then. Later the editor got the case put off when he served the country as Ambassador at a foreign capital. There were other delays. I may have been out of town myself now and then. Years passed on. I learned that I could have an apology expressed in almost any sort of phrase I chose to dictate and it would be published in the paper. I had some knowledge, more or less, of that sort of thing, and reasoned that probably the apology would not be seen by a majority of those who read the original libel, but would be sure to be absorbed by a good many who had not, and would lead them to look up the story, and talk it over. I didn't care for the apology. Ten years passed and still I had not been able to get the case into court, although some people think me rather an energetic person.

Finally the proposal to publish an apology was renewed. This I again declined, but made the counter proposition: "Next week there will appear a new issue of the Directory. I will send an advance copy to the editor. If within a week thereafter he will cause a favorable review to appear, the same to have a position at the head of his column or department of book notices, and to occupy space of not less than a third of a column, and then, within a couple of weeks thereafter, will copy from Allan Forman's *Journalist* a sketch of my life, setting it in the largest type used for editorial matter, beginning at the top of a column, with heading conspicuously displayed, the whole to occupy three or four columns, as may be required, and to appear on a conspicuous page, I will be content to let the matter drop." It had been stipulated the first time an apology was suggested, that I should be reimbursed for all legal expenses incurred, and I had the impression that this still stood; but on going over the matter afterward it did not seem to be so set down. The review appeared in space and position as specified. The biography also had place in a style that was beautiful to behold. Few persons seemed to see it. Some of those who did thought it good advertising, well done, and wished to know how much I paid for it. It really was a good bit of biography. I know that for a fact, for I wrote it all myself, and had taken a good deal of pains with its commas, semi-colons and periods. The matter was settled at last and I was quite happy—until my lawyer sent me in a bill for something more than $1,500 for his services. And after I got over feeling sore about it I felt happy about that, too. It is a curious circumstance that at the moment while I am engaged upon the preparation of this manuscript my lawyer in the case is about crossing the ocean to return from a foreign service that he has performed with honor; and the defendant in the case is about crossing over to take the place which the other surrenders. If he fills it with equal fidelity, ability and grace, there will be much occasion for Americans to think well of him.

I do not hesitate to set it down in black and white, that if any newspaper ever induces me to commence a libel suit again, it will have to abuse me much worse than the one did that I have attempted to tell about. It would be my advice, if my advice were wanted, never sue a man for libel. Never expect the courts to burnish up a character that will not shine through any amount of smoke that has no real fire at the base. Of course, if there is a foundation for the charges, one may have more occasion for being sensitive. Whenever this subject is up for discussion I like to refer to a case that I at one time particularly noted in the New York *Times*. Some political error had caused the paper to lose in circulation, and a new editor induced Mr. George Jones to allow him to put some life into it—and he did. One day there was a scare head: Colonel Cash, a South Carolinian, Had Committed a Barbarous Murder. The particulars that followed were as interesting as the story of Nan Patterson and Caesar Young. In a day or two Colonel Cash made it plain to the paper that he had not committed any murder, and then the *Times* came out with the sort of apology people usually get, who force things with a newspaper. There appeared another scare head and more reading matter—

something like this: "Colonel Cash Not the Murderer! It was Another Colonel Cash, a Colored Man—Probably a Brother of the First Mentioned." There was a libel suit sure enough. The *Times* was willing to apologize, but Colonel Cash wanted the traditional $50,000 damages in addition. After three or four years the case came to trial, and the plaintiff then perhaps learned, for the first time, that in the trial of a libel suit it is himself and not the defendant that is on trial. Before the case was ready to be committed to the jury the lawyers decided it would serve every purpose quite as well to agree upon and publish an apology and let the action drop. This was done, and next day there appeared in the *Times* as full and handsome an apology as any Colonel, white or colored, could ask for, and it was set in nonpareil or agate, condensed into the space of eight lines, had a position among ship news, or matter of that nature, and if any reader of the paper saw it at all it must have been by the merest chance.

FORTY-SECOND PAPER

There have been references to hunting and fishing. From boyhood's days nothing was so charming as a trout brook. The long tramp, taken with the flint locked Queen's arm, that resulted in the death of a chipmunk and the scaring of a partridge, was ever full of contentment and pleasure. The contemplation of others still to come—and with better luck—brightened many a waking quarter of an hour in the darkness of the night; aided, may be, by the tinkling of the rain drops falling on the shingles of the slanting roof that came so near to the head of the boy reclining there.

> What a joy to press the pillow
> Of a cottage chamber bed,
> And listen to the patter
> Of the soft rain overhead!

The first years in Boston were shortened by prospects of camp fires, and explorations in the direction of lakes and streams—famous in the talk of neighboring farmers, but as yet only known by hearsay. Occasionally realizations came, when a two weeks' vacation was allowed. Just think of the perfect enjoyment afforded to a boy of nineteen by a sixty mile ride in hot July, when all game is out of season, the steed being a three year old colt, giving to shying, and lent for the occasion by an appreciative farmer uncle; with the provisions and blanketing, requisite for a week in the woods, attached to the back of the rider, and a rifle, borrowed from a neighboring farm boy, carried all the way in one hand, with the butt resting on one foot—ever ready for instant use, in case a bear crossed the road, or a highwayman sought plunder. Did any one ever see Dixville Notch under such favorable circumstances? What pretty girls those were who, with careful parents, were touring that mountain gorge that sunny day; and how much concerned one of them seemed to be, when, in mounting to proceed into the wilderness beyond, the hammer of the rifle caught on the edge of the great boot-leg—worn outside the trousers—and shot the swab stick through the rim of my not valuable felt hat. With what joyful patience the hours till midnight at Erroll Dam were employed in fashioning, out of a goad stick—bought of a teamster for a dime—a substitute for the treasure that had been lost—with only a piece of broken window glass for the implement for removing the superfluous bulk, always paying due attention to that symmetry which the rifle barrel would demand.

The supreme happiness of the night in an improvised camp of bark at Cedar Stump on the Androscoggin—above Umbagog Lake—after the construction of which my companion and I discovered that the bottle of Medford rum, without which no New England boy would go into camp, had been broken in the tin receptacle—specially invented for this trip, and a triumph of the tinsmith's art—and not only dissolved the pound of gunpowder, the small packages of pepper, salt and sugar that constituted our total supply, but had also flavored the huge lump of salt pork—which is all a real sportsman needs to take with him into the woods in the way of provisions—so that in its present condition it was by no means satisfactory to our—may be—over-fastidious palates. There was also an additional flavor imparted by various bunches of those old-fashioned card matches that were so liberally tipped with sulphur that no one could light one and stand over it without danger of asphyxiation. The highly and miscellaneously seasoned meat was tied by a string to the stem of a leaning alder, and left over night, to be purified by the running water of the river; but was found before morning and duly appropriated by some animal less squeamish of appetite than we or more ready to recognize a good thing when he saw it.

Provisions and ammunition being gone, that hunting trip came to an inglorious end, but left none but pleasant memories. I may mention one of the most charming. We had built our camp fire against the decaying trunk of a great pine that lay in front of the spot chosen for our camp, and every now and then, as we brought fuel, or boughs for the bed, a partridge was flushed from almost under our feet. A little later we found her nest, sheltered under the other side of the log, scarcely eight feet away from where our camp fire burned. She got shot at as much as three times before we found the nest, with its ten pretty eggs; but the Yankee boy is not much of a wing shot, and after we found the nest we were so considerate that before we left camp next morning the bird would allow me to sit on the log above her and look into her wild, watchful eyes, without forsaking her post of maternal duty.

When vacations of months, instead of weeks, were to be had, many and many a time did I go over the same road, to Cedar Stump, the Middle Dam, the Upper Dam, Lakes Mollychukamuk, Welokennebacook, Mooselamaguntic, Oquossoc and what not. How many charming friendships are based upon these hunting and fishing experiences? One knows a man better after a six hours' tramp with him over a carry, a good hour's fishing in a pool that is fruitful, and one evening around a camp fire, than after years of daily meeting in the marts of business, or at the club, or at summer resorts.

I was at one time, in the late seventies, a trustee of the Oquossoc Angling Association, whose principal home was at Camp Kennebago, situated between the Richardson Lake and Cupsuptuc. We were short of members and money at that time, and one day I voted on the application of a Mr. Francis H. Leggett. Every one was admitted who would pay the initiation fee, and it was only by chance that I remembered the name, when one day, some weeks later, I was at Camp Kennebago and learned that the new member would arrive that afternoon. I saw a slim, modest, retiring man, in the early thirties, who seemed not to know so much about fishing as I did. From some impulse, I took him in hand, gave him a hundred directions, patronized him, told him his rod was too long, or not long enough, his flies too small, his reel not the best pattern—I fancied the Meek &

Millan, Frankfort, Ky., make, which no tackle dealer would ever sell if he could help it. In after years I came to know that this modest, youthful man was even then a leading merchant in New York, and one who, of all others, was the last to put up with patronage, or to seek or take advice. It is wonderful how many successes in life hinge upon sheer ignorance. If I had known the man, as I have since, I should have been slow to make any advances, and, if I had been slow to make advances, I should never have come to know him as I do now. It was so ordered that my good intentions were well received, and there began that day a friendship that has known no break, and that has given occasion for kindly offices on his part of a thousand times more importance than any I had in mind rendering him the day my eyes first rested upon the studious, thoughtful face that was a much more marked characteristic of him then than now.

It was on the shores of Plumadore, a retired little lake of the Adirondacks—reached, in those days, from Malone, by way of the State dam and a long carry—that I came into camp where my old friend Wilson was staying with two companions. One was that handsome, accomplished and vastly popular Dr. Tiffany, so long an ornament to the Methodist Church, of which Wilson was so fond; and the other a man with whom I, from that hour, began an intimate friendship that has lasted nearly thirty years. When we broke camp, the man last referred to, with Jim Bean and Amasa Washburn—two famous guides of that time—started on a tour of investigation and sport directly through the Adirondack region, coming out at The Forge, at the outlet of the stream that drains the famous Fulton chain of lakes. Many were the waits over long carries, while Jim and Amasa brought over the boats, and went again for the impedimenta; and numerous the experiences with lakes, streams, black flies and mosquitoes. On one occasion we heard an exclamation from Jim Bean, and saw him pick up a box he had dropped, and come forward, holding it above his head, with a corner downward, seeming to be imbibing a fluid stream that exuded. It soon appeared that the accidental fall had broken the only bottle of champagne left in my companion's stores, and Jim, knowing the impossibility of repairing the injury, was availing himself of the good the gods had provided.

Did any one ever see more trout on the surface than tantalized us at Blue Mountain Lake?—where not one could be induced to take the fly. And how much we were impressed with the camp equipage we passed, stacked on the shore, profusely marked with the full name and title of the famous "Bald Eagle of Westchester," the late Gen. James M. Husted of Peekskill. After a night at Pol Smith's what praise my skill with a rifle elicited when, placing the implement at my shoulder for an offhand shot, I, at the first attempt, broke one of a dozen bottles set up on pegs on a floating log anchored out in the lake. "I've been here a month," said a bystander, "and seen people shoot at those bottles every day, but no one has hit one till now." I tried no second shot, and somehow it seemed to me at the time that the bottle I broke was about three feet to the left of the one I aimed at, but I made no point of it, and we came gladly away.

If there is any dreary place in this world, it seems to me it is a hotel in the woods, where people go in crowds and wear good clothes. If there is one more dreary it is where people congregate under the name of seaside or winter resorts. I fear that my case is akin to that of the morose and sensitive Byron:

> My breast requires the sullen glen
> Whose gloom may suit a darkened mind.

At one place, where a considerable brook went through a sort of a sluice-way under an improvised bridge and, with some abrupt decline, fell into a moderate pool of still water, the pool looked so tempting that we set up our rods and cast the flies, and mine had hardly struck the water before it was taken by a pound trout, which Jim Bean deftly dipped out with the landing net. My companion, however, seemed to have a bigger job on his hands, and hard work to keep his footing and control his rod. Amasa stood by, with landing net in hand, but when it became feasible to put it into the water, he found that care was needed, for more than one fish was hooked; and a moment later—it was lucky Dr. Tiffany was not by—he exclaimed, "I'll be —— —— —— if there ain't three!" And three there were, and Amasa landed them all, and two of them were larger than mine, and one weighed nearly two pounds. We were excited. We were no fish hogs, but we were not prepared to leave that pool—not just then—and we cast and cast, but not another rise did we get, not another fish did we take and, for that matter, I think we had more pounds of trout, in the four thus taken, than the total weight of all the others killed on the entire trip.

Next day we had an experience that cast further doubt on the affair of the bottle shot from the floating log at Pol Smith's. His name is spelled Paul in his hotel announcements, but when he was an infant his mother named him Apollos, and while he attended fishermen and hunters his fellow guides called him "Pol." Although he changed the name in some degree, he ever elevated and never degraded it. Passing over a long carry, ahead of the guides with the boats, we saw a large owl on the branch of a dry spruce, about thirty yards away. As we had no fresh meat, I determined to shoot the bird, and proceeded forthwith to do so. The first shot produced no effect whatever, but a second one induced him to flap his wings and fly about half a dozen yards nearer to us, and perch again on another branch, in plain sight. My companion did not claim to be a marksman, but thought he could do better than I had done, so he took the rifle, and twice more the owl's life was endangered. At the second shot he flew again, and alighted may be twenty yards further off. But now the guides came in sight, and not wishing to delay them or trouble them with explanations we proceeded on our way and left the owl still looking after us. After that morning's effort we made no further use of the rifle, and I almost wished I had presented it to the man at Pol Smith's, whose enthusiasm my marksmanship had so wrought up the day before.

At one place while waiting for the boats to come over the carry a great green bull frog was seen perched on a rock that protruded above the water—may be three yards from shore; and my companion tempted him with a red ibis tail fly, which his frogship readily bit at, and was lifted sprawling through the air to the shore, where he was un-

RUDOLPH KAUFFMANN,   S. H. KAUFFMANN,   FRANCIS H. LEGGETT,
Vice-President.   President.   Treasurer.
JAMES D. PLATT,   GEORGE P. ROWELL,
Auditor.   Secretary.

THE PERCY SUMMER CLUB.

hitched and liberated. He returned promptly to his rock, was again tempted, again yielded, putting up his hands this time to clasp the line and save the strain of his weight on the hook, his countenance bearing a ridiculous resemblance to the Milesian caricatures so often seen in the comic papers. Again he was released, a second time he reached his rock, again he took the fly; but when released for the third time he abandoned his point of observation, and betook himself elsewhere, and we saw him no more.

Was it in Raquette Lake that the waves rose too high for our small portable boats and we landed for an hour on the lee side of a rocky islet not bigger than a freight car and opened a little game, on a flat rock sheltered from the wind, until the waves subsided and we were able to proceed? My friend told me of his home life and of a little daughter of whom he was fond, and who reposed confidence in him, as he well knew; for once at Cape May, when another little miss cried because her father with her in his arms, waded among the rolling waves; our little maid exclaimed with disapproval, "Look at that child! I shouldn't think she'd be afraid to go where her papa would take her."

It was a few years later that my friend, whose home was in Washington—and capacious—hit upon the hospitable idea that each separate member of the family might invite a guest for inauguration week, and the daughter, then arrived at the mature age of ten, insisted that her invitation should be bestowed upon me. It was with gratified pride that I accepted. It was with greater pride and gratification that I gained permission to take the little miss, in her white gown and pink sash, to her own and my first experience with an Inauguration ball. The father and I have fished in the waters of Maine, New Hampshire, New York, Maryland, Wisconsin, California, Washington, Alaska, Alberta and the Yellowstone, and it was in 1882 that we, associated with Wilson, Leggett, Kent, Congressman Ray of New Hampshire, and ex-Secretary of the Navy George M. Robeson, became founders and members of the Percy Summer Club, the most charming and successful little association of sportsmen it has ever been my fortune to know about. Camp Percy is situated in the wilds of the Granite State, north of the White Mountains, where, between the narrow fringe of settlements that cling to the Connecticut and the Androscoggin, there is a wild space, sufficient for an ordinary county, with whole townships that never had an inhabitant. It is more secluded than any point in the

350

Adirondacks, and equally abounds in the wild life of forest and stream.

My friend was not an advertising man, though he lives by advertisements. He is widely known, respected and loved by the newspaper men of America. I am speaking of Mr. S. H. Kauffmann, President of the Washington Star Newspaper Company, the Corcoran Art Gallery, and at one time of the American Newspaper Publishers' Association. I have found much to be thankful for in the twenty-eight years of close association that began with that trip across country, over lake and stream, in the pleasant summer of 1877. A better informed man, a man of a more equable temperament, a juster, or more generous—though he by no means wears his heart on his sleeve—it has never been my fortune to know.

Should I admit it, after all this advertising of a love for the life of a hunter? I will do it and get out of temptation. I have killed a hedgehog, but never a bear. I have hunted by the murderous jack light, and had an almost superstitious fear, as a great crane—that seemed so ghost-like—rose from a submerged rock, where the water was shallow, and floated away spirit-like through the wispy mist that will gather and move about—on the stillest night—over the surface of a lake when the atmosphere is colder than the water. And then the plunge, that sounded as though an elephant had dropped from the clouds into the lake just beyond where the dim candle revealed a great tree trunk, fallen from an undermined bank; and how insufficient seemed the explanation, whispered in a single word, by the guide with the paddle who sat behind. I blush to repeat it here—it was "Mushrat!" The whistle of the deer, which—although often so designated—is not a whistle at all, was heard on the shore, and his tramp, in alarm, as he scudded away through the underbrush. May be it was a fool's shot, and useless; but the men in camp heard it and counted on venison as a certainty. No, I never killed a deer, and never shot at one expecting to kill. And, will any one believe it? I have cast a fly hour after hour, day after day, with perfect enjoyment without taking a trout or a bass. And when they were hungry and most ready to sacrifice themselves for my sport I have never taken more than the mouths in camp could consume. My biggest black bass fell short of 5½ pounds. The largest trout, taken on a fly, weighed less than 4½ pounds. The one day when I and a less experienced companion brought into camp three hundred and sixty-four brook trout, and regretted, after the count, that we had not taken one more, to correspond with the days in the year, may seem an exception, yet the excuse urged by the young wet nurse in Midshipman Easy that her blame was slight because "it was such a little one," applied with cogency to our case that day. I have sometimes wondered, since the modern law about short trout has prevailed, whether the entire accumulations of forty years as an advertising agent would suffice to pay the fine that a rural justice of the peace would impose, should he be called upon to inspect such a mass of fingerlings. They scarcely more than sufficed for three meals for the half dozen ravenous stomachs that were domiciled in that little camp, covered with fragrant spruce bark, just peeled in the favoring month of June. I also expect that such wanton destruction of the pulp-producing spruce would not now be tolerated by the millionaire paper makers who have become the owners of our eastern forests.

The time for long tramps, and fishing in rocky brooks, and wading among tangled alders has nearly passed. If an effort is persisted in, now and then, the services of an experienced native are brought into requisition; and he it is who scrambles after the flopper that dropped from the hook about as soon as he was lifted over the edge of the pool, and he carries the creel and the tin box—inscribed LURE on the cover—that confines the humble angle worm until the hook threads the labyrinth of his vermiform appendix. There is no shame now in asking a hand to give a pull up a steep bank, or to grasp when venturing a short leap that will land on a rock slimy—slippery with wet mosses. Yet, after all, sitting in a boat, casting a fly over the circle where a trout rose but now, is easier work and more of it can be undertaken. It is only the wrist that gets tired there.

It is not now urged against the forest retreat where these words are written that the toot of the engine is sometimes mistaken for the hoot of the owl; nor do we enjoy the camp fire less because it burns in a wide fireplace—instead of in the open—or from the knowledge that in the room adjoining is as good a mattress as Mrs. Waldorf offers her most favored guest. On a stormy day, when it is time to break camp, no serious fault is now found that only a row of a mile, and a half a mile walk down a hill, are required to land one at a railway station from which, as some one once said of the harbor at Portland, Maine—"All the world may be visited." With increasing years one can be moderate in his demands of the wild wood, and I am quite satisfied when I know that the boy who rows my boat has put up deer no less than seven times within the past month, and that now and then, with an opera glass, we can see one, two or even four on the shore of the lake; and that it does not seem possible to walk twenty minutes without encountering the ruffed grouse, with her apparently broken wing, who flutters before our feet, tempting us to capture her, while her six to a dozen chicks make use of the diversion and escape into the greenwood. We would not hurt her if we could. Mr. Cleveland's favorite game, the rabbit, comes also every evening—about the door of the resident superintendent—with so much confidence that the man, or boy, who would shoot him would deserve to have his neck wrung, like that of the good old hen who, after being steamed to tenderness and flavored to suit the taste of an epicure, will regale us, in a brown fricassee, this very Sunday noon.

Good Izaak Walton selected a verse for a chapter heading that always impressed me as rather pretty. I quote

from memory, the reference library in camp being less well
furnished than the corner cupboard:

> The first men that our Savior dear
> Did choose to wait upon him here,
> Blest fishers were.
> And fish the last food was
> That He on earth did taste.
> And so I strive to follow them
> That he hath chose to follow him.

FORTY-THIRD PAPER

The first number of *Printers' Ink* is dated July 15, 1888. I had always an itching to have a mouth-piece through which I could speak to those whose interests were in lines parallel to mine. In the Boston days I had issued the *Advertisers' Gazette,* and whenever, in after years, I took a look at the old files, I was impressed that they contained matter of interest—much that it would be well in after times to find packed away in a shape so accessible and available. It is easy to over-estimate the importance of what we do. This thought comes to my mind as I re-read the preceding sentence; for I doubt, if aside from the one I have preserved, another volume of the *Advertisers' Gazette* is in existence. After its time the *American Newspaper Reporter* came into being, and it also bore the name *Advertisers' Gazette*—as a sub-title.

We had a printing office of our own in the seventies— the days when the *Reporter* was published. The office was specially fitted to meet the wants of our own business, without any regard to what would be the requirements of outside customers. We found it convenient to set everything in a page of uniform dimensions, so that fewer chases and forms would be needed, and a page that had done service in a circular or a pamphlet would also fit into any other circular, pamphlet or other publication that we might wish to put out. It came about in this way that the page of the *Newspaper Reporter* was identical in size with that of the American Newspaper Directory—which did not vary much from that of the general run of monthly magazines. At a later date a smaller type and style of page was adopted for the Directory, and in that way it came about that when the time came to make up the forms for the first issue of *Printers' Ink,* the old idea prevailed, and the little paper appeared with a page identical with that of the Directory in its curtailed dimensions. It was smaller and had narrower columns than any other magazine then issued. So small and insignificant did it appear when having no more than sixteen pages—and now and then only eight—that a subscriber who sent for a duplicate copy one day and afterwards discovered his regular one, made apology for troubling us, saying his got covered up under a postage stamp on his desk.

Before the little paper was launched it had been a long time incubating. I knew about what I meant it should be, but how to form and shape it, and what to call it, and who should edit it, were questions that had not been answered. I was interested in it. I thought I should put into it a good deal of my own individuality. At one time I thought of giving it my own name. I even went so far as to get up a heading composed of the word ROWELL with a small picture over it representing the act of hiding a candle under a bushel and which, may be, had the word DON'T cut into it in some way. It was surprising how well the name and design looked, and I am by no means confident that it would not have been a success; but it was a little too personal and the idea of adopting it was finally turned down. I was at this time the principal owner of the W. D. Wilson Printing Ink Company, Limited, and the manager of that company, a Mr. Eagleson, spoke to me one day about a place for a young man of eighteen or thereabouts, a son of an acquaintance of his, and who was seeking employment, preferably something akin to newspaper work. I had an interview with the youth, engaged him, told him to go ahead and get out a paper that should be "A Journal for Advertisers." We would issue the first copy whenever he got his material ready; the size of the page should be that used for everything in our printing office; the paper should be issued twice a month; the editor's salary should be $10 a week and, after a good deal of hesitation, it was decided that the name of the paper should be *Printers' Ink*.

I had been so egotistical in preceding times as to insist

that my own name had been so long and so prominently before the public, in connection with advertising, that it was to some extent a synonym for the word. As it was decided that my own name was not to be made use of what more natural than I should look to the other interest that at the time made considerable demand upon my attention?—printers' ink. *Printers' Ink* had long been used as a synonym for publicity. Much was heard of the power of *Printers' Ink.* I was a dealer in printers' ink as well as in advertising. Why not call the paper *Printers' Ink?* That question was propounded to many people. I think no single one thought well of it. Some thought it might do—it didn't matter anyway, for it would never amount to much. If there was any one thing that people did not wish to read about that one thing was advertising. What was said about advertising was commonly regarded along the line of the child's definition of faith, "A persistent belief in things that you know ain't so." Still the more my mind dwelt on the proposed name the better I thought of it and when the little paper came out July 15, 1888, the name that stood at the head was PRINTERS' INK, and a good name it has proved.

The young editor's name was Charles L. Benjamin. He is a regular contributor to the paper at this day. Mr. Kent used to relate that shortly after he had been made a Vestryman in the Church of St. Andrew's the question of music seemed to be one that caused much trouble, and he ventured the remark that he thought the Music Committee should be composed of those who knew least about music. His thought recommended itself to the Vestry and Kent was made Chairman of the Music Committee, and gave more general satisfaction than the church had enjoyed before. It was partly on this theory that I concluded my youthful editor would do very well. I think he knew that advertisements existed, thought them a necessary evil perhaps, though why necessary he did not seem to comprehend. When, not long after the paper was started, George W. Turner, then publisher of Mr. Pulitzer's *World,* bargained for the first page for an announcement of that paper, although he paid for it pretty nearly the entire cost of getting out the few hundred copies then issued—the idea of having the space prostituted to such base uses nearly broke the young editor's heart.

It so happened that one winter, several years before the establishment of *Printers' Ink*, I had been much troubled with asthma, colds, and accompanying evils, and spent a great deal of time in a sunny sitting-room, all by myself, and without any definite purpose I used up a great many pages, quires, I might almost say reams, of blank paper in writing down advertising ideas, thoughts and apothegms. There was an everlasting lot of the stuff and some of it was rather good—of its kind. At a later date, having a typewriter who needed practice and was not kept over busy, because not over-skillful, all this material was copied out on slips of half note size, and when completed, a couple of rubber bands were snapped around the bundle and it was put away to accumulate dust and cause somebody to wonder later what it was all about and what—if anything—it would be good for.

In order to give the journal for advertisers a trend in the direction of thoughts on advertising matters it seemed to be necessary that it should say more or less on the subject of advertising. The daily operations of an advertising agency furnished some material. I had ideas that I liked to ventilate, if not too much occupied with other things, but shortly after the paper was started I went away on a long vacation, and when I came back there was a pretty urgent demand made on me by the youthful and inexperienced editor for points. It was then that I thought of the bundle packed away somewhere, that represented pretty nearly one winter's work. It was looked for, fished up, dusted, turned over to Benjamin, and proved to be a veritable god-send. *Printers' Ink* became "A Journal for Advertisers," was more quoted for a time than any other paper published, and to this day I find myself able to identify wise paragraphs about advertising floating through the columns of the press, that, if they could speak, would proclaim themselves children of my—shall I say brain?

The little paper was almost immediately recognized as something new. Everybody into whose hands a copy came seemed to take an interest in it. It was the first effort ever made to discuss advertising problems seriously, thoughtfully, earnestly and honestly. It was not long before there were imitators—a good many of them. The diminutive page and absence of a cover were features that seemed to meet a long-felt want in the minds of many who would bring out a new paper, and specially so if it was anything of the nature of what is usually denominated a house organ. The amount of advertising patronage bestowed upon *Printers' Ink*, and the apparently remunerative prices it commanded, made it seem a flying in the face of providence, on the part of nearly every other advertising agency, to neglect to put out something like it; and soon there were "Journals for Advertisers" to burn. They existed by the dozen and came to be known as *Printers' Ink's* Babies. First and last there have been no less than two hundred distinct and palpable imitations of *Printers' Ink;* and it may be that as many as a quarter of the whole number have kept a foothold till the present time. The crop has not been confined to this country nor this continent. I do not know how the name the Little Schoolmaster in the Art of Advertising came to be applied to *Printers' Ink,* but it was in quite common use before the paper was two years old.

Its advertising space was held at ten cents a line and ten dollars a page, was advanced to $20, $30 and $50 a page; and at the last named prices some contracts were taken by the year for $2,600 net cash. About this time an announcement was issued offering to sell the first page for a year for $4,000, and greatly to my surprise, Messrs. N. W. Ayer & Son, the advertising agents of Philadelphia, engaged it at that price, and used it for their own announcements, until two or three years later the price of the inside pages was advanced to $100 an issue, or $5,200 by the year, and the outside pages to $200 an issue or $10,400 a year. This price Messrs. Ayer & Son considered prohibitive, but the page was taken a little later by a publisher of the most prosperous and profitable Philadelphia daily of the time, who renewed the order five times, paying for the service the very considerable sum of $62,400 for the six years' advertising. There had been an agreement that a certain proprietary article, in which I was largely interested, should place business with the paper to an amount at least as great as the sums paid in *Printers' Ink;* and it is an interesting fact that the manager of the Ripans Chemical Company asserts to-day that not only did his goods sell better in Philadelphia than they did in New York, although the latter is a much greater distributing point, but also that out of more than $2,000,000 paid for advertising the Ripans Tabules he cannot now point with confidence to any medium that, in his opinion, produced so satisfactory a result, dollar for dollar, in proportion to the price demanded.

Once while the Ayer concern had the contract for the first page, they negotiated for the last page also for a specified issue. It was at the time when the appearance of the American Newspaper Directory for that year was to be announced. When the Ayer copy came to hand the two pages were found to be devoted to the same thing. Both were announcements that on a specified day, not distant, their own imitation directory, called Ayer's Newspaper Annual, would be ready for delivery; and the weight of the argument, as well as the heading of the two pages, was "WAIT, Wait and get the Ayer Book." It was the only time that I ever saw anything emanating from the Ayer concern that seemed to savor of humor. This, however, was rather funny, for they had succeeded in making an advertising sandwich of our paper by announcing their own enterprise on it, both in front and rear. It seemed as though we actually must make some comment or protest in our own behalf, as we edited and controlled the paper, and I studied a good deal over the best manner of dealing with the problem without taking the joke too seriously. Finally, the heading of their two pages, consisting in both cases of the word "Wait," brought me thoughts of the thousand and one stories one hears of the traditional slowness of Philadelphia, and at last the editorial to be used took shape in my mind. I am not much of an editorial writer, but I made a success that time. I was given first place under the editorial head and this was the beginning and the end of my great effort. It read:

"The Philadelphia Idea—Wait!"

Is it not wonderful how much satisfaction one may sometimes get out of what he thinks a witty rejoinder or retort? and yet how little good ever comes from one, and how much harm frequently results. I am not patting myself on the back as a wit, but the efforts I have made in that direction, and my observation of others, has tended to convince me that the man who laid it down as a general proposition hit the nail pretty squarely on the head when he said that "Next to the butt of the company the wit of the company is the meanest person in it." Poor Tom Corwin realized this great truth when he spoke the injunction, "Be solemn" and ended with the assertion, "All the monuments were raised to solemn asses."

Printers' Ink was not many years old before it began to have trouble with the Postoffice Department. It was a new thing; subscribers could not be had except they knew what was offered to them. The best way to tell this was by the sample copy. The law did not limit the number that might be sent. On one occasion a Member of Congress from Rochester was known to have dispatched a train, consisting of thirteen mail cars, every one filled with sample copies of a single edition of a paper in which he was interested. I will not attempt to go over the ground. At the time we had trouble with the Postoffice Department the Postmaster-General was issuing just such a publication of his own, and in his own name, and the Superintendent of the Census, Mr. Porter, had another of precisely the same character, of which sample copies went out by the tens of thousands. Before we got through with it we got a Congressional resolution to investigate the usages of the Department, were finally reinstated in the enjoyment of the postal privileges to which we as well as every other citizen were entitled; but before that, a sum of money, falling but a few dollars short of $25,000, had been extorted from us in the way of extra postage. The case attracted a good deal of attention; we were plainly in the right, and we got some of the advantage that falls to martyrs—we were well advertised, and within a year or two after the matter was settled, the little paper carried not much less than $200,000 in advertising patronage within a single twelve month.

The last stroke of trouble we had with the Postoffice Department was a good illustration of the way those things are, or were at one time, managed. We had announced that a certain issue, in addition to the usual amount of reading matter, would contain a list of all the American newspapers that printed regular issues of more than a thousand copies, together with figures showing the regular average issue of each, and that sample copies of that number would be sent to all the people and firms mentioned on specified lists of names. In order that there should be no mistake, a dummy book was made up and submitted to the Postmaster of New York City, with a statement of precisely what was proposed to be done. He took time to look the matter over, submitted it to the authority having most experience with such questions, who said there was nothing irregular about it, and seemed to wonder why we thought there would or could be any question or trouble about it. That particular issue would contain ten or twelve times as many pages as made up the average issue. We sought advertising patronage for it and advertised it by circulars, postal cards, letters, and in the columns of the paper itself, and received many orders.

Our circulars came to the attention of Mr. Leander H. Crall, a special agent in New York for two or more excellent newspapers that were never willing to report their circulation nor to have anybody do it for them. Mr. Crall conceived the brilliant idea that what we had in mind was to secure the distribution of our Newspaper Directory at the one cent a pound rate, thus getting it out to customers for about eight cents a copy, while the book rate would be about forty cents a copy. How he got it into his mind that it would be profitable for us to give away a book we sold for five dollars to the very people among whom we would look for purchasers I have never been able to comprehend. How the Department could see anything in the case, as he presented it, I never could understand. But it did; and it held up that edition, after it had been taken into the postoffice for mailing. They tried to make me take the books away, but I had no use for them; and whatever became of them I do not know, but I brought the New York postmaster into it. He could not see why the issue was held up. The action of the Department was as great a mystery to him as to me. It turned out that there was not and had not been any ruling that would authorize the action taken and to obviate the difficulty one was promulgated that should be retroactive. It was announced in the papers of the time.

The effect of it was that a periodical might not issue one number that should be very much larger than its regular issue. And this decision got along at the very time the Christmas issue of *Life, Puck, Vogue,* and a whole lot of other periodicals that were usually sold for ten cents, but of which the public got a quarter's worth just then, although regular subscribers got the extra dose without an additional payment. The order had to be rescinded, but I believe it did kill off the practice of mailing the World Almanac, which up to that time had gone through the mails as a regular issue of the *Monthly World*—if anybody ever knew what that was.

Mr. Crall's part in the postoffice action was not known to me until some years later, when the man he employed to prepare his case for submission to the Department gave me the proof, with changes and interlineations, from which the clean copy to go to the Department had been copied. It was so preposterous that could I have known what the Department had before it I could have removed its objection in the fraction of a minute, and the laugh would have been on the department clerk who, in his ignorance had—honestly enough no doubt—thought he saw a nigger in the fence. It is the scheme of dealing with such things behind a publisher's back, without his having any knowledge that his affairs are being investigated, that has made the management of the office of the Postoffice Department, on questions relating to the transportation of second-class matter so harmful, so preposterous. *Printers' Ink* has had no trouble now for many years and feels pretty confident that it never will have any more difficulties of the same sort, unless there should be a real rather than an imaginary ground for the Department's action.

I personally appeared before a Postmaster-General and his legal adviser, the Assistant Attorney-General, on one occasion, and the Postmaster-General read aloud the law that forbids admission to the mails, as second-class matter, of publications intended primarily for advertising purposes. Then he looked at the heading of *Printers' Ink* and read there, "A Journal for Advertisers," and turning to the legal adviser at hand asked, "Does not that law exclude this paper?" The legal adviser informed him that there was nothing in the law to exclude a paper devoted to the science, business or interests of advertising as a science, business or interest, but it excluded a publication intended primarily to advertise the business of its publisher, for such a publication would be practically a circular. When the law was new, the postoffice people were inclined to construe it to mean that a paper intended primarily for the purpose of being an advertising medium would be excluded and that "primarily" would apply in all cases where it could be shown that the income from advertisements was greater than that from subscriptions; but finding that such a rendering would exclude most successful newspapers, and practically all dailies, that contention was dropped.

I am not charging Mr. Crall with any improper interest. He is a good citizen, a good man, and as such was only doing his plain duty in attempting to prevent the free distribution of a book like the Newspaper Directory—that tended to make known to advertisers the very information that the good old-fashioned papers he represents know very well it would be better for them that the public should not possess. Many publishers of periodicals that have an unlimited amount of age, character and prestige, and a quite limited circulation, resent as an impertinence any inquiries, investigations, assumptions or statements having a bearing upon the number of copies they issue.

Little *Printers' Ink* is not a large affair. Its total business, now conducted upon an absolutely cash basis, does not run into the hundreds of thousands, but its present editor and manager, Mr. Charles J. Zingg, gives it undivided and loving attention, and its owner, the writer, has not only a great fondness for it and a great interest in its growing success, popularity and influence, but furthermore, as it does not make serious demands upon his time or energy, he delights exceedingly in spending an hour or two at its office of publication and injecting a word here and there about its management. Without an excuse for going down town, the days, even in New York, would be dull and uninteresting to one in whose life a business connection has always seemed a necessity.

There is a familiar quatrain that doubtless contains much wisdom:

> Tickle the public and make it grin,
> The more you tickle the more you'll win;
> But teach the public you'll never grow rich,
> You'll live like a beggar and die in the ditch.

I have not lived like a beggar, nor do I seem likely to die in a ditch, but I am conscious that in my efforts to teach, in my efforts to show others how things ought to be done, I have ever made more enemies than friends, gathered more kicks than ha'pence. But then I like to instruct the public; and a moderate amount of misrepresentation or misunderstanding keeps one from having too good an opinion of himself, and everybody knows that the self-satisfied man is about the worst there is.

FORTY-FOURTH PAPER

Reference has been made to what might possibly have been achieved, in an advertising way, had our office been the owner of some trademarked commodity or proprietary article, having an established demand throughout the country, that might be stimulated and increased by advertising, whenever and wherever profitable contracts could be placed, or space that was in danger of going to waste could be bought at bargain prices. Some such idea was always in mind. The proprietary article that is managed with greatest ease, when the demand for it is once firmly established, is a patent medicine. The cost of production is generally small, the percentage of profit consequently large, the methods of distribution are perfected, and a demand, once established based upon merit, will continue to some extent as long as children live who can remember hearing mothers commend the article, or having seen it used, or participated in such use. I early thought I saw advantages that would accrue from the ownership and control of such an article, but the question was how to get possession of one. Those that were well established were not for sale; such as had moderate prospects were held at speculative values—probably far beyond their real worth—furthermore we had no large capital at liberty for sequestration in the way of such a purchase. We might buy some deserving article that had not been pushed far enough to become an established success; we might acquire an interest in a promising one, by purchase; or we might get up one of our own, and begin at the foundation, as had been the method pursued by most people who had made successes of this kind.

From time to time, in a half-hearted way, we experimented along the lines mentioned. One of the first proprietary articles, with the advertisements of which I had become familiar, was Redding's Russian Salve. A Boston customer of ours, who advertised two other articles successfully, had attempted to create a sale for what he called GRACE'S SALVE, which was practically the same as Redding's, but had never gained much of a position in the confidence of the public. We became possessed of that trademark; but what little advertising we did for it seemed to produce no result at all, and we finally dropped it. One of my earliest patrons was a Philadelphia druggist, S. C. Upham by name, who sold a soap known as Upham's Freckle, Tan and Pimple Banisher. Somehow I got an idea that it had possibilities in the way of popularity, and there came a time, after he had parted with his right to Demas Barnes—who was the pool or grave-yard toward which such things drifted in those days—and it had been passed on, by Barnes, to his successors, John F. Henry & Co., I made some sort of a deal with Mr. Henry by which our advertising agency became possessed of the Upham trademark; and we really did insert advertisements of the "Banisher" in a good many papers, a good many times; and succeeded in stimulating some sale; but the limited income was absorbed by the cost of management, and bore no reasonable proportion to the apparent value of the advertising done; and as the trade did not show satisfactory signs of life we finally lost interest. I do not know to-day whether I do or do not own the Grace's Salve and the Freckle, Tan and Pimple Banisher. If I do own them I will, for a dime, give to anybody who wants it a quit claim of all my interest in the two preparations—the buyer to pay for preparing the requisite papers. I do not believe I ever received ten dollars from the two combined, yet I probably advertised them to an amount that would have cost any outsider as much as $10,000.

We had a successful advertiser in Halifax, N. S., who sold a medicine known as Fellows' Hypophosphites, that proved so good that some shrewd business men in the medicine trade, who knew about it, bought the trademark, incorporated a company with a capital of $100,000, retained the original owner as manager, stopped all advertising except in medical journals, and thereafter pushed the sale only through the medical profession. I had information at one time of a young man who was heir to an uncle, recently deceased, and had come into possession of a certificate of the stock of this company, of the face value of $6,000, and made up his mind that, shrewd as the old gentleman was, he had, without doubt, acquired trash in this instance; and I heard further, that the young man began to think better of the doubtful asset, when one day a dividend check came; and when, at the end of a year, he realized that within the twelvemonth that $6,000 certificate had brought him $9,000 in dividends, he began to revise his estimate of his deceased uncle's prescience in making investments.

Our Mr. Moses, in his experience with the patent medicine trade, had knowledge that there was a considerable sale for a somewhat similar preparation known as Winchester's Hypophosphates, and knew that the owner of that trademark bought the contents of his bottles by the gallon, at a certain chemist's laboratory where anybody could do the same who would pay the price, which was hardly equivalent to half a dime for the contents of one of the Winchester dollar bottles. The medicine was a cure for consumption, and Mr. Moses proposed that we create a trade-mark on the same thing. He had experience in such matters, went ahead, got up the labels, the circulars, the wrappers, and we owned a trademark of our own—sure enough—and the copyrighted name of it was PULMONA. This, too, was advertised and had some sale. Doubtless it was good stuff, for the same people bought it over and over again, and wrote testimonials of its efficacy, but the sales did not amount to one-twentieth of the cost of the advertising, and when we one day received a lawyer's letter setting forth that we were using a trade name already copyrighted years ago by somebody else, and must stop it or buy off the previous owner, we quit. But occasional orders for PULMONA followed Mr. Moses up until the day of his death. It is said that the demand for a good patent medicine never does entirely die out.

A man from Worcester, Mass., advertised a dentifrice, through us,—I think the name was Opaline. It seemed a pretty good thing; and after a time, I made a trade with him for the trademark and paid him $1,000 on account— or something like that. When it came to executing the requisite papers he balked about something, and I felt obliged to bring suit to compel either a transfer or a refund-·ing of the money. When the case came to trial I had to go to Worcester to attend. My lawyer seemed an excellent man, and capable, but appeared rather sorry to have a New Yorker on his hands. New York was such a wicked place, a Worcester jury would hardly believe anything good of a man who lived where everything and nearly everybody was known to be so bad. He had little confidence in the result, although he personally thought I had right on my side. He gave me as good a character to the jury as could; spoke of Sodom, that might have been saved had it possessed one righteous man, but for the lack of him was burned with brimstone and fire; New York had not been burned, consequently it must have one righteous citizen, and I was the man. The argument seemed conclusive, but it did not go with that jury, they brought me in the wrong, and I not only never got back my $1,000, but I had to pay the costs of court in addition and my own lawyer as well. He was sorry, and it is my recollection that he charged me only $10 or $15 for the whole service; and yet he was a man of marked ability and stood high at the bar of his section of Massachusetts. A New York lawyer would not have let me off a single penny under $500 for the same service.

Having dentifrices in mind, what more natural than that I should look into tooth powders? We had a customer, one of the nicest men that ever lived, Dr. I. W. Lyon by name, who advertised what he called "Tooth Tablets;" and they seemed to be a good thing, and the Doctor was very much in earnest in his belief in the excellence of his product.

I became well acquainted with the Doctor; liked and respected him. We had frequent talks about the outlook of his advertising venture, and eventually agreed upon a price at which he would sell me a half interest in his trademark. The terms were fully understood and I had talks with people in the trade, telling them of my purchase; but on the morning when the papers were to be executed the Doctor came in, seemed troubled, said he was anxious about it all, and wished he had not made the trade, and wished I would be willing to call it off. He was so earnest about it that I rather thought he would in the end refuse to sign the requisite papers, but he did not say so. However, it was evident he did not wish the trade to go through, and I was quite in sympathy with his feelings, for he had managed it all his own way heretofore, and would be in a measure parting with his liberty. The trade was called off. For some reason, which I never divined, Dr. Lyon did not place his advertising through me in after years, but I am glad to know that he made an eventual success of his enterprise. His preparations are standard in the market to-day.

I have heard that persistency or consistency—one or the other—is a jewel. It cannot be the latter, for I read in Emerson that "Consistency is the weak hobgoblin of little minds." If persistency is the jewel, I think I may say I have it. I am persistent, and have always been so. For twenty-five years I had wished to own a trademark, a proprietary article that might be advertised. In 1891 I determined to own one; and will now proceed to tell how I went about it and what came of it.

I thought it most probable that what I wanted was a medicine, but I was not decided on that point. Anything would do that would meet a moderately common want. I prepared an advertisement: "Wanted—To buy a trademark, a proprietary article—something that if advertised would command a sale." This advertisement was inserted in *Printers' Ink* and in the New York *Herald*, and it brought responses. A man in Maine had a remedy for moths, another in Georgia a cure for the ague, another in

Vermont a cure for spavin on horses. There were others, mostly recipes for medical preparations. I was not working in the open,—for personal conferences were not desired until I should find myself on the track of something that seemed promising; but after a time knowledge had been gathered that seemed to warrant investigation and interviews. I had talked the matter over with a young friend, a medical student. He had leisure, and made one or two trips of investigation for me that amounted to nothing satisfactory, but as time passed he became more interested and discussed the quest with acquaintances and friends. He had some sort of a position or appointment at the Roosevelt Hospital, in New York City under that Dr. John McGaw Woodbury who has of late years gained so much commendation for his excellent work as head of the New York City Department of Street Cleaning, and mentioned there the search he was conducting, and one physician said to him, "Why don't you take so-and-so?"—a prescription found to be efficacious in syphilitic cases. This would not do, for the advertisement would be expected to appear in papers of the highest class, and such announcements, as family reading, would be objected to in some quarters.

We finally arrived at conclusions about as follows: The article, if a medicine, should be something so clean that no one could object to it on the score of impropriety; nor should any objectionable or suggestive words be needed for its exploitation. It should meet some want that exists in cold climates and in warm as well; and be in demand both summer and winter. Having to withstand all climates it should not be anything that would be liable to freeze nor likely to spoil from exposure to heat. It should be capable of being sent by mail—therefore lightness of weight would be a desirable quality—and if it could be a dry substance, the absence of fluid would be an advantage, because fluids tend to breakage, evaporation and loss of quality through exposure—and what not. If alcohol became a needed ingredient that would be expensive; furthermore, there ought not to be anything about the remedy that could alarm the temperance sentiment.

The medical student, whose leisure and good will enabled me to benefit by his knowledge, is now a physician in active practice, and to such any association with a patent medicine is "pizen." On that account I will not mention his name. When I have occasion to refer to him I always speak of him as Dr. Fred. He said to me one day: "We have a preparation at the hospital that everybody who comes there is certain to swallow more or less of, and they all complain of feeling better for it. I have talked with Dr. Woodbury about what we are looking for and he thinks it might answer our purpose as well as anything. It has a soothing effect on the stomach, and no matter what ails a man it is either a result of a stomach difficulty or it will, to some extent, induce such a difficulty. If a man eats too much, or drinks too much, it will upset his stomach. Let a man chop an axe into his foot, while splitting wood for the kitchen fire, and it will not only disable his foot, but it will immediately give him a sensation of being sick at his stomach. This particular medicine seems to act as a sweetener and soother, and, as I have said before, they pretty much all get more or less of it at the hospital, and it always seems to produce good results." When I had heard so much about this wonderful prescription I thought it must be good enough for my purpose and asked that some of it be shown to me. When this was done it almost made me sick at the stomach to look at it. Its appearance suggested that it had had its origin from putting a portion of a pulverized brick into a vial filled two-thirds full of muddy water. When "well shaken before using" it looked muddy. When at rest a dirty brick-colored sediment formed in the bottom of the bottle, but even then the upper part remained muddy and unpleasant to the eye. The bottom to all appearances might be composed of a fair quality of Jersey mud. Removing the cork there was a smell of peppermint and of something else not nearly so pleasant. Fred said that was rhubarb. "But what is the fluid?" I asked. "Oh, that's only water!" "The thing won't do," was my conclusion. "It looks nasty. It smells nasty. If it breaks it will soil anything it touches. It tastes nasty, and if it is ever exposed to 32 degrees of cold it will freeze and break the bottle—and the buyer will never want anything more to do with it." And so it was turned down hard, and more attention was paid to investigating other things. Still, Fred referred again and again to what he called "Our R. & S.

DOCTOR FRED.

Compo.," which I learned after a time to be shorthand for Rhubarb and Soda Composition, and spoke of its general application and wide use by physicians.

One day I showed the bottle to an acquaintance who had been for some years employed in a country drug store. He smelled it, tasted it, looked at it, and then said in amused surprise, "Why that's the stuff Dr. Mitchell always gives almost everybody. He writes 'G. M.' on a prescription blank, and that means 'General Medicine,' and we used to keep it on hand—all made up—and deal it out as called for. All we had to do was to shake it up, fill the bottle, write 'G. M.' on the label and how much to take and how often, collect twenty-five cents and there we were. I don't think it cost more than a cent, but then the bottle and cork cost nearly as much more.".

One day Fred told how largely his grandfather, who had been a country doctor, used to administer practically this same prescription, and how often he had seen him at the bedside of a patient measuring out the powders by taking them on the point of the blade of his pocket-knife, and putting them up in the little papers—always used for powders—and giving instructions how often they should be taken and all that. "But this stuff is not a powder!" I exclaimed. "Oh, it's more convenient for us at the hospital to have it in the form you see, but a country doctor would carry it in the form of a powder and have it put into the water when administering it. That would be the more convenient way for him." With the exception of the Seidlitz Powder, I did not know of any largely sold medicine that was put out in the form of a powder, and the powder idea did not help me any. One evening, however, Dr. Fred said, casually, "Of course, you know that R. & S. Compo. can be made into a tablet." That was just what I did not know, and what I was very glad to know. The conversation was held in the library of my house in 49th street—the one I bought of the estate of Mr. Tilford, one of the founders of Park & Tilford. He had lived in it twenty years or more. At a later time I sold it at a profit to Ogden Goelet, who lived next door, and I do not think it will do any harm to admit that it was this confounded tablet that caused me to part with the most convenient and satisfactory home it was ever my fortune to enjoy—but that is another story—or at least another part of this one. Within one minute after Dr. Fred had given expression to the tablet idea he had written a prescription, taken his hat and coat—it was autumn—and sought the nearest drug store, on Fifth Avenue, where he ordered a hundred tablets to be prepared and sent over to the house. They came next morning and looked all right. They could be swallowed without getting very much of the disagreeable taste of the Rhubarb, and I tried the things on myself and all the acquaintances I could induce to swallow one. This experimental stage brought up the question whether there might not be such a thing as taking too much of them, and I had rather high medical authority that if the stuff could have a place on the tables of the poor, who eat too rapidly of food not easily digested, and in the form of a "ketchup" be applied daily to the food as eaten, the results, instead of being harmful, would be beneficial.

Here was a prescription then that would do for a patent medicine. It was good for almost everything, was largely used by doctors, and had been for a hundred years or more. It could be put up in the form of a tablet, a form then just coming into use on account of the recent invention of machines that could compress triturated drugs and deliver them with as much accuracy as coins are turned out at the mint.

The next question then was what shall the stuff be called. The best protection for a trademark is the name of the inventor, but if the inventor ceases to be the owner that fact sometimes makes trouble for the actual proprietor. Dr. Fred was not anxious to be made famous by having his name attached to a proprietary article with which his connection was likely to be brief. I, on my part, had no wish to become widely known except as an advertising agent. Many hours were devoted to the consideration of a name. One day it was discovered that the initial letters of the six ingredients that went to make up the tablet could be so arranged that they would spell a word—a new word—one that had no recognized meaning. And that is the way that R. I. P. A. N. S. happened to be adopted.

When we had gotten up a company, and began to advertise the goods, the investor who first put his name down as a subscriber for some shares, inquired at a prominent drug store near the Grand Central Station in 42d street for Ripans Tabules. The clerk had never heard of them. An explanation followed. He would get the remedy if requested, but added gratuitously, "I guess the name will kill 'em." The name, though, meaningless, is, perhaps, as good as any. It has been found a pretty hard nut for counterfeiters or imitators to deal with. Most persons fail to note that the word Tabules is also an arbitrary word. No such word existed in any dictionary before we applied it to Ripans; but no one hearing it for the first time ever fails to understand that a tablet is meant. It was not until long after that I learned that the word Tabloid had a similar origin, was also protected by trademark, and could not be used for application to anything save the medical tablets produced by the English firm who invented and protected it in the manner prescribed by law. So naturally does the word Tabules strike upon the ear, that Dr. R. V. Pierce, of Buffalo, on one occasion, discussing the patent medicine business with me, said he was surprised to note how the sales of Tabules increased with him; that the previous year the sales had reached, I think he said, about $60,000. I thereupon said, "Doctor, you don't sell any Tabules at all." "What do you mean?" he asked in amused surprise, and I answered, "You do not sell Tabules, you sell Tablets," and he said that, actually, he had never noticed that we were using an arbitrary word.

I often wonder if any one who has not been through the mill has any idea of the great amount of work and thought involved in the preparation of the printed matter that must go with a proprietary article; and of the necessity of getting it right in the beginning; and the harm that frequently results from the most insignificant changes after people have become used to one formula. There is an unsuspected difficulty, too, in preparing advertising matter that will not seem tame and valueless beside the more glowing announcements that have been appearing daily for years in the public prints. If the medicines now on the market will do what is claimed for them there is no occasion—no room—for any other, now, nor will there ever be. It seems to be universally admitted, among those who have had most experience that in the announcements that are issued the advertiser must put it strong. "You are starting out on a long up-hill journey," said a man to me whose life had been spent in kindred lines, "and you must write your advertisements to catch damned fools—not college professors;" then, after a moment, he added, "and you'll catch just as many college professors as you will of any other sort."

I had thought it better that the article we put on the market should sell for a dollar. A dollar seemed a reasonable sum to pay for a medicine, if a medicine was needed; but when we came to make up our packages the dollar price would not seem to come right and it came about that we made a 75 cent box, the contents of which consisted of six separate glass vials, each containing six Tabules. The medicine trade seems always to have been based on the dozen and the gross. Now each vial we put up contained half a dozen Tabules, and the six vials gave thirty-six Tabules to the box, consequently four boxes would have 144 or a gross of Tabules. We decided that a buyer might have four boxes packed in one parcel for $2, thus reducing the cost of the single box to 50 cents, and, from the usual practice of figuring, to allow the retailer a profit of one-third the selling price the box, for which he was expected to get 75 cents from the consumer, would cost him but 33 cents; but the operations of cut-rate druggists made such a profit out of the question in most localities, and our practice of making a gross the integer of a transaction so mixed up the buyers in the jobbing houses that when they got an order for our goods they did not know just how to send it in, and when they filled an order the retailer rarely failed to assert that he was not getting what he asked for. Finally we made the box containing the six vials the integer, and made the price 50 cents, but it then appeared that if the box contained six separate portions, all precisely alike, it was one of those portions and not a box that the buyer at retail had in mind, consequently the druggists opened the boxes and sold the buyer what he wanted. To facilitate this division, while the retail price of the box had been 75 cents, the little vials were labeled, "Price 15 Cents," but when the reduced price of the box brought the cost of the vial down below 6 cents, 15 cents seemed too much to ask for it and 10 cents became the standard price, and soon there arose a complaint that the quantity in the vials was too small. Six Tabules for 10 cents were not enough.

All this time we were advertising largely and getting very little results. We had more than $125,000 due to us in balances that had been created against the newspapers of the country—mostly poor ones—for advertising in Rowell's American Newspaper Directory. It was determined to use this balance for the first year's advertising of the Tabules, and that was done; and, at the end of the year, the net amount of money received from the sales was found to have been precisely $976.48. It was not enough to pay the postage on the correspondence involved in managing the advertising and the cost of the electrotypes used. Next year, 1893, we advertised still more, and that year the sales amounted to $2,126.83. It was not until the fifth year that the sales amounted to as much as $2,000 in any single month. The largest sales ever made went something over $15,000 in a single day—but that was under exceptional conditions in the year 1898. The largest normal sales ever made in a month was $40,820.78 in March, 1899, but that was after numerous changes and experiments with the size of the package and the price at which it was sold.

There had been, it seemed, constant dissatisfaction with our prices, and I could note a persistent tendency in the trade toward a lower level of prices; and finding, by careful experiment, that it would be possible to make a packet of ten Tabules—with its circular wrapper and attendant packing material—at a cost of not more than one cent, we decided to introduce, experimentally, a five cent package. Ripans was the first patent medicine put up in tablet form. It was also the first five cent packet put on the market. But nobody wanted it. Nobody liked it. I went in person to the buyer at Chas. N. Crittenton & Co.'s, the principal dealers in medicines in the city, told him the story, showed the packet and he said, after looking it over, "I don't believe we will try to sell those goods," and I said, "It is an experiment, and in connection with it I will try one other. You have the standard sorts in stock and know how to get more when you want them. If at any time you think you want any of these five cent goods, we will ask you to send up the money for them before we deliver the goods."

A demand for the five cent package seemed to spring up and the enterprise took on an appearance of success. There is a sale for the Tabules in every State, although never a large one in those situated along the Southern or Gulf of Mexico region. First and last five hundred millions of them have been doled out, enough to make a string, if drilled like other pearls, that would extend from Calais, Maine, far beyond San Francisco, in fact well out into the Pacific toward Hawaii. It is still a question whether the packet with ten Tabules would not have sold just as well at ten cents. It has often been made plain that druggists do not like to handle a five cent medicinal package; and in the South, from Jacksonville to San Diego, and up along the Pacific coast and in Alaska and the Rocky Mountain towns, there is a scarcity of small coins for facilitating such transactions.

When the sale of the Tabules was at high water mark and more than fifty thousand different people were buying a package every day of the month and the wonderful virtues of the tabules were everywhere so much extolled, I used to hear that at his club and among his intimates Dr. Woodbury seemed to be immensely pleased that a suggestion of his had led to the adoption of a recipe that had become the foundation for so celebrated a medicine; but whenever he was approached for a word of commendation or approval, that might be used for advertising purposes, he seemed to be greatly pained at the suggestion, and I have reason to suppose that few physicians of high standing could be induced to stand sponsor for any advertised remedy no matter how excellent.

The goods are not advertised at all at the present time, and, therefore, the business appears to produce a handsome profit, realizing a thousand dollars every few days. Under such conditions it seems like a little gold mine. Nearly 10,000 people go every day to some drug store, somewhere, and put down a nickel to procure one of the little 5 cent cartons of Ripans Tabules. Still the total sales at the retail price have not yet reached a total of $3,000,000, and the manufacturer gets but little more than half the money paid by the buyer at retail, and the gross cost of the advertising already done does not fall very much below the full $3,000,000 specified as the gross proceeds at retail. All of which goes to show that making money in the patent medicine trade is by no means as easy as "rolling off a log."

FORTY-FIFTH PAPER

In the conduct of the ordinary affairs of an advertising agency one day is very like another. Newspaper men come in, tell of the success they are having, how rapidly the circulation is increasing, and explain how it is that this or that competitor is losing ground or has practically ceased to be a factor to be reckoned with. Advertisers have in mind introducing a new product, and believe that with the expenditure of a few hundred or a few thousand dollars, they can make their names household words; and when they learn that a one-inch advertisement costs $84 for a single insertion in one magazine that is mentioned, and that a page a year, in the same, will cost $48,000, go away with an impression that it will be well to look further into the matter before deciding to take the plunge. There will be interesting and surprising episodes now and then, more likely, perhaps, to be recalled at a later day than specially noted at the time. Sometimes unpromising customers will develop into good ones and again an apparently honest enterprise will turn out to be a trick or a fraud. Once a very shabby and, in appearance, rather stupid man wished to advertise a music box which he sold for a dollar; and the announcement said it would play eight tunes. His first investment in advertising was $1.25, but there came frequent orders afterwards, sometimes amounting to as much as $5. One day the office was surprised to see him produce four hundred very much soiled one dollar bills and authorize the insertion of his advertisement to the full amount. Inquiry elicited the fact that his "music box" was what is known as a mouth harmonica; somewhat box-like in appearance, may be, but hardly enough so to warrant being called a music box. It would certainly play eight tunes, or eighty, for that matter; or as many as the performer knew but the man said eight seemed to be a more enticing number to advertise than any other.

There were instances where some one would advertise an unobjectionable book, but so word the announcement as to lead the reader to expect something salacious. The book commonly sent would be a cheap testament or Bible; so cheap in fact, that the margin of profit would be considerable. I have heard of a man who advertised to send, for one dollar, a piece of good advice that might be the means of preventing serious injury. To those who sent the money he enclosed a printed slip reading: "Many persons have been seriously injured by the careless use of a knife. My advice to you, therefore, my friend, is 'Always whittle from you.'" A man who advertised an article most indispensable to married people or those who are about to be married, sent in return for the dollar a linen pocket handkerchief that would have been dear at ten cents. It was related that one impulsive miss, when remitting the price specially stipulated that the article should come to hand "before next Thursday night."

It was a theory with me in the early days that we stood in a position between advertiser and publisher, taking no responsibility for the thing advertised, contenting ourselves with guaranteeing to the publisher the payment for the service performed; leaving on him the onus of deciding whether or not it was a service that it would be well for him to undertake. We found ourselves obliged to recede—in part at least—from this position; for as our business was generally clean and straight, the newspapers seemed to fall into the way of accepting without question anything we might send, so long as the price was right—and sometimes when it was not. On one occasion Jacob Munsell, the antiquarian publisher at Albany, brought out a book telling a great many interesting details about a social practice that had prevailed among the early Pennsylvania Dutch, and containing some verses and details that were not just what would be chosen for family reading, although, no doubt, vastly interesting to antiquarians and those who made collections of literature that had for its object the perpetuating of the records of customs, long obsolete. This book was advertised in a few selected papers; and in a daily or any secular weekly was well enough; but it so happened that one of the papers on the list was the *Churchman*, then published at Hartford, Conn., by the same estimable gentleman who controls its fortunes to-day. He was well acquainted with our Mr. Kent, who was an Episcopalian by marriage and an important and influential member of Dr. Houghton's Little Church Around the Corner; and on account of the good understanding that existed directions had been given at the *Churchman* office that nothing coming from our agency should be subjected to censorship. The publisher was absent, his order was in force, it was press day; and when the paper appeared the advertisement of the book about BUNDLING seemed to be about the most conspicuous thing on the page where it appeared. One would hardly expect a moderate Churchman to exhibit so much indignation as that publisher displayed when he came to our office to remonstrate, and I believe that from that time forth his office censor has been much more careful to scrutinize everything offered for the advertising columns; and we, on our part, realized that we should have to assume somewhat more responsibility than we had hitherto been inclined to acknowledge.

False promises held out in advertisements have been of incalculable injury to the business of honest advertisers, and it is gratifying to notice that such announcements as are open to criticism are being gradually eliminated from the columns of the more respectable journals and magazines.

Before the foundation of our agency there was a certain advertisement that became famous from the newspaper comment that its phraseology induced. It announced that a retired physician, "whose sands of life had nearly run out," had discovered a wonderful remedy for certain serious ills, and would give the recipe, free, to anyone who cared to write to him. It soon appeared that one of the ingredients, although known to science, was not easy to procure, because it was only produced in a remote country, and no one had any very high opinion of its merits. The advertiser, however, had plenty of it; and, as a consequence, all his prescriptions came, eventually, to him to be filled. After a while the scheme played itself out, and the "old physician," a man then of about forty years, set out to discover some other thing that would tend to cause the sands of his own life to run more smoothly and pleasantly, if not more slowly. He finally hit upon a cure for epilepsy, and would come to our office from week to week, always with a differently worded advertisement; but the drawing power of none seemed to come up to his requirements. Finally, however, he began to repeat a certain formula of words which he said was a success. It also announced a recipe or a secret, and in the body of the advertisement there appeared this sentence: "This discovery was revealed to the Doctor in such a providential manner that he has felt that he should be doing wrong were he to refrain from making it generally known." He said that those words "revealed in a providential manner" were now worth a good living to him. Since that day the "old" doctor's sands of life actually have run entirely out, and no one at present appears to be giving away his providential discovery.

We had another case where the change of a word, instead of the insertion of a phrase, proved the salvation of an advertisement. A certain gunsmith in Pittsburg had built up a trade in cheap guns obtained from army sales and other sources; and succeeding so well, had bought a great number of one sort, which he advertised at a low price, announcing that they were "the celebrated Springfield Muskets." So confident was he of success that he gave an order for the insertion of his four line announcement in so many papers that the bill figured up the very respectable amount of something over $1,800; but to his surprise the responses were few; and those that did come wanted some other kind of a gun. No one seemed to care to possess a Springfield Musket; and the advertising appeared likely to result in an almost total loss of a sum that was of material consequence to a man in his comparatively small way of business. Finally he became impressed with the idea that it was the *Musket* that the people did not want, and, by his direction, the word was dropped and Barrels substituted. No sooner had the change appeared than the advertisement began to produce the effect that had been counted on, and more. While no one wished to have anything to do with "the celebrated Springfield Muskets," everybody, boy and man, seemed in haste to get in an order for a gun having the "celebrated Springfield *Barrels*" before the supply should be exhausted.

It was interesting to note, too, how a small advertiser would now and then develop into a large one. The first time I ever saw Dr. R. V. Pierce, of Buffalo, I canvassed him for an order, and we agreed upon $72 as the price. The advertisement was of a patent medicine called Dr. Sage's Catarrh Remedy. The office looked so bare and unpromising that after capturing the order I was inclined to skirmish around to see if I could not get payment in advance, and finally succeeded, by making a moderate discount. Were I still in business I should be glad to book an order to-day, from the same man, for $72,000 or $720,000 and he would not be allowed much of a discount should he offer to cash up the whole sum in advance.

There was one occasion when I was induced to go personally to a place on the east side of Broadway, below Wall Street, in response to an application. It was a small office, up three flights of stairs, in a loft over some sort of a warehouse. There, at a desk, sat a man who talked with me long and earnestly. I demanded $62.50 for the service required, and he wanted a reduction. I urged that the price named was what everybody would have to pay, and went so far as to assert that I did not think it would be fair to charge full price to the man who trusted me and gave the order in confidence, and then do the same work for a smaller sum for one who not only did not have confidence in me, but also made a great deal of trouble and annoyance by seeking to break the price. He took exception to all I

said, and asserted that the man who paid out money in a
wholesale, liberal way was generally one who also made it
in that way, while the small man, who made little, must be
careful of every cent, and was entitled to a consideration
that the other would not ask for and did not need. I did
not yield to the argument, but a remembrance of it often
recurred to me in later days. This man was a Mr. R. T.
Bush. He was then advertising for agents to sell what he
called a "Woven Wire Clothes Line," made of a galvanized
braided wire. I had known something of him previously as
selling agent for a sewing machine that was said to infringe
certain patents that were highly valued by richer companies,
who had finally succeeded in driving him out of the business. A little later—it seemed a very little while—and his
name was in all the papers, as owner of a celebrated yacht,
and he was offering a prize of $10,000 to the yachtsman who
should cross the Atlantic, or do some other specified thing,
in less time than some other had done—or something of
that sort. He was also owner and publisher of a magazine
which was just then being promoted in a manner that made
it conspicuous. The funds that had widened his views of
expenditure did not, however, come from sales of the Woven
Wire Clothes Line, but arose from his having embarked,
successfully, in oil refining, and finally negotiating a satisfactory combination with Mr. Rockefeller's enterprise. He
had a warehouse in Maiden Lane and conducted business
under the firm name of Denslow & Bush. In *Pearson's
Magazine* for May, 1905, one may read a good account of
the yacht race and see a picture of the boat that belonged to
Mr. Bush.

At one time Chesman and Moore lived at a boarding
house in the city, and became acquainted with a fellow
boarder who was interested in a baking powder. I used to
hear a good deal about it, and there was talk of advertising
it; but times changed—Moore died, Chesman married the
lady who kept the house—and has doubtless had no board
to pay for the last thirty years—and the other boarder got
himself absorbed into or consolidated with the Royal Baking

Powder Co., and at a later day rose to the control of that and of all, or practically all, the other Baking Powder interests, and is now engaged in furnishing the money to discover the North Pole, and other scientific amusements, he being no other than that Mr. William Ziegler* of whom we read a good deal in the papers from day to day.

It is customary to consider it advisable to change the subject matter of an advertisement every issue, yet I recall two examples that have appeared in papers and magazines, with some regularity, for a good deal more than forty years, without being changed at all. One of these was originally put forth by Dr. Donald Kennedy, of Roxbury, Mass., now Boston. The other appears more frequently of late years in the columns of the New York *Herald,* and a few other high grade papers and magazines. I am speaking of the complexion preparation of Dr. T. Felix Gourard, which most people will recall having seen. When I first met Dr. Gourard, about 1866, he was a little past eighty, but had recently been married to a woman whose years numbered scarcely a fourth of his; and the old gentleman was vastly proud of the baby that had come into the family, and I thought he had occasion to be so. Many years after I read in the New York *Sun,* where whatever you see is so, that —speaking of the marriage of old men—those of sixty *may* have children, those of seventy years are likely to have them and those of eighty are sure to. I then realized, this being the unavoidable outcome, there was really nothing in the case of the good old Doctor to be specially worthy of comment.

There are people now living in Roxbury who remember "Dr." Donald Kennedy, as a poor man, a laborer, who went about, from time to time, digging burdock roots, in back yards and by the roadside, wherever they chanced to grow; and later saw him, with a basket on his arm, selling his famous "Medical Discovery" from house to house and from

*Since this paragraph was written Mr. Ziegler has been called to his last account, being the sixth person mentioned in these papers who, alive at the time of mention, has passed away in the comparatively few weeks that have intervened. Verily it behooves those of us who remain to be ever ready to go hence.

store to store. It would cure every disease that flesh is heir to "except thunder humor." I have never seen any one who could tell me what "thunder humor" is, or was, but I have met more than one who has given me accounts of Dr. Kennedy's great success, the wealth that came to him, his numerous kindly acts, his willingness to extend a helping hand, and have been told that he was a good citizen, and such a man, in every way, as those who were brought in contact with him were proud to count as an acquaintance and a friend.

There was a certain Dr. Olcott, who advertised a great deal, and who, on one occasion, had asked that a representative from our office should be sent to interview him on the placing of a considerable contract. He had an office not far from Chatham Square, and gave free medical consultations. He promoted two separate remedies. One was for internal application, and known as the Pain Annihilator with great emphasis on the *h*. The other was for external use and designated as Pain Paint. I went in person to confer with the Doctor, and happened to get there at an hour when his free consultations were in full blast. The room was full of men, women and children, all in need of medical aid, and one by one they approached the Doctor, each telling his or her story; then the Doctor would ask a question or two and give his prescription. There seemed to be a great similarity in the needs of all. I listened while a distressed father related the particulars of an affliction from which a son of his was suffering; the Doctor cut him short after a time, saying "I should give him the ANNIHILATOR." "But," said the man, "his trouble is on his face, not internal." "Oh!" said the Doctor, "in that case I should apply the Pain Paint." I found that the one remedy or the other would fit every case in the room; and at a table near by, there stood an attendant, prepared to deliver the prescription—all made up, and costing a dollar a bottle. Dr. Olcott must have done a profitable business. His most successful advertisement had a picture of the head and face of a man suffering from neuralgia, who was surrounded by liliputian imps all engaged in torturing him with various instruments. One, I well remember, had a great auger with which he was boring, with much industry, into a well-chosen point on the patient's forehead, just above the space between the eyes.

Among the best advertised proprietary articles during and just after the Civil War was Drake's Plantation Bitters. The sale at one time reached very nearly a million dollars a year at wholesale. I remember very well an occasion in the early sixties, when two young men came to Boston, had a big room over a wholesale warehouse in Commercial street, and did some advertising for the Bitters. They were bright, enterprising and handsome, and with one of them I have kept up some acquaintance ever since. He is Mr. J. Morgan Richards, the first president of the Sphinx Club of London; and more conspicuous and successful than any other man has been in introducing American proprietary articles into Great Britain. He comes pretty near being an Englishman himself now, but has never lost his interest in Americans and America. A conspicuous feature of the Plantation Bitters advertising was a mysterious combination of the letters and figures which read "S. T. 1860 X.," and which was displayed everywhere, and puzzled everybody. There were many inquiries "What do they mean?" and as many explanations. One most commonly given was: "Started trade in 1860 with ten dollars capital." Mr. Drake and his partner, Mr. William P. Ward, the present head of the Lyon Manufacturing Company, owners of the old trademarks, Lyon's Kathairon, Hagan's Balm and Mustang Liniment, always asserted that there was really no meaning attached to the combination. It was said to be simply an advertising scheme to make people ask questions; but when I knew that Santa Cruz rum was the basis of the Bitters, and noted that if the figures 1860 were substituted for the letters c-r-o-i, in the word St. Croix, I have thought that those facts and conditions might be a partial elucidation of the riddle: still Mr. Drake always insisted that it meant positively nothing. Such combinations do come to have an advertising value, as is evidenced by the three R's of Radway's Ready Relief, the three S's of Swift's Syphilitic Specific, the double B of Burdock Bitters, the P. P. P. of a certain kidney remedy, the C. C. C. of Cascarets Candy Cathartic, and dozens of others that might be mentioned.

It is sometimes said that the sale of a proprietary article, after being once established, never entirely ceases; but I am told that three or four hundred dollars a year will now cover the entire demand for Plantation Bitters that were sold at the rate of nearly $3,000 a day for a period of some years. Hostetter's Bitters, introduced about the same time, are said to sell now about as well as ever, and to have been the most profitable "medicine" ever put on the market. Col. Hostetter, when he died, left a fortune of eighteen million dollars, which nearly or quite equaled that left by Dr. J. C. Ayer of Lowell, Mass., who began business earlier, owned many preparations and advertised ten times as much. Verily the secret of successful sales by advertising is past finding out. Many succeed, many fail. The man who succeeds once may fail when he tries again and to encourage the public I may as truthfully say that the man who fails many times does not infrequently hit upon an eventual success.

As further illustrating the fact that in the ordinary run of papers, in towns of moderate size, advertising had no standard of value thirty years ago, I may relate a case that came under my observation with one of the customers that came to us through the purchase of the good-will of the John Hooper advertising business. Mr. Wayre, Mr. Hooper's junior partner, brought in the list of papers, the estimate was made and given him to deliver. He looked it over and came to me, with a countenance very much perturbed, saying, "This estimate amounts to less than $2,100." "Yes," was the reply. "It will go through at those prices." "It will never do," said he. "We have been placing that order and repeating it over and over again, and at the paper's rates it comes to over $5,000, and we have been charging rates and the firm owes us to-day more than $30,000 and is not very strong. If I should take in that estimate I should never get the money due." "Very well," was the answer. "Make up the estimate yourself then," and he did so and brought in the order at the old figures, and it was paid for at that rate, too. I will not assert that the figures were not cut somewhat in sending out the order, nor that there was not some protests from publishers that it was at a lower rate than they had formerly received. I am glad to be able to say that Mr. Wayre collected the entire amount due on the old account as well as what was coming to us before he removed his domicile to mother England, and sorry to have to relate that not long after this desirable stage had been reached the Wall Street house failed.

Among the customers turned over to us by the Hooper concern was a firm, dealers in furniture and upholstery goods, B. L. Solomon & Sons by name. I had never seen any one connected with the house, but observing by the ledger one day that they had paid us something over $60,-000 for advertising in the city papers since we had obtained the account I thought it a good thing to do to make myself personally known to so good a customer. I asked Mr. Moore to go with and introduce me. We got into a discussion about some trivial matter on which Mr. Solomon and I held different views. The interview was not a thorough success. The business had gone on with perfect smoothness up to that time, but it never went so smoothly afterwards. This is an experience going to show that it is sometimes best to let well enough alone.

Before the laws were so stringent, the lottery feature was conspicuous in advertising, and great sums were expended in exploiting various gift enterprises; some of them were conducted in good faith and some were not. We had one customer whose practice seemed to be to watch the papers, and when he saw an advertisement that impressed him as attractive he would appropriate it, substitute his own name, and proceed to do business. He always paid in advance, but if on any account, or on any pretence, we were induced to trust him we would ever after have much difficulty about getting our hands on that particular sum. One day he produced an advertisement that he had found possessed pulling qualities; a list of papers was prepared and he coughed up nine thousand dollars, most of it in well worn and much soiled currency, and planked it down—in advance—for the service to be rendered; but, with or without sufficient reason, the Postoffice authorities soon stopped his mail; and before we paid him back what was coming to him on the contracts that had not been completed, we insisted upon his making good numerous items of $10, $50 or $100 that were due for orders he had left, when he didn't have the money in his pocket, and for which he would never thereafter consent to pay at all. It was pay first or never pay with him. I could never understand the theory upon which he acted.

Certain Boston houses, some of them well established merchants, did at one time a large business on a line that came to be known as the Dollar Sales. An attractive advertisement was put out inviting correspondents to invest ten cents in a scheme whereby every one who sent the money would obtain a right to buy, for one dollar, any one of several valuable things that should be named on a prize slip to be drawn after the lottery plan. Those who know what attractive things may be seen in a five cent or ten cent store, can understand that for a dollar in hand many things might be sold that would seem likely to cost much more, and out of a long list many people would be likely to select articles that would afford an excellent profit when sold for a dollar. Now and then an article would be named that would be worth many dollars, but somehow those did not come out very often, and when they did were likely to fall to the lot of some person of well-known influence living in a community where an active interest was already awakened. I would think I may have been paid as much as $100,000 in a single year for advertisements of this character, and curiously the buyers were commonly so well satisfied with what they received that they, like old Father William mentioned in "Alice in Wonderland," who continually stood on his head and finding no harm came of it:

Did it again and again.

There was a firm in New York, doing business in the Gift Enterprise line known as Elias Brothers. There were two or more of the brothers—if they were brothers—fine-looking, dare-devil Sherlock Holmes sort of fellows. They drove stylish turnouts in the park, dressed handsomely, carried themselves like gentlemen, were quiet and sober in manner, and so far as I know were not interfered with by the Postoffice people. They also invited ten cent subscriptions in a prize scheme wherein every investor had a valuable chance, and in their case every single ticket eventually drew a prize, and every prize was $200; but to get his hands on it the lucky holder was required to send in ten per cent of the face value of the prize, or $20, in pursuance of some condition specified previously, but in a manner so inconspicuous that it had generally escaped notice. Scarcely a day passed that some of our newspaper friends did not write us, confidentially, telling of the good luck that had come, asking us to advance the ten per cent, receive the prize, duly forward it and oblige. In this way we learned to know the inside of the scheme. The prize was in every case twenty $10 shares in "The Sand Hill Petroleum Company." I never knew how great was the capital stock of that company, nor where the Sand Hill was situated; but a man who came in contact with the senior member of the Elias firm used to tell of seeing him exhibit a roll containing sixty one thousand dollar bills, one day, and when putting it back in his pocket heard him remark, pleasantly, that that was some that came in after he had got done expecting to make any money. I never heard of there being any sales of those stock certificates, either at $10 or 10 cents a share, but believe the company was regularly incorporated—and that must have been some satisfaction. It seemed to me that there was a touch of grim humor in the name of that petroleum company. Once a Boston firm, dealers in cheap laces, Nottingham goods, found they had acquired an accumulation of odds and ends that it would be well to get rid of, and an advertisement was put in the papers announcing a remnant sale, and the result was so immediate, so tremendous, so satisfactory, that they cut their whole stock into remnants, repeated and extended the advertising until their bills amounted to as much as $60,000; and they had a resident buyer at Nottingham to pick up everything in the way of lace that was going. How the business came to an end I do not know, but one of the partners was that Mr. Bailey whose advertisements of peculiar and useful rubber toilet articles are seen in the best magazines from time to time. If he would write the story of the lace remnant sales for *Printers' Ink* I am confident Editor Zingg would print it and possibly pay him as much as $5 for his literary production.

Previous to the rise of the Louisiana Lottery, whose doings finally led to the laws that have driven all lottery schemes out of existence, the building of the Louisville, Kentucky, Public Library was the greatest effort in that line that came under my observation. I suppose Ex-Governor Bramlette and his associates paid me as much as half a million dollars for the announcements first and last. A part of the scheme involved the giving of concerts in metropolitan cities; and for one tour of this sort, made by P. S. Gilmore and his celebrated band, I had authority to invest $50,-000 for the advertising to be done in a single month. The effort was made to secure Theodore Thomas and his orchestra, but he would have none of it. One advertising agent made a fortune out of the placing of the advertising of the Louisiana Lottery. I did some of this advertising myself. I was too proud and too good to solicit the patronage, and not proud enough nor good enough to decline the orders when they came to me. The manager told me one day he should thereafter place the business with a neighboring agency, and I made no effort to dissuade him, and I was not sorry to see the business leave the office; but

I really wish I could look back, and think I had had the manliness to refuse to accept the orders that came to us, rather than know as I do, that I did take them, in the halfhearted way that I did, and thereby made it seem advisable to the promoters to carry the patronage where it would be received with more enthusiasm.

FORTY-SIXTH PAPER

Enthusiastic newspaper men who seek a short paragraph to fill a column sometimes set up the copy book phrase, "Advertising always pays." Advertising means to proclaim, to make known, and surely no one can do business unless he causes some others to know what he can do to serve them. Still, it is true enough that much good money is paid for advertising, that so far as the advertiser can see, is wholly barren of result. There was at one time a child's magazine, published by a firm named Hurd & Houghton, and I had been led to buy the space on the outside cover page for the period of a year, hoping to sell it at a profit. A day for forwarding copy had arrived and no copy was in hand. We had an electrotyped picture representing the counting room of our agency; and taking this, and adding a few lines to tell what an advertising agency was good for, we dispatched it, to save our space from going to waste, and that was the last we heard of it or ever expected to hear.

One day there came an inquiry from a place in Pennsylvania from a certain Dr. Shallenburger, who had a remedy for fever and ague. An estimate was prepared, and it resulted in an order for which he agreed to pay and did pay us the round sum of $8,000. After the advertising had expired and been settled for in full I was in Pittsburg one day and thought it well to visit the Doctor—his home town being situated not far away—and have a talk with him. I found him a prosperous man, living in a liberal way, a practicing physician, and not at all a practical patent medicine man. We had a long talk. He was of middle age. I think the name of his town was Beaver—a canal ran through it. When young, just starting out for the practice of his profession, the Doctor had come to this place, put out his

before; and I hardly think I had better advertise
My brother physicians do not approve of it, and
el certain that I have or ever shall get back the
ve paid to you." "How did you happen to come
next inquired. The Doctor's eyes brightened a
e said, "Sit down, I'll tell you about that. It's
It was one Sunday morning. I was ready to
ch, had my hat and overcoat on, when something
hat caused my wife to go again to her room for a
es and I sat waiting by the sitting-room table.
girl was a subscriber for *Our Young Folks*, a
published by Hurd & Houghton. A copy of it
table, with the back cover up, and on it I saw
rtisement and read it. I had often been tempted
ttle advertising, and next day I wrote to you; and
way it all came about."

other occasion I placed a large advertisement, for
ion, in the leading New York dailies; and, so far
d see, for a month, nothing came of it. It cost
One day, however, there was an inquiry from a
firm in Fulton street, manufacturers of paints.
a contract amounting to about $20,000. The firm
r been customers of ours, and after the order was
asked, one day, of one of the partners: "How did
en to come to us?" He smiled as though the query
something interesting to his mind and said, "Mr.
o"—naming his partner—"suggested one day that
be well for us to make a little trial of the effects of
ng, and I said there is a firm in the city who make
siness, and I got the paper for him that contained
ertisement. I had read it at the time it appeared;
g a little interested threw it up on top of the safe,
knew it would be likely to stay a while. We took
ur name and address, sent around to your office in
. *Times* Building, and that's the whole story."

Times used to accept a full column for insertion on
page, all the rest being reading matter. For the
his space, always a column and no less, the charge

shingle and waited for
him was an elderly wor
who sought his aid fo
which she was a great :
time; he heard how thi
scribed and done no go
just what it would be
wished she had not com
profit likely to result.
her case careful thought
for the next day. Meant
that everybody knew her
from conditions under wl
to be cured. Still, she w
wish to discourage his onl
up a prescription that wou
thing would; made it up
pills—of something less t
as she was a charity patic
gave her the medicine, tog
cautions about diet and mei

To his surprise, and no
she came again; said she
again. Soon he had a visit
canal, who had the ague an
helped the woman. The Dɑ
charged him $2, which was
receive for an office call.
ers, his companions and frie
edy; and this went on so fa
to make up the prescription i
to give out as called for—al
price. His first patient was a
thusiastic advertiser of his s
he did not like the idea of a p
the best part of his income co
package.

"But you are not an adver

advertised
any more.
I do not fe
money I ha
to us?" I
little and
interesting
go to chur
occurred t
few minut
My little
magazine
lay on the
your adve
to try a li
that is th

On ar
one inser
as I coul
$1,700.
prominen
It led to
had neve
placed, I
you happ
brought
So-and-S
it might
advertisi
that a b
your ad
and bein
where I
down y
the N.

The
the firs
use of

was $250. I at one time had in mind a small advertisement that I had thought of putting in the *Times,* and the conspicuousness of that first page position had charms for me; but my story hardly required a hundred words in the telling, and if I would have that place I must fill a column. In large type the stuff would have a straggling appearance; so I had it set in the space of one-fifth of a column, and repeated the same formula five times. A couple of days later a young man—under thirty—of stout build, and wearing a fur cap—it was winter—came in, had some conversation with me, and gave me an order to place a little advertising. After quite a talk with him I asked how he happened to come to me. "You had a column advertisement in the *Times* a few days ago," said he, "and I read it all through. It was the same thing over and over again, and it interested me; and I thought I would come in and see you." The order was not a large one, nor has the house ever become a large advertiser, but all the advertising it has done from that day to this has been placed through my office. The beginning was more than thirty years ago, and the man, through all that time, has been one of three or four of the most cherished friends of my life. I have seen his children in the cradle, and seen them married, and go to homes of their own. He and I have spent many a happy hour by a camp fire and in casting the fly to lure the speckled beauties from waters in Maine, New Hampshire, and that Lake Chateaugay that he thinks the finest sheet of water in the world. I am speaking of Seth E. Thomas, treasurer and principal owner of the great Seth Thomas Clock Company of Thomaston, Conn.

Forty years ago it was frequently said that the time for great profits from the sales of patent medicines had passed and would never come again; but since then Dr. R. V. Pierce has made a great success financially; so, too, has Brent Good, with Carter's Little Liver Pills; Dr. Kilmer, with his Swamp Root; Dr. Hartman, with P-e-r-u-n-a; Lydia Pinkham, with her Female Compound; and many others might be named. Dr. J. C. Ayer, of Lowell, had established his trademarks at an earlier date, and his success has never been equaled by any other, although Dr. Hostetter, with his Bitters, was a close second. The chances of success, however, are now so remote that he is either a bold or an imprudent man who ventures at the present day upon the introduction of a new remedy by means of advertising.

A conspicuous figure in the advertising world, when I was new to it, was Dr. H. T. Helmbold. Helmbold's Buchu was the remedy he exploited, and it was in 1865 what P-e-r-u-n-a is in 1905—the largest selling patent medicine on the market. It is rather surprising that since Dr. Helmbold's time no other person has seen a clear path toward exploiting another Buchu. It is said by physicians that Sarsaparilla has no curative qualities whatever; yet sarsaparillas follow each other in an endless procession. Dr. Jacob Townsend's was the first that I remember. Then came Isaac P. Townsend, whose beautiful house, that had in it fireplaces in every room, but no chimneys, was afterwards sold to A. T. Stewart, in whose marble palace he would have no shower bath—the guest that wanted a shower bath might go next door, he said. The place is now the home of the Knickerbocker Trust Company's offices, situated at the corner of Thirty-fourth street and Fifth avenue, in a building so wasteful in expense of construction, and in lack of room, that to merely look at it has caused more than one prudent business man to assert that if he had owned stock in the company he would have sold it as soon as that building plan became so far advanced as to let it be seen what extravagance was intended.

I do not believe Dr. Helmbold ever acquired a large fortune, but he sold an enormous number of bottles of Buchu; so much that a would-be humorist said of his store —just above the old Metropolitan Hotel and Niblo's Garden—"It is the most 'buchuful' on Broadway." He had a handsome wife, lovely beyond dispute; but any social distinction she acquired was traceable to her excellent family connections rather than to her husband's profuse expenditure and display. The Doctor used to ride in the Park daily, driving a spike team—two horses abreast and one in front. He was heard of at the watering places, and talked of to such an extent that when the bust of Humboldt was unveiled in Central Park, a lady at Saratoga, as she read of the affair, was led from a confusion of names to ask of an acquaintance just up from the city, who had attended the ceremony, "Was the Doctor present?" His pictures were as well known as those of the almost equally celebrated Dr. Munyon are to-day.

Both Dr. Helmbold and Dr. J. C. Ayer became insane in their later days, and neither recovered. Helmbold was not a good business man; Ayer, on the other hand, was exceptionally able and competent in that direction. He required a newspaper to place his advertising according to specifications and received allowance for all shortcomings; but if any error occurred he would succeed in placing the publisher so palpably in the wrong that he would gladly admit it and be quite ready to remedy his fault by a suitable allowance; and finally, when payment was made, the Doctor's well-trained correspondence clerk would write the newspaper man such a handsome acknowledgment of the value of his paper and its tremendous influence, that the delighted recipient would keep the letter at hand, exhibit it to everybody who would look at it, reprint it in his paper, and may be have it framed for preservation in his office for general inspection for years to come. Dr. Ayer had the best corps of advertising men that ever traveled in the interest of a patent medicine, and, although they never paid a newspaper any too much money for a service to be rendered, they gave as much flattery and soft soap as the publisher could make use of. The great Trinity Building on Broadway, in New York, is only one of numerous existing monuments that testify to Dr. Ayer's ability as a money-maker.

I have heard it said that titled fortune-hunters abroad were given to turning up their high-bred noses at the Ayer millions made out of "pills." Whether that be so or not, I have always understood that money made in the patent medicine business is a practical bar to social success. "Emma's papa is the man that makes —— Bitters," said a little miss to her mother, on a European steamer one day, speaking of another little miss with whom and with whose mother they had contracted an acquaintance on the voyage that promised to be pleasant all around. "We will be careful not to let her mother know that we know it," was the comment, "it might make her feel badly."

One of the first small orders I ever had, for what we called the List System, was from a New York concern named A. B. Sands & Co., and I well remember John Moore telling me, later, that it would not be renewed: "For," said he, "the house is going out of business. They are rich; used to make a sarsaparilla that had a big sale, and the heir of the family goes to Newport now, and they call him 'Sarsaparilla Sands;' and he doesn't like it, and the business is to be closed up"—and closed up it was.

I am by no means the only advertising agent who has experimented with advertising a proprietary article. Hale's Honey of Horehound and Tar was first put on the market by some men with whom James H. Bates was associated. Mr. Cooley, founder of the firm of Cooley & Dauchy, afterwards Dauchy & Co., owned a medicine known as Dodd's Nervine. No-To-Bac and Cascarets are largely the property of Mr. A. L. Thomas, of the Chicago Agency of Lord & Thomas. The Lawrence Brothers, publishers of the *Ohio Farmer,* own a proprietary article that brings a handsome income, and John B. Clarke, who long published the *Mirror and Farmer,* and besides being a successful coon hunter, thought himself pretty much the whole thing in New Hampshire, also owned a medicine that at one time had a considerable sale. N. W. Ayer & Son, of Philadelphia, are reported to have come into possession of more than one patent medicine trademark that they had advertised almost—but not quite—into financial success.

What is the value of a trademark that has been created by advertising nobody can tell. "The demand never entirely ceases," was the verdict of old Mr. Hall, of the firm of Hall & Ruckel, exploiters of Sozodont, and a man exceeding wise in such matters. I have heard Demas Barnes —once the largest dealer in that line—quoted as saying that the trademark would be worth the gross amount of three years' sales; while a more conservative estimate, from a man once a partner with Barnes, fixed the value at the gross profits on three years' sales.

Mr. J. P. Dinsmore, now eighty-two years of age, exploited thirty years ago or more a medicine that he called Iodine Water; and used to assert that a proprietary article was worth the sum of all the money that has been expended for advertising it. He spent a good deal and told me in the early part of the present year (1905), that he had not heard of an order in a dozen years. In the sixties I knew of a man, a druggist, named Marsden, who came to New York from New Orleans with a clean capital of $100,000, and blew it all in in exploiting a preparation called Marsden's Carminative Syrup, and when the money was gone he had not succeeded in creating any trade at all worth looking after. It was a dead loss.

Vinegar Bitters and Hop Bitters once sold immensely, and their owners realized a handsome profit from the exploitation of them; but it is doubtful if either remedy can now be found in the drug stores. Sanford's Liver Invigorator has not been advertised at all for twenty years, and not much in twice that time, but it still has a good sale. There is also some sale for Dr. Schenck's remedies and for Wright's, Holloway's and Brandreth's Pills. I wonder who beside myself remembers Fetridge's Balm of a Thousand Flowers, Phalon's Night Blooming Cereus, Laird's Bloom of Youth, Peruvian Syrup, or Dr. Moffatt's remedies. What has become of Spalding's Glue? Spalding, after making what was assumed to be a great success with his glue, attempted to put on the market a headache remedy called Cephalic Pills. It was his scheme to bargain for a column a year in every paper published, providing for credit for the full time—a period deemed sufficient to allow the publicity to do its perfect work. Tens of thousands of dollars' worth of advertising was done, but it is my impression that no publisher ever received a cent for his space; that Spalding did not get money enough out of the deal to pay his postage bills, and that the Cephalic Pills never got a place on the shelves of the drug stores.

Dr. Helmbold did well enough with his Buchu, but ruined himself trying to introduce something he called Grape Pills. It has been said that a medicine that has been allowed to die out for want of revivifying advertising can never be brought into a new popularity, no matter how much money may be lavished in a publicity campaign. There are many instances that could be mentioned that would go to prove the soundness of this assertion, but the versatile Mr. Wetherald showed that there are exceptions to all rules when he took hold of the Lydia E. Pinkham business, at a time when it was nearly dead, and raised the sales to a higher point than they had ever reached in the preceding time of its greatest popularity. The business, like others, is subject to fluctuations. There is no hard and fast rule that will apply to all cases.

Dr. Munyon long regretted that he could not call his Homœopathic preparations "Specifics," because Dr. Humphreys had trademarked that word in connection with remedies of the same class. Mr. Manly M. Gillam assured him that "Cures" was just as good a word—probably better—and experience has proved that Gillam was right. Munyon cut into the Humphreys sales quite seriously, and to make the matter worse, another man, a certain Dr. Hilton, brought out a "Specific" for colds that struck another blow to the Humphreys trade; but noting how successfully this had been done the manager of the Humphreys business concentrated his advertising upon a single item, No. 77, which was also a remedy for colds, and has not only circumvented the opposition, but secured a better trade on the one article than he had previously enjoyed for the whole list, while the rest of the list continues to do as well or better than before.

I have reason to believe that the sales of Dr. Pierce's remedies have exceeded a million dollars a year for many years, and that his advertising bills often come up to three-fourths of that amount. It is known that Cascarets put its promoters in a hole to the extent of nearly four hundred thousand dollars before they began to earn a profit over and above the advertising bills.

I was immensely amused one time when a man with a blood purifier paid me $20 for a ten-line advertisement for a single insertion in the New York Weekly *Tribune,* and asked how much more he would have to pay to have the word blood printed in red. The thing was then impossible, but I could do it to-day, in the Sunday edition of the New York *Herald,* without demanding a penny over the regular price.

I was talking one day with the factor in charge of the Hudson Bay Company's Post at Roberval, on Lake St. John, two hundred miles north of Quebec, and looking over the goods he had in stock for trade with Indians and trappers. "You must sell a great many patent medicines," I ventured inquiringly. "We handle but three," was the reply. One was Perry Davis's Pain Killer, another Radway's Ready Relief. The name of the third was not a familiar one, and I do not recall it. The storekeeper at Douglass Island, Alaska—where the great Treadwell mine is situated—told me of an Indian who came in one day, bought a bottle of Perry Davis's Pain Killer, removed the wrapper and the cork, put the bottle to his mouth, tipped his head back and swallowed the entire contents at one draught. He then threw the bottle through an open door and went away. "Didn't he say anything?" I asked, and the man replied, "He said 'ugh!'"

FORTY-SEVENTH PAPER

In my boyhood on the farm, so isolated, in a region of much forest and few conveniences for obtaining supplies, nothing was ever thrown away. A disused axe, a broken chain link, a rusty nail, an old thimble—every bit of odds and ends—was tossed into a corner in a disused shed; and, after a search there, my father was often heard to assert there was not in his possession any other thing that so often and so fully could be counted on to meet his urgent need as "the old iron box."

While collecting my thoughts for the preparation of these papers, I began to make memoranda of ideas and incidents, as they occurred to me, and these were used and disposed of as one paper after another was handed over to the compositor. In approaching the final wind-up, however, there remained a considerable number of such notes; that had either failed to fit in anywhere, or were afterthoughts that presented themselves when it was too late to assign them to the precise chapter in which they belonged. It has become apparent that if no material is to be abandoned as worthless—even though it may actually be so—it will be necessary to string the incidents and ideas that compose the aftermath—the left over part—of this junk shop of memories, without any particular regard to sequence or connection. The last two or three papers have been somewhat of this order, and so also will be most of those that follow, to complete the contemplated series of fifty-two. If any one finds in them matter of interest, it is well; if nothing of the sort is discovered, it may still be hoped that little harm will have been done.

How well I remember the expensive desk I bought for my private office, in the Times Building, at the time I took possession there, that cost a hundred and fifty dollars, and

seemed a piece of unpardonable extravagance. Mr. Kent
has it at his house at the present day and I am glad it has
never found its way to a second-hand shop nor an auction
room.

How vivid is the picture, to my mind's eye, of the time
when it seemed wise to cut off something from the length
of the day at the office; how it was with something like a
guilty feeling that I went away, in broad day-light—perhaps not later than four o'clock of a summer afternoon; and
one day, when there was snow on the ground, and a coachman in livery came for me, with a handsome pair of horses,
a sleigh with brightest varnish and luxurious bear-skin
robes, I sincerely hoped no one would see me, as I took my
proprietor's seat and was driven away.

One thing after another comes to mind, the older in
point of time the more distinct the memory of the details.

There was an experience with the old firm of Bent &
Bush, fashionable Boston hatters, who cheerfully paid a bill
for advertising a certain style of hat, and it occurred to me
to wonder that the profits on that particular article could
warrant so large an expenditure, and was told that the retail price of the entire invoice would not cover half the advertising outlay; but the venture had been satisfactory, because not one in ten of the customers the announcement
brought to the store bought the hat they came to see, but all
were glad to have seen the new thing, and most of them
bought some other hat, out of stock, and there was a reasonable likelihood that some would become regular customers. Also the similar experience of a clothing dealer in
Dock Square whose advertisement of an all-wool overcoat
for $15 brought the great Edward Everett there to fit out
his coachman, and how, although pleased with the garment
shown him, he finally paid $25 and secured a better one.

Among the Boston memories there was Curtis Guild,
then as now publisher of that sterling business paper, the
Commercial Bulletin, which is one of the small number to
which Rowell's American Newspaper Directory has long
accorded that emblem of excellence, the so-called Gold

Mark. Tall, young, handsome, energetic, earnest, Mr. Guild was one of the few newspaper men I have known who early believed there would be a profit in advertising his own wares. He made his paper a success and acquired a prosperity that surprised those who did not observe the excellence of his methods and the earnest attention he paid to the conduct of his affairs. His canvassers went everywhere, and from among them more than one successful man of business has been developed. I suppose his son, Curtis Guild, Jr., recently elected Governor, is something like what his father was then.

Mr. Guild wrote two books of travel—"Over the Ocean," and "Abroad Again"—that I thought excellent specimens of that kind of literature. I crossed with him on one of his trips and remember being introduced to a Mr. C. A. Richards, who became conspicuous in connection with the early Boston street car extension, but at that time had the best example, in that city, of a store where good things in bottles could be bought. Guild had a stateroom, with Richards for a neighbor on one side and a department marked "W. C." on the other, and had remonstrated at the steamship office against being sandwiched between two "Wine Cellars." Richards was wealthy, and I recall his standing one day on the deck, smoking a pipe—his daughter leaning on his arm—when Guild came up, filled his briarwood from Richards' pouch, and turning to me, but glancing at the girl, made the apt remark, "Richards has a pretty daughter—and capital ter-back-er."

His brother, Ben Guild, long associated with him, was, to the end of his life, one of the newspaper men who were in the habit of now and then dropping in on me at the office, and I was always glad to see him. He had a larger fund of good stories than almost any man I ever met. I never think of him without having my mind carried back to the charming figure of a girl, whom I, as a boy, had noted on Washington street, from time to time, as one of the most attractive to be seen upon the promenade of that day; and who afterwards became his wife. He had a keen sense of humor, and any one who remembers the peculiar walk that was characteristic of Henry G. Parker, who succeeded Billy Clapp as publisher of the *Saturday Evening Gazette,* will appreciate the point he had in mind when he told of walking down Water street one day past the old paper warehouse of Rice, Kendall & Co., where two men were unloading a truck and, as Parker went by, one nudged the other in the ribs, directed his attention to the passerby, by pointing over his shoulder with his thumb, and said in a loud whisper "Jack the Giant Killer!"

I have spoken of Curtis Guild as young, active, handsome. That must have been some time ago, for I called at his office the last time I was in Boston, and on inquiring for him was told, "The old gentleman don't come down very often. I don't think he has been here for a month. He is not very well and is rather lame." Alas, we get over being young and handsome—let us hope the soul is and will be ever young and ever beautiful.

On the occasion of the dedication of the statue of Daniel Webster that stands in front of the State House, in Boston, Edward Everett was to deliver the oration. It was a stormy day and there was talk of a postponement. I remember hearing the subject discussed. "The Mayor wants it postponed, but Billy Clapp doesn't want it postponed and it won't be." This was W. W. Clapp, so long publisher of the *Saturday Evening Gazette,* and—after Charley Rogers' time—of the Boston *Journal.* It may be mentioned—in passing—that the ceremonies were *not* postponed. I further remember in connection with that occasion that Mr. Everett, apotheosizing the statue, said, "It is him, as he stood, as he looked, as he wished to be remembered, as we would wish to see him represented." Critics wrote to the papers criticising Mr. Everett's grammar, but Col. Greene, of the *Post,* had the opinion that Mr. Everett knew what he wanted to say.

In the early years of my business career I had that confidence that is so conducive to success to the extent that when I went out to see an advertiser who contemplated

placing an order I would hardly thank a man to insure me
that I would get it. One day I went to Hartford, where
the subscription book men were then doing a lively business. My principal competitor, Mr. Pettengill, was on the
same train, but I did not know it. I went into one office on
Asylum street, while he visited another. I secured my
order, while in his case it was arranged that he should call
again later in the day. His next call was where I had preceded him, and it so chanced that he followed me over the
entire route. My last call was at the place where he made
his first one, and there I also secured a small order. We
met at the station; I had taken six orders, he not one.

The Directory newspaper circulation ratings were always getting me into trouble. There was a time when
Harper's Weekly seemed to be the leading newspaper in
the country, from an advertiser's standpoint. Ours was a
leading agency, probably it had become *the* leading one.
On every estimate we mentioned *Harper's Weekly*. If a
man would make an experiment in advertising, but would
spend little money at the start, we put him into this paper,
even if he took no other. Advertisements in it cost $2 a
line each insertion, and for the outside page $4 a line. We
were paying the paper, possibly, as much as $5,000 a month,
but as circulation statements from the office fell short of
being definite there came a time when the rating accorded
by our Directory failed to be satisfactory to the publishers
of the paper, and I went to Franklin Square one day to talk
the matter over. The original members of the firm had
passed away. It was the second generation that took part
in the conference. I explained that we had to have the
same sort of statement from one paper as from another.
What we asked from the "Bungtown Banner" we were
obliged to require from *Harper's Weekly*. There was a
pause, the gentlemen looked at each other and one quietly
said to the others, "It seems to me that if Mr. Rowell talks
that way we don't want to continue to do business with
him;" and the others, in a rather indifferent way, appeared
to coincide with that view. There was nothing more to be

ld fill the require-
When they came
e firm of Scribner
he outcome. Mr.
business side, Dr.
arose friction that
me to the *Century*
t a pace that had
sible for the high
ich the American
ng it to be almost

for the *Century* a
ith sat by the Gen-
George W. Childs
he General whether
n a description of
ld have been possi-
interest, and Grant
est. Such a story
rican people," said
ns, written by you,
rest, even more in-
h flattered and con-
desired and did so.
irculation to a high
vas a question what
and Mr. Smith's at-
f inducing Mr. Lin-
the Martyred Pres-
n was outlined. The
and it was decided
a figure, and then all
tment of ideas thus
lip of paper the fig-
. Messrs. Nicolay
gratified. They did
ith and the Century

said, and I came away, and the next advertising order sent from the Rowell Agency was refused. There was no serious difficulty about securing the insertion by sending the order through another agency, and, as the paper was named on all the estimates we had out and in most of the letters we had issued recommending this paper and that, we for a time received about as much business for it as ever. Naturally, however, we became less urgent in our recommendation of it; perhaps we even began to suspect that we might have been overvaluing it. The publishers and I were on good terms enough. The one who made the suggestion to close the account, afterwards visited me at my house and invited me to his. By and by the rule was rescinded, and that part of the difficulty removed, but in the meantime we had gotten out of the habit of recommending the paper, and a time came when instead of sending advertising to it to the amount of $5,000 a month I doubt if so much as $5,000 went to it, upon orders from our Agency, in some periods of five years. When, a long time after, the old house of Harper & Brother failed, I could but wonder whether the firm had been as successful in shutting off streams of revenue from numerous other sources as they had been in the one case in which I had been so intimately concerned.

I was discussing the circumstance with one of the senior members of the house of D. Appleton & Co. once, and he said I was wrong; that I would be justified in considering the character of the publisher, and not being so exacting when that was high as I had to be in other cases. His firm was at the time issuing an excellent weekly, called *Appleton's Journal*, that, like *Hearth and Home*, for some reason, failed to gain public favor. It did not live many years, and it would be my impression that its publishers never did make a satisfactory circulation report. Publishers of high character owning papers, also of high character, that appeal to an exclusive and specially intellectual constituency, are given to being super-sensitive on the subject of circulation.

The only time I can recollect having a circulation report from Mr. Henry C. Bowen, long owner and publisher of

that superlatively excellent and ex
ligious paper, *The Independent,* he
piece of white paper, about half a
upon which was written in pencil th
man said—that Mr. Bowen said—t
tion of his paper, and that he sent
application for a statement upon wl
might be based. I knew Mr. Bowe
it is quite possible I ought to have
with confidence; but if I had, and ta
faith, I feel certain the reputation of
veying reliable information would
that it has to-day. In after years M
me, and on my appearance at his offi
desire to be freed from the annoyance
nually for a circulation statement, a
there did not exist some method wh
an affliction that had become distaste
he could hardly express. Being told
that to stop the publishing of his pap
effective remedy for the evil of whi
shrugged his shoulders, but expresse
the plan suggested. He adopted it,
later—at the age of eighty-four. Cl
not allow himself to be annoyed by s
familiar with the uses of a waste basl

The persistency with which many p
cellent papers will decline to tell the I
he would like to know, and how willing
is to tell him a great deal that he doe
never fails to amaze me. One conspicu
ent time is that of *Vogue,* the fashion
of New York. The publisher of this
lieves its publishers are honest and the
mental work. He is ready to throw
show his circulation not only for a ye
years, and to prove the accuracy of the
receipts; but he will not personally writ

Mr. Smith suggested that may be he wo
ment, and the Doctor thought he would.
back to New York they negotiated with
& Co., and *Scribner's Magazine* was
Smith controlled the magazine on the
Holland was editor, and eventually there
led Smith and Holland to change the n
and to go out by themselves. They s
never been dreamed of and are respo
plane, the magnificent plan, upon wl
magazine of to-day is conducted, maki
one of the wonders of the world.

General Grant long declined to writ
history of his campaigns. Once Mr. Sn
eral at dinner, at the hospitable table of
at Long Branch, and happened to ask
if Napoleon or Wellington had writt
Waterloo, with so much of detail as wo
ble, such a book would possess much
said, "It would be of surpassing inte
would be invaluable." "To the Ame
Smith, "such a story of your campaig
would be of even more surpassing inte
valuable." Whereupon the General, bo
vinced, promised to prepare the articles

The *Century* war articles lifted its
figure. When they came to an end it
could take their place as an attraction,
tention was directed to the possibility of
coln's two Secretaries to write a life of
ident. Negotiations were opened, a pla
question of compensation was broache
that each party in interest should mark
should be compared and a fair adjus
arrived at. Mr. Smith wrote on his
ures $50,000. No others were so hig
and Hay were not only satisfied, but
their work and with the result Mr. Sr

Company were both gratified and satisfied. Mr. Smith never quite forgave the Scribners for starting a rival magazine. He thought they had no right to do so. Probably they were within their legal rights, however.

Mr. Smith and I served on the Charities Committee of the New England Society at one time, and that Committee did not have much to do. The Directors always met at the Union League Club, and I occupied a suite of rooms there that were very comfortable, and in that pretty little sitting room, with our cigars, the Charity part of our work being soon disposed of, Mr. Smith told me many experiences in publishing that were interesting to a high degree. The Century Dictionary was then under way, and the Company had, up to that hour, paid out more than six hundred thousand dollars toward the production of the work, and not only had not received a penny in return, but could not expect to receive a penny for several months to come.

One of the pleasantest newspaper acquaintances I ever made was Amos J. Cummings, the first editor of the *Evening Sun*. He had been a compositor, then a reporter. When Mr. Dana bought the *Sun* Robert Bonner lent Amos money to enable him to secure some of the *Sun* stock, Bonner holding the certificate as security. The *Sun* made money, and Bonner was paid. Amos was threatened with pulmonary disease, and spent some time in Florida, where he dressed like the poor whites, went fishing and lived out of doors. One day he did some service for a Western Congressman, who gave him a quarter and was much chagrined when Amos reminded him of a former meeting when he sat by him later at a banquet at Charleston. He brought home a paroquet from Florida, one out of a flock which he had shot into—for the birds are good to eat you know—but this one was only stunned and not seriously hurt, and became so thoroughly domesticated, that, when I met Amos for the first time, the paroquet would follow him about, flying from tree to tree, or post to post, never losing sight of his protector, and if a hawk or other bird appeared of which he was afraid he would fly to a haven he knew of and crawl into seclusion through an opening left for him in the bosom of the man's flannel shirt. This was on the occasion of a visit to a great pigeon roost in Western Pennsylvania, the last of those remarkable manifestations that has occurred. Amos wrote a very pretty magazine story called "The Bird That Was Fond of the Man Who Shot Him." Later he became a Congressman himself and continued for many terms, and one day when I was in Washington and had read glowing words about his oratory, I asked him if it didn't amuse and amaze him to find himself counted as an orator, and he said it did. He was a capable and lovable man, an exceptionally brilliant journalist, and had a sense of humor hardly excelled by Nasby or Mark Twain.

I once said to that Mr. Cyrus Curtis, who owns the *Ladies' Home Journal* of Philadelphia, who has done as much as any man living to place advertising on a high plane and has found his profit in it, "Why, Mr. Curtis, do you, when you are making more money than you know what to do with out of one paper that you already own, go and buy another paper, and compel yourself to work harder and run an opposition to yourself?" Those who see Mr. Curtis never connect him with the idea of work. He is always at leisure, never seems to have anything to do or appears to have ever done anything. He listened to my remark with a mere suggestion of a smile, then he—being a Yankee from Maine—asked me a question. "Admitting for the sake of argument," said he, "that I make more money than I care to spend, which is better for me, to invest the surplus in a business that I understand and control, or to put it into one that I don't understand and other people control?" I am not asking Mr. Curtis many questions since that day—his answers have a tendency to shut off conversation—but I was reminded of his apparent habit of never doing anything by a reference to him one day made by a Philadelphia acquaintance who had crossed the ocean with Mr. Curtis, and, on their arrival at Southampton, seeing no movement on in the direction of going ashore, he spoke to him about his apparent delay, and was told, "No! I'm not going ashore. I came over for a rest and am going back with the vessel."

When a man remains in one business a long time and makes little display, it commonly happens that he leaves a good estate. I know one instance where a dealer pursued one line of trade nearly as long as I have been an advertising agent and always considered that he had done well when his profits for a day amounted to so much as $1.25 or $1.50.

1864.   1904.

J. WESLEY BARBER, THE BOSTON ADVERTISING AGENT.

His place of business was on Park Row. When I took the office, No. 40, in 1868, he stood on the sidewalk near the entrance and announced vocally that he sold needle threaders. I never saw anybody buy one until about thirty-five years later. I did the thing myself. He stood in the same place, looked no older than when I saw him first, said he made a good enough living—couldn't afford to go to Delmonico's—took a day off whenever the weather did not suit him. Probably many men doing business on a larger scale have had a smaller store of content than he.

Those who read these pages may occasionally come across the names of advertisers once conspicuous, now forgotten. In New York there was Leary the Hatter and later Amidon. Union Adams was a name once conspicuous in the daily papers, so, too, were those of Devlin & Co., and Baldwin the Clothier and the Great American Tea Company. The medicine men stop advertising when they go broke, and, generally, either stop or incorporate the business, so as to change the name, when they get so rich that their sons and daughters feel encouraged to attempt to get into society.

It is rather queer that there should be such a thing as an appropriate style of advertising for a particular line of business, yet such is developed now and then. Wherever a tailor's advertisement is seen the influence of the Rogers, Peet & Company announcements is plainly discernible. Whoever saw the representation of an autograph on a sign board that was not the name of a photographer?

It is good advice to a young man to bid him to aim high. A schoolmate of the late William C. Whitney has been heard to relate that it was a peculiarity of Whitney's, even in boyhood, to seek the society of those who would have the ability, if they had the wish, to be of service to him. Advice not to be too modest in my aims would have been beneficial to me in my boyhood. I wished to go to college, but thought that a consummation beyond my power to accomplish, but have known in later years that a good friend stood ready to help me, but waited to see me exhibit the desire—which I never did. Many a man has advanced himself by marrying a rich wife, and it is a fact that the daughters of the rich, out of families of assured position, are as a rule better brought up, better trained and make better wives—even for a poor man—than the average miss from humbler homes—furthermore they are often passed by, as unattainable, by a deserving youth who need only have spoken to be accepted. Such girls, if they have sense, and most of them have, know that character and ability in a husband can do more for them than all the power of papa's money can do.

I have often had occasion to notice that one man can do what another cannot. That the way—the method—that is successful with one man will not work at all when adopted by another. I have always had a way of saying Yes or No, cutting the answers short, only making certain that the inquirer got the answer and knew what it was. So far as I know my methods gave no offence. I am certain that few or none have kept friends or customers better than I did, but hundreds of enemies and cords of dislike have been created for my office by my employees attempting to deal with people precisely as they had seen me do.

"Calculation!" was the terse response attributed to the Squire, who had married a widow a few months before, when the lady expressed to him a fear that a condition had arisen that might have been foreseen considering the intimate relation that existed. When the writer was recently told by a brother advertising agent—that Mr. J. Wesley Barber of Boston, whose photographs in 1864 and 1904 show how forty years can change a man—that he seemed to have raked his memory for every incident that ever occurred, and to have set them all down in these papers— with a smaller faculty for condensation, he felt inclined to say in reply, "That has been the calculation!"

FORTY-EIGHTH PAPER

I was out walking one Sunday afternoon during the early years of my residence in New York, and in a retired street, west of Washington Square, came across a sign, occupying a position over a narrow passage, that impressed me as curious. The name was O. Stickheim which I Americanized as O. Stick-him. The business announced was CARPENTER, and the sign would seem an invocation to charge a high price; but between the line that expressed the name and the one that designated the business there was another line, composed of very small letters, enclosed in parentheses, that spelled out the words (in the rear).

. Early in my business career I had experiences with newspaper men, who had had dealings with advertising agents who may have had signs similar to that of the carpenter; and, if not actually stuck "in the rear," yet had not wholly escaped injury. A burnt child dreads the fire, but the publisher of a country paper hungers after advertising. He wants to be paid for it; but in spite of serious losses and annoyances he will take chances. Once when I was sending out new business to papers with which I had not before had any open account, there came a six-page letter, written in a business-like hand from a publisher in Pennsylvania, who went at length into the question whether he would or should, or would not or should not, open an account with my firm. He stated the case pretty well, rather plaintively, but seemed on the whole to lean towards the chance, and finally closed by signing his name,—O. Stuck.

I thought it a joke at first, but on investigation found it was not, for there was his name on his letterhead, set in conspicuous type that I had not noted, and in his paper it was also announced. I long had satisfactory dealings with Oliver Stuck, publisher, but it is so long ago that I do not now remember in just which town in the Keystone State he was domiciled.

Church & Goodman published a religious paper in Chicago; Steele & Eaton was the less sanctimonious designation of a firm that published another religious paper. Ham & Carver owned a daily at Dubuque, Iowa. Walking through William street from Spruce, toward Wall, many years ago, I saw over the door of a saloon, evidently the proprietor's name, A. Christian, and on the very next corner another, A. Goodman. On a sign in Dublin, Ireland, over a meat shop, was the name of the firm who conducted it, Lamb & Bullock. There was long a sign in Fifth avenue, New York City, which I thought noticeable. It bore the name of Salmon Skinner.

The first time I ever saw Broadway I discovered, not far from the Metropolitan Hotel, a sign that bore the words:

HAPPY
TAILOR.

In later years the man changed his location and also the lettering of his sign, and it then read G. D. HAPPY. We all know the story of the German who subscribed to an agreement the name, A. Schwindler, and when some one suggested that he should acquire the habit of writing out his first name in full, replied that it would not help matters any and, to illustrate, wrote his name in full, A-dam Schwindler. Our firm long had dealings with a man named Liberty Hall. There was the old and very respectable firm of brokers in Wall Street, Ketchum & Cheatum, who were said to have attempted to alleviate the suggestiveness of the combination by adding the initials of the given names of the partners, Isaac and Uriah.

That Mr. Dwight, who made a fortune of the Cow Brand of Soda, and was the founder or at least a benefactor of Mount Holyoke College for young ladies, in Western Massachusetts, had three daughters who married husbands named respectively Walker, Leggett and Ketchum. There was long to be seen from the cars of the Sixth Avenue Elevated two conspicuous signs on one building, one below the other. The first had the single word COFFINS and the other the compound word SHOW-CASES. Not less gruesome was an exhibition in the window of an undertaker's shop where was shown a child's casket, lined with white satin, and well centered in it were the words, To Let, the same being the shadow of a part of the wording in gilt letters on the window that set forth the fact that there were Carriages To Let. I will not omit to mention the firm of Somebody & Huggs who had a school of which it was asserted that Mr. Somebody taught the boys, and Huggs the girls.

There was long a sign in Centre street, not very far from the Tombs, that read, "We Paint Your Eye for 50 Cents—While You Wait." It has been displaced by the changes that have come to the location. In Dr. Henry M. Field's time the sign bearing the name of his paper on the building, No. 5 Beekman street, came into unfortunate juxtaposition with that of a saloon keeper who had the store under Dr. Field's offices. The two signs were on a level and the passerby might read

REGAN—THE EVANGELIST.

The first time I ever noticed the combination my eye also took in the wording of a card in Regan's window—it was winter—which read, HOT WHISKEY A SPECIALTY.

Of course there have been newspapers and magazines with curious names. The *Ram's Horn* is an influential religious paper to-day. There was once a magazine issued in Portland, Maine, denominated *The Chariot of Wisdom and Love*. Somewhere I have seen a magazine called the *Pleasure Boat*. There is one issued in Boston at the present time called the *Black Cat*.

The correspondent of the London *Times*, in his comment upon the newspapers seen at the Philadelphia Centennial Exhibition in 1876, was impressed that the following names were rather curious: the *Union Spy*, the *Jolly Giant, Aurora Brazileira, Broad Axe of Freedom, Unterri-*

fied Democrat, Painted Post Times, Roman Citizen, Homer Iliad, Horseheads Journal. To these might be added the Anniston, Ala., *Hot Blast;* Tombstone, Ariz., *Epitaph;* Hot Springs, Ark., *Thomas Cat;* Estero, Fla., *Flaming Sword;* Tarkio, Mo., *Avalanche;* Irrigon, Ore., *Irrigator;* Jefferson, Tex., *Jimplecute;* Kosse, Tex., *Cyclone;* Rosenberg, Tex., *Silver X-Ray;* Laramie, Wyo., *Boomerang* and the Pinedale, Wyo., *Roundup.*

Readers of Dickens often express surprise at the incongruous names that are found in his pages and yet, it is said, he used none that he had not known in actual life. I remember that to me the name Dombey seemed a synonym for pompous dullness, and the surprise I felt at seeing it with my own eyes on a tailor's sign in High Holborn, London. Dombey & Son was the firm.

I have had a Dickens-like experience with the names of the tradespeople with whom I have dealt for nearly fifty years. In Boston I had boots made by a shoemaker named Bisbee. He removed to New York about the time I did and I continued to make use of his services. · I found a tailor at the corner of Broadway and Eighth street who served me pretty well and whose name was Bagg. As I grew prosperous I bought neckties, stockings and handkerchiefs of Budd, who still does business at the corner of Twenty-fourth street and Broadway. I became dissatisfied with the sartorial efforts of Bagg, after a time, and went to Bowne at 182 Fifth avenue. That was in 1876. Bowne died at a later period, but was succeeded by his nephew, also named Bowne. Bisbee died and a workman of his continued to make boots for me and his name is Bihler. I see progress, however, toward other letters of the alphabet, for I buy trunks of late years of a man named Cherry, and my shirts are made by Caskel & Caskel, although they change the initial from C to K—perhaps to help me along—for life cannot endure forever, and the space between sixty-seven and the traditional three score and ten is not much, and it is still a far cry to X, Y and Z, unless my connection with Editor Zingg may be taken as closing the list.

It is wonderful with what facility I forget the happenings and incidents of the past six weeks and recall those that might have been overtaken by oblivion a score and a half or two score years ago. I recall Barnabee of the Bostonians as a good singer, a noted raconteur and a very fair salesman in a retail clothing store in Boston; how the name of the Boston Theatre, after a successful season of Italian Opera, became the Academy of Music; and after being closed for a time and reopened by James M. Nixon, and the Menken—reputed wife of John C. Heenan who fought Tom Sayers—clad in tights and tied to the back of a horse, represented the hero of Byron's poem "Mazeppa," and another scene in which the horse seemed to find stepping stones that enabled him to ascend with his pinioned burden straight up the face of a great waterfall; and how everybody was thrilled with the scene, and in the mouths of the people the name of the Academy was changed again and now became "The Horse Opera."

What a furore there was in Boston when the great organ was put in place in the Music Hall, and how villainous it was in the man who described an Oratorio rendered there by the Handel and Haydn Society, asserting that on the right there stood a group of forty old maids, every one screeching, "And unto us a son is given," and on the left forty other old maids, likewise screeching, "And unto us a child is born," when, at that point, a little man, with black hair and broad shoulders, rushed excitedly forward into the center of the stage, looked at the maidens at the right, and the maidens at the left of him, noted their skinny proportions, and in a powerful bass voice at last expressed his admiration in thunderous words, "'Tis wonderful! 'Tis Wonderful!"

It was at the Music Hall that the lady, commenting upon John of Bologna's statue of Mercury, standing on one foot with arms extended, admitted that she was not well up in classical Mythology and had always understood the figure represented Col. (Tom) Chickering.

I must not get away from Boston without at least mentioning the name of "Collins the Pants Man." There comes up the memory of seeking an interview with "Young America Train," just returned from a residence in Australia, for the purpose of collecting three years' accumulated subscriptions for the Boston *Post,* and the surprise at the office at the success that crowned the effort. He was the celebrated George Francis Train of later years. Then there came Paul Du Chaillu with an exhibition, in School street, of trophies of his African travels, and what a brilliant imagination we thought he had when he told us about the gorilla, not previously admitted to exist—and not admitted then, for that matter. In the same connection stands a memory of Henry M. Stanley, young, black-haired—with not a gray one in his head—standing strong, vigorous, confident, at a reception given him at the Lotos Club, relating the story of his discovery and meeting with Dr. Livingstone in Central Africa, when he advanced, took the old gentleman by the hand, and said—as though meeting him in a drawing room—"Dr. Livingstone, I presume." I admired the man's nerve, but did not believe a word he said. He was, I thought, just a *Herald* reporter, bluffing through the biggest hoax of the time. Truth is stranger than fiction, and we think better now of both Du Chaillu and Stanley; but neither are on earth to read my apology—and neither probably was ever aware that I existed.

How people would persist in calling Orange Judd's *Agriculturist* the *Agriculturalist.* How every man who wanted to advertise thought his copy should occupy "about a square," but never could give any idea of how much space he thought a square would call for. How much remark there was about, and what a catch phrase the closing line of the announcements put forth by "Jones of Binghamton," became. He was afterwards Lieutenant-Governor of the State, and later lost his eyesight. I believe he is still living, but we see his advertisements no more ending with the statement: "Jones, He Pays the Freight." Not the Kodak catch line, "You Press the Button and We Do the Rest," nor the Hook and Eye query, "Do You See That Hump?"

nor the "Smile That Won't Come Off," nor "We Are Advertised by Our Loving Friends," nor even Sunny Jim has become more familiar. I wonder, by the way, what would happen to an advertising agent who should induce a client to take up and exploit and spend tens, yes hundreds of thousands on an idea like that of Sunny Jim.

There was a time when it seemed that a satirical or comic illustrated paper could not be made profitable in America, but when *Puck* appeared that idea was put at rest. Many people in New York City will recall the circumstance that *Puck* was at one time advertised by painted signs, and that Mr. Comstock, or some other guardian of the public morals, took alarm at the naked figure of the person whom Shakespeare made to assert that he would or could put a girdle round the earth in forty minutes, but who had failed to find time to put even so much as a belt round about himself. He was more naked than the man who supports the great clock in front of Tiffany & Company's new store at the corner of Fifth avenue and Thirty-seventh street. In response to urgent demand the painter of the *Puck* announcements added a black Prince Albert coat to the figure, and *Puck* has continued so clad, with no other garments, since that day. Being successful, and of Democratic politics, there was a demand for an attempt to produce a rival of Republican principles and *Judge* came into existence, and has remained a good second. Some people have supposed that without these two periodicals no barber's shop could do business, but since the advent of the Yellow Kids, Buster Brown and their kindred in the Sunday editions of the dailies, we begin to wonder if the days of *Puck* and *Judge* are not nearing their end. Their principal competitor in the barber's favor, the *Police Gazette,* is not much seen now. Later came *Life;* keener, sharper, lighter, more sarcastic, without any political bias beyond being anti-automobile. It was a profitable venture almost from the first and is really a dear—but like other infants it loses something of its cuteness with advancing years.

Among the papers of promise that have failed, *Every*

Saturday should be remembered. It was a brisk rival of *Harper's Weekly* for a time. It brought Bret Harte from California, but could not make him profitable. He was later induced to move on, and went to England from whence he never came back. Finally the losses on *Every Saturday* caused the collapse of its publisher, James R. Osgood, who was later taken on by the Harpers and died as the London representative of that house.

Although the rent account was vastly reduced and the quarters much improved and made more convenient by the removal of our office from the Times Building to Spruce street, it is probable that from a business point of view the change was not a good one. The new office was scarcely two hundred feet away from the old one, but it was less conspicuous. It seems to be in the nature of an advertising agency that it should be approached by one or more flights of stairs—ours was now on the ground floor. The price paid for the building was $40,000 in 1876. The store was occupied by a dealer in leather who had a lease with a year to run. We tried to buy him off, offered him $1,500 to move, but he would not. We gutted the building overhead and made so much dust that our tenant took a trip South to visit his customers and clear his lungs. He bought an insurance ticket at the railway office for $5,000, paying five dollars for thirty days' insurance. He was alone in the rear car of a train in Georgia that fell through a railroad bridge, and he was killed. He proved to be insolvent, his family got the $5,000 insurance, which was all they did get, and we got possession of the store without any payment for cancelling the lease. "It's an ill wind that blows nobody any good."

The money was in bank to pay for the building, but there was a mortgage on it of $20,000 that could not be paid off until after thirty days' notice; and in order not to have the money laying idle it was invested in the stock of the Delaware & Lackawanna Railroad, which was sold later, netting a loss of $4,000. The same stock to-day would be worth more than $300,000, and the income from it all these

thirty years would go far toward paying the $11,500 rent
which Mr. Jones of the *Times* was exacting of us when
we came away from his building. Moral: When you move
a place of business be certain to go to a more rather than
to a less conspicuous situation. We spent $15,000 in reno-
vating our new home, and it proved one of the most com-
modious and convenient offices I have ever known. My successors, however, have given it up and moved next door
and up stairs—so as to be more in the fashion.

For a great many years we had a printing office of our
own. It took tons of type to keep the Directory pages
standing and thereby save a large part of the composition
bills. Now and then some requirement would run counter
to the rules of the Typographical Union. I would be surprised that ours was a Union office, would insist that it
should not be; some men would go away, others would
come and ours would be an open shop. After a year or two
there would come notice that this or that thing would not
be permitted by the Union. My surprise would break out
again, again we had the open shop and again—a little later
—the Union would be in command. I finally gave up, concluding that on the whole Union rule was most economical.
Sometimes we needed fifty men, at other periods three or
four or even two would do. The Union had no soul or
body. A man could be dismissed the moment work was
slack. The Union provided no two weeks' vacation. No
Union man expected to be paid when he did not work. It
was go by rule and no favors either way. I have always
thought that were I a workman I would have nothing to do
with any Union; that the Union is a leveler that holds poor
workmen up and keeps good workmen down. Still, on the
whole, as I look on the matter in the best light I have, I
cannot but admit that I think the Labor Unions have improved the condition of working men. I like to think that
the world grows better, that conditions tend to improve
rather than to retrograde, and it is a pleasure to me to know
that I am not required to regulate the affairs of the world.

I remember that in the story of Rasselas, Imlac had to

remind the prince, when he was discontented, that he could not, at one time, drink from both the source and the mouth of the Nile; and that the wise man who had gained the power to regulate the weather, found that while one man wanted rain, another did not; and try as he would he could not conduct matters in a manner that proved any more satisfactory than they went on in the hands of the Divine Ruler before the possessor of so much earthly wisdom had undertaken to favor him with his assistance.

I once heard an Arabian Nights sort of anecdote of a Sultan of Bagdad who had an inordinate appetite for listening to stories, and never could hear one that was long enough to satisfy him, so he promised his daughter in marriage and the half of his kingdom to whosoever would relate a story that was long enough to satisfy him; but the competitor for the prizes would lose his head if he broke down in his attempt. Whereupon a youth who loved the maid appeared at court and sought an audience. He had a story to tell. It was about a great king who feared a famine and built a warehouse wherein he lodged such a store of corn that it seemed ready to burst, and no one had ever heard of so much corn being brought together since the world began, and the people knew that beyond peradventure famine could have no terrors for them. But, behold, one day there was a cloud in the East, it came nearer and nearer, and when at hand it was not a cloud, but a swarm of locusts, and about the warehouse it gathered; and finally, a locust discovered a crevice through which it was able to enter and he went in, and soon returned, bringing with him a kernel of corn; and thereupon another locust went in, and soon came out, bringing with him also a kernel of corn; and the swarm of locusts was uncountable and the supply of kernels innumerable; and the king, who was never tired of detail, listened day after day to a continuation of the statement that another locust went in, and came out, bringing with him another kernel of corn; and enjoyed it all so much that he gave his daughter to the raconteur, and the other rewards as promised, so that while he continued to delight the king with other and still other repetitions, he might also, in his hours of rest, learn and practice the science of government, and gain experience in the raising and management of a family.

This story of mine, which has already extended to four dozen chapters, threatens perhaps to be another one of the "Another locust went in" variety; but in my case the swarm, although numerous, is not uncountable, and the supply of kernels, although not inconsiderable, is not inexhaustible. My story will have an end and that end is not very distant.

FORTY-NINTH PAPER

In the *Advertisers' Gazette* for December, 1866, one may read a paragraph stating that "Charles H. Sweetser, founder and for some time manager of the *Round Table*, has retired from the ownership and editorship in order that he may at once carry out his favorite idea of a cheap evening paper in New York." That was the origin of the New York *Mail*. The paper he started was called the *Gazette*. And what an ideal paper it was—a tea table paper—clean, literary, well written, brisk, sharp, thoroughly likable and good; but it requires money to found a new paper in New York City, and Sweetser and the brother associated with him had but little. There was a man in the counting room of the *Evening Post*, a prudent, saving, red-haired Scotchman named Johnson, who had accumulated some capital, and he, after a time, acquired an interest in the *Gazette*. He was a man who disliked putting out a dollar without seeing a pretty certain chance of getting back more than a dollar next day, and his economies made the Sweetsers so wild that they could not put up with the condition they found themselves in, so one day there appeared on the streets a new paper called the *Mail*, that was the very counterpart of the *Gazette*, and the Sweetsers were managing it. They took to it the features that had gained the *Gazette* the good will of many people, and it seemed likely to prosper. The *Gazette* meantime quickly lost what hold on the community it had obtained and soon ceased to appear. I do not know what became of Johnson. Probably his savings were dissipated in the venture. The *Mail* seemed to prosper, but it had no Associated Press franchise, and after James and Erastus Brooks died there was a consolidation, and we had the *Mail and Express*. Sweetser did not live long, but the paper still appears, and there are many people who think highly of it. In later times the name of the *Express* was dropped from the heading, and in name and character the paper is something like what the Sweetser Brothers hoped to make it, only there is nothing of the old-time snap in it.

In those early days I used frequently to have luncheon at Mouquin's restaurant, in Ann street, and often saw Robert Bonner there, and noted his frugal meal, and realized that the successful man soon loses the capacity to enjoy champagne and many other good things, or loses his health. The man who has a rosy face and fills out his belt is one who goes sooner to his account. Nat Goodwin, in one of his plays, used to make a successful comment upon the need of giving up wine, women and song, or some of them, and stated that he, not wishing to attempt too much had decided as a starter to give up song. It is really the one thing of the three that men can stand the most of.

When Charles A. Dana abandoned the Chicago *Journal* and came to New York to start a daily paper, he intended calling it the *Telegraph,* and had gone so far as to have printed matter, books, etc., prepared with that name; but a day or two before he was ready to issue his prospectus or get out his paper Mr. Bennett launched the *Telegram;* and probably was the means of insuring Dana's success; for the latter thereupon bought the *Sun* of Moses Y. Beach, a paper already established, and put new life into it at once. It was more Yellow than the *World* was later or the *Journal* is now, only the term "Yellow Journal" had not then been coined. The phrase came from a series of pictures, of the Buster Brown order, of a baby, that, because of being dressed in a long yellow skirt or petticoat, came to be spoken of as the "Yellow Kid," and was exploited so much, so voluminously and so continuously, that it became famous. and led the papers that exploited it to be referred to by an after-dinner speaker somewhere as the "Yellow Journals." I think Senator Wolcott, of Colorado, was the man. The series began in the *World,* but later the *Journal* seduced the artist from his allegiance and carried the illustrations much further—very far indeed.

When I was a boy the neighboring farmers' wives spun their own wool and made flannel, and the baby's petticoat was of that material, colored with the blossoms of the golden rod. Without doubt the Yellow Kid came from a memory of the custom of that period—but how many are living to whom the thought would occur?

When the pink *Telegram* first appeared on the street it was supposed that misfortune had come to a batch of paper that was needed for immediate use, and considerable fun was poked at it on that account; but it has been a distinctive feature of it ever since. Until within quite recent years the *Telegram* was not a financial success. It is the judicious policy of the *Herald* not to tell its circulation. It was a great and prosperous paper—everybody admitted that. The *Telegram* actually printed as many copies as the *Herald* did. It is the tendency of evening papers to acquire larger circulations than morning editions attain; but nobody believed it in the case of the *Telegram;* advertisers had no use for it, and one day, not long ago, Mr. Bennett ordered its publication to be discontinued. I think it did fail to appear for one or two days, but an exchange of cablegrams between New York and Paris resulted in permission being given to keep it alive; and not long after, Mr. F. James Gibson, the father of the Sphinx Club, and at present a useful adjunct to the business-getting force of the successful New York *Times,* was made business manager, and persuaded Mr. Bennett to allow a circulation statement to be made to Rowell's American Newspaper Directory. The accuracy of the statement was not doubted; everybody was surprised that the issue was so large, and from that day forward the *Telegram* has been earning Mr. Bennett a handsome income.

I have spoken somewhere of the wonderful power and success that sometimes reward the efforts of the ignorant and inexperienced. The origin of the Sphinx Club, that best example of an association of advertising men that has numerous imitators in this country and abroad, was a case in point. Mr. Gibson, its founder, was a Canadian without much acquaintance with advertisers or advertising, but was at the time in charge of the publicity department of the great Oriental Mart of A. A. Vantine & Co. He thought such a club would be a good thing; communicated with a dozen or so of men whom he did not know, but whose names were familiar to him in connection with advertising. Went straight ahead to form the association; sat down to the first dinner with five others—well content with that as a beginning. This was only nine years ago. To-day the Sphinx Club numbers more than three hundred members, and its monthly banquets at the Waldorf-Astoria are notable occasions and invitations are sought by men interested in advertising the world over.

The *Sun* was a success from the day it passed into Mr. Dana's hands, but I can recall no other paper that has been more thoroughly abused than it was for some years. People asserted that it was impudent, saucy, scurrilous. I hardly realize the full meaning of the last word, and do not believe it could ever have been properly applied to Mr. Dana's paper, for the *Sun* was never indecent; and it surely gave its readers the best English that had ever been seen, with regularity, in an American newspaper. To me the *Sun* is often irresistibly funny. No paper likes to get into an argument with it. If it is attempted the opponent is likely to find himself high and dry, and to be seen to be in that position by others before he begins to realize it himself. I read an editorial in the *Sun* once that proceeded to relate the doings of a wise, gentlemanly man—in the City Hall Park. There were seats in the park in those days, and this dignified gentleman was seen to buy two papers of a newsboy; he thereupon proceeded to an unoccupied bench, carefully spread the *Herald* upon it, and then sat down on the *Herald*, and read the *Sun*.

The *Advertisers' Gazette* for June, 1867, announces the formation of the American News Company at 119 & 121 Nassau street. Before that there had been a continual rivalry among competing interests. After the consolidation the company became a great power and remains so to-day. It was often thought that the handling of advertising patronage might be much more economically controlled by a similar combination of scattered agencies, but no step in that direction has ever seemed to promise even a remote prospect of success.

The Sunday papers practically came in with the Civil War. They are something between the daily and the weekly in character, have tended largely toward making the old weekly an obsolete back number, and have so absorbed the advertising patronage of the dailies as to lead some to characterize a majority of them as Sunday papers with daily supplements.

The passing of the weekly paper is a comparatively recent development. The New York Sphinx Club is not yet ten years old, yet at one of its meetings when the writer had been asked to speak on the comparative value of the daily and the weekly as advertising mediums, and pronounced the daily by far the best, there was not a single member present who agreed with him. To-day not a single member would take issue with his conclusion. In the days when the great encroachment of the daily upon the weekly field was setting in there arose some very curious conditions. I can recall cases where the owner of a prosperous weekly felt impelled to put out a daily, and found it so hard to dispose of the advertising space in his newest venture that advertising agents were able to contract for an appearance in every issue, daily and weekly, for less money than they had formerly been compelled to pay for the weekly alone.

As illustrating the hard times daily newspapers sometimes had, I often think of a man named Tripp, who issued a daily in Fall River, Massachusetts, and never came to Boston without dropping in on me for an advertisement order; and it used to seem that there could be no price named that would be low enough to cause him to decline what was offered. Wondering what sort of a proposition I might be up against, I said to him one day, "Mr. Tripp, there was a Fall River printer in here last week, that knows all about you and your paper, and he assured me that you only print seventy-five copies." The poor man gave a start. His face expressed pain. He was silent for a moment, then rose, walked to the window, looked out, turned and came solemnly back to me and said impressively, "Mr. Rowell, I give you my word of honor I have never printed so small an issue as seventy-five copies since my paper was started." He paused for fully half a minute and then adding a saving clause—"Unless it may have been on a very rainy day."

I am a believer in the newspaper as the best advertising medium. It is the only one I ever recommend; and it hurts me to have to admit that the best advertising my firm ever did, the advertising we heard from most, and longest, was accomplished by printed posters pasted on a fence. It was at the time when the present New York Postoffice was in course of construction. The contractor, in an ill-advised hour, sold for a very moderate sum and to a rank outsider who did not understand the business the right to cover that fence with posters. He made a beginning with one or two, but the system by which that sort of thing is now managed had not then come into being and the space was going to waste. He came to me, and I authorized him to print on a large poster in large letters the statement that all the newspapers published could be found on file at the Advertising Agency of Geo. P. Rowell & Co., No. 41 Park Row, and advertisements would be received and forwarded to any or all of them at publisher's rates. He was to print enough of these posters to cover the fence throughout its entire length on Mail street, Broadway and Park Row and to be paid a specified sum for the service, and have a right to cover my posters with others as fast as new customers could be secured. It is my impression that there was difficulty encountered, the right of the contractor to sell the space was questioned, perhaps, and the contract was eventually rescinded, as was the case more recently with the fence around the Public Library in Fifth Avenue and Bryant Park. Anyway, however, my posters went up and stayed up a good many days, and everybody seemed to see them and to speak to me about them; and I do not believe there has been a year since that they have not been mentioned to me by somebody, although the time of their appearance was more than thirty years ago.

In one of the early papers of this series the story was told of the success of the Richardson Brothers of the Davenport, Iowa, *Democrat.* They were known to be poor, so people were surprised when it began to appear that they were rich. Each new property acquired by them became a topic for surprised comment. It began to be believed in Davenport that they could buy anything. I was there on one occasion, in the days when the Chicago *Times* was a great property—the most conspicuous newspaper west of New York—and Mr. Story, its founder and owner, had recently died. What would become of the paper was nearly as much of a question as the fate of the New York *Herald* would be if Mr. Bennett were to die to-day. I was in Davenport, as I have said, and a rumor went about the street, the Richardson Brothers have bought the Chicago *Times!* It was heard with open-mouthed amazement. What did they pay for it was sure to be asked, and in the answer was the gist of the story. The price paid was five cents. Jenness had not bought the plant of the *Times,* but had been seen to buy a copy of that paper.

I often wonder to what extent some highly respectable people are ignorant of certain stories about them that have wide currency among those who do and those who do not know them. I have had knowledge of or some acquaintance with numerous persons who were known to be rich, or appeared well to do, and of whom their intimates, or such as assumed that relation to some degree, would from time to time assert that in the period of the Civil War, this person, associated with that other, had early knowledge of the government intention to put an internal revenue tax of two dollars a gallon on whiskey, and thereupon purchased numerous barrels at the then current price of about eighteen cents a gallon, and thereby made a thousand per cent profit on every gallon on hand before the tax on future product would go into effect. The first time I heard the story the successful speculator was a gentleman named Holmes, whose two sons married the two most beautiful girls I had any recollection of ever having seen.

The next successful operator, as the story came to me, was that Mr. Tilton, who long maintained, at Sanbornton Bridge, N. H. (now Tilton), a replica of the Apollo Belvidere, held in place, on a grassy bank near the railroad track, by a strong wire securely anchored in the rear, and attached to an iron staple inserted in the back between the magnificent shoulders of the god-like youth; and also maintained an imitation of the Arch of Titus—as it exists in Rome—which sheltered a lion, carved in granite, all standing conspicuous on a hilltop, in view from the railway station, and reported, by the proud citizens, as Mr. Tilton's idea of giving publicity to a metaphysical discovery made by him and thought to be best expressed by the words:

PEACE HATH HER VICTORIES NO LESS RENOWNED THAN WAR.

Next I had the story that Alfred Cowles of the Chicago *Tribune* made a fortune in the way indicated above. Then that Horace White, long editor of the *Tribune,* and later of the New York *Evening Post,* had been fortunate enough to do this very thing, and finally that a certain rich New Yorker, originally a Cape Cod boy, and still spending his summers near its sandy shores, once known as the able president of the First National Bank of Chicago—Nickerson by name—made the foundation of his great fortune in a whiskey venture, as already specified. Then some one who had definite knowledge, or said he had, enlarged upon the story. Said White was clerk of the Ways and Means Committee of the United States House of Representatives when the decision was arrived at; that he telegraphed to Cowles, Cowles interviewed Nickerson; so while one furnished the information, another supplied the capital, and the other was useful enough to make his claim respected for a square divide—something like the sequence in the story of "The House that Jack Built." I tell the story, as I have often heard it, without any knowledge of the truth or whether truth is in it. I have often wondered what Mr. Rockefeller and Miss Ida Tarbell would think of the transaction, provided it took place at all as outlined here.

There have been frequent references to an early residence in the northern county of the Granite State, above the White Mountains, the sparsely settled Coos County, the cap sheaf of New Hampshire. I am here reminded that the Horace White above mentioned came from this region, and we are so proud of the fact that we take pains to mention it whenever occasion occurs. Major Bundy, so long the editor of the New York *Evening Mail,* was of the same origin. So also was Mr. Charles A. Dana of the New York *Sun;* Vice-President Hobart, later of New Jersey; the eminent Stilson Hutchins, now of Washington, and finally, that Mr. Henry W. Dennison, for a quarter of a century legal adviser to the Emperor of Japan. Artemus Ward, the humorist—not he of Sapolio fame—as well as the writer of these lines, were not so fortunate as to be natives of "old Coos," but we were both of us doubtless strengthened and improved by an early residence there. It was not Artemus Ward that originated the assertion that it was because of the statement made by doctors that hot water increases the circulation that made the practice, in country newspaper offices so universal of keeping an iron kettle, half filled with it always on the top of the stove that was counted on to moderate the winter temperature wherever such offices existed. Ward has been dead nearly fifty years, but the circulation joke was musty a generation before he was born.

I once listened to an instructor who enlarged upon the need of concentrating the mind upon the matter in hand and keeping it from flying off in this direction and that, to the detriment of the work set out to be performed. "If you should assign yourself the task," said he, "of writing down all the facts that would have a bearing upon the origin, history and final disposition of the old log school house where your earliest lessons were learned, you will need to have a care that you do not get sidetracked by leaving the house for a moment to wander with this one or that one of the inmates you remember to have met there. There was the studious boy whose mind was always on his books, who is now the president of a university; and what a pretty girl Lucetta Gilbert was, and what an ambitious marriage she made, and how long afterward it was that we heard of her in a distant place—poor, deserted, degraded, friendless. Oh, horrors! I cannot bear to think! The subject to be considered has been forgotten and you are traveling over the earth with Lucetta who was not at all the object to be dealt with."

Notwithstanding this caution, which I remember so well, I have not been able, in setting down these recollections, to avoid now and then forgetting all about the subject chosen and wandering off with Lucetta and Bill and Jim, and bringing in a thousand and one matters that

Have nothing to do with the case.

I am getting very close to the end, however, and shall not err any more. Three more papers will complete the allotment of fifty-two, and in the completion of these the teacher's charge to concentrate the thought and keep the pen from wandering shall not for another moment be forgotten.

FIFTIETH PAPER

I have mentioned that my start as an advertising agent came from exploiting the merits of the country weeklies and the dailies in the smaller cities, and that before me the Boston Agency of Evans & Lincoln had gained a foothold·by directing attention to the excellence of a neglected medium, the religious papers. Carlton & Smith in New York, through the connection of Carlton's father with the Methodist Book Concern, had their energies bent in the same direction; and N. W. Ayer & Son of Philadelphia, in the beginning, worked in the same vein; as did also E. N. Freshman & Brother, two young Hebrews in Cincinnati, who developed a pretty lively agency out of an engagement to canvass for a few Methodist papers in that city.

A new advertising agency must specially represent something; must be headquarters for something, and depend upon that special representation to gain a hearing. These are days of specialization even more than in the past. Advertisers are not looking for people who can do everything, they are more interested in those who can do some one thing well that nobody else can do at all. When the new man has made good on what he asserted, there is often no limit to the extent to which the pleased advertiser will trust him, nor to the endorsement he will give him to every acquaintance who may be on the lookout for some one to place advertising for him.

A great many efforts have been made in times past to define what constitutes an advertising agent, and entitles him to recognition as such. Publishers and agents have discussed the subject in convention, over and over, but no definite conclusion has ever been arrived at. Some have suggested known responsibility, others a proved capacity for the work; finally it seems to have been agreed that no more than two things are necessary and these are, first, that the claimant for recognition should assert that he actually is an advertising agent, and, second, that he should have a printed letterhead with the address of an alleged office thereon set forth. There seems to be a wide tendency, however, on the part of newspaper men to assume that the first requirement specified is enough and that the second is asking rather too much.

One of the prettiest lines of business I have ever known to be in the hands of one agent was controlled many years ago by John Manning, who got his foothold as a canvasser for the New York *Tribune*. If he had any office I never knew where it was. For his correspondence he commonly used the stationery of his clients. He doubtless did have a billhead. He controlled the advertising of such houses as Tiffany & Co., Brewster & Co., the carriage makers; Robins, Appleton & Co., makers of the Waltham Watch, and numerous other accounts of a similar high grade, and did a business running up into hundreds of thousands annually. He is still living (1905), but has long disappeared from the scenes of his former activity. Manning used to assert that there is much in the sound of a name; that Tiffany and Delmonico could never have attained the height of popularity they acquired had their names chanced to be Murphy and O'Donahoe instead of what they were.

Mr. N. W. Ayer was never much known among advertising men. He had been a school teacher, but that occupation had failed him. It was his son, Francis Wayland Ayer, a handsome red-cheeked, dark-haired youth of twenty years, that did the work and created the great agency of N. W. Ayer & Son, the greatest institution of the sort that has thus far come into being in any part of the world. The Ayer agency is the only one I have ever known anything about that claims to have had capital to do business with in the beginning. Mr. F. W. Ayer asserts, and I think truthfully, that he and his father had $250 in hand, and he tells how he earned it. I think it came from canvassing for advertising for the list of papers controlled of late years by the Religious Press Association of Philadelphia.

thought the biggest lie came wonderfully near to absolute accuracy. When my mind attempts to deal with the subject of names of agencies, it immediately reverts to the days of Palmer, and Joy, Coe & Co. When I progress as far as Scriven and Cook; Coburn & Co. of Chicago; L. P. Fisher of San Francisco; S. H. Parvin of Cincinnati; Pettengill of Boston and New York; John Hooper of New York; Mather & Abbott; Abbott & Co.; Hudson & Menet, F. J. Fontaine, J. Viennot & Co., John F. Phillips, Bates & Locke, all of New York; S. R. Niles, Evans & Lincoln, T. C. Evans, Horace Dodd, all of Boston; Coe, Wetherell & Smith and Coe, Wetherell & Co., of Philadelphia; Griffin & Hoffman of Baltimore; E. N. Freshman & Brother of Cincinnati; Sheffield & Stone of St. Louis, and realize that not one of these is now doing business, and not many have a representative living to-day, I realize I am certainly very much behind the times.

No one now claims to be the successor of Palmer; Mr. Ayer paid something for the right to call himself successor of Coe, Wetherell & Co., but never called himself so; W. W. Sharpe of New York has the right to say he succeeded to Joy, Coe & Co., but does not say so; and if he did few would know what he meant, for the old name is forgotten. The Lyman D. Morse agency has corraled whatever remnants there are of the once great business of S. M. Pettengill & Co. and Bates & Locke, while U. K. Pettingill in Boston still does something under the old name, shortened by the omission of the initials, and with the "i" in the middle instead of the "e;" and he, too, I think, owns the right to call himself successor to S. R. Niles, whose agency was undoubtedly the successor to that of Palmer, in Boston, and was always one of the most conservative, most profitable and most satisfactory to owner, patron and publisher of any that ever existed. Niles was a square man and the soul of honor.

The Freshmans disappeared from the advertising field and left no successor. I had the good fortune to run across one of the brothers in Southern California five years ago,

With the probable exceptions of John Hooper and L. F. Shattuck, Mr. F. W. Ayer is now, and has long been, the richest man in the business. It is quite possible that there need be no exceptions made. Of late years he seems to pay most attention to the Merchants' National Bank, of which he is president; and which has increased its line of deposits since he took hold of it from less than three to nearly five times as many millions. He is an indomitable worker; thinks of work all the time, eats little, drinks nothing but

F. W. AYER.

water; has no vices, small or large, unless overwork is a vice; is the picture of health; and I sometimes think a good deal such a man as Oliver Cromwell would have been had Oliver been permitted to become an advertising agent.

Mr. Ayer cannot put his hand to anything without being in dead earnest. He bought a farm at one time, as a place where he could retreat from business cares; and before he knew it was running a profitable milk route and selling butter in Philadelphia at a higher price than anybody else could get; and the farm, instead of proving an expensive toy, as it pretty uniformly is when owned by a business man was, almost from the beginning, adding to his wealth. He has been vastly blessed in one of his partners, Mr. McKinney, who looks older than his senior, although he is not so. Mr. Ayer is fifty-seven this Year of Our Lord, 1905. It is told of McKinney that in his youth he attended Eastman's Business College at Poughkeepsie; and said to the principal that it was his ambition to secure the 100 mark on every point of excellence; was told that it was a commendable ambition, but would indicate a degree of merit to which no student has ever yet attained. McKinney still said he would do it, and my informant says he did do it. There is a great deal of inaccuracy of statement floating around among human beings, but Mr. McKinney is one man in a thousand, and I would believe of him that what man has done he could do—still the college principal said no man *had* done it.

It was the success of *Scribner's Magazine,* afterwards transformed into the *Century,* that first gave magazine advertising the impetus that has grown to be so great. I have stated that *Harper's* was established for the deliberate purpose of advertising the books that were published by the firm. In the early days the reading matter was largely made up of what might be called advance notices of forthcoming publications. Advertisements from outsiders were declined, and an offer of $18,000 a year for the last page, in the early seventies, for an announcement of the Howe Sewing Machine, did not tempt the managers to remove from that position the prospectus that told on what terms the *Magazine,* the *Weekly,* the *Bazar* and the *Round Table* could be had, either together or separately. I had this information from a member of the firm of whose general truthfulness I never had any doubt, although at the same sitting I heard him tell another man about the peculiarities of that part of Long Island where the Harpers originated, and assure him that ague prevailed there to such an extent that all his ancestors had quinine put into their graves to keep the corpses from shaking the sand off.

The original firm of Carlton & Smith changed in time to W. J. Carlton, and Carlton in turn was succeeded by J. Walter Thompson, but had previously enlarged his list of religious papers and become the first agent who sought advertising for a list of magazines. It is Thompson, more than any other agent, who has developed the magazine field, and he has found his profit in it, too. He has fully deserved whatever success he has attained, and it has been very great. Conditions are vastly different now from what they

U. K. PETTINGILL.

were when he began. John Wanamaker spends more money for advertising every week than A. T. Stewart ever did in a year.

If I should attempt to enumerate the successful advertising agents of to-day I should doubtless reveal the fact that I am not up to date on the subject. Now and then I hear of some agency, with the sound of whose name my ear is wholly unfamiliar, but which is said to place more business every month than I should suppose any agent ever attempted, and occasionally I find that the story I ha and was pleased to learn that he was president of a railroad. Few persons are aware that Mr. N. M. Sheffield, the New York special agent—who is never seen without an umbrella—of whom nothing is ever said that is not a nice thing, was once the senior member of the St. Louis advertising agency of Sheffield & Stone. While it was in the field, there have been few more lively competitors than they were for such business as was going.

Out of a list of over two hundred names furnished in the early part of 1904 by Chas. H. Taylor, Jr., of the Boston

N. M. SHEFFIELD.

Globe, then president of the American Newspaper Publishers' Association, I can enumerate fifty of which I have some personal knowledge. Naturally they are mostly made up of the oldest firms, although there may be exceptions arising from circumstance of our being thrown together through the accident of business or social association. In this list will doubtless be found the leaders of the business at the present time, although I am not prepared to assert that it does not contain names of much less importance than numerous others that are omitted:

Edwin Alden, Cincinnati.
A. A. Anderson, New York.
Arnold Advertising Agency, Philadelphia.
N. W. Ayer & Son, Philadelphia.
J. W. Barber, Boston.
George Batten & Co., New York.
Calkins & Holden, New York.
Nelson Chesman & Co., St. Louis.
Danielson & Son, Providence.
Dauchy & Co., New York
Stanley Day, Newmarket, N. J.
E. B. Dillingham, Hartford, Conn.
E. N. Erickson Advg. Agency, New York
Albert Frank & Co., New York.
Geo. Ethridge Co., New York.
Charles H. Fuller, Chicago.
W. N. Gates & Co., Cleveland.
J. J. Gibbons, Toronto.
Ben B. Hampton Co., New York.
William Hicks, New York.
W. H. H. Hull & Co., New York.
H. B. Humphrey Co., Boston.
H. I. Ireland, Philadelphia.
H. W. Kastor & Sons, St. Louis.
Kaufman Advertising Agency, New York.
Long-Critchfield Corporation, Chicago.
Lord & Thomas, Chicago.
A. McKim & Co., Montreal.
Mahin Advertising Co., Chicago.
Converse D. Marsh, New York.
Chas. Meyen & Co., New York.
Lyman D. Morse Advg. Agency, New York.
O'Flaherty & Co., New York.
Pettingill & Co., Boston.
Geo. G. Powning, New Haven, Conn.
Frank Presbrey & Co., New York.
Proctor & Collier Co., Cincinnati.
E. P. Remington, Pittsburg.
T. P. Roberts, Chicago.
Geo. P. Rowell & Co., New York.
Geo. M. Savage, Detroit.
Frank Seaman, New York.
W. W. Sharpe & Co., New York.
C. E. Sherin Co., New York.
J. L. Stack, Chicago.
M. Lee Starke, New York.
J. P. Storm, New York.
J. Walter Thompson Co., New York.
M. Volkmann Advg. Agency, New York.
James T. Wetherald, Boston.
Wood, Putnam & Wood, Boston.

At the time of my first recollection of Chicago as an advertising field one Charles H. Scriven had it all to himself. This was in 1865. He was a capable man I have always heard. The only time I ever saw him was at a sort of free lunch reception given by H. T. Helmbold in his Broadway store near the old Metropolitan Hotel in New York City. Mr. Scriven did not live very long after. If he has been as happy since as he appeared to be at the time I refer to he

CARLOS A. COOK.

has no kick coming against the fate that is his.

The next agency to get a foothold in Chicago was that established about the year 1865 by Carlos A. Cook, who had associated with him at various times E. A. Carr, C. E. Coburn, E. B. Mack and A. H. Taylor; Carr, Coburn & Mack having interests in the Chicago office, while Taylor had the management of a Cincinnati branch, established later, where he divided the patronage with honest old S. H. Parvin, of whom it may be said that no agent ever deserved better of the newspapers than he did. An old associate and friend of Mr. Cook's has furnished the following historical data concerning him:

Carlos Allen Cook was born June 23, 1828, in the town of Preston, New London County, Connecticut.

His years up to young manhood were spent on his father's farm, and in his father's woolen factory.

Leaving these employments, he went to Lowell, Mass., and learned to be a druggist in the drug store of Dr. J. C. Ayer.

Then followed some years in travel, selling goods in the provinces and States, and finally he had a drug store in Rock Island, Illinois.

In 1859 he was in the sewing machine business in Chicago, and in 1862, he, in partnership with a relative, had a brewery in Peoria, Ill.

In 1863 he secured the agency of Dr. Roback's Bitters, and coming back to Chicago, made his headquarters with the wholesale drug house of Fuller, Finch & Fuller, and in addition to selling bitters started an advertising agency under the name of C. A. Cook. There was but one other advertising agency in Chicago at this time, that of C. H. Scriven. Mr. Scriven died very soon, thus leaving Mr. Cook the only advertising agent in Chicago.

Later E. A. Carr was admitted as a partner, and the firm became Cook, Carr & Co.

On Mr. Carr's leaving the business Mr. C. E. Coburn became a partner and the firm was then Cook, Coburn & Co. This was in 1864. Mr. Coburn remained in the business ten years, and, on his retiring, the firm was again called C. A. Cook & Co., and so continued until Mr. Cook went out of the business in 1886 or about that date. Mr. Cook had no partner after Mr. Coburn left the firm.

A branch house was established in Cincinnati in 1866 under the firm name of Cook, Coburn & Taylor, Mr. A. H. Taylor becoming a partner, but this branch agency was discontinued in 1871.

Mr. C. A. Cook died at his home in Chicago, September 27, 1898. Mr. C. E. Coburn is still—in 1905—in Chicago engaged in the insurance business.

Mr. A. H. Taylor is also in Chicago in the advertising business, being employed in the agency conducted by Theodore P. Roberts, who places most of the Sears, Roebuck & Co. advertising.

Mr. Cook's family are all gone from Chicago except a son. It was of this young man that Mr. Cook used to tell that as a boy he developed artistic tendencies and, thinking perhaps he should be given an education on the line of his tastes, sought advice from a friend thought competent to give it and who, after listening to all the pros and cons, volunteered the information that if the boy with such tastes was his own he would put some bricks in the seat of his trousers and let him sit down in the lake.

The firm of C. A. Cook & Co. was unfortunate at the end of its career. The cause of its decline was the advertising of Lawrence & Martin "Tolu Rock and Rye." When that firm failed they owed C. A. Cook & Co. $69,000, entirely unsecured. After discontinuing as much advertising as possible the net loss was $47,500, and not a cent of it was ever paid. This was more than Mr. Cook could stand, and, after adjusting matters as far as possible, an effort was made to continue business with but indifferent success; the agency made no money and younger men coming into the field and new ideas coming up the struggle was a hard one, and finally Mr. Cook ceased to be an advertising agent.

Mr. Richard S. Thain, the present editor of *Agricultural Advertising*, had a pretty close connection with Chicago agency matters in the late sixties and early seventies. Previous to its sale to Lord & Thomas, Mr. Thain was editor of *Mahin's Magazine*. He took up the advertising business in 1868 and has been at it pretty steadily since. There are not many now in the business who have been engaged in it longer than he.

In a recent communication, Mr. Thain writes:

In 1868 I was advertising manager of *Western Rural*, published in Chicago, and during that year the firm of Sharp & Thain was organized. We remained together in business until 1871. The firm was dissolved after the Chicago fire. We did quite an extensive business—especially with religious papers. We purchased one column from *The Interior, Advance, Northwestern Christian Advocate, New Covenant*, and the Episcopal paper that was published here. We usually kept from three to five columns filled with good advertisements. At that time, Field, Leiter & Company (now Marshall Field & Company) advertised extensively in these publications, and it was my pleasure to meet Mr. Field nearly every Saturday afternoon at 1.30 o'clock and get his copy for the following week. Before the Chicago fire, Mr. Field wrote his own advertisements, and he certainly knew how to write good ads—i. e., judging by the standard of the times. I had the pleasure of chatting with him not long ago regarding the old days of advertising, and find that he takes quite a lively personal interest in advertising at the present time.

George W. Sharp, my old partner, was an Englishman of the pure John Bull breed. He used to keep me busy fixing up his quarrels with publishers. I got rather tired of this and when the Chicago fire occurred I thought it a very opportune time to dissolve the partnership. I happened to be in New York City at this time, getting advertisements for the *Elgin Almanac*, October, 1871. Sharp & Thain were handling the advertising of the Elgin Watch Company, and they issued an Almanac to be handed out by the various jewelers throughout the United States. The issue was one million copies. We placed over $20,000 worth of advertising in the Almanac. The plates were ready, but were burned up in the great fire, and when I went back to New York I made a contract with James W. Sutton, of the Aldine Press, to get out the Almanac.

After the dissolution of Sharp & Thain, I went into business for lished a Newspaper Directory which the New York *Tribune* considered much better than mine; and said so, in its editorial columns. Editors are uniformly truthful and impartial. That's what makes the calling so elevating.

At one time, when my interest in the advertising business was most active, we had a pretty lively competitor in a neighboring agency conducted under the name of Hudson & Menet. They were weak financially, and one day when passing their office I saw a sign of theirs being elevated to a higher position on the building they occupied, and, with that desire to be funny that has often got me into hot water, I wrote a paragraph for the *Newspaper Reporter*—the *Printers' Ink* of that day—which said, "Last week there was a sign of Hudson & Menet's going up." Newspaper men read the paper and took alarm. Bills poured in on the unfortunate concern, and before another week I had a libel suit on my hands. It never came to trial, for before it was reached the concern had failed; but my lawyer exacted a $500 fee for his services in my behalf and I realized then, and have often thought since, that it was more than such a poor joke was worth.

In concluding what I have to say about conducting an advertising agency I may make mention of the fact that it is one of the easiest sorts of business in which a man may cheat and defraud a client without danger of discovery; and also note that no agent who was not superior to this temptation has ever been permanently successful. The high reputation for honor and probity uniformly enjoyed by those who have been most conspicuous in the business has been gained by strict integrity—a determination to secure a fair deal for every patron.

FIFTY-FIRST PAPER

In the year 1900 I was led to secure a country home that should be within such easy reach of the office as would make it possible to go and come daily, should that seem desirable. Influenced by an advertisement in the *Evening Post* I went one day in early spring to look at a place, of some historic interest, that was announced to be for sale. The day was sunshiny, the buds were bursting into leaf; a little brook so glistened in the sun that I was impressed that this was the very spot I had in mind and that no other one would do; and it came about that I bought it, and went there to live. It was in a community of millionaires, and I was not a millionaire. I found that I minded the twenty odd miles travel, between house and office, more than I should have done when I was younger; and on the whole my new possession proved so much of an establishment, and cost so much to keep going, that there never seemed to be any money left over for excursions, travel, amusements or charities. If we could afford to have this, and half a dozen other places, and to shut them all up and go away when we liked, this would be delightful, but to live here day in and day out, to the end of life, was a prospect with too much monotony in it for perfection. It was eventually decided that we must part with our acquisition, and as it was an advertisement that had directed my attention to it I depended on another to bring me a buyer, and with this in mind, I prepared a description to be used to tell the story to interested inquirers. I reprint the wording of the leaflet here, partly as a specimen of an effective real estate advertisement of my own construction, and partly because the place advertised did for several years absorb a pretty large proportion of my thoughts and interests.

WILLOW BROOK

"On the banks of the Hudson, in a beautiful country."—
Washington Irving's Life and Letters, Putnam, Vol. IV, p. 407.

Ten acres is the answer usually given to the inquiry as to the area of Willow Brook. It is not, in fact, quite so much; but it is more than nine and a half, and round figures make a shorter story.

The place is bounded on the south by Sunnyside Lane, on the west by a private road from the lane to extensive acres composing the former home of a one-time famous New York merchant, Moses H. Grinnell; but more recently known as the Banker place. This private road separates Willow Brook from historic Sunnyside, the home of Washington Irving, which reaches down to the Hudson River. The Banker place forms the northern boundary, the eastern side is marked by the Croton Aqueduct, separating it from Shadow Brook, the beautiful residence of Mr. Henry Graves, Jr., which fills out the space to Broadway, as the high road between New York and Albany is known throughout its length.

All the places mentioned were once parts of a farm owned and occupied by Oscar, an older brother of Washington Irving, and the Willow Brook house was the home of Oscar before Sunnyside came into being.

"I am more and more in the notion of having that little cottage below Oscar's house."—*Extract from a letter written by Washington Irving to his sister in November, 1832. Life and Letters, Putnam, Vol. III, p. 30.*

"You have been told, no doubt, of a purchase I have made of ten acres, lying at the foot of Oscar's farm, on the river bank. It is a beautiful spot, capable of being made a little paradise."—*Life and Letters, Putnam, Vol. III, p. 75.*

It was at Willow Brook that Washington Irving lived while his house was building, and here he liked to come in his latest days, to eat a Sunday dinner with his nearest neighbor, in the old familiar dining-room, as is well remembered by a son, still resident of Irvington, then a youth not yet in his teens.

Something more than fifty years ago Edward S. Jaffray acquired the Oscar Irving place and made of it a summer home. It was from the Hudson at the foot of Sunnyside Lane that Mr. Jaffray embarked and disembarked for daily trips to and from New York upon his steam yacht, being the first to set the fashion that afterwards became quite general among wealthy residents along the river's banks. It was in the middle of the last century that, by Mr. Jaffray's order, a landscape gardener marked out the sites where pretty little groups of luxurious foliage have stood and grown, until now the separate bunches of Spruce, Larch and Lindens are something to make glad a lover of trees; and single specimens of Sugar Maple, Tulip and Linden elicit admiring exclamations. A Copper Beech has a girth of nearly eight feet, two Cucumber trees (Magnolias) are of almost equal girth; there is one graceful specimen of the Kentucky Coffee tree; and, by the brook side and vicinity, Black

FIFTIETH PAPER

I have mentioned that my start as an advertising agent came from exploiting the merits of the country weeklies and the dailies in the smaller cities, and that before me the Boston Agency of Evans & Lincoln had gained a foothold·by directing attention to the excellence of a neglected medium, the religious papers. Carlton & Smith in New York, through the connection of Carlton's father with the Methodist Book Concern, had their energies bent in the same direction; and N. W. Ayer & Son of Philadelphia, in the beginning, worked in the same vein; as did also E. N. Freshman & Brother, two young Hebrews in Cincinnati, who developed a pretty lively agency out of an engagement to canvass for a few Methodist papers in that city.

A new advertising agency must specially represent something; must be headquarters for something, and depend upon that special representation to gain a hearing. These are days of specialization even more than in the past. Advertisers are not looking for people who can do everything, they are more interested in those who can do some one thing well that nobody else can do at all. When the new man has made good on what he asserted, there is often no limit to the extent to which the pleased advertiser will trust him, nor to the endorsement he will give him to every acquaintance who may be on the lookout for some one to place advertising for him.

A great many efforts have been made in times past to define what constitutes an advertising agent, and entitles him to recognition as such. Publishers and agents have discussed the subject in convention, over and over, but no definite conclusion has ever been arrived at. Some have suggested known responsibility, others a proved capacity for the work; finally it seems to have been agreed that no more than two things are necessary and these are, first, that the claimant for recognition should assert that he actually is an advertising agent, and, second, that he should have a printed letterhead with the address of an alleged office thereon set forth. There seems to be a wide tendency, however, on the part of newspaper men to assume that the first requirement specified is enough and that the second is asking rather too much.

One of the prettiest lines of business I have ever known to be in the hands of one agent was controlled many years ago by John Manning, who got his foothold as a canvasser for the New York *Tribune*. If he had any office I never knew where it was. For his correspondence he commonly used the stationery of his clients. He doubtless did have a billhead. He controlled the advertising of such houses as Tiffany & Co., Brewster & Co., the carriage makers; Robins, Appleton & Co., makers of the Waltham Watch, and numerous other accounts of a similar high grade, and did a business running up into hundreds of thousands annually. He is still living (1905), but has long disappeared from the scenes of his former activity. Manning used to assert that there is much in the sound of a name; that Tiffany and Delmonico could never have attained the height of popularity they acquired had their names chanced to be Murphy and O'Donahoe instead of what they were.

Mr. N. W. Ayer was never much known among advertising men. He had been a school teacher, but that occupation had failed him. It was his son, Francis Wayland Ayer, a handsome red-cheeked, dark-haired youth of twenty years, that did the work and created the great agency of N. W. Ayer & Son, the greatest institution of the sort that has thus far come into being in any part of the world. The Ayer agency is the only one I have ever known anything about that claims to have had capital to do business with in the beginning. Mr. F. W. Ayer asserts, and I think truthfully, that he and his father had $250 in hand, and he tells how he earned it. I think it came from canvassing for advertising for the list of papers controlled of late years by the Religious Press Association of Philadelphia.

said, and I came away, and the next advertising order sent from the Rowell Agency was refused. There was no serious difficulty about securing the insertion by sending the order through another agency, and, as the paper was named on all the estimates we had out and in most of the letters we had issued recommending this paper and that, we for a time received about as much business for it as ever. Naturally, however, we became less urgent in our recommendation of it; perhaps we even began to suspect that we might have been overvaluing it. The publishers and I were on good terms enough. The one who made the suggestion to close the account, afterwards visited me at my house and invited me to his. By and by the rule was rescinded, and that part of the difficulty removed, but in the meantime we had gotten out of the habit of recommending the paper, and a time came when instead of sending advertising to it to the amount of $5,000 a month I doubt if so much as $5,000 went to it, upon orders from our Agency, in some periods of five years. When, a long time after, the old house of Harper & Brother failed, I could but wonder whether the firm had been as successful in shutting off streams of revenue from numerous other sources as they had been in the one case in which I had been so intimately concerned.

I was discussing the circumstance with one of the senior members of the house of D. Appleton & Co. once, and he said I was wrong; that I would be justified in considering the character of the publisher, and not being so exacting when that was high as I had to be in other cases. His firm was at the time issuing an excellent weekly, called *Appleton's Journal,* that, like *Hearth and Home,* for some reason, failed to gain public favor. It did not live many years, and it would be my impression that its publishers never did make a satisfactory circulation report. Publishers of high character owning papers, also of high character, that appeal to an exclusive and specially intellectual constituency, are given to being super-sensitive on the subject of circulation.

The only time I can recollect having a circulation report from Mr. Henry C. Bowen, long owner and publisher of that superlatively excellent and exceptionally successful religious paper, *The Independent,* he sent a man to me with a piece of white paper, about half as large as a postal card, upon which was written in pencil the figures 67,000, and the man said—that Mr. Bowen said—that that was the circulation of his paper, and that he sent it to me in reply to my application for a statement upon which a circulation rating might be based. I knew Mr. Bowen very well indeed, and it is quite possible I ought to have accepted the pencil slip with confidence; but if I had, and taken others in like good faith, I feel certain the reputation of the Directory for conveying reliable information would fall something short of that it has to-day. In after years Mr. Bowen once sent for me, and on my appearance at his office, expressed an ardent desire to be freed from the annoyance of being called on annually for a circulation statement, and wished to learn if there did not exist some method whereby he might escape an affliction that had become distasteful to him to a degree he could hardly express. Being told that there was a way; that to stop the publishing of his paper would be found an effective remedy for the evil of which he complained, he shrugged his shoulders, but expressed no appreciation of the plan suggested. He adopted it, however, some years later—at the age of eighty-four. Clarence, his son, does not allow himself to be annoyed by such requests. He is familiar with the uses of a waste basket.

The persistency with which many publishers of most excellent papers will decline to tell the Directory editor what he would like to know, and how willing the same man often is to tell him a great deal that he does not care to know, never fails to amaze me. One conspicuous case at the present time is that of *Vogue,* the fashion paper *par excellence* of New York. The publisher of this excellent weekly believes its publishers are honest and the Directory a monumental work. He is ready to throw open his books and show his circulation not only for a year, but for several years, and to prove the accuracy of the figures by his cash receipts; but he will not personally write down a statement of what his circulation is and sign it. The Directory editor, on his part, says that if he should undertake to present himself in person for the purpose of examining the books of all the 20,000 papers he attempts to rate, he would not only be overworked, but before he got through he believes some one of the 20,000 would succeed in fooling him. On this account he never attempts making an examination until after a publisher has made a report and somebody has doubted its accuracy.

How well I remember the beginning of the Sapolio advertisement. I saw the first one in the New York *Times,* more than thirty years ago. There was a small picture of a man's head, next day a picture of a sauce pan, frying-pan or some other kind reflected in the supposed to be shining surface of the pan of character not fully determined, and finally the appearance of the then new and strange word SAPOLIO, followed by the information that applied to the pan as directed a reflection would be or could be produced as shown in the picture. The article must have been good. It must have had some immediate sale, but it is my impression that it was many years before the income equaled the outgo; and, if the owners never got over the brink of bankruptcy, I am confident they were for a considerable time on the ragged edge. It is a satisfaction to know of late years they are on velvet, and have been ever since the versatile Artemas Ward was placed at the helm and took command in all their subsequent voyages of publicity.

Roswell Smith, the founder of the *Century,* was an Indiana man who had had something to do with publishing and selling books and had made some money. While on a vacation trip abroad he formed the acquaintance of Dr. J. G. Holland, whose literary reputation was rather wide. He was the Timothy Titcomb of the Springfield *Republican,* wrote the poem, "Bitter Sweet," and was an author somewhat after the E. P. Roe type, having a great circle of readers among the better sort of the common people. Dr. Holland had an ambition to control a magazine. He had some capital and wished he knew an ideal publisher, whereupon

Mr. Smith suggested that may be he would fill the requirement, and the Doctor thought he would. When they came
back to New York they negotiated with the firm of Scribner
& Co., and *Scribner's Magazine* was the outcome. Mr.
Smith controlled the magazine on the business side, Dr.
Holland was editor, and eventually there arose friction that
led Smith and Holland to change the name to the *Century*
and to go out by themselves. They set a pace that had
never been dreamed of and are responsible for the high
plane, the magnificent plan, upon which the American
magazine of to-day is conducted, making it to be almost
one of the wonders of the world.

General Grant long declined to write for the *Century* a
history of his campaigns. Once Mr. Smith sat by the General at dinner, at the hospitable table of George W. Childs
at Long Branch, and happened to ask the General whether
if Napoleon or Wellington had written a description of
Waterloo, with so much of detail as would have been possible, such a book would possess much interest, and Grant
said, "It would be of surpassing interest. Such a story
would be invaluable." "To the American people," said
Smith, "such a story of your campaigns, written by you,
would be of even more surpassing interest, even more invaluable." Whereupon the General, both flattered and convinced, promised to prepare the articles desired and did so.

The *Century* war articles lifted its circulation to a high
figure. When they came to an end it was a question what
could take their place as an attraction, and Mr. Smith's attention was directed to the possibility of inducing Mr. Lincoln's two Secretaries to write a life of the Martyred President. Negotiations were opened, a plan was outlined. The
question of compensation was broached and it was decided
that each party in interest should mark a figure, and then all
should be compared and a fair adjustment of ideas thus
arrived at. Mr. Smith wrote on his slip of paper the figures $50,000. No others were so high. Messrs. Nicolay
and Hay were not only satisfied, but gratified. They did
their work and with the result Mr. Smith and the Century

With the probable exceptions of John Hooper and L. F. Shattuck, Mr. F. W. Ayer is now, and has long been, the richest man in the business. It is quite possible that there need be no exceptions made. Of late years he seems to pay most attention to the Merchants' National Bank, of which he is president; and which has increased its line of deposits since he took hold of it from less than three to nearly five times as many millions. He is an indomitable worker; thinks of work all the time, eats little, drinks nothing but

F. W. AYER.

water; has no vices, small or large, unless overwork is a vice; is the picture of health; and I sometimes think a good deal such a man as Oliver Cromwell would have been had Oliver been permitted to become an advertising agent.

Mr. Ayer cannot put his hand to anything without being in dead earnest. He bought a farm at one time, as a place where he could retreat from business cares; and before he knew it was running a profitable milk route and selling butter in Philadelphia at a higher price than anybody else could get; and the farm, instead of proving an expensive toy, as it pretty uniformly is when owned by a business man was, almost from the beginning, adding to his wealth. He has been vastly blessed in one of his partners, Mr. McKinney, who looks older than his senior, although he is not so. Mr. Ayer is fifty-seven this Year of Our Lord, 1905. It is told of McKinney that in his youth he attended Eastman's Business College at Poughkeepsie; and said to the principal that it was his ambition to secure the 100 mark on every point of excellence; was told that it was a commendable ambition, but would indicate a degree of merit to which no student has ever yet attained. McKinney still said he would do it, and my informant says he did do it. There is a great deal of inaccuracy of statement floating around among human beings, but Mr. McKinney is one man in a thousand, and I would believe of him that what man has done he could do—still the college principal said no man *had* done it.

It was the success of *Scribner's Magazine*, afterwards transformed into the *Century*, that first gave magazine advertising the impetus that has grown to be so great. I have stated that *Harper's* was established for the deliberate purpose of advertising the books that were published by the firm. In the early days the reading matter was largely made up of what might be called advance notices of forthcoming publications. Advertisements from outsiders were declined, and an offer of $18,000 a year for the last page, in the early seventies, for an announcement of the Howe Sewing Machine, did not tempt the managers to remove from that position the prospectus that told on what terms the *Magazine*, the *Weekly*, the *Bazar* and the *Round Table* could be had, either together or separately. I had this information from a member of the firm of whose general truthfulness I never had any doubt, although at the same sitting I heard him tell another man about the peculiarities of that part of Long Island where the Harpers originated, and assure him that ague prevailed there to such an extent that all his ancestors had quinine put into their graves to keep the corpses from shaking the sand off.

The original firm of Carlton & Smith changed in time to W. J. Carlton, and Carlton in turn was succeeded by J. Walter Thompson, but had previously enlarged his list of religious papers and become the first agent who sought advertising for a list of magazines. It is Thompson, more than any other agent, who has developed the magazine field, and he has found his profit in it, too. He has fully deserved whatever success he has attained, and it has been very great. Conditions are vastly different now from what they

U. K. PETTINGILL.

were when he began. John Wanamaker spends more money for advertising every week than A. T. Stewart ever did in a year.

If I should attempt to enumerate the successful advertising agents of to-day I should doubtless reveal the fact that I am not up to date on the subject. Now and then I hear of some agency, with the sound of whose name my ear is wholly unfamiliar, but which is said to place more business every month than I should suppose any agent ever attempted, and occasionally I find that the story I had thought the biggest lie came wonderfully near to absolute accuracy. When my mind attempts to deal with the subject of names of agencies, it immediately reverts to the days of Palmer, and Joy, Coe & Co. When I progress as far as Scriven and Cook; Coburn & Co. of Chicago; L. P. Fisher of San Francisco; S. H. Parvin of Cincinnati; Pettengill of Boston and New York; John Hooper of New York; Mather & Abbott; Abbott & Co.; Hudson & Menet, F. J. Fontaine, J. Viennot & Co., John F. Phillips, Bates & Locke, all of New York; S. R. Niles, Evans & Lincoln, T. C. Evans, Horace Dodd, all of Boston; Coe, Wetherell & Smith and Coe, Wetherell & Co., of Philadelphia; Griffin & Hoffman of Baltimore; E. N. Freshman & Brother of Cincinnati; Sheffield & Stone of St. Louis, and realize that not one of these is now doing business, and not many have a representative living to-day, I realize I am certainly very much behind the times.

No one now claims to be the successor of Palmer; Mr. Ayer paid something for the right to call himself successor of Coe, Wetherell & Co., but never called himself so; W. W. Sharpe of New York has the right to say he succeeded to Joy, Coe & Co., but does not say so; and if he did few would know what he meant, for the old name is forgotten. The Lyman D. Morse agency has corraled whatever remnants there are of the once great business of S. M. Pettengill & Co. and Bates & Locke, while U. K. Pettingill in Boston still does something under the old name, shortened by the omission of the initials, and with the "i" in the middle instead of the "e;" and he, too, I think, owns the right to call himself successor to S. R. Niles, whose agency was undoubtedly the successor to that of Palmer, in Boston, and was always one of the most conservative, most profitable and most satisfactory to owner, patron and publisher of any that ever existed. Niles was a square man and the soul of honor.

The Freshmans disappeared from the advertising field and left no successor. I had the good fortune to run across one of the brothers in Southern California five years ago, and was pleased to learn that he was president of a railroad. Few persons are aware that Mr. N. M. Sheffield, the New York special agent—who is never seen without an umbrella—of whom nothing is ever said that is not a nice thing, was once the senior member of the St. Louis advertising agency of Sheffield & Stone. While it was in the field, there have been few more lively competitors than they were for such business as was going.

Out of a list of over two hundred names furnished in the early part of 1904 by Chas. H. Taylor, Jr., of the Boston

N. M. SHEFFIELD.

Globe, then president of the American Newspaper Publishers' Association, I can enumerate fifty of which I have some personal knowledge. Naturally they are mostly made up of the oldest firms, although there may be exceptions arising from circumstance of our being thrown together through the accident of business or social association. In this list will doubtless be found the leaders of the business at the present time, although I am not prepared to assert that it does not contain names of much less importance than numerous others that are omitted:

Edwin Alden, Cincinnati.
A. A. Anderson, New York.
Arnold Advertising Agency, Philadelphia.
N. W. Ayer & Son, Philadelphia.
J. W. Barber, Boston.
George Batten & Co., New York.
Calkins & Holden, New York.
Nelson Chesman & Co., St. Louis.
Danielson & Son, Providence.
Dauchy & Co., New York
Stanley Day, Newmarket, N. J.
E. B. Dillingham, Hartford, Conn.
E. N. Erickson Advg. Agency, New York
Albert Frank & Co., New York.
Geo. Ethridge Co., New York.
Charles H. Fuller, Chicago.
W. N. Gates & Co., Cleveland.
J. J. Gibbons, Toronto.
Ben B. Hampton Co., New York.
William Hicks, New York.
W. H. H. Hull & Co., New York.
H. B. Humphrey Co., Boston.
H. I. Ireland, Philadelphia.
H. W. Kastor & Sons, St. Louis.
Kaufman Advertising Agency, New York.
Long-Critchfield Corporation, Chicago.
Lord & Thomas, Chicago.
A. McKim & Co., Montreal.
Mahin Advertising Co., Chicago.
Converse D. Marsh, New York.
Chas. Meyen & Co., New York.
Lyman D. Morse Advg. Agency, New York.
O'Flaherty & Co., New York.
Pettingill & Co., Boston.
Geo. G. Powning, New Haven, Conn.
Frank Presbrey & Co., New York.
Proctor & Collier Co., Cincinnati.
E. P. Remington, Pittsburg.
T. P. Roberts, Chicago.
Geo. P. Rowell & Co., New York.
Geo. M. Savage, Detroit.
Frank Seaman, New York.
W. W. Sharpe & Co., New York.
C. E. Sherin Co., New York.
J. L. Stack, Chicago.
M. Lee Starke, New York.
J. P. Storm, New York.
J. Walter Thompson Co., New York.
M. Volkmann Advg. Agency, New York.
James T. Wetherald, Boston.
Wood, Putnam & Wood, Boston.

At the time of my first recollection of Chicago as an advertising field one Charles H. Scriven had it all to himself. This was in 1865. He was a capable man I have always heard. The only time I ever saw him was at a sort of free lunch reception given by H. T. Helmbold in his Broadway store near the old Metropolitan Hotel in New York City. Mr. Scriven did not live very long after. If he has been as happy since as he appeared to be at the time I refer to he

CARLOS A. COOK.

has no kick coming against the fate that is his.

The next agency to get a foothold in Chicago was that established about the year 1865 by Carlos A. Cook, who had associated with him at various times E. A. Carr, C. E. Coburn, E. B. Mack and A. H. Taylor; Carr, Coburn & Mack having interests in the Chicago office, while Taylor had the management of a Cincinnati branch, established later, where he divided the patronage with honest old S. H. Parvin, of whom it may be said that no agent ever deserved better of the newspapers than he did. An old associate and friend of Mr. Cook's has furnished the following historical data concerning him:

Carlos Allen Cook was born June 23, 1828, in the town of Preston, New London County, Connecticut.

His years up to young manhood were spent on his father's farm, and in his father's woolen factory.

Leaving these employments, he went to Lowell, Mass., and learned to be a druggist in the drug store of Dr. J. C. Ayer.

Then followed some years in travel, selling goods in the provinces and States, and finally he had a drug store in Rock Island, Illinois.

In 1859 he was in the sewing machine business in Chicago, and in 1862, he, in partnership with a relative, had a brewery in Peoria, Ill.

In 1863 he secured the agency of Dr. Roback's Bitters, and coming back to Chicago, made his headquarters with the wholesale drug house of Fuller, Finch & Fuller, and in addition to selling bitters started an advertising agency under the name of C. A. Cook. There was but one other advertising agency in Chicago at this time, that of C. H. Scriven. Mr. Scriven died very soon, thus leaving Mr. Cook the only advertising agent in Chicago.

Later E. A. Carr was admitted as a partner, and the firm became Cook, Carr & Co.

On Mr. Carr's leaving the business Mr. C. E. Coburn became a partner and the firm was then Cook, Coburn & Co. This was in 1864. Mr. Coburn remained in the business ten years and, on his retiring, the firm was again called C. A. Cook & Co., and so continued until Mr. Cook went out of the business in 1886 or about that date. Mr. Cook had no partner after Mr. Coburn left the firm.

A branch house was established in Cincinnati in 1866 under the firm name of Cook, Coburn & Taylor, Mr. A. H. Taylor becoming a partner, but this branch agency was discontinued in 1871.

Mr. C. A. Cook died at his home in Chicago, September 27, 1898. Mr. C. E. Coburn is still—in 1905—in Chicago engaged in the insurance business.

Mr. A. H. Taylor is also in Chicago in the advertising business, being employed in the agency conducted by Theodore P. Roberts, who places most of the Sears, Roebuck & Co. advertising.

Mr. Cook's family are all gone from Chicago except a son. It was of this young man that Mr. Cook used to tell that as a boy he developed artistic tendencies and, thinking perhaps he should be given an education on the line of his tastes, sought advice from a friend thought competent to give it and who, after listening to all the pros and cons, volunteered the information that if the boy with such tastes was his own he would put some bricks in the seat of his trousers and let him sit down in the lake.

The firm of C. A. Cook & Co. was unfortunate at the end of its career. The cause of its decline was the advertising of Lawrence & Martin "Tolu Rock and Rye." When that firm failed they owed C. A. Cook & Co. $69,000, entirely unsecured. After discontinuing as much advertising as possible the net loss was $47,500, and not a cent of it was ever paid. This was more than Mr. Cook could stand, and, after adjusting matters as far as possible, an effort was made to continue business with but indifferent success; the agency made no money and younger men coming into the field and new ideas coming up the struggle was a hard one, and finally Mr. Cook ceased to be an advertising agent.

Mr. Richard S. Thain, the present editor of *Agricultural Advertising,* had a pretty close connection with Chicago agency matters in the late sixties and early seventies. Previous to its sale to Lord & Thomas, Mr. Thain was editor of *Mahin's Magazine.* He took up the advertising business in 1868 and has been at it pretty steadily since. There are not many now in the business who have been engaged in it longer than he.

In a recent communication, Mr. Thain writes:

In 1868 I was advertising manager of *Western Rural,* published in Chicago, and during that year the firm of Sharp & Thain was organized. We remained together in business until 1871. The firm was dissolved after the Chicago fire. We did quite an extensive business—especially with religious papers. We purchased one column from *The Interior, Advance, Northwestern Christian Advocate, New Covenant,* and the Episcopal paper that was published here. We usually kept from three to five columns filled with good advertisements. At that time, Field, Leiter & Company (now Marshall Field & Company) advertised extensively in these publications, and it was my pleasure to meet Mr. Field nearly every Saturday afternoon at 1.30 o'clock and get his copy for the following week. Before the Chicago fire, Mr. Field wrote his own advertisements, and he certainly knew how to write good ads—i. e., judging by the standard of the times. I had the pleasure of chatting with him not long ago regarding the old days of advertising, and find that he takes quite a lively personal interest in advertising at the present time.

George W. Sharp, my old partner, was an Englishman of the pure John Bull breed. He used to keep me busy fixing up his quarrels with publishers. I got rather tired of this and when the Chicago fire occurred I thought it a very opportune time to dissolve the partnership. I happened to be in New York City at this time, getting advertisements for the *Elgin Almanac,* October, 1871. Sharp & Thain were handling the advertising of the Elgin Watch Company, and they issued an Almanac to be handed out by the various jewelers throughout the United States. The issue was one million copies. We placed over $20,000 worth of advertising in the Almanac. The plates were ready, but were burned up in the great fire, and when I went back to New York I made a contract with James W. Sutton, of the Aldine Press, to get out the Almanac.

After the dissolution of Sharp & Thain, I went into business for a short time with Wm. H. Fitch, of New York, who was at that time advertising manager of *American Agriculturist.* The firm name was Fitch & Thain. In 1872 I came back to Chicago, when the firm of Thain & Paine was organized. Inside of a year I bought out Mr. Paine's interest and merged the agency with the firm of Chandler, Lord & Company. Mr. H. H. Chandler is now the publisher of *Farmers' Review* of this city; and Mr. D. M. Lord was head of the firm of Lord & Thomas for a number of years up to the time of his retirement from the business two years ago. I sold out my interest in the firm of Chandler, Lord & Company about ten months before they failed, and after the organization of the firm of Lord & Thomas I went to work for them in 1882 and was with them for seven years, occupying the position of what they termed their "right-hand" man.

In 1889 I left their employ and was the first Special Representative in Chicago. My list of publications composed the *Ladies' Home Journal, Christian Herald,* the Frank Leslie publications, *Golden Rule,* and I was also advertising manager of *Advance, Living Church,* and *Union Signal* of Chicago.

In 1893, having invested in unimproved real estate in a manufacturing district of Chicago, I sold out my special representative business to two of my employees and gave my time to the real estate business. My experience cost me about $15,000, and at the end of about twelve months I concluded that the advertising business was good enough for me and I went back into the game again. I am pleased to say, however, that I did not lose all of the money which I had made in the advertising business. During my connection in this business, dating from 1868 to the present time, I have always been able to pay one hundred cents on the dollar.

I believe there is a better chance in the advertising business to-day than there ever was for a young man who is willing to learn the business and play the game square.

The firm of Louis Lloyd & Co. also conducted a considerable business in Chicago, but finally the great Agencies of Lord & Thomas and C. H. Fuller grew up and overshadowed all others. Furthermore, the advertising business underwent a revolution to such an extent that while, forty or thirty years ago, scarcely five per cent of the so-called foreign advertising, that is advertising that was not local, emanated from points west of New York and Philadelphia, to-day forty-five per cent of all such advertising comes from west of Buffalo. At the time of the retirement of Mr. Daniel M. Lord, late of Lord & Thomas, he was the only living example of an advertising agent who had quit the business with a competence. Horace Dodd, who was my first partner in Boston, and who was succeeded by J. W.

Barber, is still living and has not, probably, any occasion to complain of being oppressed by either poverty or riches. Those who note Mr. Lord's smiling countenance are inclined to believe that the alleged competence with which he is credited is something more than a moderate one.

When Nelson Chesman commenced business in St. Louis I was his partner. The firm name was Rowell & Chesman. When I proposed withdrawing, Nelson believed the credit of the concern would receive a heavy blow. I told him he would never notice a shade of difference, and the result showed I was right. When a newspaper has

NELSON CHESMAN.

once got an account opened it requires something equivalent to an act of God to induce it to shut off the channel through which a golden stream may possibly flow in, and out of which—most of them think—nothing can escape that costs the publisher anything.

With one exception, no advertising agency has ever become prominent while doing business in a city of much less than half a million inhabitants. The exception was Mr. H. P. Hubbard, of New Haven, who first exploited Lydia Pinkham and her compound. He managed many campaigns that were successful and, led on by prosperity, finally took risks that resulted in his eventual collapse. He pub-

lished a Newspaper Directory which the New York *Tribune* considered much better than mine; and said so, in its editorial columns. Editors are uniformly truthful and impartial. That's what makes the calling so elevating.

At one time, when my interest in the advertising business was most active, we had a pretty lively competitor in a neighboring agency conducted under the name of Hudson & Menet. They were weak financially, and one day when passing their office I saw a sign of theirs being elevated to a higher position on the building they occupied, and, with that desire to be funny that has often got me into hot water, I wrote a paragraph for the *Newspaper Reporter*—the *Printers' Ink* of that day—which said, "Last week there was a sign of Hudson & Menet's going up." Newspaper men read the paper and took alarm. Bills poured in on the unfortunate concern, and before another week I had a libel suit on my hands. It never came to trial, for before it was reached the concern had failed; but my lawyer exacted a $500 fee for his services in my behalf and I realized then, and have often thought since, that it was more than such a poor joke was worth.

In concluding what I have to say about conducting an advertising agency I may make mention of the fact that it is one of the easiest sorts of business in which a man may cheat and defraud a client without danger of discovery; and also note that no agent who was not superior to this temptation has ever been permanently successful. The high reputation for honor and probity uniformly enjoyed by those who have been most conspicuous in the business has been gained by strict integrity—a determination to secure a fair deal for every patron.

FIFTY-FIRST PAPER

In the year 1900 I was led to secure a country home that should be within such easy reach of the office as would make it possible to go and come daily, should that seem desirable. Influenced by an advertisement in the *Evening Post* I went one day in early spring to look at a place, of some historic interest, that was announced to be for sale. The day was sunshiny, the buds were bursting into leaf; a little brook so glistened in the sun that I was impressed that this was the very spot I had in mind and that no other one would do; and it came about that I bought it, and went there to live. It was in a community of millionaires, and I was not a millionaire. I found that I minded the twenty odd miles travel, between house and office, more than I should have done when I was younger; and on the whole my new possession proved so much of an establishment, and cost so much to keep going, that there never seemed to be any money left over for excursions, travel, amusements or charities. If we could afford to have this, and half a dozen other places, and to shut them all up and go away when we liked, this would be delightful, but to live here day in and day out, to the end of life, was a prospect with too much monotony in it for perfection. It was eventually decided that we must part with our acquisition, and as it was an advertisement that had directed my attention to it I depended on another to bring me a buyer, and with this in mind, I prepared a description to be used to tell the story to interested inquirers. I reprint the wording of the leaflet here, partly as a specimen of an effective real estate advertisement of my own construction, and partly because the place advertised did for several years absorb a pretty large proportion of my thoughts and interests.

WILLOW BROOK

"On the banks of the Hudson, in a beautiful country."—
*Washington Irving's Life and Letters, Putnam, Vol. IV, p.
407.*

Ten acres is the answer usually given to the inquiry as to the
area of Willow Brook. It is not, in fact, quite so much; but it is
more than nine and a half, and round figures make a shorter story.
The place is bounded on the south by Sunnyside Lane, on the
west by a private road from the lane to extensive acres composing
the former home of a one-time famous New York merchant, Moses
H. Grinnell; but more recently known as the Banker place. This
private road separates Willow Brook from historic Sunnyside, the
home of Washington Irving, which reaches down to the Hudson
River. The Banker place forms the northern boundary, the eastern
side is marked by the Croton Aqueduct, separating it from Shadow
Brook, the beautiful residence of Mr. Henry Graves, Jr., which fills
out the space to Broadway, as the high road between New York and
Albany is known throughout its length.
All the places mentioned were once parts of a farm owned and
occupied by Oscar, an older brother of Washington Irving, and the
Willow Brook house was the home of Oscar before Sunnyside came
into being.

"I am more and more in the notion of having that little
cottage below Oscar's house."—*Extract from a letter written
by Washington Irving to his sister in November, 1832. Life
and Letters, Putnam, Vol. III, p. 30.*

"You have been told, no doubt, of a purchase I have made
of ten acres, lying at the foot of Oscar's farm, on the river
bank. It is a beautiful spot, capable of being made a little
paradise."—*Life and Letters, Putnam, Vol. III, p. 75.*

It was at Willow Brook that Washington Irving lived while his
house was building, and here he liked to come in his latest days, to
eat a Sunday dinner with his nearest neighbor, in the old familiar
dining-room, as is well remembered by a son, still resident of Irvington, then a youth not yet in his teens.
Something more than fifty years ago Edward S. Jaffray acquired
the Oscar Irving place and made of it a summer home. It was from
the Hudson at the foot of Sunnyside Lane that Mr. Jaffray embarked and disembarked for daily trips to and from New York
upon his steam yacht, being the first to set the fashion that afterwards became quite general among wealthy residents along the
river's banks. It was in the middle of the last century that, by Mr.
Jaffray's order, a landscape gardener marked out the sites where
pretty little groups of luxurious foliage have stood and grown, until
now the separate bunches of Spruce, Larch and Lindens are something to make glad a lover of trees; and single specimens of Sugar
Maple, Tulip and Linden elicit admiring exclamations. A Copper
Beech has a girth of nearly eight feet, two Cucumber trees (Magnolias) are of almost equal girth; there is one graceful specimen of
the Kentucky Coffee tree; and, by the brook side and vicinity, Black

Walnut and Butternut trees furnish food for a colony of squirrels that seem ever happy and prosperous. There are also notable Catalpas, Red Maples and numerous symmetrical Horse Chestnuts. Probably the number of trees on the Willow Brook estate is not fewer than six hundred, and chiefest among them is an English Cherry, still bearing good fruit, that measures more than sixteen feet in circumference, at the point just below where its branches spread. This tree must have been planted at a date preceding the American Revolution by many years, and to the same period may probably be ascribed the tall Box borders that still divide the old-fashioned garden into parallelograms, although lapse of years and winter frosts have made sad gaps in their once solid walls of miniature foliage.

Those who care for such things note that a Wistaria vine, that covers the branches of several tall trees over-arching a roadway, has a circumference of more than two feet at a considerable distance from the ground, and a wild grape as long, and probably older, serves as a hand-rail for a log bridge across the brook and ascends a great Ash tree at an apparently impossible distance from its root stock.

A note recently taken of the size of some of the larger trees, at the point within seven feet from the ground where the girth of the bole was smallest, revealed circumference as follows:

Tulip	167 inches.	Cucumber	79 inches.
English Cherry	159 "	Sycamore	78 "
Elm	129 "	Linden	74 "
Sugar Maple	114 "	White Pine	71 "
Black Walnut	113 "	Butternut	62 "
Catalpa	106 "	White Ash	55 "
Willow	99 "	Honey Locust	51 "
Chestnut	99 "	Sweet Birch	51 "
Horse Chestnut	95 "	Dogwood	32 "
Norway Spruce	91 "	Wistaria Vine	26 "
Copper Beech	85 "	Wild Grape	19 "

These do not exhaust the list, and it would be difficult to find a spot that, in sunshiny October days, so fully exhibits the variety and gorgeous beauty of American autumn foliage.

The brook, with the log bridge mentioned, and with other bridges at other points, has given the names to Willow Brook and Shadow Brook and is the principal ornament of Sunnyside, at which place it loses itself in the great river. The banks of the Hudson being hills of considerable magnitude, the little streams that come down abound in pretty cascades. The one now spoken of flows by Sunnyside Lane through the entire width of the Willow Brook estate, and a more clean, flowery and attractive wooded ravine might not be easily discovered, nor could one who loves seclusion ask for a more effective screen than its foliage affords from the eyes of passers-by. The brook has no dead water. Sometimes it is a torrent, but the rim of the ravine is ten times higher than the highest flood; and in severest summer drought there is still a crystal stream over the little rock-formed cascades that vary in fall from half a dozen inches to a large number of feet. In springtime great patches of blue violets hide the grass from sight by this brookside, and later the gray Stone Crop, the blue-eyed Gill-over-the-Ground and the so-called Yellow Strawberry furnish masses of pleasing color that give a charm to the ravine.

When Willow Brook changed hands about four years ago, for the only time in sixty years, the architect told the buyer he could build a new house for less money than it would cost to put the old one in as good condition as would be demanded. The answer was an expression of doubt about being brave enough to construct a new one on a plan that would be as pleasing and satisfactory as the old. At a later day, when the new possessor visited the just completed house of a friend, erected at barely half the cost of the repairs at Willow Brook, the thought that the architect had been right obtruded itself; but after mature deliberation, the conclusion was arrived at that the new house would not have been as satisfactory. Two hundred and fifty feet of a ten-foot piazza seems a good deal, but it is an invigorating reflection, when taking a constitutional walk in its glass-enclosed space on a winter day, that ten times around and ten times back make a mile.

A hall twelve feet wide, on every floor, extending the full width of the house, seems to furnish space for breath; and if two are engaged in an interesting conversation it is a comfort to walk up the wide stairway, side by side. A drawing-room 20x35, a dining-room 18x35, a library of a similar size, with five windows facing the South and West, all have advantages in their way. Five bath-rooms, with additional water-closets and wash-hand rooms, may not be needed every hour, but they give a feeling of satisfaction to guests that makes them willing to come again. "I have never visited at nor been in a house where every room in it is as nice as it is here, and where I am so uniformly comfortable," was the comment of a visitor whose city house is worth a fortune and who has expended a quarter of a million in making a country place just what he would like to have it.

That the servants' rooms are by themselves, separate and apart from the rest of the house though conveniently approached, is not found a disadvantage; and, although small and compact, the fact that each may have a separate room, a hanging closet, neat and tidy, with bath and water-closet close at hand, may possibly do something to explain why servants who occupy them like to stay, like to show them to their friends and, if they have gone away, seem rather anxious to come back.

Although the house is lighted by electricity it is found that having a gas machine is at times a convenience and a reliance; for the gas range in the kitchen can be turned off when not in use, and when in use, in place of the coal range, it promotes coolness in summer and tends to make the cook good-natured and contented; and then the gas log in a bed-room on a frosty October morning, before the furnace is at work, is about as much of a comfort as it is to be able to get along without candles at the infrequent times when the wires are witched, and, for an hour perhaps, neither the electric light nor the telephone service is doing duty.

Many persons have remarked the beauty of the Colonial mantels that surmount the fireplaces in drawing-room, dining-room and library, and speak of the prodigality of the three-foot sticks that make such attractive back logs. It seems almost like economy, however, to be able to burn the occasional tree that wind or age destroys and the fact that more of this sort of fuel is produced yearly than the fire-places will consume, is a circumstance that has weight in explaining why Willow Brook is even more attractive as a winter home than it is in summer. With a book, a cigar and an open fire in the library of a winter evening, a cold wind howling outside, tends to make one contented and happy. Possibly the fire-places would not seem so all sufficing were not the temperature of halls and corners helped out by the soothing influence of the most efficient Lord & Burnham double boiler hot water system, that, ensconced in the cellar and burning anthracite, gives the Willow Brook house as even a temperature as its owner has ever found in a home.

Those who see the stables at Willow Brook for the first time are led to expect great things in the way of horses, for there are stalls for more than a dozen; but the surplus room does not embarrass the coachman, who has only a modest pair in his charge, and as for too much room in a carriage house, no one has ever heard of such a thing. It is surprising, too, how handy this extra room is found to be for storing hay, straw, wood, boxes, barrels and what not; and so long as the roofs are kept painted, it costs nothing to keep up buildings that are better and larger than actual needs demand. The great stable yard with its substantial stone walls on sides where buildings are not, and the cleanly coating of blue stone, is always an attractive spot.

The water supply at Willow Brook is that of the town of Tarrytown, and is ample and excellent; but, inasmuch as those who have a superior thing are bound to use it, the occupants of Willow Brook avail themselves largely of a notable spring that in severest drought never flows less than twenty gallons to the minute of a delicious table water. The Sunnyside place has a sister spring of which Washington Irving speaks lovingly in the first chapter of "Wolfert's Roost." He called his place Wolfert's Roost before the prettier one of Sunnyside recommended itself to him. He says:

> "Each stream that flows down from the hills of the Hudson had its petty sachem who had his seat of government at its mouth. The chieftain who ruled here was not merely a great warrior, but a medicine man or prophet or conjurer, for they all mean the same thing in Indian parlance. Of his wizard powers we have a token in the spring which wells up at the foot of the bank which, it is said, was gifted by him with rejuvenating powers, something like the renowned Fountain of Youth in the Floridas, so anxiously sought after by the veteran Ponce de Leon. This story, however, is contradicted by an old Dutch matter-of-fact tradition which declared that the spring was smuggled over from Holland in a churn by the wife of one of the first settlers, and that she took it up by night, unknown to her husband, from beside their farm house, near Rotterdam, being sure she would find no water equal to it in the new country—and she was right."—*Wolfert's Roost, Putnam, 1864, p. 10.*

In connection with water there comes always the less attractive subject of sewage. Imperfect sewage is the bane of many a country place, and in times past Willow Brook has not escaped the need of creating and caring for adequate cesspools; but that has happily been done away with since the corporations of Tarrytown and Irvington have constructed an efficient sewer down from Sunnyside Lane, carrying to the Hudson River, down an incline of possibly two hundred feet, every bit of waste and fluid filth from house, stable or gardener's cottage. This is a matter of enormous importance, but one often lost sight of by those who seek a country home. Everybody knows that where the drainage is perfect there are no mosquitoes. There are no mosquitoes at Willow Brook.

One of the most charming features about Willow Brook is the great number of birds. To look out on the lawn and count fifty Robins is not an experience difficult to compass. No bird beside the Robin is more persistent in his visits than the Wood Thrush; and, strange as it may seem, he is even the more domesticated of the two. He builds his nest so low down that it may be looked into, and is not worried by the proximity of humans who come near in pursuance of work or play. The first morning his musical note announces his arrival is a joyous event in spring. Then there is the Wren, smallest of the feathered visitors excepting the Humming Bird, but what a song he has. It is perhaps the sparkling of the brook that secures his presence, for scarcely any other bird is so attracted by running water; but when a box with a hole in it is mounted on the piazza cornice, he loses little time in making a home of it; and how he will strain his throat with song as he swings on a string that controls the piazza awnings. It is pleasant to put out pieces of twine and thread or yarns in the hope that the Oriole will use them for his hanging nest, and, if a great bunch of Maple concludes to die this year, there is a possibility that a Yellow Winged Flicker will find its wood soft enough next spring to permit him to hollow it out and raise a family in the space he excavates. The Song Sparrow seems to find a good perching place in the pear tree, and pours out his soul in the sunshine; and in winter the Nut Hatch walks head downward on the trees and lets it be known that he is alive by a note that, to state it mildly, is much too big for him. The Scarlet Tanager, if it does not come often, is conspicuous while he is in sight, and little Red Starts actually appear in dozens now and then. These small visitors, always cheerful and always young, do not add taxable value to real estate, but the place where they are is worth ever so much more than the other one where they are not. Although plentiful on Broadway, the English Sparrow does not come to Willow Brook. He likes city life or village society, and Willow Brook, although scarcely an hour from Wall Street, is too much like the Adirondacks to suit his taste. And yet the butcher, the baker, the candlestick maker come almost too often, and even respond promptly to a hurry order by telephone for an item forgotten in the morning.

The architect who overhauled the house not long ago, as a circumstance having a bearing on the fact that the expenses had exceeded double his estimate, mentioned that the plumbing was absolutely new and the most expensive he had ever been permitted to put into a house, and that the heating apparatus had cost more than the entire outlay sometimes appropriated to construct a very considerable country home. As both appeared to be of good quality and to accomplish the work expected, the explanation was thought plausible if not satisfactory.

When it was noted that the roads and paths generally escaped damage from washouts so common after a storm in towns along the Hudson, the contractor who put them in order, a few years ago, explained that the paved gutters were of themselves pretty good and durable but were underdrained with pipes of sufficient size to carry off the overflow at numerous taps and that, under such conditions, no serious washouts could take place, and with a light dressing of blue stone now and then, the roads ought to be permanent and enduring.

The view of the Tappan Zee, over the trees of Sunnyside, is pretty and looks better from the windows of the upper rooms. That towering structure to the North, just beyond the Banker place, is Lyndhurst, the home of Miss Helen Gould, of whom it may be said that Irvington has no citizen so much beloved.

Irvington is 23 miles from New York, and the fastest Hudson River trains consume 40 minutes in reaching it. To climb the main street, going north on Broadway, taking Sunnyside Lane (the first turning to the West) uses up 15 minutes more before Willow Brook is reached. The distance from the station must be fully a mile, but people who like short cuts, find satisfaction in a walk down Sunnyside Lane to the railroad track. It was by this route that Washington Irving frequently returned to Sunnyside after visits to the metropolis, walking the few hundred yards of cinder path that intervened between his loved retreat and the railroad station, the name of which had, in 1845, been changed from Dearman to Irvington.

> "Yesterday I alighted at the station within ten minutes' walk of home. The walk was along the railroad, in full sight of the house."—*Irving's Life and Letters, Putnam, Vol. IV, p. 135.*

To those who love the country and the life out of doors, Willow Brook exhibits many scenes of enchantment. In the days of spring the ever-recurring miracle of swelling buds and opening leaves; the dotted veils of the spice bush; the white sprays of the Dogwood; tne great masses of crimson that envelop the Maple and the delicately gorgeous beauty of the Wistaria; all of these equaled, if not excelled, some winter mornings, when every twig may be surmounted by a lacework of snow, or encased in glittering ice, brilliant in the early sunrise to a degree that is beyond belief.

For a summer home it is all that need be desired; but in winter, to quote quaint Izaak Walton, it is "too good for any but a very honest man."

Any one who has taken the pains to read the entire specimen of a real estate advertisement, constructed by the writer—if there be any such—may be further interested in knowing that the story was so effective—or that chance so ordered—that the very first man who ever saw and read the leaflet became the purchaser of the place. It should ·be still more interesting to be assured that the new owner is widely known as precisely the sort of man indicated in the last paragraph—that the place is not too good for.

FIFTY-SECOND PAPER

It has been made plain in the papers that have preceded this concluding one that the time when I pursued the business with so much attention as to exclude all thought of other things was limited to the first six years of the existence of the Advertising Agency, which I had established in 1865. In 1871 the practice of taking a four months' vacation out of every year was begun and there was rarely any variation from it, and if any such occurred it seemed certain to be in the way of adding to rather than curtailing the period of relaxation.

After twenty years of this I realized that I dominated the business without giving it the personal attention necessary to insure its success. We published Rowell's American Newspaper Directory, and that made work in the office that was different and separate from the ordinary business of conducting an advertising agency. We were issuing *Printers' Ink,* a weekly paper devoted, it is true, to the interests of advertisers, but involving work that was outside the regular lines of an advertising agency. We had established a patent medicine—a trademark—a proprietary article—that would need to be advertised, and to that extent were getting away from the legitimate business of an advertising agency, which is to place advertisements for clients —not for itself.

We had with us several men whose terms of service had extended over periods of from ten to twenty years—more or less—and each of these had ideas as to the way an advertising agency ought to be conducted; that were more or less at variance from the methods that prevailed with us. These men were Mr. E. D. Wayre, the bookkeeper; Mr. B. L. Crans, the collector and outside man; Mr. E. F. Draper, the estimate clerk; Mr. B. F. Newton, whose term of service had been longer than that of any other employee, and who was the best letter writer and correspondent for conducting negotiations with newspapers that we had ever had in our employ. Lastly, there was Mr. F. C. Ringer, whose term of service had possibly been shorter than that of any of the others, whose general usefulness in the office had not always seemed to be up to the average of any of the others, and yet, on account of a certain aptitude he displayed in sketching out and emphasizing the points of an advertisement, and perhaps more than all, because for a year or more he had been kept at work in a position that brought him and me into almost hourly conferences, he seemed to be the one most likely to be able to organize and carry out the scheme I began to have in mind of disposing of the business to selected employees, incorporating it, thereby avoiding personal liability, and making it possible to have the conduct of affairs managed on the different lines that were from time to time brought before me by these employees, or some of them, as the methods that were up to date and ought to supersede ours that had become obsolete and somewhat down at the heel.

It was to Mr. Ringer, therefore, that I eventually—in the year 1892—made the proposal by letter, naming the men whom he might or might not associate with him. He immediately discussed the matter with Mr. Draper. Both were enthusiastic about the prospects—thought it the opportunity of their lives. They were agreed that Mr. Newton was needed in the combination, as office man and executive, but that it would be a pity to divide the pie into too many pieces, and consequently, Mr. Wayre and Mr. Crans ought not to be invited to join the new arrangement, but might remain on the salaries being received at the time. In the conferences that ensued Mr. Draper promptly rose to the position of apparent leader, although Mr. Ringer appeared to have as much real influence in determining a course, while Mr. Newton, saying little, not anxious to be in any way prominent, seemed always to have a good reason for everything he proposed, and his good sense was much deferred to.

No one of the three had any capital. It has scarcely ever been my fortune to be associated with anybody in a business way who brought any capital into an enterprise at its inception. We fixed the capital of the corporation at $50,000. Ringer, Draper and Newton were assigned $8,000 each, and to each I loaned $8,000 in cash, holding their stock certificates as collateral for the loan, which was to bear interest at six per cent. I kept $8,000 of the stock myself, and put in that amount of money, and was elected president of the corporation at a nominal salary of $600 a year. Mr. Kent took $8,000 of the stock, paying cash for it, and was made vice-president, he also drawing a nominal salary of $600. This left $10,000 of stock in the treasury, but it was promptly taken by a Wall Street man who knew about it, had the money to spare, and thought the opportunity too good to let slip. It perhaps has at no place been made plain that at some time previous to this I had acquired the interests of my two partners, Mr. Kent and Mr. Moses, but such was the fact, and at the commencement of the negotiations I was sole owner of the business and all its belongings.

The stockholders, now having $50,000 on hand, paid over to me the entire sum in consideration of the purchase of the good will of the business, the office furniture and the right to use the name. They began with such orders as came to them the opening day, with no money of their own in hand, but with an agreement on my part that in case of need I would advance them whatever was required up to $10,000 for a period of two years.

I tell the story in detail. It may interest some other younger men to whom a chance may come some day as it had to these.

The new managers worked cheerfully, with good heart; did things their own way, and it was not a bad way. Neither Kent nor I interfered We were there to give advice, if it was asked, but volunteered none. Kent and I occupied the office with them. He edited the Directory—which remained my property—receiving an agreed upon compensation for the service. *Printers' Ink* was managed in the same office, but the corporation had no interest in the paper nor the book.

The three new managers of the Advertising Agency soon found the salaries they had been receiving scarcely adequate to the new dignity belonging to their positions as principals, and the probable earnings appearing to justify these were advanced about sixty per cent. At the end of a year there had been a profit, but it was not a large one. It sufficed to pay a dividend to the stockholders that was at least enough to pay the interest on the notes I held. The second year showed something better, but the dividend was not increased, because it was thought a surplus fund would be a convenient thing to have. Another year, and another, and another, and things were better. The dividends had been sufficient to pay the interest on the notes, to pay the notes themselves, and the Wall Street man had six per cent interest on his investment, had received his investment back again, had a fifty per cent surplus on it in the shape of an extra dividend—and even a little more.

The business under new methods had grown. In the beginning there had been a multitude of small orders. In the old days straggling orders for small amount of advertising would count up a thousand dollars a day for a summer month, and three-quarters of it would consist of commissions from schools and summer resorts, each affording a moderate percentage of profit. The name of the concern appeared to be known everywhere. Every new man who thought of doing a little advertising was certain to come to us first. Whenever an advertising agent tried to explain the nature of his not very widely understood calling, if he made a success of it, he would commonly be greeted, toward the end of his explanation, with the query—something like Rowell's! Isn't it?

The younger men secured larger orders. They paid better. Smaller customers received less attention than formerly, and when they dropped off were neither missed nor mourned. Expenses increased. Attention to business diminished. There came a time when there was a scarcity of large orders and the small ones did not return. Expenses still increased and business not being brisk there was more leisure. In all business it is found that the less a man has to do the greater income he requires. The old method of paying to-day the bill that came in to-day for payment was less stringently adhered to. Dividends ceased. One day it was made to appear that there were unpaid bills in the office amounting to a good deal more than half as much as had been paid to me for the name and good will; and an examination of the books showed that the amounts due to publishers exceeded the total due from advertising patrons.

I had arranged the corporation to relieve myself of responsibility. I was not personally responsible to its creditors, but the name of the corporation was my name—The Geo. P. Rowell Advertising Company. I would have preferred to have the affairs wound up and wipe my hands of a business that for thirty years I had taken pride in; but this meant leaving newspaper publishers, who had trusted to the name, to lose a good many thousand dollars, and the concern to end in bankruptcy. The managers could see the situation and were aghast; but no remedy was in sight. The conclusion was soon arrived at that I should take up the burden again. The corporation met, agreed to sell its assets to me for one dollar, I agreeing to assume all obligations. This wiped out the stockholders. Two of the three managers went elsewhere, one remained. The Wall Street man submitted to the cancelling of his stock without a murmur. He had often come out worse—and rarely better; had had his money back, had interest on it, and a fifty per cent bonus, and a trifle over beside. There was no kick coming from him. One of the managers was not quite satisfied with the condition that confronted him, but there did not appear to be any remedy.

Mr. Kent, whose stock was wiped out, thought the arrangement a mighty good one for me. The belief was not expressed in a complaining spirit, but in good faith. He had a son, engaged in the business, who liked it. Kent had ample capital for the purpose. I had no son and was five years his senior. "Supposing the arrangement to be, as you say, a mighty good one for me," said I to him, "it would be equally so for you, and you have a son to go with you. The thing to make everybody happy, is for you to step into my place. Then the business will be yours absolutely." For as much as an hour I believe he thought he would do it; but he is a cautious man, and after walking around a block half a dozen times he determined that he would not risk a certain competence for a responsibility that might bring large earnings, but would entail responsibilities, which he would thereafter carry without me to share them with him; and the negotiations resulted in his severing a connection with me that had lasted for more than thirty years. No one can know how much I missed his always cheerful greeting, his always patient listening to any plan I had to propose. He was a restful partner for a man to have—always faithful in his attention to affairs, always outspoken with his opinion, and, if overruled and the thing turned out badly, was never the man to say, "I told you so!" but if, on the other hand—as was sometimes the case—the thing turned out well, it seemed to be his pleasure to recognize the fact, admit that he had not thought well of the plan in the beginning, and to say how glad he was that the better way had prevailed.

After the change the bills were paid in full, and every day thereafter as in former years, but never again was I able to take the old-time interest in the business, and it was not prosperous in any very large way. There is a homely proverb that says:

> He who by the plough would thrive,
> Himself must either hold or drive.

I was more interested in the Directory, in *Printers' Ink,* in the Ripans Chemical Company, in going fishing, and in travel than in the Advertising Agency. It was during the year 1897 that two of the men who had been with me longest retired from the office. They were capable, but remiss in some matters. I once heard of a firm of wholesale grocers in Louisville that dissolved, to the surprise of everybody, and it was not everybody who saw the logic of the explanation given by the senior partner for the retirement of the junior. He said he did not think a good business man should spend the whole day selling champagne at $2.50 a bottle and the whole night in buying it back at $5 a bottle.

Mr. Kent, who had been thirty years with me, always working with a faithful assiduity that was beyond praise, had also retired with a moderate and well-earned competence, and was spending most of his days with his family, or in the garden of his Long Island residence or with the books in his library where he was always happy.

Again I was alone in the conduct of the business, but not carrying it on with anything like the vim and energy of former years. There seemed to be a vast difference in the ambition of fifty-nine as compared with that at twenty-nine. I relied mainly upon subordinates—more or less well instructed; was interested in other matters more or less disconnected with the business; still made an effort to keep up the old-time vacation system of four months' absence out of every year; and to some extent, doubtless, the business suffered for want of a head. Finally, in the autumn of 1903, it was practically turned over to the management of two gentlemen in the early thirties, Mr. W. F. Hamblin and Mr. F. W. Tully.

Mr. Hamblin had for some years been business manager of the New Haven, Conn., *Register,* and Mr. Tully for a considerable time advertising manager for the model, growing Boston department store of William Filene's Sons. Both men had been earnest students of advertising, had had a training in it from their boyhood's early years; both were hard workers, men of pleasing address; both of the best possible age, a little over thirty. Although I remained a general partner and favored them with sage old-fashioned counsel, when they asked for it, I was even less active in the management of the agency than I had been before, and fully realized that I should never again resume anything of the old-time interest. On the 31st of August, 1905, my connection with the firm ceased absolutely. The business was reincorporated, without counting me as a director or stockholder, and its offices were removed from No. 10 to No. 12 Spruce street. The old offices at No. 10 with their five thousand square feet of floor space have since been leased, for a term of years, by the F. Wesel Manufacturing Company of Brooklyn, who are so well known to newspaper men as dealers in about everything in the implement way that printers have to spend money for.

If in years to come the business of the Advertising Agency expands far beyond any state of prosperity it has ever known the credit will not be mine. Conditions are changing and only young men can be expected to keep up with the times. I have passed the age of ambitious initiative and reached the reminiscent stage, a period which I fully realize is like that wherein a happy couple celebrates a golden wedding, and every one present knows that not very long after a funeral is inevitable.

My life has contained few incidents that seemed to me so wonderful as the beautiful banquet given in my honor in the Astor Gallery of the Waldorf-Astoria, on the evening of Tuesday, October 31, 1905, to commemorate my retirement from the business of conducting an advertising agency. That so many as one hundred and sixty-two gentlemen from various sections of the country could be induced to come together and pay ten dollars a-piece for the privilege of dining with me seemed almost too wonderful to be true. When Mr. Frank Presbrey, president of the Sphinx Club, that important association of advertising men that had once honored me with the office he now holds, addressed to me the sentences that follow, I could not feel otherwise than honored to a high degree.

Addressing the guest of the evening, Mr. Presbrey said:

It has been your privilege, Mr. Rowell, to observe from your important position on the field the transition of advertising from a chaotic, unsystematic attempt at publicity to an established business in which many of the best trained and most intelligent minds of the country are engaged. You have seen a mighty commercial battle waged for the supremacy of the markets of the world. You have seen the weekly papers which, in your early career, were the infantry on the firing line, fall back to make room at the front for the cavalry brigade of dailies, and you have seen the batteries of the magazine wheel into line and come into action with their heavy guns, whose reverberations are heard around the globe. It has been your privilege, sir, to witness and bear an honored and notable part in the greatest commercial battle ever known—that of conquering the markets of the world by the well-directed fire of publicity through the Gatling guns of the newspapers and the more ponderous long-distance guns of the magazines. I feel that I am within the lines of truth when I say to you, sir, that wherever and whenever the history of this battle is written the name of George P. Rowell will be written down as one of the greatest of the field marshals who stood the heat and turmoil of the conflict. Now that you have withdrawn from active participation in the advertising business and enlisted in the ranks of retirement, let me assure you, sir, that you carry with you the good wishes, the admiration and the respect of every one gathered here to-night, and of each one of your hosts of friends from one end to the other of this broad land.

If I could call up from this board, by telephone, every daily newspaper office in this country; if I could have Central put me in touch with every weekly paper, from the rocky shores of Maine to the sunny slopes of California, and say that George P. Rowell was at the 'phone, I promise you that in not one instance would I have to explain your identity. Your name is in the business office what Hoe's is in the press room and Mergenthaler's in the composing room. Your reputation and association with advertising runs back so far that some who have more recently come upon the advertising stage may consider you an inheritance from the times of Greeley, Thurlow Weed and the elder Bennett. If there be one man whose life history is woven into the very warp and woof of American publicity, it is you whom we are here to honor to-night.

During the period of your active business life advertising has developed from a timid, unsystematic, hope-it-will-pay-me venture into one of the greatest commercial certainties whose aggregate, measured in dollars, is next in volume to the banking and insurance business of the country. In this wonderful development the one man who has ever been a dominating factor, whose personality has always stood for advancement and progress, who has always been on the firing line of controversy and discussion, is George P. Rowell. Through the columns of your *Printers' Ink* you have exercised a greater influence on the general subject of advertising, have developed and made more new advertisers than any other man who has ever lived. If credit is due to him who makes two blades of grass grow where one grew before, you, our honored guest, are entitled to the respect, the admiration and the esteem of every man here to-night, and of every man engaged in advertising or publishing in the United States.

Mr. Artemas Ward, another ex-President of the Sphinx Club, seemed to be in sober earnest when he said:

Born of sturdy New England stock, of the uncompromising kind, the guest of the evening has some sharp edges; so has a diamond. He has tried more experiments in advertising systems than any man in the world. When he disagreed with any popular system he walked off alone; if the system did not suit him he would not suit himself to the system.

Successful though he has been, he has within himself resourcefulness, industry and genius enough to have made his success colossal had he been more pliable. Yet why should we wish him to be other than himself? He shall remain a character apart by itself, a life that has passed through opportunities without number and has still held on to one central fact—which is not opportunity nor opportunism—integrity. The business of advertising, which has passed from its initial strength of purpose till it includes too many devious, weak, and even disreputable forms, can look back and thank God that one Rowell lived. He may have missed much that he might have gained. I believe he did, but whenever his road parted from ours we missed more than he did.

Mr. Louis Wiley of the New York *Times,* who has never been President of the Sphinx Club, but stands in the regular line of promotion asserted:

Our distinguished guest began his career in the very infancy of the advertising business, and its wonderful development and expansion are largely due to his initiative and enterprise.

You have been told by the able gentlemen who have preceded me to-night of the remarkable efforts and the remarkable success of this advertising propagandist. All his efforts and all his success have had an important bearing on the prosperity and the influence of the American press. The great modern newspaper is now sold at a price much smaller than the cost of production, and its success depends largely on its advertising revenues. These make possible the engagement of able writers, the installment of fast presses and linotypes, and the many other requisites for the daily newspaper.

Among the men who have instilled in the minds of the merchants and manufacturers of America the knowledge of the value of advertising and have educated them in the way to advertise, the name of George Presbury Rowell leads all the rest.

We have met here to testify to our admiration for a great career, to show that we appreciate the services of Mr. Rowell in the cause of education, for advertising, all of us must admit, is a great educating influence.

I hope the guest of the evening may continue for many, many years to shed his light upon *Printers' Ink*, Rowell's American Newspaper Directory, and all the other agencies he has employed for the benefit of the American people.

Appreciative allusion has been made by Mr. Noyes, president of the Associated Press, to Mr. Rowell's great work in the American Newspaper Directory, that Webster's Dictionary of American news-

papers. This book has for many years been an absolute requirement in the office of every newspaper publisher and of every advertiser. And yet how many bitter controversies has it engendered?
How many newspaper publishers there are who claim to have suffered injustice at its hands! This has all resulted from the insistence of Mr. Rowell that each newspaper wishing a rating should
make a statement of its circulation for every day of the year, and
many newspaper publishers who were reared to believe that lying is
a sin refrained from making the statements required.

It was the speech of Mr. Frank B. Noyes, editor and
publisher of the Chicago *Record-Herald* and President of
the Associated Press, that gratified me more than any other
words that were spoken. Mr. Noyes said, in part:

It is as a publisher that Geo. P. Rowell has pre-eminently done
the work that in my judgment entitles him to the thanks in the fullest measure of all those who believe that thanks are due to one who
has been the main moving cause of the revolution that has raised
the advertising side of the newspaper business above the level of the
green goods game.

Prior to his strenuous efforts it is true that here and there isolated
newspapers had recognized an obligation to advertisers to make
known to the buyers the measure of the goods they were selling
them, and on the other hand then and now many honorable newspapers did not regard it as compulsory nor in accord with their
interests to make known the amount of their circulation.

With these latter I have no quarrel, nor has Mr. Rowell had;
but as a matter of fact it is not very many years back that in many
quarters direct lying concerning circulation was regarded as a venial
sin, and the buncoing of the succulent advertiser caused apparently
no twinge of conscience.

With this condition of affairs existing Mr. Rowell began
through his Newspaper Directory and later through *Printers' Ink*
his many years' fight for honest circulation statements.

Week by week, month by month and year by year he has pilloried
the circulation liar relentlessly, treating him exactly as a swindler
should be treated.

By this course, made effective only by the merciless manner in
which it was pursued, a revolution has been wrought in the ethics
of circulation statements, and, speaking broadly, the circulation
statement of to-day is as essentially honest as are the representations
made by the seller in other business enterprises.

I would not be understood as asserting that all is well with us
and that the day of the necessity for the Rowell scourging has altogether past. In common with other lines of endeavor we still have
our bad eggs, and we hope that Mr. Rowell will continue to ruth-
lessly expose them to the contempt of men.

Personally I have no doubt that so long as life remains to him he
will continue to do just this thing, and for myself and my brother

publishers I wish to put on record our deep appreciation of Mr. Rowell's great work in our behalf.

If I left you, however, with the impression that in my mind George P. Rowell is pictured as the stern, impartial, incarnate punishment of wrongdoing, I should signally fail in doing justice to myself.

It was my fortune to become known to Mr. Rowell at about the time that I was able to sell papers across the counter of the Washington *Star*, without being elevated on a high stool.

I came to know him through the beautiful friendship that has long been between Mr. Rowell and one who has been a second father to me, and when I say a second father the depths of tender, sympathizing helpfulness have been sounded. As some of you know, I refer to Mr. S. H. Kauffmann, and I am sure that to our guest of this evening and to many others here it is a great sorrow that his health does not permit him to be with us on this occasion.

And so it has happened that for many years I have felt that I really knew George P. Rowell, and have held him in deep affection. He has ever been a kindly, loyal, truth-telling friend, and I thank God that it has been my privilege to know him, to respect him, to love him.

Commenting on the affair, the Brooklyn *Eagle*, in its issue for Wednesday, November 1, 1905, said, editorially:

A NOTABLE HONOR MERITED BY A NOTABLE MAN.

George P. Rowell, the pioneer and the master in the field of the art and enterprise of advertising, has retired from the business in which he has won merited distinction. He was last night honored by a dinner in Manhattan. The occasion was notable for affection, admiration, gratitude, friendship and good wishes. The guest, Mr. Rowell, was an honor to his hosts, and his hosts comprised men of integrity, influence, ability and distinction, alike for character and for achievement, in many useful and inciting fields of intelligent and uplifting endeavor. The *Eagle* wishes for Mr. Rowell many years of happiness. He eminently deserves them. He has won his right to them. No man has better illustrated fine standards, high ideals and a clean-hearted courage, as well as indomitable confidence in justice and in right in the field of labor and of life. In that field he has conquered and held the pinnacles. His history is an incentive and a vindication, as well as a model and a stimulation, to all his fellow workers as well as to all his legion of friends outside the lines on which he has wrought.

If I should fail to admit that I was gratified and vastly proud of the expressions of good will that culminated on that happy Hallowe'en, I should only omit to mention what was conspicuously evident to every one who looked into my face on that occasion.

Those who have read these papers, already stretched out to an interminable length, will have noted that they are not written in a complaining or a repining strain, and there is no reason why they should be, for the world and the Ruler of it have dealt more than kindly with me. It is natural enough, perhaps, to be sad when we think of those who started out with us and have fallen by the wayside, but is there not still more reason for cheerful thankfulness when we realize that thus far our strength has been sufficient to sustain us, and give us a longer period than falls to the common lot to enjoy the sunshine and the blossoms of this beautiful world? That a day will soon come when I, too, shall step forth is not a thing to regret, for surely no one would be willing to be here when all early friends are gone. The old man of whom Dr. Holmes spoke may possibly have lived too long when it was said of him:

> The mossy marbles rest
> On the lips that he has pressed
> In their bloom.
> And the names he loved to hear
> Have been carved for many a year
> On the tomb.

I realize that I am no longer young, but when I recall that my good mother; a brother of my father; and two of my grandparents each lived from twenty to twenty-five more years than I have enjoyed, I regard it as not impossible that, in connection with the Newspaper Directory and *Printers' Ink,* I may be heard of for some time yet. I am rather amused than annoyed when I hear references made to my numerous years.

One day only a few weeks ago I was sitting by a lakeside in a northern New Hampshire forest, concealed by the foliage of the shore, and listened to a conversation between two men in a boat; one a Princeton graduate and the other a native youth who was rowing the collegian for fly-fishing. They were discussing the matter of ages. The Princeton man said, "Why, I think my grandfather must be very much older than Mr. Rowell," and the other responded, "I know Mr. Rowell must be very old, for he taught school in this county more than fifty years ago, and my grandmother went to school to him." It was an overstatement. It was only forty-nine and a half years since I taught that school. I remember it well, and that although I was but sixteen years of age at the time no less than eight of my thirty-five pupils were more than twenty-one; and I think, perhaps, the boy's grandmother may have been one of these.

When the genial George H. Daniels, as President of the Sphinx Club, asserted that I was referred to in Washington's farewell address, he said what was not true. Still my life has been a long one. I have told here the story of that part of it that has had to do with advertising; have told much that seems trivial, but have classic authority that men are interested in whatever concerns a man. My career has been one of half successes. I have phrased the story as well a I am able, and as completely, although there may be many things that I might mention—but to attempt more would be to go on and on for ever and ever. To avoid an outcome so undesirable I will now stop short.

> There's a divinity that shapes our ends,
> Rough-hew them how we may.

INDEX

A

B

D

F

G

H

INDEX

J

K

L

495

M

N

O

INDEX

Q

R

INDEX

INDEX

513

U

V

W

Index

515

Y

Z

Titles in This Series

9.
C. Samuel Craig and Avijit Ghosh, editors. The Development of Media Models in Advertising: An Anthology of Classic Articles. 1985

10.
C. Samuel Craig and Brian Sternthal, editors. Repetition Effects Over the Years: An Anthology of Classic Articles. 1985

11.
John K. Crippen. Successful Direct-Mail Methods. 1936

12.
Ernest Dichter. The Strategy of Desire. 1960

13.
Ben Duffy. Advertising Media and Markets. 1939

14.
Warren Benson Dygert. Radio as an Advertising Medium. 1939

15.
Francis Reed Eldridge. Advertising and Selling Abroad. 1930

16.
J. George Frederick, editor. Masters of Advertising Copy: Principles and Practice of Copy Writing According to its Leading Practitioners. 1925

17.
George French. Advertising: The Social and Economic Problem. 1915

18.
Max A. Geller. Advertising at the Crossroads: Federal Regulation vs. Voluntary Controls. 1952

19.
Avijit Ghosh and C. Samuel Craig. The Relationship of Advertising Expenditures to Sales: An Anthology of Classic Articles. 1985

20.
Albert E. Haase. The Advertising Appropriation, How to Determine It and How to Administer It. 1931

21.
S. Roland Hall. The Advertising Handbook, 1921

22.
S. Roland Hall. Retail Advertising and Selling. 1924

23.
Harry Levi Hollingworth. Advertising and Selling: Principles of Appeal and Response. 1913

24.
Floyd Y. Keeler and Albert E. Haase. The Advertising Agency, Procedure and Practice. 1927

25.
H. J. Kenner. The Fight for Truth in Advertising. 1936

26.
Otto Kleppner. Advertising Procedure. 1925

27.
Harden Bryant Leachman. The Early Advertising Scene. 1949

28.
E. St. Elmo Lewis. Financial Advertising, for Commercial and Savings Banks, Trust, Title Insurance, and Safe Deposit Companies, Investment Houses. 1908

29.
R. Bigelow Lockwood. Industrial Advertising Copy. 1929

30.
D. B. Lucas and C. E. Benson. Psychology for Advertisers. 1930

31.
Darrell B. Lucas and Steuart H. Britt. Measuring Advertising Effectiveness. 1963

32.
Papers of the American Association of Advertising Agencies. 1927

33.
Printer's Ink. Fifty Years 1888–1938. 1938

34.
Jason Rogers. Building Newspaper Advertising. 1919

35.
George Presbury Rowell. Forty Years an Advertising Agent, 1865–1905. 1906

36.
Walter Dill Scott. The Theory of Advertising: A Simple Exposition of the Principles of Psychology in Their Relation to Successful Advertising. 1903

37.
Daniel Starch. Principles of Advertising. 1923

38.
Harry Tipper, George Burton Hotchkiss, Harry L. Hollingworth, and Frank Alvah Parsons. Advertising, Its Principles and Practices. 1915

39.
Roland S. Vaile. Economics of Advertising. 1927

40.
Helen Woodward. Through Many Windows. 1926